Dialogues in Arab Politics

Dialogues in Arab Politics

NEGOTIATIONS IN REGIONAL ORDER

Michael N. Barnett

Columbia University Press   NEW YORK

Columbia University Press
Publishers Since 1893
New York   Chichester, West Sussex
Copyright © 1998 Columbia University Press
All rights reserved

Library of Congress Cataloging-in-Publication Data
Barnett, Michael N., 1960–
    Dialogues in Arab politics : negotiations in regional order /
Michael Barnett.
        p.   cm.
    Includes bibliographical references (p. 339) and index.
    ISBN 978-0-231-10918-5 (cloth). — ISBN 978-0-231-10919-2 (pbk)
    1. Panarabism.   2. Nationalism—Arab countries.   3. Arab
countries—Politics and government.   4. Arab countries—Foreign
relations.   I. Title.
DS63.6.B35   1998
320.54'089'927—dc21
                                            98–12600

Contents

Preface

Albert Hourani, the distinguished historian of the Middle East, once observed that any book on twentieth-century Arab politics must "express a dialectic of unity and variety." Local interests and geopolitical imperatives pull Arab-speaking peoples apart, while the persistence of inherited traits, historic memories, and the attempt to address certain shared problems of identity bring them closer together.[1] Hourani was not alone among historians of Arab politics to note how the tension between transnational bonds and territorial divides has produced a rich mixture of conflict and cooperation among Arab states. For many observers, inter-Arab politics can be defined by the search for integration among Arab states and peoples, inspired by the belief that they are members of the Arab nation, only to be undermined by the existence of latent mistrust and manifested conflict. Such antagonisms, however, never fully extinguish the promise of integration, for the Arab states almost always return to solidarity after such conflict. Inter-Arab politics exhibits an inescapable rhythm of conflict and cooperation, itself a product of the dialectic of unity nurtured by the existence of transnational bonds and of the variety generated by rivalries that are part and parcel of territorial possessiveness and personal jealousies.

Scholars of international relations have another way of characterizing inter-Arab politics. Quintessentially realist. Perhaps with good reason. Arab politics has seen more than its share of wars, conflicts, and unfriendly acts. The region boasts of a number of strategically skilled and savvy leaders who are noted for their acumen at exploiting the political environment and regional ideology in order to pursue their goals of state power. Gamel Abdel

Nasser of Egypt. Hafiz al-Asad of Syria. King Hussein of Jordan. These and other Arab leaders have a well-earned reputation for their survival skills, derived in part from an appreciation of the international and regional forces and the direction in which the wind is blowing, and the flexibility to adjust their policies accordingly. Because security dominates all other concerns, given the prominence and persistence of inter-Arab conflict, transnational loyalties and "unity" slogans do not have any appreciable effect on interstate patterns.

Realism's view that Arabist sentiments fold in the face of anarchy contrasts decidedly with Hourani's insistence that Arabism animates the very texture of inter-Arab politics. A consequence of these obverse starting points is that observations of the region and explanations for those observations sometimes are startlingly different. Where Hourani finds an inescapable rhythm to the region that is generated by a dialectic of diversity and unity, realists note cycles of power whose origins reside in anarchy and the self-help behavior that it generates. Where Hourani implies that inter-Arab conflict derives in part from Arabism, realists respond that such conflict is a predictable manifestation of anarchy and power politics. Where Hourani and other seasoned observers of the region imply that what makes Arab politics Arab is Arabism, realist-inspired interpretations usually dismiss the claims that Arabism is causally consequential and that Arab politics has a social or cultural foundation, and instead advance the explanatory power of anarchy and the distribution of power. These substantial differences have led to divergent conversations and, at the extreme, to mutual dismissal: those concerned with theory tend to treat closely observed historical narratives as interesting but ultimately idiographic, and students of the region frequently indict theoretically generated interpretations as offering some important insights but ultimately contorting history. Any effort to narrow these differences must recognize that Arab politics has a social foundation that is culturally distinctive yet theoretically recognizable. This is my starting point. The claim is that doing so can generate an historically intuitive and theoretically inspired account of inter-Arab politics. My reinterpretation of the history of inter-Arab politics aspires to approach that lofty goal.

I view Arab politics as a series of dialogues between Arab states regarding the desired regional order—the ongoing debate by Arab states about the norms of Arab politics and the relationship of those norms to their Arab identities. Since the beginning of the Arab states system, Arab states and societies have been negotiating the norms of Arabism. Can Arab states conclude strategic alliances with the West? Are they expected to work for unification? Is it permissible for them to negotiate or have relations with Israel? Arab states have addressed and debated what the norms of Arabism should be as they have responded to the important events of the day, and as they have done so they have asserted that certain norms are expected or proscribed because of their shared Arab identity. By organizing Arab politics according to the debates about the desired regional order, I am offering a decided alternative to how we typically tend to think about Arab politics—or international relations, for that matter.

Arab states have had strikingly different views of the desired norms. Although such differences might be attributed to principled beliefs, the more prominent reason was regime interests, beginning with but not exhausted by survival and domestic stability. As a consequence, over the years Arab leaders have vied to draw a line between the regimes' interests, the norms of Arabism, and the events of the day. They attempted to do so through symbolic technologies. A defining feature of these moments of normative contestation was that Arab states competed through symbolic means to control the foreign policies of their rivals and determine the norms of Arabism. Nasser's ability to define the agenda and to rally the people in the streets in Damascus and Amman in his favor came not from the barrel of a gun but from his ability to deftly deploy the symbols of Arabism. Although students of international relations will probably receive this observation warily because of their tendency to assume that military and economic instruments define the technologies of influence, scholars of the region will quickly recognize this feature of Arab politics. And once the norm of Arabism was stabilized, few Arab leaders possessed the brazenness or recklessness required to defy them. Indeed, the rivalry and sometimes vicious name calling that marked the period of normative contestation usually yielded, however awkwardly, to speeches of solidarity and a general coordination of their policies. The conflicts between Arab governments have concerned the norms of Arabism and not the balance of power; their weapons of influence and control have derived from the symbols of Arabism; and they have impressively demonstrated their solidarity over the years because of their desire for social approval, which comes from being associated with the Arab consensus. To recognize these fundamental features of Arab politics requires an appreciation of the power of Arabism and its capacity to invite both conflict and cooperation among Arab governments, which possess a keen sense of self-preservation.

But Arab politics is not what it used to be. The unity that was defined by the presence of Arabism appears increasingly elusive, and the diversity defined by acreting statism appears increasingly prominent. The post–Gulf

War debate in Arab politics about whether some version of "Middle East-ernism" is supplanting "Arabism" exemplifies how Arab states are orienting themselves in new directions and identifying new interests that are enabled by the decline of Arab nationalism. Although scholars are in general agree-ment that a revolution in the organization of the Arab states system has oc-curred, the debate about its causes is considerable. I argue that how Arab states conducted themselves during these dialogues goes a long way toward explaining the map of the Arab world today. This is a world of their own making and unmaking. Of course, major transformations in regional sys-tems are a product of many different forces and factors, including wars and, most important here, changes in state-society relations. But, surprisingly, inter-Arab interactions have not been given their due.

This book examines the ongoing debates about the desired regional order, how Arab states repaired or revised the norms of Arabism through symbolic exchanges, and how the legacy of those exchanges is the fragmen-tation that currently defines the Arab states system. I begin the exploration of these themes in 1920 with the establishment of the mandate system and continue through today. Rather than treat the history of the Arab states sys-tem as one uninterrupted story, however, I identify five periods defined by different conversations about the desired regional order: from 1920 to the es-tablishment of the League of Arab States in 1945; from 1945 through the de-bate about the Baghdad Pact in 1955; from the 1956 Suez War through the 1967 Arab-Israeli War; from the 1967 war through the 1990 Gulf War; and the post–Gulf War period. The content of these dialogues has changed consid-erably over time, which suggests nothing less than a change in the underly-ing structure of Arab politics; by tracing these dialogues since 1920, we can follow the dynamics that have defined, shaped, and transformed the Arab states system.

This narrative is informed by sociological theory and contributes to the growing constructivist scholarship on international politics. Arab politics is generally viewed as realist terrain. But the prominence of identity politics, certainly familiar to even the most casual observer of the region, demands that we move beyond realism to consider other approaches that better rec-ognize the fundamentally social character of global politics. The challenge, however, is to acknowledge this social character without forgetting that ac-tors are frequently strategic and manipulative. Indeed, they could not be strategic and manipulative if there were no social foundations and norma-tive expectations to exploit and use for ulterior purposes. I draw from a reservoir of sociological theorizing, most prominently from the work of Erving Goffman, to explore this relationship between the normative and the strategic as it pertains to the debate about the desired regional order in Arab politics. In this fundamental way, international orders are an ongoing accomplishment and subject to continuing negotiations, which are defined by the strategic and symbolic interactions that are the factory of new environments. Structure through process.

This book goes beyond simply redescribing what scholars of Arab politics already know. Many excellent treatments of Arab politics are available, and I rely heavily on them. But resituating the "facts" of Arab history in an alternative narrative generates a different way of understanding these facts and of providing a systematic way of thinking about Arab politics. This narrative invites us to pull back from the details of the events and reflect on the more enduring processes that have defined how Arab states have conducted their relations, to consider how they have debated and revised the norms of Arabism. It therefore allows us to untangle the meaning of Arabism, to recognize its conceptual elasticity and the social and political forces that are responsible for its changed meaning. We also become more attentive to the ways in which the current climate in Arab politics is a product of the Arab states' own handiwork; if statism now overshadows Arabism, this is largely because of how Arab states conducted themselves during the heyday of Arabism. These concerns and claims are enduring controversies in Arab historiography, and the focus on inter-Arab interactions and the debate about the desired regional order, I claim, address each of them. The dialectic of unity and diversity that is widely noted by seasoned observers of the region requires a greater understanding of how that rhythm is generated through the strategic and symbolic interactions among Arab leaders that occur within a social context defined by Arabism—and how those interactions did not necessarily return Arab states to the starting point of unity but rather helped to redefine the meaning of unity and, ultimately, generated a path toward greater diversity.

This book also contributes to the emerging dialogue between international relations theory and the study of the Middle East. Scholars of the region write accounts that look idiographic to theorists of international politics, and theorists of international politics frequently compress the history of the region to the point that it looks exotic to scholars of the region. But it need not be that way. By drawing on international relations theory and by listening carefully to the politics of the region, I am attempting to craft an account of inter-Arab politics that is both theoretically informed and historically intuitive. Although scholars of international relations have been somewhat late to recognize that international relations transpire within a social environment, the idea that relations between states are affected by transnational norms is no surprise to students of the Middle East. Although scholars of the Middle East sometimes suggest that theirs is a region that is unique, international relations theory can help us recognize what is distinctive and what is generalizable. International relations theory can learn much from the politics of the Middle East, and Middle Eastern politics can be fruitfully informed by international relations theory.

I have accumulated many debts during the last few years and imposed myself on many colleagues; a real pleasure is being able to acknowledge their assistance and guidance. Alex Wendt and Emanuel Adler have read more versions of some chapters than either I or they probably want to recall. Greg Gause was a patient and generous reader and friend. Marc Lynch, Malik Mufti, and Bruce Maddy-Weitzman read the manuscript in its entirety and offered important correctives to my interpretation of Middle Eastern politics. Marty Finnemore, Andrew Grossman, Roger Haydon, Steve Heydemann, Ron Jepperson, Peter Katzenstein, Baghat Korany, Keith Krause, Jack Levy, Yagil Levy, Joel Migdal, Craig Murphy, Charles Tilly, and Marco Verweij read various portions of the manuscript. Gehad Auda, Laurie Brand, Bud Duvall, Dana Eyre, Ellis Goldberg, Robert McCalla, Avraham Sela, Ellie Podeh, and Mark Tessler offered advice and suggestions along the way. Kate Wittenberg expertly shepherded the manuscript through the various states of the process. Polly Kummel had the unenviable task of copyediting my prose and rose to the challenge.

I delivered portions of this argument in various places over the years: conferences sponsored by the Social Science Research Council (SSRC) at Brown University, the University of Minnesota, and Stanford University, as well as at other events at Rutgers University, the University of Washington, the University of North Carolina, Cairo University, Ain Shams University, and the Al-Ahram Press Institute. I have benefited from the criticisms and comments that I received in various corridors, forums, and e-mails.

The book was partially supported by the MacArthur Foundation—SSRC's International Peace and Security Fellowship. This unique program provided research support and the opportunity to read widely in other disciplines. I spent a year at the New School for Social Research, where Charles Tilly graciously hosted my stay and patiently answered my many questions about sociological theory. The SSRC Fellows' conferences provided another venue in which I was challenged by others from outside my discipline; I thank those who listened to my presentations in the bars and at the formal panels. I also want to thank the research assistance of Michael Malley in Madison, Wisconsin, Avi Muallan and Dina Cohen in Tel Aviv, and Ashshraf Rady in Cairo.

I immensely enjoyed my abbreviated time in the field because of the good friends who hosted my stay and pointed a *khawaga* in the right direction. In Tel Aviv the Dayan Center for Middle East Studies provided both tremendous resources and infinite hospitality. In Amman I was taken care of by several friends, including Khalid Mufti. In Cairo Jocelyn Dejong and Tariq Tall generously opened their home to me; I received a home away from home and a trenchant critic in Tariq. At each locale I knocked on the door of many policy makers and scholars. I learned much from them, and I thank them for submitting themselves to my interviews and many questions.

I dedicate this book to Victoria. She has offered support, relief, humor, and comfort in various places, through various phases, and in various ways. The joy of her conversation and her many qualities deserve a better return. But this is the book I wrote, and with all its flaws it is Victoria's.

Dialogues in Arab Politics

[1]

A Narrative of Arab Politics

Many of the best-known accounts of Arab politics are informed by a realist narrative. Realism's defining and cyclical narrative—the ongoing pursuit of states to provide for their security in an environment that is uncertain and dangerous because of the condition of anarchy, conflict as a way of life, and war as ever present or looming—seems to capture Arab politics.[1] Arab politics is renowned for its contending bids by Arab states for leadership, shifting alliances, steady stream of crises, occasional war, and ongoing pursuit of security and survival in a very rough neighborhood. If Arab politics has any distinguishing traits, it is the dramatic relief of the supposed existence of a community and shared identity against the harsh reality of anarchy and rivalry. Arab states ranked their survival and security ahead of Arab sentiments, and when they pledged their devotion to Arabism, the pledge usually came with empty rhetoric and false promises, a manipulative attempt to shore up a domestic situation, or an effort to bludgeon and embarrass an opponent.[2] Realist imagery dominates our understanding of Arab politics, and Arab politics "best fits the realist view of international politics" for good reasons.[3]

But realism has a difficult time addressing some fundamental features of Arab politics. Consider realism's reliance on hegemonies, balances of power, and alliances for understanding international stability. Realists would expect that in such a high-threat environment Arab states would attempt to increase their security against each other by accumulating arms and forming military alliances. But where are the arms races? Curiously, Arab states have shunned any noticeable effort to enhance their security by amassing weapons.[4] That they have refrained from this classic security-building option is not because they lack the wherewithal, for they certainly have raced with their non-Arab rivals, or because they have forged arms-control agreements, for there were none. Much of the history of Arab politics shows few recorded instances of an Arab government's taking cover or trying to bolster its security against an Arab rival through military accumulation. Exceptions to this observation exist, but such exceptions only animate the anomaly.

Perhaps Arab states chose not to develop their military arsenals but to increase their security through alliances. But a neorealist student of the region concluded his exhaustive survey by noting with some curiosity that "a different form of balancing has occurred in inter-Arab relations" as Arab states allied to protect their image and not in response to shifts in military power.[5] Security, in other words, was not tied to material power but to presentational politics. The unification of Syria and Egypt in 1958 is a case in point. The establishment of the United Arab Republic (UAR) sent shivers of insecurity throughout the Hashemite palaces in Iraq and Jordan, but Iraqi and Jordanian leaders did not fear the military power of the UAR; rather, they were concerned about their image as conservative states amid a tidal wave of support for pan-Arabism and unification. They responded as would any leader seeking survival under such circumstances: they unified their states— in other words, they did not construct a security alliance—in the hope of answering their domestic and regional critics. The case of the UAR is not alone in the annals of Arab politics; few alliances among Arab states were a response to shifts in military power, and many more were efforts at impression management.

The relative absence of arms races and security alliances is tied to another feature of Arab politics that appears peculiar from a realist view: Arab leaders were more practiced in the ways of symbolic politics than they were in the ways of military politics. More often than not Arab leaders deployed symbolic power, not military power, to enhance their security and to control each other's foreign policies. Simply put, Arab politics was symbolic politics. Arab leaders frequently took to the airwaves to portray their adversaries as outside the Arab consensus as a result of policies they had recently enacted or proposed. They took such charges seriously, expended tremendous energy pleading innocent of such crimes, and often adjusted their policies to avoid the appearance of impropriety, because they knew that to be perceived as violating a norm of Arabism could easily summon regional censure and, more consequentially, domestic turmoil. A defining feature of Nasser's foreign policy was his masterful use of the Voice of the Arabs radio broadcasts to accuse his rivals of threatening the Arab nation. In countless instances he mobilized people in the streets of Amman in his favor and made life difficult for King Hussein by portraying him as forsaking the Arab nation. Nasser did this not because it was good sport but because it was a highly effective way to control Hussein's foreign policy. Nasser was not unusual among Arab leaders in his use of symbolic tools, just more expert. In Arab politics sticks and stones had little effect, but words could really hurt.

Or consider the events leading up to the 1967 Arab-Israeli War. We have little evidence that military considerations drove Nasser to undertake a series of provocative actions toward Israel that pushed the region closer to war. Rather, he knowingly risked an unwanted war with Israel to preserve his image as the leader of Arab nationalism. Nasser was not alone in deciding to sacrifice state power for impression management; King Hussein calculated that if he went to war with Israel the worst that would happen was that he would lose Jerusalem and the West Bank, but if he stood on the sidelines an unforgiving Jordanian public would demand his crown. The king later reflected that the Arab mobilization for war was merely "propaganda, radio speeches, and talk."[6] If ideologies such as Arab nationalism are simply instruments of state power, as realists contend, why would Arab leaders sacrifice state power on the altar of Arab nationalism?

Finally, a widely observed transformation has occurred in Arab politics during the last few decades. To capture such changes scholars and politicians speak of the "new realism," the "maturation of the system," the "return to geography," the "end of pan-Arabism," the "fragmentation of the Arab world," "Middle Easternism," and the shift from the language of *qawmiyya* [national identity] to *wataniyya* [state identities].[7] These different labels represent different ways of describing normative fragmentation in Arab politics: whereas Arab states once were oriented toward each other because they presumed that their shared Arab identity generated shared interests, Arab states now are suspected of having state identities with separate interests that potentially orient them in distinct directions.

To explain this outcome realists elevate shifts in the distribution of power, notably the decline of the power of Egypt, Arab nationalism's champion, and the rise of the conservative oil states. But even when the shifts are judged on the realists' evaluative criteria, this view wilts: changes in the regional distribution of power do not correlate with the decline of pan-Arabism. Indeed, different accounts identify radically different moments for Arab nationalism's passing: one identifies the failed unity talks of 1963 between Egypt, Syria, and Iraq, another elevates the 1967 Arab-Israeli War, and still another argues for the swing in power from Egypt to Saudi Arabia in the mid-1970s.[8] Shifts in the distribution of power are a poor predictor of this fundamental change in Arab politics.[9]

Realism's inability to explain regional stability, the strategic interactions between Arab states, and the fragmentation in Arab politics are not simply inconvenient omissions but severe theoretical deficiencies. Perhaps realism is not the problem—maybe it is the region; after all, a long-standing tradition treats the region as irrational and therefore inexplicable using the theories that explain the histories of other regions. But we have no reason to presume that the region is unique and impervious to theorizing. Only a poor social scientist blames the subject for a faulty instrument.

That said, the scholarship on Arab politics lends implicit and explicit support to realism in several ways. The analytical frameworks offered almost always derive from realism. Few frameworks explicitly attempt to construct an alternative approach to Arab politics; the result is that realism maintains a privileged theoretical place.[10] Moreover, many historical accounts implicitly accept realist categories; shifting alliances, bids for leadership, and the onset of war generally mark historical time and thus implicitly lend support to a realist narrative that organizes history in much the same way. Furthermore, an unstated assumption is that the mere existence of conflict and the actors' attempt to maintain their security are properties of realism alone. But conflict is part of all social relationships and can have a source other than anarchy, few social theories presume that actors are not protective of their security, and we have no reason to assume that a shared identity necessarily and always leads to harmonious relations.

It is unfortunate that the scholarship on Arab politics is usually associated with realism because historical accounts of Arab politics depart significantly from how realism understands international life. Few narratives of Arab politics look to anarchy and the distribution of power to understand the state's foreign policy; most begin with Arab nationalism and discuss how it constrained and shaped the Arab state's foreign policy. Few accounts of Arab politics argue that the state's interests stemmed from anarchy; most discuss Arab national interests that derived from their shared Arab identity. Most accounts of Arab politics highlight those rare moments when an Arab state used military means of influence and treat as a matter of course how Arab states routinely used symbolic technologies to embarrass their opponents into submission. In general, scholars of international relations write that Arab politics is realist politics, even though these scholars are unable to account for some gaping omissions. And scholars of Arab politics write narratives of the region that defy realist categories, even though they are generally read and advanced as supporting a realist imagery.

This book advances a narrative of Arab politics that is theoretically distinctive and historically instinctive. Beginning in 1920 with the period of the establishment of the mandate system and continuing through the contemporary era, I examine the dialogues among Arab states concerning the desired regional order, that is, the rival imaginings about the relationship between the desired regional order, the norms of Arabism, and their identities as Arab states. These dialogues have been an enduring feature of Arab politics. The creation of the Arab League, the 1955 Baghdad Pact, Egypt's path to Camp David—these and other events triggered a hailstorm of debate among Arab states and societies about the norms of Arab nationalism. Does Arab nationalism demand political unification? Under what conditions can Arab states ally with the West? How should Arab states organize their activities to confront the Zionist threat? Arab states had rival opinions of what these norms should be, and a defining feature of these dialogues is that the Arab states competed through symbolic means to determine the norms of Arabism. But the legacy of these dialogues has been normative fragmentation in Arab politics. To understand the fragmentation that defines contemporary Arab politics requires a detailed understanding of how Arab leaders have related and competed over the years. By following these dialogues we are positioned to understand the dynamics that have defined, shaped, and transformed the Arab states system.

This narrative is informed by a constructivist approach to international relations theory. Building on various strands of sociological theory, constructivism posits that the actions of states, like individuals, take on meaning and shape within a normative context, that their interactions construct and transform their normative arrangements, that these norms can in turn shape their identity and interests, and that the "problem of order" is usually "solved" through social negotiations and a mixture of coercion and consent.[11] By adopting a constructivist approach, we are able to reconceptualize the history of inter-Arab politics, approach the debate over the desired regional order as Arab states and societies did, understand why Arab states competed through symbolic means to establish the norms of Arabism, and recognize how and why those ongoing struggles over the desired regional order caused the fragmentation in the Arab states system.

Dialogues and Regional Order

I organize Arab politics according to the ongoing negotiations about the desired regional order. States can be understood as engaged in a never-ending process of negotiating the norms that are to govern their relations. All groups of actors, including states, have norms that regulate their relations, govern their conduct in public life, and delimit the types of behaviors and actions that are permissible, prohibited, and desirable. Regional order, in this view, emerges not only because of a stable correlation of military forces but also because of stable expectations and shared norms.[12] But such normative arrangements are not givens; they are the result of political contestations and social interactions.[13] An additional feature of these struggles frequently goes unappreciated by scholars of international politics: states implicate their identities as they defend or advance a regional order. Norms, in short, might be not only regulative of their interests but also expressive of their identities. As is evident in the post–cold war shuffle, states are sorting out their future arrangements by asking who they are and what the ties that bind should be.

Arab states and societies have been involved in a continuous negotiation about the desired regional order, the norms of Arabism, and the Arab state's identity. Since the creation of the mandate system Arab states have been actively debating how they should organize their relations to achieve their shared concerns, which have largely revolved around the desire to protect the Arab nation from the West, confront Zionism, and strengthen the political community. Although Arab states defined these three issues as the consummate Arab interests, they had a more difficult time determining the appropriate means to further those goals. Should Arab states be allowed to negotiate separately with Israel? Can they conclude strategic alliances with the West? Must they work for integration to strengthen the Arab political community, or can they cooperate as sovereign states? As Arab states debated the answer to these questions, they usually claimed that some policies were proper for and expressive of their identities whereas others were not.

These debates about the desired regional order are most evident during a dialogue, an event that triggers an intensified discussion among group members about the norms that are to guide their relations.[14] At such moments states become fixated on the norms that define the regional order and how those norms are related to their identity. Arab politics has had many such instances. The creation of the League of Arab States in 1945, rumors that Jordan was considering relations with Israel in 1950, the 1955 Baghdad Pact that established an alliance between Iraq and Turkey, the Arab unity experiments of 1958 to 1963, the Arab summits of the mid-1960s, the Khartoum meeting after the 1967 Arab-Israeli War, the contest over the Camp David accords, the tremors from the Iraqi invasion of Kuwait in 1990—these and other events unleashed a dialogue about the desired regional order, which norms should organize their relations, and how those norms related to their identity as Arab states.

THE GAME OF ARAB POLITICS

A defining feature of these dialogues was that Arab states fought about the norms that should govern their relations. Understanding the creation, repair, and transformation of the norms of Arabism requires a detailed exploration of the interactions between Arab states. Social processes, not social structures, produce norms.[15] Norms do not operate behind the backs of actors; rather, actors determine what the norms are. Actors struggle to determine these norms because they have differences of opinion that stem from divergent principled beliefs and from opposing political calculations. But scholars are justified in looking first to instrumental reasons. After all, the norm that is advantageous to one actor can be detrimental and constraining to another. Arab leaders vied to promote a definition of the situation and to repair or reform the norms of Arabism that were connected to the desired regional order, because doing so could further their various interests and control the foreign policies of their rivals.

Defining the norms of Arabism was an exercise of power and a mechanism of social control. Some international relations scholars have an unfortunate tendency to portray norms as married to cooperation. Indeed, Arab leaders frequently claimed that these norms were intended to allow them to further the collective aspirations of the Arab nation. But frequently lurking beneath the lofty expressions of cooperation was the more base desire to determine the norms of Arabism because doing so would establish the parameters of what constituted legitimate action and thus represented an act of power. Nasser's power derived not from Egypt's military capabilities but from his ability to impose a meaning on the events of his time, to establish the norms of Arabism, and to weave a compelling image of the future. Arab leaders did not compete to increase their "relative gains," as measured in terms of military or economic power, but they did compete to establish the meaning of events and to define the norms of Arabism. A corollary was that the "threat" was not from the barrel of a gun but from the establishment of a norm or vision of political life that was contrary to the regime's interests.

Jordan and Iraq did not view the creation of the UAR in 1958 as a threat because of Syria and Egypt's newly combined military power but because the UAR offered a powerful vision of how Arab politics should be governed, and this had immediate implications for domestic stability.

A central ambition of this book is to explore how Arab states competed to define the norms of Arabism. To do so we must examine the social and strategic interactions between Arab states.[16] What makes these interactions social is that Arab leaders were in a structural condition of mutual dependence: because of their shared Arab identity they determined the norms of Arabism collectively and could hardly declare a sovereign prerogative over such matters, were expected to honor those norms, and generally did so because of their desire for social approval and the recognition that they were Arab leaders in good standing. What makes these interactions strategic is that Arab governments recognized that achieving their goals depended on the norms that were established and the actions of other Arab leaders, and they manipulated information and images in order to increase the likelihood that their preferred definition of the situation was accepted and that their desired norm was stabilized.

These social and strategic interactions inform what I call the game of Arab politics. The concept of a game, which dominates international relations scholarship and informs most analytically driven analyses of Arab politics, recognizes that states are in a social situation defined by the distribution of power; it assumes that states attempt to maximize security, survival, or power because of anarchy; and it attempts to determine the logic of their choices and the pattern of their interactions as prescribed by their preferences and identified constraints.[17] Many scholars of international politics have implicitly adopted this approach to organize their reading of Arab politics.[18] In this view Arab states were attempting to foster their security and survival, which depended on their assessment of the goals and determinations of other Arab leaders and on the distribution of power.

An alternative understanding of games, however, is that they are normative structures, that is, they contain the socially determined norms that restrict and guide what is considered acceptable. This approach suggests that the social situation contains norms that constrain the behavior of states; the social situation not only constrains these self-interested and faceless states but also is a source of identity and interests; and the logic of their choices and the pattern of their interactions is shaped by the normative structure that constitutes their identities and constrains their behavior. By embedding state action within a normative structure, I am attempting to blend *homo economicus* with *homo sociologicus;* if economic humans are calculating, utility-maximizing agents, sociological humans—though still calculating and pursuing interests—define their interests and modify their behavior within a normative context.

Arab leaders were embedded in a structure defined by Arabism and sovereignty that shaped their identities, interests, presentation of self, survival-seeking strategies, and strategic interactions. It all begins with Arabism. International relations theory has a penchant for treating the social fabric of global politics as either an instrument in the hands of self-interested actors or as a constraint on their behavior, but in both cases it gives priority to the material foundations of the environment. But the structure of international politics is comprised of normative and material elements, and that structure might not simply constrain but also constitute the identity and interests of states. Arabism was why Arab states were expected to pursue Arab national interests and act in concert to achieve their shared goals. In this way Arab leaders were regarded as representatives of the Arab nation and not only of the territorial state and were expected to be agents of the Arab political community and not only of their citizens.

Yet these were Arab leaders who frequently demonstrated a greater concern for their survival than for Arab nationalism. The observed gap between theory and practice has encouraged scholars of the region to conclude that Arab leaders proclaimed their commitment to Arab nationalism but through their actions demonstrated a greater commitment to themselves.[19] From such observations come realist conclusions. But ample historical evidence exists that Arab nationalism shaped the foreign policies of Arab states in consequential ways. So how should we conceptualize the relationship between the norms of Arabism and the actions of Arab officials who honored, exploited, and ignored these norms?

I draw from the work of Erving Goffman and others to claim that although Arab leaders occupied social roles that derived from the Arab nation as they interacted on a regional stage, they also maintained some autonomy from their roles that allowed them to be creative occupants and cynical manipulators. I assume that Arab leaders were deeply committed to their own survival. Recognize that at issue here was not the survival of the state that dwelled in anarchy but the survival of the Arab leader who dwelled in Arabism.[20] But because their legitimacy, popularity, and sometimes even survival depended on whether they were viewed as adhering to the norms of Arabism, Arab leaders expended considerable energy conveying the image that they were genuine disciples of Arab nationalism.[21] Such

4) Arab leaders were likely to honor stabilized norms because of a sense of self and a sense of survival.

NORMATIVE FRAGMENTATION

How Arab leaders played the game of Arab politics had the potential to transform that game. By focusing on dialogues as sites of norm creation and historical change, I am highlighting how their interactions generated a map of potential roles and worlds. In this respect events can be moments of change, bounded periods of time when a transformation of thought, experiences, and social relations occurs.[24] Recognizing that events can be transformative moments shifts our attention away from structural explanations to the microprocesses upon which structures are built and transformed, away from the language of structural determination and to that of social negotiation. This event-centered and process-oriented approach is generally consistent with many previous studies of Arab politics. These accounts have produced detailed considerations of the idiosyncrasies, diplomatic intrigues, and nuances of various events, which typically are selected because they are understood as turning points in Arab history. The creation of the Arab League, the Baghdad Pact, the rise and demise of the UAR, the 1967 war, the Camp David accords, the Iraqi invasion of Kuwait—these and other events are frequently forwarded as moments of rapid change when Arab leaders reconsidered the meaning of Arabism and their relationship to one another.

I hope to contribute to our understanding of these events in two ways. First, by focusing on the mechanisms that produced the observed outcomes, I am suggesting how these individual dynamics are indicative of more enduring and fundamental processes. Second, many studies implicitly or explicitly favor a realist explanation even though they concentrate less on how the regional balance of power shapes interstate interactions and more on how social processes shape regional structures. Therefore my reading of the historiography of Arab politics is that it is more consistent with constructivism than with realism. The focus on the social interactions between Arab states as a source of change provides a more consistent and compelling understanding of how and why these were transformative events in Arab history.

To chart the changes in the norms of Arabism is to consider the different meanings of Arab nationalism and to uncover why Arab nationalism underwent the conceptual transformation that it did. Scholars of Arab politics have implicitly recognized that Arab nationalism has demonstrated tremendous conceptual elasticity and has always been a work in progress, but surprisingly few studies have traced the changes in its meaning and its political implications. Much early work on the emergence of Arab nationalism has been generally attentive to its socially constructed nature, carefully considering the social and political processes, and the external challenges and intellectual movements, that were responsible for its emergence. But the debate over the "end of Arab nationalism" has been rather polemic and has had an essentializing tone that revolves around Arabism as unification or as nothing at all. I hope to offer a modest corrective to that debate. By examining the sinews of Arab nationalism as it has evolved during the debates about Zionism, the West, and Arab unity, I am attempting to provide a more nuanced understanding of the influence of Arab nationalism on inter-Arab dynamics and how the strategic interactions between Arab states were responsible for Arab nationalism's changing and recently declining fortunes. In general, by detailing and following the debate about the norms of Arab nationalism, I am allowing for the possibility of collective mobilization for political projects short of political unification, recognizing that various norms have been associated with Arab nationalism over the years, exploring how these changing norms had varying effects on state behavior and regional politics, and isolating how these norms were sustained or transformed as a consequence of inter-Arab interactions.

Scholars generally agree that Arab politics is not what it used to be. Whereas Arab states once were actively considering how to strengthen their ties and to integrate their polities at all levels, the defining theme of the past few decades has been normative fragmentation to the extent that Arab states are no longer as pressed toward mutual orientation because of underlying shared identities and interests. I observe two analytically distinct but historically related issues. Some rules of the game that have emerged revolve around sovereignty and its norms. A dramatic development in Arab politics is the greater agreement among Arab states that regional order should be premised on the norms of sovereignty. And the emergence of sovereignty in this instance is descriptively and analytically connected to the rise of statist identities that are better able to compete with an Arabism that generates alternative expectations. Indeed, the features that once defined Arab politics and Arabism—confronting Israel, shunning strategic alliances with the West, and territorial unification—have declined in prominence and have left many wondering what is distinctive about Arab politics.

The debate has been considerable among scholars of Arab politics regarding how to explain this fragmentation. Whereas some look to systemic politics and the shift in the distribution of power, and others look to domestic politics and state formation processes, I argue that the fragmentation was a result of how Arab leaders played the game of Arab politics. The strategic and symbolic exchanges that occurred between Arab leaders during a dialogue led to differentiation and fragmentation. Whereas Arab states professed an eternal devotion to the cause of Arab unity, their mutual suspicions and symbolic competition led to the creation of separate identities, roles, interests that encouraged Arab leaders to adhere to the norms of sovereignty and to privilege the discourse of state interests over Arab national interests. The strategic interactions between Arab leaders were largely responsible for the fraying fabric of Arab politics.

The claim that strategic and symbolic interactions were responsible for this normative fragmentation challenges the most compelling alternative: that state formation processes created a more "realist" environment.[25] Simply stated, this literature claims that the softer the state is, the more it will gravitate toward transnational ideologies to bolster its domestic and regional standing; the harder the state is, the easier it finds the forwarding of its interests. Conversely, that societal actors are no longer responding to the prospect of unification in the same way or demanding that their governments be associated with the norms of Arabism suggests a transformation in state-society relations and relatively successful state formation projects.[26] In general, this literature properly notes that Arab states were more likely to lean on transnational forces if their societies perceived these states as artificial, that Arab leaders attempted to reduce their vulnerability to the dictates and demands of other Arab leaders by encouraging their citizens to identify with the capital city and the regime in power through state formation processes, and that as a general rule the search for integration at the local level correlated with the increased fragmentation and decreased sense of collective obligation at the regional level.[27] State formation processes are connected to the changes that have taken place in the Arab states system for good reasons.

But this second-image approach suffers from two limitations that point to the necessity of examining the interactions between Arab states to understand the cause of this normative fragmentation. First, this literature nearly assumes that "stateness" must be theoretically and logically linked with a particular set of practices tantamount to realism and realpolitik. Yet stateness can be related to a host of practices. Nasser, who presided over the Arab world's only "national state," was Arab nationalism's most articulate and forceful spokesman. Although the European states rank high on indexes of legitimacy and capacity, they exhibit a pattern of politics that is far from the realist model now forwarded by some students of Arab politics. Indeed, the same European states that have high levels of stateness have been integrating—that is, in the exact opposite manner of Arab states. Second, state formation processes are decades-long developments and do not correspond directly with many of the important events usually identified as having transformed Arab politics. In a subtle recognition of this gap many explanations that center on domestic politics first examine how domestic politics shapes the state's foreign policy but then quickly shift attention to interstate interactions to understand the outcome. Domestic structures are not the wellspring of international norms; rather, they emerge from interstate interactions. The quality of inter-Arab interactions was what contributed to the differentiation among Arab states and not to successful state formation alone.

In sum, Arab politics can be understood as a series of dialogues concerning the relationship between identity, norms, and regional order, and by tracing these dialogues over time we are in a position to understand the fabric of Arab politics. Dialogues represent a moment when Arab leaders think aloud about the norms that should govern their relations; during these dialogues Arab states act strategically and deploy symbols to repair, stabilize, or transform the norms of Arabism that are consistent with their various interests; and these exchanges led to the widely observed fragmentation in Arab politics. These dialogues about the regional order animated Arab politics for years, and by tracking them through time we are positioned to follow the debates and dynamics that defined, shaped, and transformed the Arab states system.

Which Dialogues Among Which Arab States?

I am offering a narrative of Arab politics as the ongoing debate about the desired regional order. Briefly, a narrative concerns a story that is joined by a plot.[28] All theories of international politics have an implicit narrative. In realism that narrative is associated with the state's struggle for survival, balancing behavior and the ever-present threat and preparation for war; history, in this sense, is cyclical, and events are logically and causally connected by virtue of the story that realism tells. In this fundamental respect my approach is no different than realism; a narrative provides a way of approaching and organizing history, and realism represents one such approach.

Whether my narrative is more convincing, however, depends on the evidence that I bring to bear and how compellingly I connect these events causally and theoretically. I am not uncovering new facts, but I am generating an alternative interpretation and understanding of these events by situating them within an alternative narrative. For instance, if the Baghdad Pact receives relatively little attention in Stephen Walt's realist interpretation of Arab politics because it has little demonstrable influence on the balance of power, its standing is elevated once it is connected to the debate about the desired regional order. These events, moreover, are causally connected to the changes that follow in the debate about the desired regional order. The Baghdad Pact reestablished the parameters of Arab politics as it inaugurated the radical Arab agenda. That is, its causal consequence is not tied to the balance of power but to a change in the desired regional order. Although the narrative might be distinct, the social science methods that I use to provide theoretical leverage over these individual events and to causally and theoretical connect them in an intelligible way are quite familiar.

Thankfully, I do not have to examine all the dialogues among all the Arab states in order to gauge the changing content and nature of the debate about regional order. Although the League of Arab States has twenty-three members, I limit my investigation of the dialogues about regional order to Egypt, Lebanon, Syria, Jordan, Iraq, Yemen, and Saudi Arabia for both practical and theoretical reasons. On the practical level these countries, the original members of the League of Arab States, were at the forefront of and defined the debate about regional order. On occasion other Arab states entered the discussions, including the Persian Gulf and the North African states by the late 1960s, but by and large these seven Arab states provide a fairly good if not exhaustive representation of Arab politics over the decades. The other principal contributor to this debate was the Palestine Liberation Organization (PLO). Before the creation of the PLO in 1964, various leaders from the Palestinian community were important to this debate, particularly as it pertained to the confrontation with Zionism; however, Arab states largely vied for the claim to represent the Palestinians. The emergence of the PLO, however, gave the Palestinians an organization recognized by other Arab states, and eventually by non-Arab states as well, as their sole and legitimate representative. Beginning in 1964, therefore, the PLO played an increasingly prominent role in shaping inter-Arab dynamics and the debate about the desired regional order. These eight actors—seven states and one nonstate actor—were most important in shaping the dynamics that I observe. In this respect my goal is not to tell the complete and definitive history of Arab politics but to understand one important feature—their dialogues about regional order. To do so convincingly does not require a complete survey and accounting of the positions and foreign policies of all Arab states but rather a structured and selective slice.

My exploration of the ongoing negotiation of Arab states about regional order through dialogues has three layers. First, I examine the Arab states system from the beginning of the mandatory period in 1920 through today in order to trace the debate about regional order both at a particular moment and its historical development. Rather than treat the history of the Arab states system as one uninterrupted story, however, I divide it into periods according to the dominant debate about the desired regional order. Different periods have a different theme to their conversation. I have identified five distinct periods: from the mandate period up to the establishment of the League of Arab States in 1945; from 1945 through the debate about the Baghdad Pact in 1955; from the Suez War through the 1967 Arab-Israeli War; 1967 through the Gulf War; and the post–Gulf War period. Thus the content of these dialogues has changed over time, which suggests nothing less than a change in the underlying structure of Arab politics; tracing these dialogues provides something of a magnetic resonance device for examining the texture of Arab politics.

Second, within each period I examine three defining issues—the Arab states' relationship to unification, the West, and confrontation with Zionism—as a way of gauging the debate about the desired regional order and the goals and the socially acceptable means to pursue those ends. A celebrated and infamous point of contention is Arab nationalism's relationship to state sovereignty and whether Arab states were expected to work to bring the national identity and political authority into correspondence. Far from honoring the correspondence between statehood and sovereignty, a central debate in Arab politics involved whether its fundamental organization should rest on Westphalia, a gift from the West, or an alternative arrangement of the Arabs' devising.

Another enduring issue concerns whether and under what conditions Arab states could enter into strategic arrangements with the West. Western intrusions, interventions, and imperialism gave Arab nationalism a kickstart, and consequently a defining concern was how to increase the Arab states' power and security vis-à-vis the West. Beginning in the mandate period with anticolonialism, picking up steam in the mid-1950s (thanks to Nasser and his concept of positive neutrality), an article of faith among Arab leaders became they should shun strategic alliances with the West and practice the art of Arab self-reliance. Consequently, if realism assumes that states can enter into any alliance as they see fit, an emerging property of Arabism cautioned against alliances with the West not simply because it might reduce the state's autonomy but because it might jeopardize the security of the entire Arab nation.

And then there is the Arab-Israeli conflict. That Israel represents a threat to the Arab nation is derived from the Arab identity, and over the years the Arab states have established a series of norms that not only helped to overcome collective action problems but also served to define the meaning of Arabism. Regardless of how Arab states calculated their strategic or material interests, what Mohamed Heikal described as the taboo in Arab politics left unquestioned (until recently) the assumption that relations with Israel or a separate peace could never happen.[29]

Unity, the West, and Zionism have been salient, defining, and identity-expressive issues in Arab politics for several reasons. These were not simply foreign policy issues; they also were domestic issues, and in this respect they were not simply about domestic politics but also about identity politics. Because Arab leaders depended on Arabism to authenticate and support their rule of citizens who saw themselves as Arab nationals, the leaders' domestic legitimacy depended on how they conducted, presented, and carried themselves on these matters. Moreover, because these were Arab issues, they properly belonged to—and should be decided collectively by—all Arab states. A central feature here was that an Arab leader could hardly insist on his right to act unilaterally because of state sovereignty. It was bad form to act unilaterally on these issues, and other Arab states were quick to remind the would-be renegade that it also was bad politics. Finally, Arab leaders were forced to take a stand on these matters and judged accordingly, and through their collective positions and interactions on these issues they waged, defined, and transformed the debates about the desired regional order. Because these issues provided a litmus test for an Arab state's attitude toward Arabism, they also presented a moment when historical transformation was possible.

Third, rather than survey all the events that might be covered by, say, the relationship between the Arab states and Israel in the 1956–1967 period, I examine those that were decidedly salient and causally consequential for the future path of Arab politics. In other words, although I examine some events that led to the repair of a norm, most of those I examine were consequential for understanding the path and development of Arab politics. I want to understand events theoretically and causally, and instead of treating them as mere data points, I dissect them to understand how they represented moments at which norms were established, debated, and potentially transformed and when new historical roads opened up and others became more difficult. I emphasize the importance of path dependence—that when things happened and how they happened matter for what follows and what is subsequently possible or unlikely.[30] Therefore within each period I examine specific regional crises and events to observe both the nature of the dialogue and to consider whether and how its dynamics led to the creation of new normative arrangements and shifts in the desired regional order. Understanding the contemporary map of Arab politics requires following the trail of the states' interactions, the historical turning points at which Arab states reconsidered their relations, and how those turning points became consequential, given the subjective understanding of those moments in relation to earlier turning points.

Organization of the Book

Chapter 2 presents my framework for conceptualizing the dialogues in Arab politics as Arab states debated the norms of Arabism. The central concern here is to consider how the normative structure of Arab politics, constituted largely by Arabism and sovereignty, shaped the strategic, symbolic, and social interactions that ensued between Arab states in this encounter. Specifically, while Arab leaders maintained a strong interest in regime survival, Arabism and not anarchy provides leverage over the Arab governments' central objectives, presentation of self, and strategies; the technologies of power that they used as they debated the norms that were to govern their relations; and why their interactions repaired or reformed a norm and contributed to normative fragmentation in Arab politics.

The five periods categorized by the debate about the desired regional order comprise chapters 3 through 7. Chapter 3 examines the historical evolution of the Arab states system and the events leading up to the establishment of the League of Arab States. The breakdown of the old order—a consequence of the demise of the Ottoman Empire, the emergence of nationalism, and the spread of the world economy—and the fight for the "Ottoman succession" caused the region's inhabitants to consider how the Middle East should be organized and ordered—who constituted the political community. Anticolonial and Arab nationalist movements emerged in this context, and their meaning cannot be divorced from how individuals responded to and attempted to make sense of these fundamental transformations. These forces offered different visions of the future and had different prospects for success, given their relationship to institutionalized power and the state. In many respects this is the genesis of the Arab states system, when Arab nationalism's defining issues are crystallized: the West's segmentation of the Arab nation into separate mandates and territories, thus creating the fledgling demand for territorial unification; Britain's and France's hold over these states, establishing an Arab nationalism that became associated with anticolonialism and independence; and the increasingly strong Zionist presence, particularly the Great Palestinian Revolt of 1936, which placed Palestine on the map as an Arab issue. The defining and closing event of this period is the debate about the League of Arab States. Arab leaders gathered in Cairo to consider—and then rejected—an institutional architecture that would be more favorable to the idea of territorial unification; indeed, an inescapable feature of the League's charter was its nod toward sovereignty and nearly possessive statism.

Chapter 4 examines the period from the establishment of the League of Arab States through the yearlong debate about the Baghdad Pact in 1955. I examine three issues. The first, revolving around the relationship between Arab nationalism and Zionism, had two defining moments: the decision by the Arab states to invade Palestine upon the termination of the mandate in May 1948, and the subsequent decision by the League of Arab States to prohibit a separate peace with Israel in April 1950. What is striking about both cases is that the embryonic norms of Arabism and symbolic accumulation led Arab states to alter their policies in decided and highly consequential ways. Although Arab leaders expressed an array of attitudes toward Zionism—including moderate hostility, indifference, and seeing a potential political ally—the desire to be associated with the norms of Arabism, the use of symbolic sanctions against one another, and symbolic competition led them down the path of prohibition.

The second issue concerns the relationship between Arab nationalism and unification. Although Egypt, Saudi Arabia, and Lebanon hoped that the League of Arab States would place an institutional blanket on this possibility, leaders of the Fertile Crescent circulated various proposals to this end for more than a decade. The most important motion occurred in the fall of 1949 when Iraq and Syria seriously contemplated unification. Egypt derailed a primary motivation for Syria's unification drive, security and fear of Israel, by ingeniously proposing a collective security pact. This proposal led to the 1950 Arab Collective Security Pact and the first glimmer that Arab states might coordinate their foreign and security policies in a much more forthright manner. But it also put a momentary end to unification bids. The third issue concerns the relationship between Arab nationalism and strategic relations with the West. The Baghdad Pact represented a turning point in Arab politics; until that moment the dynastic rulers had largely kept the lid on radical Arabism. Iraq's decision to ally with Turkey and the West, however, stoked the embers of Arabism, catalyzed a regional debate about the relationship between the Arab world and the West, led to the norm prohibiting alliances with the West, marked the passage to a more radical version of Arab nationalism, and crowned Nasser as the unchallenged leader of Arab nationalism.

Chapter 5 examines the third period, which is framed by the 1956 Suez and 1967 wars and defined by the clash between state and nation, which is symbolized by the rise and decline of unification on the political agenda. The Suez War's principal effect was to institutionalize tendencies that were already present in the system, namely, the eclipse of the British Empire and the West and the undermining of all Arab leaders who were their political allies. During this period Arabism became synonymous with positive neutrality and self-reliance among the Arab states. The emergence of radical forces, however, also produced a greater interest among some societal forces and state elites for territorial unification. The shining moment was the creation of the UAR by Egypt and Syria in 1958, which completely altered the region's political debate. Its ignoble demise in 1961 notwithstanding, the demand for unification retained some force and underwrote the tripartite talks of 1963 involving Egypt, Syria, and Iraq. These talks, which began with much fanfare and ended in wicked acrimony, had two consequences. The first was a general decline in the belief that unification was possible in the near future or even desirable. In short, the legacy of these failed experiments was greater suspicion of pan-Arabism and a growing acceptance of sovereignty. The second consequence was the elevation of Israel on the Arab agenda, symbolized by the era of summitry. Beginning with the Cairo summit in January 1964, the Arab states temporarily overcame their differences to convene a series of meetings intended to forge a collective Arab response to the Israeli challenge. The era of summitry soon descended into regional acrimony in 1966, and by late December and continuing through June 1967 Arab states engaged in symbolic competition intended to demonstrate their allegiance to Arabism through their strident actions toward Israel; the dance of symbolic competition, however, sashayed into symbolic entrapment and the 1967 Arab-Israeli war.

Chapter 6 examines the post-1967 period. What is striking is that the issues of the West and unification began to disappear from dialogues about the desired regional order. For the most part, the Arab-Israeli conflict took center stage and became, for all intents and purposes, how Arab leaders defined and demonstrated their credentials and the symbols of Arabism that they sought to accumulate; indeed, at roughly the same moment that they were converging on the norms of sovereignty, they entered into a more divisive and open-ended debate about how to organize the Arab-Israeli conflict. I begin with the aftermath of the 1967 war and the events leading up to and resulting from the Khartoum conference of September 1967; the significance of Khartoum was that it signaled Nasser's withdrawal from radical politics and a further step toward sovereignty. The Jordanian Civil War of 1970 further institutionalized sovereignty; placed in the difficult position of either allowing King Hussein to bludgeon the PLO, the new symbol of Arabism, or intervening and perhaps undermining the principle of sovereignty, Nasser and other Arab leaders supported Hussein. For the next several years the defining events revolved around the Arab-Israeli conflict. Although the Arab states responded to their defeat in the 1967 war with a semblance of solidarity, the victory of 1973 stirred them toward the opposite direction as Anwar Sadat's thinly veiled unilateralism—beginning with the 1975 Egypt-Israel disengagement agreement and continuing through the 1977 flight to Jerusalem, the 1978 Camp David accords, and the 1979 peace treaty—starkly challenged the norms of Arabism. Although the Arab states responded by ostracizing Egypt for its heresy, for the next decade they failed to act proactively to Egypt's challenge, because Libya, the PLO, Syria, and Algeria (collectively known as the "Steadfastness States") held virtual veto power and blocked anything other than the status quo. No other Arab state dared to venture publicly outside this consensus. Still, the emergence of statist identities and acceptance of the norms of sovereignty to organize regional politics were related to a growing disagreement among Arab states over both broad principles and short-term strategies concerning the Arab-Israeli conflict. Two other developments suggest a growing fragmentation of Arab politics. The first is the emergence of subregionalism, which first appeared with the establishment of the Gulf Cooperation Council in 1981. The second is a continuing effort to develop some common norms of interaction, although these norms are increasingly indistinguishable from those of international society. These post-1967 events, in short, signal the emergence of statist identities, a centrist definition of Arab nationalism that is consistent with sovereignty, and acceptance of sovereignty as the basis for regional order.

Beginning in the 1970s political Islam became part of the mix of political challenges confronted by modernizing and religious states alike.[31] But I will pay relatively little attention to political Islam because Islam's principal challenge has been to domestic governance rather than regional governance. I am not denying that Islam has a transnational component. Westphalian sovereignty rests on a territorial logic that is denied by Islamists who assert that the authority of the state derives from religious principles and practices that know no territorial boundaries. Islamic movements also have strong ideas about how the state should conduct its foreign policy, particularly on the question of Israel and the West as a religious and cultural threat rather than as a nationalist threat. There is the Organization of Islamic Countries, and Saudi Arabia has sponsored various Islam-based interstate organizations to act as a counterweight to Arab-based organizations. And Islamic movements have received financial backing from outside and constructed cross-state organizations. But Islamic movements in contemporary practice have targeted their energies at state-society rather than interstate relations, demanding domestic rather than regional reforms.[32] Simply put, if the divide in regional politics is statism versus Arabism, in domestic politics it is Islam versus secularism.

Chapter 7 considers the question of whether the end of the Arab states system is at hand. The Gulf War unleashed a flood of discussion about the Arab regional order and what, if any, sorts of exclusive arrangements should be constructed in the ashes of Arabism. Whereas the decades-long debate about the desired regional order revolved around the premise that as Arab states they shared certain fundamental objectives that should be properly handled collectively, the Gulf War—coming on the heels of rising statism, sovereignty, a centrist definition of Arab nationalism, and political Islam—undermined these assumptions. Indeed, the post–Gulf War debates question whether an *Arab* states system is disappearing, for Arabism is no longer the defining principle of regional politics; the marker to differentiate membership in the group and its associated organizations; or able to make the same claims on or have the same force regarding the practices of Arab governments. The post–cold war debate about the concept of Middle Easternism and the readiness to acknowledge Israel's legitimate place in the region and potential inclusion in regional institutions and organizations speaks to these issues.

In sum, these five periods are defined not simply by a change in the debate about regional order but, more specifically, by a changing relationship between the Arab states and the underlying structure of regional politics. My goal is to demonstrate how and why these fundamental changes have occurred in the underlying structure of Arab politics and the norms that guide and define the Arab states system and to show that such changes point to a shift in the game of Arab politics and the desired regional order. This transformation occurred through dialogues among Arab states and state formation processes. Both processes led to the relative salience of state-national identities over alternative political loyalties; a growing differentiation between Arab states; a growing interest by Arab leaders in presenting themselves in ways that are statist and more consistent with the demands of sovereignty; and a willingness by Arab leaders to more consistently occupy the roles and norms associated with sovereignty. But my central concern is to demonstrate the causal contribution of interstate interactions to these very developments. Such developments do not imply a termination of this debate over the desired regional order. Far from it.

Chapter 8 identifies several themes that suggest how constructivism helps us recognize what makes inter-Arab politics distinctive and familiar. To examine inter-Arab politics with a constructivist spirit is to reacquaint international relations theory and the study of the Middle East. Various features of inter-Arab politics have remained inexplicable from a realist perspective but intelligible from a constructivist perspective, including the prominence of symbolic exchanges, the character and quality of alliances and institutions, and the social processes responsible for transforming the character of Arab politics. But this study of inter-Arab politics also contributes to international relations theory in various ways and elevates several themes likely to be as present in other regions as they are in Arab politics.

The Game of Arab Politics

Arab states have been engaged in a continuous, often bitter, and divisive debate about regional order, the norms that should regulate their relations, and how those norms express their Arab identities. Although these debates were an almost daily feature of the political landscape, they became dramatically visible, heated, and politically consequential at certain historical moments. When an event triggers an intensified discussion among the members of the group about the norms that are to guide their relations, I call such moments *dialogues*. The Baghdad Pact of 1955, the establishment of the United Arab Republic in 1958, the Arab summit meeting of 1964, the disengagement agreements between Israel and Egypt in the mid-1970s, the Camp David accords of 1979, the Iraqi invasion of Kuwait in 1990, and other events catalyzed a fervent debate about the relationship between the Arab state and the Arab nation.

These dialogues about how to handle relations with the West, integrate their states, and confront Zionism invited participation from all Arab states because the outcome of that debate would affect their interests. These were Arab issues, connected to their shared Arab identity, blurring the distinction between the domestic and the international and thus arresting any claims of sovereign prerogatives and making their behavior accountable to a regional audience and part of a collective undertaking. Arab states had every reason to take part in debates whose outcome would determine what policies were and were not available to them. But Arab states had a more immediate reason to register their opinions: they leaned heavily on Arab nationalism to legitimate their rule and justify their actions and generally honored the norms of Arabism because they desired the social approval and symbolic capital that came from being identified by their societies as Arab leaders in good standing. Arab governments were more animated by a challenge to the norms of Arabism than they were by a shift in the distribution of military power because the former, and not the latter, was a more concrete and direct threat to their various interests. Predictably, then, they competed fiercely to draw a line between the regime's interests, the norms of Arabism, and the events of the day. Determining whether a norm applied in a social situation was an act of power, closely attached to the government's popularity and future plans, and a mechanism to control the foreign policies of other Arab states.

Dialogues can be understood as moments of strategic interaction, when actors are "in a well-structured situation of mutual impingement where each party must make a move and where every possible move carries fateful implications for all of the parties."[1] At such moments of interdependence the ability of actors to obtain their preference depends on the choices made by other actors. As a consequence, actors will select a course of action that incorporates the probable choices of other actors. But they also are likely to try to find ways to increase the likelihood that they will obtain their preference. Actors attempt to coordinate their actions, and to manipulate each other's choices, in order to achieve the best result possible. Arab leaders were in a social situation defined by mutual dependence: because of their shared Arab identity, they determined the norms of Arabism collectively, were expected to honor those norms, and generally did so because of their desire for the social approval that came with being associated with Arabism.

Social scientists typically liken such social and strategic interactions to a game. For scholars of international relations such game metaphors are closely associated with game theory. Game theory examines the strategic choices among self-interested rational actors who operate under a specified social situation in the context of interdependence of choice among other utility-maximizing actors. Many realist-inspired analyses of Arab politics approach inter-Arab relations in ways that parallel game theory's basic approach to international politics. Specifically, they proceed on the belief that Arab states attempt to maximize their security or power, that their ability to achieve these goals depends on the actions of other Arab states, and that the structures that condition their choices are anarchy and the distribution of power.

Sociologically minded students of strategic interaction provide an alternative understanding of a game: a "normative structure" that is both external and internal to each player.[2] The game is external to the players because they tend to treat the social situation as a constraint on their ability to achieve their goals; thus the game encourages them to act strategically. But the game also is internal to the players because the normative structure establishes the culturally and historically specific terms in which actors think and relate and thus is a source of the players' collective beliefs and strategies. Following this tradition necessitates an attempt to identify the rules of the game, that is, the socially determined norms that restrict and guide what play is considered acceptable, to "display the associated normative expectations, and thus attempt to understand action as doing of what is normatively expected in a situation structured by rules."[3] Sociological conceptions of a game, then, begin not with the asocial actor but with a social whole that determines the normative enactments and rule-governed conduct that actors are expected to follow during their social encounters. In this view the choices made by actors are linked not simply to private wants but also to societal expectations.[4]

This sociological approach departs from realist-inspired assessments of inter-Arab politics in three important ways. First, the normative structure defined by Arabism and by sovereignty is why Arab states identify themselves as Arab and delineate a set of Arab national interests. In other words, whereas realist approaches bracket the identity and interests of the players and treat the environment as a constraint, constructivist approaches treat the environment as a source of identity and interests for the players of the game.[5] This move, however, is only meant to balance out the stark asocial view of actors advanced by many microeconomic approaches, not to replace it with an equally artificial view of actors as completely socialized and domesticated. Actors are not simply the bearers of social roles and enactors of social norms; they also are artful and active interpreters of them. Such a view allows for the possibility that the actors can both honor and manipulate those norms. Arab leaders were not simply instruments of the will of the Arab nation. They also were active interpreters of that will, spinning interpretations that frequently incorporated their other agenda items in a highly manipulative way. States are still calculating strategic egoists a fair bit of the time. But the underlying normative structure shapes their calculations and strategies.[6] Not all is fair in love and war. And not all was possible in Arab politics. The normative structure constituted and constrained Arab states, generating incentives for state action and presenting the states with opportunities to twist these social roles for ulterior motives.

Second, the normative structure shapes the technologies of power that actors use to influence the actions of other actors. Students of Arab politics have frequently described how Arab leaders attempted to control the policies of their rivals through discursive means and the manipulation and deployment of symbols, but they have failed to explicitly theorize how such technologies are possible because of a normative structure that leaves actors susceptible to such technologies. The more general point is that international relations theorists tend to focus on material means of influence because they conceive of the environment as asocial, defined by the distribution of power, and populated by "billiard-ball"–like actors who care about their military and economic standing and little else. But if international politics is understood as social, defined by a normative structure, and populated by actors who care about their reputation, the means of influence can include discursive, symbolic, and communicative action.

Third, the analysis of strategic conduct must be attentive to how actors "draw upon structural properties" as they make and unmake their relations.[7] Because Arab states are addressing whether to revise or repair a norm of Arabism, their strategic interactions conceivably can lead to a transformation of the norms that govern their relations. Normative structures, then, are not fixed and permanent entities but are produced through social interactions and social processes. Social processes and not social structures, interstate interactions and not the distribution of power, are responsible for normative change. But unlike most approaches to strategic interaction in international politics that hold constant the identities and interests of states, the constructivist approach adopted here allows for the possibility that during a dialogue Arab states are reconsidering their political identities as they reconsider the norms that govern their relations. Strategic interaction could lead to normative integration or normative fragmentation, and a central concern here is why it led to the latter in Arab politics.

Beginning with the normative structure and not with realism's simplifying assumptions regarding the interests of states and their constraining environment certainly complicates the effort to generate a precise and deductive model of strategic interaction. But the promise is that such complications are generously compensated by the presentation of a more accurate understanding of inter-Arab politics. Although Arab leaders maintained a strong interest in regime survival, Arabism and not anarchy provides leverage over the Arab governments' central objectives, presentation of self, and strategies; the technologies of power that they employed as they debated the norms that were to govern their relations; and the reasons that their interactions, which allowed for repair or reform of a norm, led to fragmentation in Arab politics.

This chapter begins by considering how the structure of Arab politics, a structure defined by social and material elements, represented a source of identity and interests for Arab states. Arab leaders, however, were not bearers of these structures; they were at once constrained by and manipulated the norms of Arabism. But the content of these norms was a matter of debate. Because these norms of Arabism were connected to the regimes' various interests, the regimes competed to determine their content. The next section argues that Arab leaders competed to establish the norms of Arabism through symbolic exchanges, discusses why symbolic exchanges were so prominent in Arab politics, and outlines the distinct characteristics of these symbolic exchanges. The concluding section considers how these dialogues were sites of normative change and, in the case of Arab politics, led to normative fragmentation.

The Structure of Arab Politics

The structure of any regional or international society is comprised of both material and normative elements.[8] Although international relations theorists sometimes have a penchant for reducing political life to its base material components and for eradicating the social, the structure of any politics—whether it is interpersonal, domestic, or international—always has a defining social element that must be situated alongside the material. But this structure is not only part of the environment that actors confront as they attempt to pursue their interests. The environment is also a source of their identities and interests.

These issues are central for considering the structure of Arab politics. To be sure, Arab states lived in a formal anarchy, but these were hardly states that could easily and clearly distinguish the "inside" from the "outside"— that could discriminate the political community that resided within its borders from that which existed on the other side—and whose societies clearly and consistently differentiated between "us" and "them" based on territorial markers. The boundaries of the Arab identity and the territorial lines drawn by the colonial powers pushed and pulled the debates in Arab palaces and cabinets. We call these Arab states with Arab national interests for a reason, and the reason is Arabism.

That the normative structure of Arab politics is comprised of both sovereignty and Arabism, and that this structure is a source of identity and interests can be best appreciated through the concept of social roles and norms.

Social roles concern a position in a set of social relations and therefore are autonomous from and can exist apart from the individual actor who might occupy that role.[9] Roles, in other words, are socially recognized positions accompanied by normative expectations and demands; the normative expectations attached to the social roles constrain the behavior of actors. Norms are expectations that constrain action within a specific social context.[10] In this way, "when an individual follows a norm, she acts in a way learned by familiarity with previous accepted instances or examples. The intention is to act in proper analogy with those examples."[11]

The analytic distinction between regulative and constitutive norms is useful for thinking about Arab politics.[12] Regulative norms enable actors to overcome collective action problems associated with interdependent choice. In other words, even when actors desire some degree of cooperation to further their self-interest, they still need to negotiate explicit rules to encourage compliance and reciprocity. Constitutive norms, on the other hand, are a direct expression of the actor's identity—they tell actors how to enact a particular identity and how to present themselves. Actors frequently behave in certain ways and not others because of the relationship between such behavior and their identity. As Erving Goffman observes, to follow a norm is a communicative act, expressive of one's self and self-understanding in the situation.[13] In this way constitutive norms provide a link between agency and structure to the extent that they instruct players how to enact their identity and accompanying social role.

The norms that animated the debates in Arab politics largely concerned how they would enact their identities to accomplish their collective aspirations. In one sense these norms were intended to help them overcome collective action problems. But at a more fundamental level these norms were tied to their very identity as Arab states and allocated to them their very interests. Arabism, for instance, did not simply instruct them to avoid bilateral settlements with Israel, although it did; it also helped to construct Zionism as a threat and as a defining element of the Arab national interest. To contemplate relations with Israel, to violate the taboo of Arab politics, was to invite public ridicule and charges of having betrayed the Arab nation. Although various Arab governments privately believed that they gained little from the state of war with Israel and might profit materially from a reduction, if not resolution, of the conflict, they knew better than to air such ideas in public. In 1950 King Abdullah of Jordan calculated that Jordan's economic and political interests might be better served by ending the state of war with Israel, concluding some commercial agreements, and arranging for an outlet to the sea; a Jordanian and Arab public that viewed such agreements as blasphemy overruled such material calculations. The norms of Arabism sanctioned some strategies and placed others outside the normative reach of Arab states, regardless of their capabilities or how they calculated their material incentives.

Arab leaders occupied social roles that contained normative expectations as they performed on the regional stage. In fact, they occupied two roles: agent of a sovereign state and agent of the wider Arab political community.[14] What are the normative expectations associated with sovereignty? Such norms have varied considerably over the years, but at a minimal level they accord a measure of possessiveness and exclusivity to the state. It has authority over its domestic space and the authority to act as a legitimate member of international society, and such entitlements are embodied in the principle of noninterference. As John Ruggie has argued, the development of the institution of sovereignty differentiated "among units in terms of possession of self and exclusion of others," and created an international order that enabled states to become the principal unit of international life.[15] Being recognized as sovereign amounts to a social permission granted by the community of states to act with certain powers and implies a certain measure of self-restraint by other members of this community, that is, a live-and-let-live attitude.[16]

Arab states were sovereign states, and their leaders had a strong interest in defending the territorial and sovereign basis of their authority and power. The mandate system and colonialism created the territorial boundaries of these states, and the anticolonial tide in these countries largely demanded immediate independence and sovereignty rather than rewriting the borders that were a gift of the West. Having worked so hard for their independence, Arab governments were hardly excited about turning over their newly won sovereignty to a larger entity in which they would have reduced political power. From such considerations came the decision by the Arab states to construct a charter for the Arab League in 1945 that made generous references to their sovereign basis of authority and the sanctity of their territorial confines. As Arab leaders competed on the regional stage, they did so as heads of sovereign states, and they wielded sovereignty as a normative shield against encroachments from other Arab leaders.

Arab states were formally sovereign states, but they also were *Arab* states. What made them Arab states was their shared identity. Because of a confluence of historical processes Arab nationalism emerged from its standing as a romantic movement at the beginning of the twentieth century to tower over the political landscape and shape the region's political identity and discourse of political protest.[17] Quite simply, this is why these were Arab states with Arab national interests.[18] Arab states presented themselves as Arab because of their shared language, heritage, and future; they shared a common story line that enjoined them and separated them from non-Arab states. As Arab states they also had shared interests, which largely concerned the struggle for formal independence and autonomy from the West, the struggle against Zionism, and search for unity. Because these interests derived from the shared Arab identity that enveloped the separate Arab states, these interests frequently overrode those of sovereignty to the extent that sovereignty provided a degree of possessiveness that Arabism denied. As Walid Khalidi has observed, "Raison d'état no less than raison de la révolution can invoke raison de la nation, while even raison de la status quo can invoke both these latter. Only explicit or transparent raison d'état is heresy."[19] An Arab state that attempted to claim a sovereign prerogative when it sought a strategic alliance with the West was quickly reminded by other Arab states that such an alliance was a public and not a private matter because it concerned the Arab nation. Most famously, an Arab nationalism that demanded territorial unification represented a direct challenge to the sovereign authority and territorial basis of Arab states. In these and other ways, although Arab states were formally sovereign, they had to work out the meaning of sovereignty in practice, in conflict, and in relationship to a (prior) set of claims that derived from Arab nationalism. Arabism and not anarchy was why they had a shared Arab identity and interests.

If Arab leaders had automatically pursued these Arab interests and mindlessly conformed to the norms of Arabism, we would study Arab politics for its impressive solidarity and awe-inspiring cooperation, and Arab leaders would have a reputation for subordinating their personal interests to the Arab nation. But Arab politics is renowned for its conflict, and Arab leaders are famous for caring more for themselves than for the Arab nation. I am certain that many students of the region would be willing to extend what the historian Kamal Salibi has called the "confidence game" of Lebanese politics to all of Arab politics: "The game involved a succession of devious transactions between players who invariably pretended to stand for nationalist ideals and principles aimed at the common good, while they strove to outwit and overturn one another, motivated by atavistic loyalties and insecurities for which the professed ideals and principles normally served as a mere cover."[20] If they could act so cynically, if not instrumentally, with regard to the norms of Arabism and be more accomplished at demonstrating their commitment through words than through deeds, how meaningful were these norms? And, more to the point, how can such norms, if they are as ephemeral as they seem, shape the game of Arab politics?

A good place to begin is with the recognition that structures make possible and circumscribe what actors can do in concrete situations, but they do not determine action. In this regard individuals are not cultural dupes; they are not perfectly mannered representatives of a static, harmonious, and securely anchored society. "Structure provides the condition for the possibility of action and guides how actions are to be performed, but it is agents who produce and reproduce this structure by means of activity."[21] The roles and norms that they are expected to follow demand interpretive activity on their part. But this interpretive activity also allows actors to be skillful and willful manipulators of those societal expectations. Rather than construct an image of a normative structure that is honored at all times or is pronounced as meaningless, it is better to conceive of a normative structure that provides incentives for actors to honor and manipulate the social roles and norms of that structure. The gap between theory and practice in Arab politics is as expected here as in any social setting.

Erving Goffman's classic *The Presentation of Self in Everyday Life* offers a synthetic, sophisticated, and systematic statement concerning the relationship between self-interested actors, the roles they perform on a public stage, and the underlying moral order.[22] Goffman recognized that although actors occupy roles as they interact on a public stage, they also maintain some autonomy from their roles that allows them to be creative occupants and cynical manipulators. Social roles are generally permissive and provide the actors who occupy them some degree of autonomy; the actors can be expected to follow norms some of the time but disregard them at others. Actors, in short, maintain "role distance."

Although actors are likely to try to ensure that their performances are consistent with the expectations of their audience, they frequently want to satisfy not only their audiences but also themselves—and they will use their roles for such a cause. Actors can exploit their social roles, manipulating them to serve ulterior ends. Goffman's concluding statement is worth quoting at length:

> In their capacity as performers, individuals will be concerned with maintaining the impression that they are living up to the many standards by which they and their products are judged. Because these standards are so numerous and so pervasive, the individuals who are performers dwell

more than we might think in a moral world. But, *qua* performers, individuals are concerned not with the moral issues of realizing these standards, but with the amoral issue of engineering a convincing impression that these standards are being realized. Our activity, then, is largely concerned with moral matters, but as performers we do not have a moral concern with them. As performers we are merchants of morality. Our day is given over to intimate contact with the goods we display and our minds are filled with intimate understandings of them; but it may well be that the more attention we give to these goods, then the more distant we feel from them and from those who are believing enough to buy them. To use a different imagery, the very obligation of profitability of appearing always in a steady moral light, of being a socialized character, forces one to be practiced in the ways of the stage.[23]

Goffman brilliantly highlighted how actors are performers who interpret their roles and occasionally exploit them for purposes for which those roles were not generally intended. Yet actors are able to manipulate their image because a moral fabric exists (something denied by materialist approaches), and they understand these normative expectations. Goffman's dramaturgical imagery, in short, suggests how actors manipulate the underlying moral framework in the service of ulterior ends.

But all this cynical manipulation can be dangerous: actors might soon have their reputations and moral character called into question. To avoid this outcome they will engage in "face work" and "impression management" to convince their audience that they are operating according to society's moral framework. Not only does such maneuvering reveal that society has a normative character but a convincing performance requires more than talk—it requires action that is consistent with these expectations. Therefore actors will abide by social norms for a host of reasons—including self-interest and self-image—but in either case their desire to be viewed as moral creatures, to be operating according to society's standards, will shape their behavior.[24]

This understanding of society—that actors stand distant from their social roles and can manipulate them for ulterior purposes, though for reasons of self-interest and self-image are prone to act according to society's normative expectations—is a cornerstone of my approach to Arab politics and provides theoretical leverage in regard to how Arab states are likely to handle and conduct themselves on the public stage. I begin with the assumption that Arab leaders were fundamentally concerned with regime survival. Regime survival and domestic stability were daily concerns for state elites that governed societies that openly questioned the legitimacy of the state and the government's ability to accomplish the myriad tasks expected of state building in the modern era. Accordingly, when peeling back the layers of motivations that drove the Arab governments' policies, regime survival was nearly always at the top of the list.[25] Indeed, sometimes Arab leaders knowingly and willingly subordinated the "logic of anarchy" and state power to the logic of regime stability and personal power; the creation of the UAR in 1958 and the 1967 Arab-Israeli War were driven by the logic of regime survival and not the logic of anarchy. As former Jordanian ambassador Adnan Abu Odeh put it, "The survival instinct dominates all else."[26]

Arab governments worked daily and strenuously to maintain political stability and quickly found that they could harness Arab nationalism for the cause. Arab leaders desired the social approval and prestige that came from being associated with Arabism because it could help bolster political stability and infuse their regimes with the social purpose and legitimacy unavailable from domestic foundations.[27] These were Arab regimes standing at the helm of Arab states that were porous and shot through by transnational forces, states that they and their societies frequently described as artificial, illegitimate, and agents of the Arab nation. Accordingly, Arab societies judged their governments according to how well they defended a "national interest" defined by an Arab nation that enveloped the state's territorial borders.

Arab officials, then, had every conceivable reason and incentive to present themselves as acting on behalf of the Arab nation and to articulate a discourse that referred to the Arab nation and shunned the language of state interests.[28] They studiously cultivated the image that they were Arab leaders in good standing. By attending Arab league meetings, contributing to collective Arab causes, speaking out on behalf of the Palestinians at international gatherings, in these and other ways Arab governments could support the collective good and better their political standing. Although adhering to these norms and articulating the discourse of the Arab political community was no guarantee of political stability, I argue that they had no better way to invite trouble than to deviate from such expectations. Even if an Arab leader cared little about the Palestinian conflict, only a leader with a strong self-destructive streak would publicly confess such views or pursue policies that hinted at such betrayals.

In general, Arab leaders had both private preferences that concerned political stability and social preferences that concerned the norms of Arabism. This perspective suggests that the normative structure in which actors are embedded shapes their public pursuits and that actors can be expected to

appropriate these norms for their private interests. Arabism shaped the social interests of Arab leaders, and Arab leaders used these norms to further
their personal objective of regime survival; as representatives of the Arab nation they were expected to pursue its interests, but as flesh and blood politicians they manipulated its norms for more secular concerns. These were social actors with private preferences who recognized that obtaining their
private preferences depended on effecting and pursuing social interests.[29]

Arab leaders sought the social approval that came from being identified
with the Arab cause because such approval could further their other domestic and foreign policy objectives. In other words, Arab states desired the symbolic capital they could amass from their association with Arab nationalism
because they could exchange it for capital that they needed for their other
objectives. Different strands of sociological and anthropological theory observe that capital (sometimes referred to as resources) can take different
forms—symbolic, economic, political, and cultural—that are acquired by
the actor's activities in different networks that generate social status and material rewards.[30] These different forms of capital can be exchanged for one
another. Some actors will exchange economic capital for political capital,
others will exchange political capital for economic capital, and still others
will exchange the capital that they generate from being associated with the
aspirations of the community for other highly valued objectives.

Arab leaders pursued a strategy of symbolic accumulation in part to advance or protect their domestic political situation. This highlights an important facet of Arab politics: power was associated less with accumulating
military force than with accumulating the symbols of Arabism, presenting
and projecting a particular image, and demonstrating an alliance and affin-
ity with a vision of political life. Arab leaders attempted to attach themselves to and become identified with the symbols of the political community—and in this instance those symbols largely derived not from domestic
but from transnational politics—not only because the leaders were dedicated to the cause but also because such identification would strengthen
their domestic standing.[31]

This suggests one reason that Arab governments competed for the privilege of being recognized as the leader of the Arab world: a government could
exchange the symbolic capital that accompanied this status for its other objectives. Consider, for instance, Egypt's long-standing desire to maintain a
leadership position in Arab affairs. Among the various reasons Egypt coveted this role was that it could exploit this status for its other objectives. During the 1950s Egypt intentionally played up its role in Arab politics to in-

crease its bargaining leverage during its negotiations with Britain regarding the Suez Canal. During the cold war Egypt promoted itself as the leader of the Arab world as a way of generating greater military and economic assistance from the superpowers. Syrian leaders promoted Syria as a rival to Egypt's leadership position, in part because they recognized that such a position could generate substantial military assistance from the Soviet Union, economic assistance from Saudi Arabia, and prestige from Syrian society.

In general, Arab leaders wanted to be associated with the norms of Arabism for reasons of self-image and self-interest. Because they were *Arab* leaders, they could be expected to genuinely express Arab nationalist sentiments. Although some academic circles find it fashionable to dismiss the possibility of transnational obligations and identification, is it so absurd to suggest that Arab leaders were committed to Arab unity, fearful of Zionism, and mistrusting of the West? Intuition and evidence suggest that such sentiments could be quite genuine. But if their self-image did not encourage them to work for collective causes, self-interest surely would. Because they were Arab *leaders* whose popularity depended in part on adhering to the Arab consensus, they presented their policies and themselves in ways that were consistent with society's expectations. And Arab leaders, like all actors, maintained some distance from the roles that they occupied, and such distance allowed them to be creative and cynical occupants of them. These were mannered and manipulative politicians, not unlike politicians of other times and places who will fashion themselves and their policies in ways that are consistent with the community's expectations in order to remain popular and in office.

All this presupposes that Arab leaders agreed on what the norms of Arabism were. But this was hardly the case. The norms of Arabism have never been fixed; Arab states never attained a concrete consensus. Over the years Arab states and societies debated long and hard about what constituted the practical and political meaning of Arab nationalism. Arab politics is not unique in this regard. All social orders are contested, and the norms that define that order are negotiated, repaired, and transformed during social interaction.[32]

These negotiations over the regional order are particularly pronounced when an incident forces actors to consider whether a norm properly applies. To properly follow a norm, as Barry Barnes has observed, is to extend an analogy. But not all analogies are identical, self-evident, or taken for granted. "Although it is equally possible to assimilate the next instance to a norm by analogy with existing examples of the norm, it is equally always possible to resist such assimilation, to hold an analogy insufficiently strong, to stress the differences between the instance and the existing examples."[33] A defining feature of a dialogue was the attempt by Arab leaders to determine whether a norm properly applied to a social situation. Did the Baghdad Pact between Iraq and Turkey violate the norm of Arabism that regulated strategic alliances with the West? Did the 1975 disengagement agreement between Israel and Egypt violate the normative prohibition against bilateral arrangements? Arab states and societies held differing views regarding such matters, whether the present instance was analogous to earlier instances or whether extenuating circumstances made the present instance a legitimate exception.

Controversy nearly always accompanied a debate about whether a norm properly applied. Sometimes these divisions were driven by principled differences. After all, individuals can have genuine disagreements about what constitutes proper and legitimate behavior. This might be particularly so in Arab politics because Arab leaders occupied the social roles of sovereignty and Arabism that might instruct them to follow potentially contradictory expectations or, at the least, provide some measure of indeterminacy about how they should behave. For instance, although Arab nationalism instructed Arab states to proceed cautiously with regard to their ties to the West, what the states had to determine on a case-by-case basis was what *caution* meant. Arab states could be expected to have genuine differences of views regarding what constituted caution or caprice. Indeed, a defining feature of inter-Arab politics was the attempt by Arab states to reconcile the potentially competing expectations of Arabism and sovereignty, and they had different views over how such reconciliation should best be accomplished. But the controversy that ensues during a debate about norms also can derive from more immediate and worldly concerns. After all, whatever norms are established will determine the boundaries of appropriate action, rendering some action possible and raising the costs of others. Arab states always asserted that their positions were driven by unadulterated principles. Perhaps. But their more secular concerns nearly always colored these principled positions. Not without good reason: the public judgment would affect their various interests and future freedom of action.

Accordingly, Arab states competed to fix an interpretation of events—to determine whether a norm applied—that was consistent with their interests.[34] Simply put, they attempted to draw a line between the regime's various interests, the norms of Arabism, and the events of the day. Because this was a collective undertaking—whatever norm emerged would constrain their future freedom of action and potentially implicate their political stability—and because Arab states had divergent views of these norms, they competed to impose their interpretation of the social situation.[35] Actors are oriented toward objects based on the meaning that they have for them. But meanings of these events and objects are not given and do not stand outside experience. Instead, they are constructed through a social and political process. Was the 1975 disengagement agreement between Egypt and Israel a violation of the norm of Arabism that prohibited bilateral arrangements, as Syria claimed, or was it consistent with Arabism, which allowed for the reclamation of Arab territory, as Egypt claimed? Did the Baghdad Pact violate a norm of Arabism, as Egypt claimed, or was it consistent with Arabism and Iraq's sovereign prerogatives, as Iraq asserted? Arab leaders competed long and hard to construct the meaning of these events, to determine the interpretation of the social situation, because doing so would protect their various interests and control the actions of other Arab states.

To define the situation was an act of power. Power was not generally manifested through military coercion or economic sanctions but rather through symbolic means. Perhaps one of the defining characteristics of inter-Arab conflict was that Arab leaders used symbolic technologies to construct the norms of Arabism to circumscribe the actions of other Arab states; a highly effective way to halt an action of an Arab leader was to portray him as violating the norms of Arabism, as harming the Arab nation. The question is how Arab leaders arrived at their definition of the situation and stabilized those norms.

Symbolic Exchanges

Arab leaders attempted to define the social situation, determine the norms of Arabism, and control the actions of their rivals through strategic framing and symbolic exchanges. These means derived from a cultural tool kit made available by the normative structure of Arabism.[36] The "thicker" the normative environment is—that is, the more embedded actors are in a network of relations that are invested with symbolic content and that provide a source of identity—the more dependent the actors will be on each other for social approval and the more susceptible they will be to symbolic and affective mechanisms of control. In other words, if Arab politics was symbolic politics, it was because Arab states were embedded in a shared normative structure in which they were mutually dependent on each other for social approval.[37] This dependence on social approval in turn increased their susceptibility to normative suasion and symbolic sanctions.

The presence of this normative structure, moreover, reduced the efficacy of the military and economic instruments of statecraft. This position is in direct contrast to realism's golden rule: those that have the gold make the rules. No immediate or causal relationship existed between military and economic power and the ability to establish the norms of Arabism. I am not suggesting that economic and military power were inconsequential or insignificant to the outcome, but I am arguing that the normative structure defined and constrained the forms of power, for several reasons.

First, because the norm under discussion was part of the public process, it became connected to public and community-wide aspirations and withdrawn from the domain of private calculations and choice.[38] Arab leaders had to offer reasoned and persuasive arguments directly tied to existing norms and ideas that were in turn connected to community-wide standards.[39] Arab leaders appealed to a regionally situated audience, justified their actions in relationship to Arab nationalism, and thus were constrained in what they could do. Second, Arab states wanted their decisions to have the veneer of legitimacy; receiving this legitimacy meant subjecting themselves to a legitimation process, and this process gave state and nonstate actors plenty of opportunities to shape the result. One consequence of this process was that in countless instances the more powerful state was constrained by the previously established set of norms and was unable to revise those norms to fit its current plans. Third, an informal decision-making rule was that any change in a norm should be done through consensus. This consensual decision-making principle evened the playing field and handed less powerful states and nonstate actors, like the PLO, important decision-making power. In general, in this game the military and economic tools of statecraft were not the generally accepted and used means of influence; instead, Arab states attempted to stabilize a set of norms through means that were available from a cultural tool kit that was available to all other Arab states.

We begin with the earlier observation that Arab leaders attempted to draw a line between their various interests, the norms of Arabism, and the meaning of the events of the day. But because events do not have an objective meaning, Arab leaders attempted to make them politically meaningful and intelligible by locating them within an overarching narrative that provided a link between an interpretation of the past and an image of the future.[40] This is achieved through a frame. Frames "are specific metaphors, symbolic representations, and cognitive cues used to render or cast behavior and events in an evaluative mode and to suggest alternative modes of action."[41] To frame an event means to situate it within a particular story line in order to locate that event, organize the experience, and guide the action.

This suggests a close connection between frames and interests. Although frames and interests are independent concepts logically, frames will shape interests and actors will select certain frames based on their interests.[42] To frame an event or action is potentially to alert others that their interests are at stake. When Palestinian Arabs framed Zionist immigration as a threat to the Arab nation, they galvanized support for their cause from Arabs in other lands; this frame, in other words, nurtured the image of Zionism as a threat to those living in Baghdad or Damascus even though they might not find that their lives or livelihood were immediately at stake. This also suggests that actors carefully select frames based on their interests. The Palestinian Arab leadership attempted to frame Zionist immigration as a concern for the entire Arab nation in part because the leaders recognized that they would be more likely to generate diplomatic and financial support from Arab states. Frames became a way to "discover" interests, and interests are frequently advanced by the careful and strategic adoption of a frame.

Frames have three key characteristics that are particularly relevant here. Actors compete to frame the event because how the event is understood will have important consequences for mobilizing action and furthering the actors' interests. This competition can be understood as a strategic framing process: the "conscious strategic efforts by groups of people to fashion shared understandings of the world and of themselves that legitimate collective action."[43] Political elites attempt to mobilize collective action by drawing on "cultural symbols that are selectively chosen from a cultural toolchest and creatively converted" into frames for action.[44] Arab leaders attempted to frame an event by locating it within a narrative of Arab history that included some reference to the norms of Arabism and the desired regional order. Their selection of a frame and their references to past historical experiences, moreover, were generally the product of strategic calculations intended to galvanize regionwide support for their position. Although state officials were not alone in their efforts to frame the events of the day— various social movements and intellectuals also played an important part— for a variety of reasons, including control of the media and other perks that attend to rule, state officials had a decided and consequential advantage.

Also, during this framing process Arab officials implicated themselves and other Arab leaders in that narrative. As actors tell stories to each other, they define each other in various ways—the actions that are permissible and comprehensible, and a "map of possible roles and of possible worlds in which action, thought, and self-definition are permissible (or desirable)."[45] As Arab leaders offered their interpretation of the challenges at hand, they usually blanketed their speeches with references to their Arab nationalist credentials and the failings of their rivals, and as they did so they tied themselves to an interpretation of Arabism that elevated their fortunes and hurt their rivals.'

Finally, Arab officials usually framed the event as part of a long history of injustices and injuries to the Arab nation. Arab politics is not unique here: collective mobilization is frequently accomplished by framing events in terms of injustice.[46] Although Arab nationalism was not animated and defined by injustice and grievances alone, these were powerful and ever-present themes. If part of Arab nationalism was the promise of a political and cultural renaissance that is uplifting and empowering, the flip side was that the West committed a series of historical injuries through acts of imperialism, beginning with colonialism and continuing through the present day, that has crippled the Arab nation. A related frame was that the Arabs were weak in relationship to the West, and they were weaker still when they were divided and fragmented; therefore they had to act collectively to protect themselves against further intrusions and to achieve their interests. Consequently, a powerful line in Arab politics was to frame an event or another Arab leader as potentially threatening the goal of Arab unity, dividing the Arab ranks, and providing an opening for the West. Usually, another Arab leader was responsible for provoking the challenge or making matters worse, so to frame the event as potentially weakening the Arab nation invariably involved accusing another Arab leader of being an accomplice to the crime.

By framing the event within a story line, Arab leaders transformed it into a symbol, its meaning produced by virtue of its connection to and placement within a cultural context.[47] Arab politics was symbolic politics. Nasser turned the Baghdad Pact into a symbol of Western imperialism and Arab treachery. During the 1980s Syria referred to many diplomatic efforts to achieve a breakthrough in the peace process as "Camp David," transforming such efforts into a symbol of selling out the Palestinians and dividing the Arab ranks. During the Gulf War Arabs who were opposed to Desert Storm portrayed it as akin to San Remo (which established the mandate system), thus transforming the Western-led force into a symbol of imperialism and drawing symbolic boundaries between Arabs and non-Arabs. An international relations discipline that has been raised on the centrality of force for regulating political life will be suspicious of the claim that symbols are anything but cosmetic. But few political orders are ever successfully contested or sustained by force alone; many if not most political contests are often waged over and through symbols. Rare is the act of collective mobilization that is without symbolic content, and actors attempt to guide and constrain action through symbolic means and technologies.

What are symbols? Symbols can be generically understood as standing for or representing something else. The earlier examples suggest how symbols, which derive from a shared historical memory, language, and culture, are rooted in political community and bound up in identity. The symbols are intelligible because they have a cultural resonance and define the group and its boundaries. Therefore, although symbols stand for something else, they cannot be drawn from thin air; that "something else" must be part of reality if such symbols are to be consequential in political struggles.[48] Although Arab leaders might exploit the language and symbols of Arab nationalism to further their domestic and regional standing, they could exploit only what existed and could do so because it was generally consistent with the sentiments and historical memories of their citizens.

Symbols do not merely stand for something else. They are made meaningful by political actors. Political actors use symbols to galvanize sentiments, mobilize and guide social action, and control the direction of political change.[49] Symbols become part of political struggles as elites attempt to use them, often in a strategic and manipulative way, to communicate with and mobilize members of society.[50] In this central way symbols are part of social control, capable of being manipulated and deployed in order to stir emotions—to mobilize action in one's favor and do so at the expense of one's rivals.[51] But part of what makes symbols politically effective is their ambiguous nature. This ambiguity allows diverse interests to mobilize around shared symbols to which they might well bring contested meanings. For instance, the symbols revolving around anticolonialism could unify both those who adhered to an Arab nationalism that demanded territorial unification and those who offered a vision that kept the territorial configuration intact. In general, during a dialogue Arab leaders attempted to appropriate and wield the symbols of Arabism for collective mobilization, to define the meaning of events, and to influence their domestic and regional audience.

These symbolic exchanges had three different forms: symbolic sanctioning, symbolic competition, and symbolic entrapment. Arab states attempted to undermine their rivals and control their foreign policies through *symbolic sanctioning*: the attempt by one actor to influence the actions of another by deploying the symbols of the community.[52] "When a movement organization chooses symbols with which to frame its message, it sets a strategic course between its cultural setting, its political opponents and the militants and ordinary citizens whose support it needs."[53] Time and time again Arab leaders took to the airwaves to broadcast a message that used the various symbols of Arabism to communicate how the actions, both anticipated and taken, by other Arab leaders were either permitted by or inconsistent with the norms of Arabism. Gamal Abdel Nasser had few peers on this score. When he spoke "the streets emptied as everyone went into their houses to listen to him on their radios."[54] And sometimes when they returned to the streets, they demanded that their governments follow Nasser's directions. Accused of destabilizing Lebanese politics in 1958, Nasser was asked by the United Nations to suspend his Voice of the Arabs broadcasts. His response was highly revealing of the power of symbolic sanctioning: "If you ask me for radio disarmament, you are asking for complete disarmament."[55] When Arab states sought a détente, their first step was to put down their weapons, which in this case was to suspend their highly inflammatory and destabilizing communiqués; such developments were to be expected in a social setting where power derived from the deft and destabilizing deployment of symbols. Sticks and stones might hurt, but Arab leaders were particularly threatened by symbols and speeches.

Two factors made symbolic sanctions an effective strategy. One necessary condition is that actors be embedded in a shared normative order that leaves them mutually susceptible to and dependent on each other for dignity, honor, and approval. In this view actors can be pressed into action, solidarity, and conformity because of their concern with nurturing their self-image and protecting their self-interest. Actors use norms and symbols to influence the actions and directions of others, and they are able to use such means because others are susceptible to them and desire to maintain a public face. The care that Arab leaders took to guard their images reflected a more generalized desire for social approval; such desires steered them away from crudely self-interested behavior and encouraged them to contribute to the maintenance and collective goals of the group. And if one leader's behavior seemed out of step with the emerging consensus, the other Arab leaders were more than willing to remind him of his obligations.

Second, Arab governments directed their message not only at other Arab leaders but also at their societies. If an Arab government wanted to use persuasion to convince another Arab leader of the error of his ways, they could always use private, discrete, diplomatic démarches. But their public broadcasts and pronouncements were also targeted at other Arab societies. In short, one way to influence another Arab state's foreign policy was to press the norms and symbols of Arabism in order to mobilize its citizens, thus raising the domestic political costs (or benefits) of a particular course of action. This suggests one way that Arab public opinion shaped the policies and actions of Arab leaders. But Arab leaders did not always wait until the populace was mobilized to factor public opinion into their decisions. Arab leaders were constantly managing their impressions and images, and they understood from past examples of transgressions that their behavior would be judged harshly if they were perceived as venturing outside the consensus. Stated somewhat differently, they engaged in "role-taking behavior."[56] Arab leaders saw themselves as others saw them; they recognized that their societies expected them to conform to the social roles that they occupied, and so they came to accept those roles. In general, symbolic sanctions were effective because the actors wanted to maintain their dignity, honor, and face, and if self-image was not enough to bring them along, survival instinct surely would.

This raises an important consideration. Although all Arab leaders participated in the game of Arab politics, not all were equally active, equally desirous of accumulating the symbols of Arabism, equally likely to discharge them against their rivals, or equally vulnerable to such symbolic weaponry. The historical and regional variations on such matters are obvious, and a key variable here is domestic politics in general and the domestic vulnerability of Arab governments to symbolic sanctions in particular. It will be difficult to provide an a priori linkage between domestic configurations and foreign policy outputs because of foreign policy and domestic policy substitutability,[57] and because no immediate or well-defined relationship exists between Arabism and the Arab state's position during a dialogue outside a specified historical setting. This recognition begs for a healthy dose of induction.

Still, Arab states were more likely to participate in these dialogues, and were more involved in symbolic accumulation and susceptible to symbolic sanctioning, under two conditions. The first was when the political identities of the population were more stirred by the symbols of Arabism than they were by the symbols of the state. Arab states' interest in appropriating the symbols of Arabism was piqued to the extent that those symbols resonated with the citizenry at large and key societal actors; under such conditions Arab governments had a direct political incentive to be associated with and to appropriate such symbols. The second condition was the extent to which the norm that emerged from the dialogue affected the regime's political, strategic, or economic interests. An Arab government was more likely to become embroiled and enmeshed in these dialogues when its interests were implicated. Not all conversations were of equal interest or importance to Arab leaders because they were not equally threatened by or likely to profit from the outcome.[58] In general, Arab states were more likely to be involved in these dialogues if the symbols of Arabism challenged the symbols of the state and the eventual definition of the event affected the government's interests.

Because Arab leaders were involved in a competitive situation, the possibility of *symbolic competition* was ever present. This form of symbolic exchange occurred when Arab leaders wanted to demonstrate that they were more ready to commit and contribute to Arab nationalism than were other Arab leaders. Consider the following description of the symbolic competition before the 1967 Arab-Israeli War:

> In the campaign Nasser was saying that Wasfi Tal [the Jordanian foreign minister] was a spy for the British and the CIA. The Jordanians were being branded all the time as imperialist tools, traitors, and spies. The continuous and severely hostile campaign affected the stability of the regime and its very survival. So they [the Jordanians] had to reply. They devised this method of trying to show that it's not they who were allies of Israel and imperialist tools but that Nasser was not actually serious in wanting to confront Israel or in being the real champion of the Palestine cause, because he was shielding himself behind UNEF [the United Nations Emergency Force, which separated the Israeli and Egyptian armies in the Sinai]. Of course, many people, many wise people, in Jordan realized that indeed this was playing with fire, because it would push Nasser into taking action which they knew was detrimental to the Arab cause. But there was no way, or no other way, let me say, of defending themselves against the charges that were pouring out against them day and night from Egypt and other propaganda machines.[59]

Symbolic competition could ensnare even those Arab leaders who believed that such competition was harmful to their collective and personal fates. But resisting the lure of competition was difficult because resisting meant inviting charges of being a charlatan and of being unwilling to contribute to the cause. Call this the logic of a "symbolic" security dilemma.

An artifact of this competition was that Arab leaders created a more austere interpretation of Arabism. Who was ready to sacrifice his sovereignty for unification? Willing to wage war against Zionism and for Palestine? Committed to no alliances with the West? Arab leaders had no better way to demonstrate their leadership credentials, candidacy, or character than by proclaiming a defiant or strident stand on such issues, and they had no better way to embarrass an opponent than by claiming a willingness to sacrifice when others exhibited reluctance to do so. In this competitive dynamic, Arab leaders were continually forced to decide whether to fold 'em, see 'em, or raise 'em. Symbolic competition, then, was a high-stakes poker game: to fold was to allow another Arab state to determine the norm of Arabism and to acknowledge one's shortcomings, to see that bid might be to commit to a unwanted course of action, and to raise it was to hope that one's bluff would not be called and that action would not be required. Such competitive moments are reminders that all encounters are something of a gamble, for they are laden with opportunities and dangers because of having to lay oneself on the line and because of the potentially dramatic consequences for one's relationship to others after the encounter is over.[60]

Yet sometimes those who live by the symbol and the speech are expected to deliver with action and material commitments. An Arab leader who identified with the symbols and slogans of Arabism might at some point be asked to make good on this talk or endanger his reputation and standing. This can be understood as *symbolic entrapment* because during the "decision making process . . . individuals escalate their commitment to a previously chosen, though failing, course of action in order to justify or 'make good on' prior investments."[61] In other words, an initial association with the wider normative expectations later restricts what the actor can do because of reputational considerations. Arab officials sometimes called this one-upmanship: as they competed to demonstrate who was the most loyal supporter of Arabism, they risked having to make good on their promises in order to maintain their reputation, even at the sacrifice of their other interests. As Nasser found to his subsequent horror in the events preceding the June 1967 war, his attempt to maintain his Arab nationalist credentials by acting defiantly and aggressively toward Israel led to an unwanted war, which subsequently undermined the Egyptian state's and his regime's interests. Using the symbols of the wider community to portray themselves as adhering to, and a rival as departing from, the goals and aspirations of Arab nationalism meant that at some level they were obligated to honor its norms even when doing so might sacrifice other valued interests. Symbols could be double-edged swords.

Perhaps the distinguishing sign that the dialogue was coming to a close was the yielding of conflict to exchanges of congratulations for having demonstrated eternal commitment to the Arab nation. The intense episode of conflict, then, frequently succumbed in a somewhat clumsy manner to proclamations of solidarity. However contrived this spirit of cooperation might appear, once Arab states agreed on a norm, they oriented themselves in each other's direction and coordinated their policies.[62] The stabilized norm, then, served as a focal point for organizing their actions and for considering their identity. To be sure, the level of commitment was not awe inspiring much of the time, but such evaluative measures run the risk of denying the very real and impressive movement toward solidarity and the substantial political and material contributions to central and defining Arab issues.[63]

Inter-Arab cooperation is best approached from the vantage point of the relationship between the interests of actors and the structure in which they are embedded. Collective action was not a testimony to heroic efforts of atomized actors who stood outside society or who acted because of norm internalization, socialization, or value consensus. Rather collective action and mobilization were largely accomplished by Arab officials who recognized that they were vulnerable to enforcement action and sanctions if they violated the norms of Arabism. The sanctions might be financial, political, military, or symbolic, and sometimes the methods of enforcement were formally institutionalized, whereas at others they depended on spontaneous and informal organization. The enforcer of these norms might be international and/or domestic actors. But in any event enforcement mechanisms and sanctions usually encouraged compliance with the group's norms.[64] The rhythm of the dialogue was defined by a prolonged period of normative contestation, followed by a rapid burst of normative consensus.

The game of Arab politics was played by self-interested Arab leaders whose understanding of how to play the game was shaped by the underlying structure defined by Arabism and sovereignty. This game commenced when an event forced Arab leaders to reconsider a norm of Arabism. Arab governments used strategic frames to situate the event in a particular way; as they situated it conceptually and historically, they attempted to draw a line between their proposed response, the norms of Arabism, and the regime's interests. As they framed that event, moreover, they transformed it into a symbol that could enhance their own standing and be wielded against their rivals. In this fundamental way symbolic politics was bound up with social control, a defining element of the state's attempt to protect its domestic situation and influence the foreign policies of other Arab states. Through strategic framing and symbolic exchanges Arab leaders competed to stabilize the norms of Arabism.

The norms of Arabism encouraged and sometimes dragged Arab governments toward cooperation, collective action, and some show of solidarity;

provided a symbolic and literal brake on the centrifugal tendencies toward narrow self-interest; and represented a principal reason behind the sustained cooperation amid apparent acrimony. Any tendency toward crass self-interest among Arab leaders and centrifugal tendencies in Arab politics were checked by the recognition that the stated goals of Arab leaders and their available means were guided and limited by the norms of Arabism, as defined at that particular historical moment. As occupants of social roles, Arab leaders, like all actors, could manipulate them. But only within reason. Their desire to be associated with the symbols of Arabism, to be viewed as operating according to its norms, and their susceptibility to symbolic sanctions explain why they would subscribe to the norms of Arabism, whether they were sincere champions or not.

The Changing Game of Arab Politics

During a dialogue Arab states were discussing whether to repair or revise a norm of Arabism. Thus normative structures were not fixed and permanent entities but were produced through social and strategic interactions. Arab nationalism was always a work in progress, pushed along and amended by the strategic and symbolic exchanges by Arab states. But such changes were not an everyday occurrence. Not every interaction and exchange produced a new set of arrangements and rules of the game; powerful forces made it quite likely that the status quo would prevail. After all, the structure in which Arab states were embedded constrained their behavior and provided incentives that increased the probability that the previously established norms would be repaired.

But in some instances Arab states revised a norm of Arabism, and when they did so, they also reconsidered their political identities. Crises and dialogues, in this regard, can be a place of "punctuated equilibrium," a point of passage from one identity to another.[65] Because Arab states were addressing the relationship between the desired regional order, the norms of Arabism, and their own political identities, the repair or transformation of the norms of Arabism also implicated their identities. As G. H. Mead observed:

> The changes that we make in the social order in which we are implicated necessarily involve our also making changes in ourselves. The social conflicts among the individual members of a given organized human society, which, for their removal, necessitate conscious or intelligent reconstruc-

tions and modifications of that society by those individuals, also and equally necessitate such reconstructions or modifications by those individuals of their own selves and personalities.[66]

The norms of Arabism were tied to their Arab identities, and as they made adjustments in those norms, they also revised how they understood and presented themselves. The post–Gulf War debate about the parameters of the region—whether it is Mediterranean, Arab, or Middle Eastern—testify dramatically to how the debate about the regional order was inextricably tied to their identities. The historical analysis therefore will consider how Arab states revised their identities as they revised the norms of Arabism.

A central claim of this book is that there is new environment to Arab politics, one largely created by and through the actions of Arab states; this environment can be characterized as normative fragmentation because Arab states are no longer as pressed toward mutual orientation because of the decline of underlying shared values and identities. The extent to which Arab leaders feel the weight of expectations derived from the norms of Arabism, the degree to which they are more concerned with being perceived as working for the Arab nation than for the state, their desire to determine the understanding of the event, their necessity of appearing to act in concert with other Arab leaders in the pursuit of common ends—these and others features of Arab politics have dissipated in the recent past and reflect a decline in the salience of the Arab identity.

Why did the interactions of Arab states, although seemingly informed by a sense of community and shared purpose, lead to estrangement rather than collaboration, difference rather than fraternity? The reasons can be found in a structure of Arab politics that encouraged survival-seeking Arab leaders to act in ways that hastened individuation. Arab leaders wanted to be associated with Arab nationalism for a variety of reasons, including the accumulation of the symbolic capital that was vital for regime survival. But the more they leaned on Arab nationalism to legitimate their rule, and the more their societies held them accountable to the norms of Arabism, the more vulnerable they were to the encroachments and symbolic sanctions of other Arab leaders. The result was that Arab nationalism was both an aid and a threat to domestic stability, the government's autonomy, and perhaps even the state's sovereignty.

Under such circumstances Arab leaders could be expected to first try to create an Arab nationalism that could legitimate their separate authorities and second to portray other Arab leaders as potential threats. By stressing the legitimacy of each Arab state and the differences between them, and by doing so in fairly aggressive ways, Arab leaders created the conditions for individuation and fragmentation. Although the remainder of the book explores the dynamics that led to this outcome, let me offer two preliminary observations.

Arab leaders frequently attempted to define the norms of Arabism and to frame the events of the day in a manner that would protect the regime's interests. This framing process often included Arab leaders distinguishing their interpretation of these events from those of others. Sometimes this attempted distinction was done through more passive and defensive strategies; for instance, they appealed to sovereignty and pluralism in Arab politics in order to protect themselves from the normative interventions, assaults, and symbolic sanctioning of other Arab leaders. King Hussein, for example, continually echoed a theme, strongly voiced during the heyday of unification, that Arab nationalism allowed for different political "experiments." Sovereignty here was premised on the recognition that although Arabs were, after all, Arabs, they were also citizens of particular territorial states to which they owed additional political obligations and loyalties that must be recognized.

But this framing process was competitive, and Arab governments sometimes adopted a more aggressive stance as they championed their interpretation by portraying a rival as part of the problem, not the solution, and perhaps even covertly complicit in the threat to the Arab nation. Most of these dialogues brought out the worst brand of unity among Arab leaders, one based on mutual animosity and name calling. Accordingly, Arab leaders encouraged differentiation to the extent that they portrayed each other as threats. Although they were usually careful to distinguish between the population and the regime, the overall result was to accentuate their separate paths. Differences and threats contributed to the development of distinct identities and normative fragmentation.[67]

Further, Arab governments frequently viewed all-Arab institutions and projects as an unwanted constraint on their actions and as a potential threat to domestic stability. The result was that they had an incentive to create alliances and institutions that preserved the appearance of collective action without really delivering it—or at least delivering it to its fullest, and expected, expression. By creating institutions that gave the appearance of action but delivered little of it, Arabism came to be identified with the self-interested and manipulative acts of Arab states. Arabism soon acquired a normative deficit. This is most famous in the constant refrain that a gap existed between ideology and practice in Arab politics and that this gap manufactured widespread and regionwide disillusionment with Arabism.[68] Thus the danger for Arab governments was that by routinely failing to follow through on Arabist-inspired rhetoric and promises, they undermined the symbols and norms that they used to prop up their legitimacy. The end result was to tarnish such projects. As individuals came to have less confidence in the viability of Arabism, or at least as long as this generation of leaders was in power, individuals increased their identification with and orientation toward the territorial state.

Yet the transformation of these norms was not a wholly interstate affair. If over time Arab leaders were presenting themselves differently, if they appeared less inhibited about asserting the interests of the state, we can thank not only strategic interaction but also state formation. Although nearly all Arab states relied on the language of Arabism to further their domestic and foreign policy objectives, they also engaged in state formation that was designed to transfer subnational and transnational identities to the state and therefore to enhance the state's legitimacy and domestic stability. State formation projects were instrumental in producing new political identities, shrinking the salience of transnational loyalties; to the extent that such ideational shifts occurred among the population Arab governments had a greater incentive to act consistently with broad parameters of sovereignty and to articulate the discourse of state, as opposed to Arab national, interests. As a general rule, the search for integration at the local level has translated into increased fragmentation and a decreased sense of collective obligation at the regional level.[69] But to understand why state formation in this instance led to fragmentation requires a focus on inter-Arab interactions. The historical analysis therefore focuses on dialogues as a source of norm creation and inductively traces how state-society relations contributed to the state's foreign policy at such moments.

In general, interstate interactions and state formation processes begin to suggest why dialogues about regional order encouraged (1) a revolution in identities—a transfer of loyalties from subnational and transnational affiliations to the state; (2) a closer identification by citizens with the symbols of the state relative to other transnational symbols; (3) the development of a centrist understanding of Arabism that was consistent with sovereignty and statist identities; and (4) normative fragmentation. Regional and domestic practices transformed the structure in which future interactions played themselves out and unfolded.

This chapter offered a conceptual framework for analyzing dialogues in Arab politics and observed how these dialogues offer both a window into the debates about regional order and a method for tracing the change that has taken place in the organization of Arab politics. The remainder of the book uses these categories to observe how Arab states have been involved in an ongoing series of negotiations over their desired regional order, to understand how these negotiations shaped basic patterns of conflict and cooperation as Arab leaders attempted to frame the events of the day and used symbolic exchanges to stabilize a particular order, and to explore how and why these dialogues represented a source of normative transformation and ultimately fragmentation.

[3]

The Creation of "Arab" Politics, 1920–1945

          Arab politics emerged during the tumultuous twenty-five-year period between the imposition of the mandate system in 1920 and the establishment of the League of Arab States in 1945. In this relatively brief span Arab nationalism sprang from the pan-Arab clubs and its standing as a rather minor and politically inconsequential movement to become a dominant force in formal politics and to tower over the political landscape. Many factors contributed to this rapid rise, but foremost were a series of seismic shocks surrounding the death of the Ottoman Empire, and World War I, that caused the region's inhabitants to reconsider the boundaries of the political community and the political organization of the region. Arab nationalism surfaced from the debris of these geopolitical changes, as political elites, urban notables and masses, and the intelligentsia slowly converged on the language of Arabism to frame the events surrounding them, organize political action, secure their various interests, and contemplate the emergent regional order.

       At the outset Arabism was better understood as a sentimental movement than as a political project with well-defined objectives. "Arabism was a romantic notion," wrote Kamal Salibi, "whose full implications had not been worked out."[1] For some, Arab nationalism meant cultural revival, for others it meant political autonomy for those in different Arab lands, and for others still it meant one state for one nation. The ambiguity inherent in the concept had a decided virtue because it allowed for multiple meanings and thus helped to mobilize those who held conflicting interests. Arab societies were increasingly mobilized around the cause of Arab nationalism even before it had a meaning that was reasonably consistent across the Arab world.

By the late 1930s, however, Arabism slowly yielded to more specific sets of meanings that revolved around the quest for independence, the cause of Palestine, and the search for unity. That Arabism came to be defined by these issues owed not to abstract debates but to the practical, daily, and ongoing challenges posed by colonialism and Zionism. This chapter explores the construction of Arab politics by examining the dynamic and reciprocal relationship between the growth of the Arab identity; how Arab political elites responded to the growth of Arabism among the masses by cultivating these new symbols of political expression to further the elites' domestic and regional aspirations; how independence, Palestine, and unity came to be connected to Arabism; and the increasingly transnational character and institutionalization of Arab politics. The outcome of these historical processes was truly transformational: whereas at the turn of the century *Arab* was not a highly consequential category of political identity and action, within a half-century there emerged Arab states with a set of interests that flowed from the Arab identity. These states became mutually vulnerable to the symbols of Arab nationalism, and Arab leaders tried to accumulate these symbols and deploy them against their rivals in the pursuit of their domestic and foreign policy objectives.

Arab Nationalism

Until the late nineteenth century the inhabitants of the region existed within a variety of overlapping authority and political structures. The Ottoman Empire, Islam, and local tribal and village structures all held sway over various features of peoples' lives and consequently gave shape to their political identities.[2] Arabism was hardly heard on such matters. Yet within a few short decades Arabism became increasingly popular in the discourse of political protest and the politics of identification and association. Arabism's impressive rise is a testimony to a series of historical shocks that began at the turn of the twentieth century and continued for the next several decades. These shocks caused the region's inhabitants to rethink the nature of the political community, their political loyalties, and their political projects.

The central forces spurring the development of Arab nationalism can be described briefly. Beginning in the late nineteenth century, various Westernized elites, many members of which were educated at the American University of Beirut, in Constantinople, and in Europe, began to borrow from intellectual developments in European thought that concerned the development and desirability of the nation-state. Mostly influenced by German and French theorists who argued that language was the wellspring of a national identity, a number of Arab intellectuals, including luminaries like Sati al-Husri, began to expound that all those who spoke Arabic had a common mentality and shared a past, present, and future. Such claims, however, were not at all intuitive. Most individuals identified themselves according to familial and tribal affiliations, local residence, or religion, and the idea that these political, geographic, and religious divisions could be and should be superseded by the Arabic language they shared was radical. Arab nationalism could scarcely be heard in formal political settings in the late 1800s and was largely limited to the growing number of pan-Arab clubs of Damascus, Beirut, Baghdad, and Cairo.

Arab nationalism first became part of the language of political protest and cultural renaissance as a consequence of a series of reforms planned by the Ottoman Empire.[3] The Young Turk Movement of 1908 proposed a Turkification program in the Fertile Crescent that many Arab elites saw as a potential political, economic, and cultural challenge. In response, they called for full instruction in the Arabic language, greater local autonomy and the protection of Arab rights within the Ottoman Empire, and the promotion of Arab unity and with it a sense of its historic past and a restoration of its glory. Yet absent from the list of demands was statehood or sovereignty; most political elites were content to remain within the Ottoman Empire so long as these other goals were met.[4] But the episode stimulated greater interest in Arab history, generally known as *al-nahda* [the Arab revival], a growth in pan-Arab clubs and associations, and a heightened sensitivity to a common identity based on language and ethnicity.[5] Arab nationalism now entered the lexicon of identity and protest.

World War I unleashed several tremors that forever changed the political and territorial landscape, nurtured the Arab identity, and boosted the Arab nationalist movement. The first was the death of the Ottoman Empire. Even before World War I many Arab elites began debating what political arrangements should emerge once the "sick man" of Europe succumbed to its widely anticipated death. Such conversations took on an air of urgency as the Ottoman Empire's status went from critical to fatal because of the war, and its rather hasty demise resulted in a political vacuum that many political movements hoped to fill. As Albert Hourani wrote:

The political structure within which most Arabs had lived for four centuries had disintegrated. . . . These changes had a deep effect on the way in which politically conscious Arabs thought of themselves, and tried to define their political identity. It posed questions about the way in which they should live together in political community. Wars are catalysts, bringing to consciousness feelings hitherto inarticulate and creating expectations of change.[6]

War caused the region's inhabitants to reconsider their political identity and what sorts of political arrangements would be most meaningful and desirable.

The Great Arab Revolt of 1916 offered one answer to the question of what life would be like after the Ottoman Empire. In an attempt to enlist the Arabs in its campaign against the Triple Alliance, the British approached Sharif Husayn of the Hijaz (a semiautonomous region on the Arabian Peninsula that was controlled by the Ottoman Empire) to determine whether and at what price he would be willing to join the fight. To side with Christians in a rebellion against the Ottoman Empire, the holder of the caliphate, would require a non-Ottoman identity, a grand narrative, and a cause that might silence critics. Although not an Arab nationalist of outstanding credentials (a few years before Sharif Husayn had sided with the Ottomans against the cause of Arabism), he offered himself as the leader of the Arabs and demanded their independence; his price of entry into the war was that he be acknowledged as ruler of the Arabs.[7] These negotiations, an exchange of eight letters between July 1915 and January 1916 commonly known as the McMahon-Husayn correspondence, led the "Arabs" to declare war on the Ottomans in return for certain guarantees, some of which the British kept (independence for much of the Arabian Peninsula), some of which remained under a hail of controversy (whether Palestine was promised independence), and some of which the British undeniably broke (independence for the rest of the Fertile Crescent). By waging a war against the Ottomans and in the name of independence for the Arabs, Sharif Husayn triggered tremendous excitement and captured the imaginations of many in the Fertile Crescent.[8] In a few short decades Arab nationalism had grown from a minor intellectual movement to become associated with the demand for political independence and statehood.

Britain made two subsequent pledges during the war that countered the spirit and completely abrogated the other promises of the McMahon-Husayn Agreement, resulting in a boost to Arabism. The first concerned the future of Palestine. In November 1917 British foreign minister Lord Balfour announced that his government would look favorably on the establishment of a Jewish homeland in Palestine. Subsequently known as the Balfour Declaration, it had the illustrious distinction of angering both the Zionists and the Arabs. The Zionists, though pleased that their aspirations had gained a measure of legitimacy from a Great Power, were disappointed that the declaration sanctioned only a "homeland" rather than their sought-after sovereignty and statehood. The Arabs protested that the declaration was inconsistent with the McMahon-Husayn Agreement, which they believed promised Palestine independence, and objected to the idea of a foreign power's handing an Arab territory over to an alien and minority population. Although whether McMahon-Husayn pledged independence for Palestine remains a matter of historical controversy, Arab political elites of the time quickly concluded that a promise by Britain had been broken. Accusations of betrayal by the Arabs spilled over into increasing suspicions of the West. Their suspicions were well-founded.

The second pledge, an unambiguous break with McMahon-Husayn, was the secret agreement concluded between Britain and France in 1916 that concerned the division of the spoils of the Middle East. Known as the Sykes-Picot Agreement, the two imperial powers conspired that after the war France would inherit Syria and Lebanon, and Britain the remainder of the region (Iraq, Palestine, and the soon to be created territory of Transjordan). Britain was well aware that Sykes-Picot violated its earlier promises to Husayn, but such sacrifices were necessary to maintain its strategic goals and to satisfy France, its wartime ally. The Sykes-Picot Agreement obtained the luster of legitimacy at the San Remo conference of April 1920 and then was absorbed into the mandate system of the League of Nations; Britain and France now became colonialists with a mission—they were to instruct these territories in the art of self-rule, that is, to ensure that their eventual independence would maintain the interests of the Great Powers.[9] The period surrounding World War I introduced two external elements that favored Arab nationalism: a duplicitous Western diplomacy that betrayed the cause of Arab independence and imposed the mandate system and then legitimated the Zionist movement with Britain as its nominal guardian. Arab nationalism now possessed what all nationalisms thrive on—a threat.

Arabism began to emerge as an important political movement because of the massive political and social upheavals that accompanied World War I and the death of the Ottoman Empire. I want to stress three related points, the first two brief and the other occupying the remainder of the chapter. The first is the relationship between Islam and Arabism. Arabism was intertwined with Islam in many respects. Although many early champions of Arabism were Christians who stressed Arabism's ethnic and secular content, Arabism's symbols often drew from Islam, and its rapid rise can be partially attributed to its piggybacking on an existing Islamic identity. Whether Arabism and Islam were so intertwined that they were indistinguishable to the region's inhabitants is a matter of historical and scholarly dispute. Less controversial, however, is that over time the religious content of Islam lost out to the secular and statist tenets of Arabism.[10] Arabism quickly gained greater currency as the guiding force behind the independence campaigns and nearly all of the most consequential proposals for considering the desired regional order. Arabism rather than Islam became the language of protest and politics for many reasons, but chief among them was that Arab leaders found Arabism to be a better instrument for political survival. For instance, the caliphate disappeared with the Ottoman Empire, which meant that no "political or religious figure could claim allegiance from anyone outside his own country's boundaries. To win such status—which also carried enhanced domestic prestige—Arab leaders became avid participants in the search for a new source of authority."[11] This search led them to Arabism.

Second, Arabism's rise was attributable to more than external shocks and threats. The region's inhabitants and political elites began to contemplate their response to these challenges through the lens of Arabism because this Arab identity was being nurtured by an expanding transnational network. Arab nationalism benefited from new means of communication, transportation, and education. Newspapers multiplied, and Arabs began to travel more frequently throughout the region, to be educated in each other's schools, and later saw the Egyptian films that were shown throughout the Arab world. Such transnational and cultural movements "helped to create a shared world of taste and ideas."[12] Social movements and political elites, capitalizing on a political and intellectual vacuum and on the inability of the political institutions to confront the challenges of the day, began to nurture and promote an Arab identity.

Third, Arab nationalism's emergent meaning was contingent on its relationship to wider sociopolitical forces. Arab nationalism began as a romantic movement that stressed the singularity of an Arab identity but was generally unattached to any concrete political programs. To be sure, some championed a single Arab state for a single Arab nation, but Arabism's political popularity grew, and its political projects came into focus in response to daily practicalities, not because of abstract debates. Arab nationalism's inaugural political moment came in response to the Turkification programs and with the demand for autonomy. For the next several decades Arabism's political salience rose and its political projects crystallized as political elites and societal groups dealt with the international challenges of political independence, Palestine, and unity while standing vigilant over their domestic political interests.

Arab Nationalism and Independence

> A map anticipated reality, not vice versa. . . . A map was a model for, rather than a model of, what it purported to represent.
> —Benedict Anderson, *Imagined Communities*, p. 73

The mandate system unleashed two somewhat countervailing nationalisms. The less prevalent of the two was pan-Arabism, which stressed Arab sentiments and the demand for political unity as far as the political identity stretched, that is, wherever Arabic was spoken. In this view the mandate system had territorially divided a singular Arab nation, creating the demand to rejoin what had been dismembered. Sometimes the fight for statehood and the desire for unity could be strategically merged in a single stream; for instance, Arab nationalists were at the forefront of the struggle for political independence, viewing the independence of the separate Arab states as the first step toward political unification. But they refused to coin terms that could conceptually and historically accommodate the separate struggles for political independence as part of distinct nationalisms, preferring to treat all independence drives as one step toward the larger goal of political unification.[13] The growing stature of pan-Arabism was one consequence of the mandate system that divided the Arab nation.

The second and dominant strand was territorial nationalism. Between the wars many residents came to define Arab nationalism as anticolonialism and independence for the separate Arab states.[14] The territorial segmentation channeled political energies to the local rather than the regional level, feeding into existing regional rivalries and differences.[15] That is, the mandates did not exactly divide what the region's inhabitants understood as once integrated, and in some cases these areas already had core constituencies that reflected more localized identities. Moreover, the establishment of the mandate system made political independence the key issue for all Arab governments, and in most instances Arab elites used the language of Arab nationalism in the struggle for statehood. The combination of these existing differences and the new institutional environment meant that most power-ful political movements had as their guiding inspiration territorial indepen-dence rather than political unification.

Although Arab nationalism obtained a territorial character during the mandate period, the degree of satisfaction with the territorial arrangements was generally associated with the degree of societal segmentation and the salience of the Arab identity in relationship to other political identities. As a general rule territorial nationalism grew in popularity relative to pan-Ara-bism as one traveled away from the Fertile Crescent. Saudi Arabia, Yemen, Egypt, and (to a lesser extent) Lebanon adhered to territorial nationalism and remained distant from pan-Arabism. Saudi Arabia, which emerged from a marriage of military prowess (Saudis) and religious creed (Wahab-bis) and received its independence in 1921, presented itself as the homeland of the original Arabs but expressed an Islamic religious identity rather than a secular national identity.[16] Any support for Arabism among the ruling elite was dissipated by the knowledge that the Hashemites of Transjordan and Iraq, a family that Saudi Arabia had defeated in battle in 1925 and evicted from the Hijaz, were among Arabism's chief champions. Yemen also achieved independence at this time and was far removed from the unifica-tion spirit.

Lebanon was a creation of French strategic machinations, severed from historic Syria in 1920. In 1861 France helped to secure a special status for the Maronites of the Mount Lebanon region within the Ottoman Empire and backed by Western guarantees, specifically French military and political power. From then on, the Maronites actively pressed to expand their politi-cal and territorial claims. A winning opportunity came with the collapse of the Ottoman Empire and the assumption by France of the Syrian mandate; France created present-day Lebanon from Mount Lebanon and part of Syria. Now two communities, the Western-leaning Christian Maronites and the Arab-leaning Sunni Arabs, undertook a struggle over Lebanon's national identity, with the Maronites reaching back to a Phoenician heritage and claiming for Lebanon a historical authenticity and the Sunnis challenging the legitimacy of the state and expressing a preference to join with their Arab neighbors. Indeed, of the five states that were "artificial creations and hand-ed their constitutions by the Great Powers," only in Lebanon did a local pop-ulation "seriously advance a thesis in support" of the country's national va-lidity.[17] However, what might have become a clash of national destinies eventually yielded to a gentlemen's agreement to acknowledge Lebanon's sovereign—but Arab—character, reflected by the National Charter of 1943.[18]

Egypt, which was not a mandatory country and had been ruled by Britain since 1882, was disposed toward territorial nationalism and distant from Arab nationalism through the mid-1930s. Indeed, Egyptians generally did not identify themselves as Arabs, and if they thought about those in the Fertile Crescent, they often held rather uncharitable views.[19] Accordingly, Egyptians demonstrated little interest in the important Arab events of the 1920 riots in Palestine, the Arab Congress in Damascus in 1919 and 1920, and the French takeover of Syria in 1920. When the Egyptian nationalist leader Sa'ad Zaglul met the Arab delegates at Versailles in 1918, he insisted that their struggles for statehood were not connected: "Our problem is an Egyptian problem and not an Arab problem."[20] Many Egyptian intellectuals and politicians treated Arab nationalism warily; even the author Taha Husayn, who supported an increase in Egypt's ties to the Arab world, opposed unity lest the Egyptian personality be diluted.[21] In any event, Egyptians exhibited a strong territorial nationalism and saw their drive for independence as distinct from the other independence campaigns in the Fertile Crescent.

Nearly all surveys of Iraq, Transjordan, and Syria begin by stating how these countries were inventions of the colonial powers and, relatedly, highlight the problems of governance of ethnically and religiously divided societies whose people had little political identification with the state.[22] Arabism's popularity is closely connected to this environment. As a result of the Turkification programs, Arabism was already part of the political vocabulary in this region before World War I. But its stature grew in connection with the postmandate struggle for independence and the attempt to forge some political cohesion from a population whose primary political identifications derived from their religion, tribe, or village. As residents of countries that were created by Great Power machinations, they could hardly see themselves as, for instance, Syrians or become enthusiastic about Syrian independence. Confronting a situation in which the traditional sources of authority and legitimacy were quite weak, political elites found that Arabism made them politically useful, could create some commonality where only divisions existed, and raised a banner that could lead the struggle for independence. Appeals to nationalism, Clifford Geertz once remarked of new states, are based on hopes and not on descriptions.[23]

Britain promised Syria independence and then denied it in deference to France. In fact, Syria actually experienced a brief moment of political independence between its liberation in 1918 and the French military conquest in July 1920. Notable here was the series of congresses that occurred in 1919 and 1920. The last congress took place in March 1920 and offered Faysal, the son of Sharif Husayn, the whole of Syria. His reign was brief. In July French forces took Damascus, expelled Faysal, and established a republican regime.[24] From this point on the Syrian political elite cultivated Arab nationalism for three related purposes. First, Arabism could legitimate the elite's rule in a way that no other ideology or program could. Syrian leaders began to portray themselves as leaders of an Arab struggle in order to make themselves politically relevant and to link themselves to a past, present, and future. Second, Arabism proved relatively effective in the attempt to meld a single political community from the mélange of ethnic, tribal, and religious communities that was now Syria. To be sure, Arabism could not erase their differences outright, but it could lessen the existing political divisions. Third, Arabism proved highly useful in the struggle for independence. To rally the population for "Syrian" independence was politically difficult because its populace viewed Syria as an artificial creation of the West; to rally the population for Arab independence, however, tapped into a historic past and a tangible political identity. This independence was largely territorial, despite the prominent exception that many Syrian political elites insisted on the restoration of Greater Syria, which would include parts of Transjordan and Lebanon, territories that they viewed as ancestral parts of Syria severed by colonial whims.[25] Arabism had an additional advantage in the anticolonial campaign: it could attract the backing of other Arab states in their struggle against France. That Arabism could tie together these three political programs became particularly evident at various moments; for instance, the Great Revolt in Syria of the mid-1920s was anti-imperialist and territorially nationalist in character, and the nationalist elite channeled the traditional nonnational loyalties and growing discontent of many residents into an anticolonial campaign.[26] Such campaigns highlight not only the multifunctional use of Arabism but also the territorial character that the language of Arabism had in Syria, Arabism's cradle.

Iraq, cobbled together from various areas of the old Ottoman Empire, contained three significant and regionally defined populations: the Kurds in the north, the Sunnis in the central areas and Baghdad, and the Shi'ites in Baghdad and in the south. It was left to a foreigner from the Hijaz and a self-proclaimed Arab nationalist, Faysal, to govern this divided polity. After the French ousted Faysal from Damascus, the British, attempting to repair relations with him and to use his close association with Arabism to legitimate their mandate, made him king of Iraq.[27] Although the Kurds and the Shi'ites were suspicious of Arabism and their new king, Arab nationalism gained a foothold in Baghdad because of the spread of Arab clubs, the Turkification programs and Ottoman insensitivities, and, perhaps most important, the English military invasion in 1914–1918, which brought together Shi'i and Sunni in a common political cause for the first time in centuries.[28]

Iraq now had an Arab and Hashemite king who faced a dual challenge: reducing British control and creating a national identity among a people who had no shared political community.[29] From the moment of Iraq's creation Britain hammered out a series of treaties that guaranteed for Britain various rights and hinted at greater Iraqi autonomy and the prospect of independence. Iraq gained formal independence in 1930, but Britain continued to cast a long shadow over Iraqi life through various treaty provisions. Britain's presence, coupled with the ongoing governability question, meant that the political history of Iraq before World War II is in many respects a tale of the coalitions and cliques that formed around three different nationalisms in the fight for *istiqlal tam* [total independence]: Iraqi nationalism and the attempt to forge an Iraqi national identity that could envelop the three principal demographic groups; Arab nationalism, which was territorial in character and envisioned an independent but Arab Iraq; and pan-Arabism, which was bound up with the palace's long-standing aspirations but was viewed suspiciously by the Shi'ite and Kurdish populations, which saw it as a threat to their cultural and religious autonomy. The "Iraqi first" version of nationalism eventually lost out to a growing pan-Arab spirit that was closely bound up with the ambitions of the palace and was particularly strong among the officer corps.[30] But the palace's heavy reliance on Britain for financial and military support eventually clashed with nationalist currents; the palace responded to the greatest of these domestic challenges, the Rashid Ali coup of 1941, by leaning on British military power to support its rule, injuring the palace's legitimacy and Arab credentials.[31] Still, Iraq remained the home for various unification and Fertile Crescent schemes.[32]

The history of Transjordan is bound up with the personal ambitions of Abdullah, the son of Sharif Husayn and the older brother of Faysal. Watching the French conquest of Syria in 1920 from the Hijaz, Abdullah reacted by initiating a military campaign against the French. This act was a potential embarrassment to Britain and a source of friction between Britain and France because Abdullah was conducting his raids from British-controlled areas. Britain, hoping to quiet Abdullah and to be seen as making good on some of its earlier promises to the Arabs, lopped off the eastern part of the Palestine mandate, dubbed it Transjordan, and made Abdullah its emir. Beginning in April 1921, Abdullah ruled a land with no jewel for a capital city and few natural resources; it was all but landlocked and highly dependent on

Britain for military and financial support.[33] Abdullah, an unabashed Arab nationalist of the unification variety who named his army the Arab Legion, made the best of the situation by clamoring for political independence and circulating an endless number of Greater Syria schemes that featured Abdullah as the prospective king of Damascus. Although he gained some prestige by his association with Arabism, his Arabism was born not from domestic pressures but from his personal and territorial ambitions. Indeed, he faced little substantial domestic opposition to his rule, thanks to his skillful manipulation and use of patronage politics, but what opposition existed concerned not his Arabism but the demand for constitutional mechanisms to check his power.[34] Abdullah and Faysal, the bearers of Hashemite ambitions, ruled from Amman and Baghdad but continued to covet Damascus and to dream of a unified Fertile Crescent that bore their family crest.

Arab nationalism was a growing force throughout the region, but Arab societies and elites maintained varying degrees of allegiance to the existing territorial states. As a general rule the Arab societies in the newly created states of Transjordan, Iraq, and Syria had little emotional attachment to the state and were more likely to favor unification than were the Arab societies of Lebanon, Egypt, and Saudi Arabia. These latter societies were more removed from unification as a tenet of Arab nationalism and more closely identified with the existing state. Arab political and ruling elites tended to adopt a stance that roughly reflected these currents of opinion; those in Syria, Transjordan, and Iraq were more likely to wield a unification theme in the struggle for independence and in their contest for political power with domestic rivals than were those in Egypt, Saudi Arabia, and Lebanon.

But in all cases the mandate system and the searing drive for independence represented a powerful force behind territorial nationalism and statism. To be sure, some Arab political elites and social movements came to embrace the demand for unification as they struggled against colonialism, but in other instances the practical goal of immediate independence gave way to an attachment to the territorial state. Unification might be possible and desirable, noted many Arab political elites, but such goals depended first on territorial independence.[35]

Although Arab nationalists might have differed on whether they should work for unification or live within the confines of existing state boundaries, they were unified in the belief that independence implied not simply juridical statehood but also the elimination of foreign control. Statehood meant little if the colonial power retained its privileges and prerogatives; therefore all vestiges and residues of colonialism must be removed as well. But agreement on the need to remove foreign control yielded to disagreement on the types of relations permitted with the West. Many Arab leaders, because of pragmatism, a desire to keep aid flowing, or a genuine desire to emulate the model of the nation-state of the West, were resigned to, if not desirous of, maintaining relations with the West. But such a relationship had to be based on equality and respect, if only for domestic political purposes.

The demand for real rather than rhetorical independence came alive during the ongoing and highly controversial treaty negotiations between the Arab states and the mandate powers. Two features of these negotiations are worth highlighting. Britain and France were attempting to preserve their control over the region and to further their interests as much as possible; the Arab states were attempting to achieve independence and to maintain the flow of foreign assistance without sacrificing their autonomy. Soon after the imposition of the mandate system the British and the French became enthralled with the idea of replacing their formal rule with informal treaties that would generate the same package of benefits without the increasing political costs.[36] Arab political elites were open to a treaty relationship because they were pragmatic and wanted financial and strategic assistance, but they were unwilling to sign on to a treaty that seemingly continued colonialism in all but name. Arab leaders were eager to conclude an agreement, but they were not so impatient that they were willing to make concessions that would leave them vulnerable to domestic rioting or subject to humiliating conditions from the Great Powers.

In addition, the spread of Arab nationalism meant that these treaty negotiations were linked across the region at both the bargaining table and within the various societies. Those negotiating in Cairo kept a keen eye on the negotiations reached in Baghdad, Abdullah in Amman would routinely insist on terms that resembled what his fellow Hashemites in Baghdad received, and Syrian politicians could hardly accept an agreement with France that was less than what other Arab leaders gained from Britain. The conclusion of a treaty, moreover, was cause for commentary throughout the region, including cables of congratulations from one Arab leader to another and pronouncements that the independence of one Arab state was a victory for Arabs everywhere. Conversely, a treaty viewed as conceding too much to the colonial power was met with catcalls and protests in capitals across the region. When Iraq concluded the Portsmouth Agreement with Britain in 1948, an agreement widely interpreted as allowing Britain to maintain its colonial prerogatives, rioting erupted in Baghdad and elsewhere; Abdullah's treaty with Britain in 1947 led many Arab politicians and newspapers to comment that Transjordan's independence was compromised by concessions made to Britain.[37] The treaty negotiations between Arab states and the mandatory powers were the subject of regional commentary because of the view that the security of the Arab states was interdependent and that the fate of the Arabs was intertwined.

In sum, the first concrete and politically consequential meaning associated with Arab nationalism was anticolonialism and political independence. Arab leaders began to cultivate, appropriate, and accumulate the symbols of Arabism as a way of legitimating their rule, those symbols were largely displayed during the fight for independence and statehood, and the fight for independence in the name of Arabism helped to deepen and legitimate Arabism. Political independence, however, need not entail the severing of ties. Most Arab political elites contemplated a continued relationship with their colonial patron after statehood, but they also were determined to ensure that the relationship was viewed as equal if only because a perception of dependence could leave them vulnerable to domestic discontent and regional ridicule. To be an Arab nationalist meant to be committed to independence and freedom from foreign control.

Arab Nationalism and Palestine

Before 1936 the struggle in Palestine was hardly the stuff of regional politics. Palestine took a backseat to the more pressing and immediate demands of political independence. And even if Arab governments had wanted to become more engaged in the conflict, they could hardly pursue whatever foreign policy they wanted; not only were they occupied but the regimes in power had to fear that becoming too vocal might jeopardize their independence campaigns. Finally, for residents of Baghdad or Cairo to associate with the plight of an Arab-speaking resident of Jaffa generally required that they view their political circumstances as intertwined because of their shared Arab identity. But this was hardly the case. Except for the well-publicized clashes of 1921 and 1929, the drama in Palestine largely occurred in isolation and without political mobilization in other Arab lands; seldom did Arab societies demand that their governments take a stand on these events, and Arab leaders found little political advantage to be gained by doing so.

By the late 1930s, however, Palestine had become an Arab issue. Three factors contributed to this development. Arab nationalists increasingly framed the Zionist challenge as an Arab issue, as situated alongside the regionwide struggle for independence from the West. As the Arab identity emerged in relationship to the struggle against colonialism, Arabs fighting for their independence in Baghdad, Damascus, and Cairo began to identify with the similar story unfolding in Palestine.[38] Palestinian leaders in fact were actively educating their brethren about the connection in order to further their struggle against Zionism; by playing the Arab card, they could mobilize regional support on their behalf.[39] In general, various Palestinian and Arab activists were framing Palestine as an Arab issue, attempting to build an identity-based bridge between those in different Arab lands and Palestine.

Further, the growing attention to Palestine contributed to and reflected a deepening Arab identity. During the 1930s more newspapers throughout the Arab world reflected a stronger voice for Arab unity, and more pan-Arab clubs and political associations reported on events in Palestine as a matter of concern to all Arabs.[40] As individuals began to identify themselves as Arabs, they also began to make connections to the Arabs of Palestine, and the tendency to frame Palestine as an Arab issue led to the further attachment to an Arab identity.

The third factor contributing to the making of Palestine as an Arab issue was the watershed event of the Palestine strike of 1936. The background of the strike is bound up with the long-standing grievances of the Palestinians against Zionism, and the trigger for the strike was the murder of two Jews by Arab assailants, followed by Jewish retaliation that left two Arabs dead and more widespread violence. The result was an instantaneous and unplanned revolt among Palestinians in April 1936, peaking later that year and continuing with decreasing strength through 1939. The Palestinians organized strikes, demonstrations, and clashes with the Zionists and British authorities that were intended to assert Palestinians' claims and to publicize their plight.[41]

And that they did. Occurring at a moment of growing support for Arab nationalism, the strike captured the attention of a region that had remained politically uninvolved in the Palestine conflict. That the strike was a major, if not the single most important, factor in the growth of Arab nationalism was the result of timing—it occurred during greater identification with Arab nationalism.[42] In Syria the spontaneous popular support for the Palestinians resulted from a growing awareness of the place of Palestine in the future Arab world and the fear that an independent Zionist state might create an obstacle to Arab unity, establish a dominating economic presence, and represent a threat to the Arabs because of Zionism's Western ties and origins.[43] Iraqis generally shared the Syrians' concerns and beliefs. Arab societies were racing ahead of their governments in support of Palestine, representing one of the first instances of social mobilization for a political project outside the state's territorial boundaries.[44]

Such mobilization placed immediate pressure on Arabs governments to formulate a coherent and concrete Palestine policy. Indeed, domestic opposition groups found that they could advance their fortunes and embarrass the regime in power by challenging its Arab credentials and policy on Palestine. In Iraq the Palestinian strike quickly became part of domestic politics and the struggles among the rival factions for political power.[45] The Syrian populace's demand that the government aid the Palestinians challenged the political program of the National Bloc, the major political party in Syria, tipping Syrian nationalism—that is, the struggle for independence—into Arab nationalism, a connection to transnational obligations.[46] Domestic political pressures pushed Arab governments everywhere to take a more active stand on Palestine.

But Arab governments also found that Palestine could become a source of symbolic capital, a way to bolster their domestic and regional prestige. Iraq now became "a vital center of Arab nationalist activity, enhancing Baghdad's reputation among the Arabs. In Transjordan the ambitious Amir Abdullah, while not at all pleased by the use of his territory as a conduit for arms and fighters, sought to benefit from the revolt by expanding his influence in Palestinian politics."[47] Though driven less by nationalist than by religious identification, Saudi Arabia's regional prestige swelled because of its visibility on the Palestine issue.[48] Arab political elites could gain or lose politically depending on how their societies viewed them in relationship to the cause of Palestine; accordingly, the elites had every reason to attach themselves to the cause.[49]

Developments in Egypt highlight the growing identification of Palestine as an Arab issue, the insertion of Palestine in domestic politics, and the attempt by state officials to take the lead on Palestine for domestic and foreign policy purposes. Before the 1930s most Egyptians did not identify themselves as Arab and accordingly perceived Zionism with a blend of indifference and some modest concern, driven by an Islam-based fear that the Jews would control the Muslim holy sites in Jerusalem.[50] During the 1930s, however, Egyptians began gravitating toward Arabism, and by the time of the Palestine strike what had once been indifference had become "interest, identification, and involvement."[51] In fact, the 1936 strike inaugurated Egypt's new Arab orientation.[52] At the grassroots level various movements began to organize public demonstrations and relief committees. But grassroots politics quickly became part of formal politics. The principal political opposition, the Wafd, found that Palestine was an effective way to embarrass the palace and score political points. The regime in turn found that becoming more involved was both politically necessary and a potential source of prestige.[53] "Thus the question of Egypt's political identity and orientation," wrote Yeshohua Porath, "became deeply intermingled with its internal political strife, all the more so since the Palace and the politicians connected with it did whatever they could to outbid the Wafd on this matter."[54] Economic and strategic interests also pushed the regime to become more involved in the conflict: some Egyptian businessmen feared that a more financially and industrially advanced Jewish population would have easier access to the markets in the Arab east; the alienness of a potential Jewish state represented a strategic threat; and Egypt might generate some political clout with Britain if it became identified with the cause of Palestine.[55] The palace, in short, found that a pro-Arab line was both popular at home and potentially consistent with its various interests.[56] Symbolic capital could be exchanged for other highly valued goals.

Now that Arab states were more actively involved in the Palestine crisis, they began to coordinate their Palestine policy, engage in symbolic competition, and face growing normative constraints on their foreign policy. The Palestine strike caused Arab states to embark on their maiden effort to construct a common foreign policy on Palestine. In October 1936 Iraq, Transjordan, Saudi Arabia, and Yemen appealed to the Arab Higher Committee (the nominal leadership of the Palestinian community) to call off the strike. Soon thereafter Arab states routinely participated in informal discussions and consultations and attempted to coordinate their policies. By the waning days of the strike and the time of the St. James Conference of 1939, Arab states took it almost as a matter of course that they should coordinate their policies on Palestine and attempt to forge a collective position.

Because the Arab states were becoming more involved in Palestine, Palestine was becoming part of inter-Arab politics. Arab leaders competed not only with their domestic rivals to demonstrate their commitment on Palestine but soon they were doing the same vis-à-vis other Arab leaders. Finding that they gained incredible regional prestige if they were identified as a leader on the Palestine issue, prestige that could translate into domestic popularity, Arab officials now engaged in symbolic competition.[57] But taking a stand on Palestine was not a risk-free proposition. After all, Arab leaders who "staked their prestige on saving Palestine for the Arabs risked being discredited if they could not produce results."[58] For the moment, however, those risks were minimal because Arab states were committed to little more than diplomatic support.

The regionalization and institutionalization of Palestine as an Arab issue meant that Arab leaders were increasingly constrained not only by domestic public opinion but also by "Arab" public opinion. One of the first instances of this came when Abdullah of Transjordan responded favorably to the 1937 Peel Commission's proposal that Palestine be partitioned between the Zionists and the Palestinians, with the latter becoming part of Transjordan. He became the target of outrage for a stand that Arabs viewed as defeatist and acceding to the Zionists.[59] To rally public opinion against the Peel Report and to increase pressure on the British, several hundred Arab nationalists from around the region gathered in the Syrian town of Bludan in September 1937.[60] This unprecedented development—the attempt to mobilize Arabs across the region to change the foreign policy of an Arab leader—would soon become a permanent feature of Arab politics. Arab leaders increasingly found themselves accountable to Arab public opinion.

In general, the growth of an Arab identity led to greater involvement in Palestine, and events in Palestine, notably the 1936 strike, contributed to the rise of Arab nationalism. Although the influence of the revolt differed from place to place, it had the uniform effect of pushing and pulling Arab leaders toward greater involvement in the Palestinian conflict. Residents of the region were now defining themselves as Arabs, supporting Arabs in Palestine, and expecting their governments to do the same. And so they did. Although Arab leaders might have been genuinely concerned with developments in Nablus, Jaffa, and Jerusalem, considerable evidence exists that their involvement derived from domestic political calculations and the desire to accumulate symbolic capital tied to Arabism. By the late 1930s Arab governments had uniformly declared their commitment to justice in Palestine, staked their Arab credentials on it, begun to coordinate their policies and decisions, and found themselves politically accountable not only to their societies but to those in other Arab states. Palestine was now an Arab issue.

Arab Nationalism and Unification

By the late 1930s, as an independent Arab world emerged, the race for statehood among Arab states was "taken over by the struggle for unity."[61] Newspapers, popular magazines, and general political commentaries increasingly featured the topic of Arab unity and the practical steps that might foster this outcome. Arab leaders were beginning to speak of life after colonialism, and the political opposition in many Arab countries began using the theme of Arab unity to embarrass the government and score easy political points.[62] Although strong divisions existed among Arab leaders, social movements, and intellectuals concerning what unity meant and what practical form it should take, the consensus was emerging that an Arab association of some sort was necessary for an Arab revival and commendable on strategic, political, cultural, and economic grounds.[63] The mix of anticipated independence and Arab nationalism steered the conversation among Arab states and societies toward the future regional order.

At the heart of this debate was the meaning of Arab unity. *Unity* was one of those catchall words that few could define and even fewer could object to. Still, there were two distinct camps. The maximalist camp defined unity as entailing unification or federation among the Arab states to bring the state and the nation into correspondence, erase the residues of colonialism, and fulfill Arab nationalism's ultimate aspirations. But even where unification was most favored—largely in Transjordan, Syria, and Iraq, and among the lower and middle classes—the support was hardly overwhelming. Few politically consequential mass demonstrations for unification were staged.[64] Moreover, Syrian and Iraqi leaders could hardly be counted as genuine and diehard supporters. Most Syrian political elites resisted concrete calls for unification because of their fear of Hashemite designs, their desire for a republican rather than a monarchical regime, and their reluctance to trade French for British guardianship, which would have occurred with any association with Iraq or Transjordan.[65] Iraqi officials proceeded cautiously toward unification or federation, fearing that it might ignite political instability among a population whose majority was Kurdish and Shi'ite and therefore suspicious of Arabism.[66]

But Iraqi, Syrian, and Transjordanian political elites kept unification alive—indeed, Arab officials matched, and sometimes outpaced, their societies—because of personal, political, and strategic calculations. King Abdullah of Transjordan aired various Greater Syria plans, primarily to achieve his long-standing personal ambition of being crowned king of Damascus and to lay claim to part of Palestine and secondarily to encourage Britain to expedite the timetable for Transjordan's independence.[67] Beginning with King Faysal and continuing over the years, the Iraqi palace saw Syria as having been promised and then denied to the Hashemites and held that a reclaimed Syria also would advance Iraq's economic interests and leave it more secure from Turkey and Iran.[68] Iraq's interest in some sort of federation increased with formal independence in 1930, when the rather ambitious Nuri al-Said was prime minister, when such proposals might increase Iraq's other foreign policy objectives vis-à-vis Britain or the other Arab states, and on occasion for domestic political purposes.

In general, these and other Arab officials might have been sincere champions of unification, but it just so happened that the discourse of unification served to legitimate their rule. And in the highly unlikely event that their proposals became reality, the result would be an increase in their political power. After all, these proposals had one common feature: the official forwarding the recommendation stood to be an immediate beneficiary.[69]

Saudi Arabia, Yemen, Lebanon, and Egypt comprised the minimalist camp, as they opposed unification and pressed for a regional association that exhibited some modest moves toward cultural, economic, and political cooperation within the constraining parameters of sovereignty. Saudi Arabia was suspicious of Arab nationalism or any related scheme that increased the political power of the Hashemite states of Transjordan and Iraq. And with good reason. The Saudis had ousted Sharif Husayn from the Hijaz in 1925, and ever since the Hashemites had been quite vocal about their desire to return.[70] From then on Saudi king Ibn Saud viewed Arab nationalism as a potential threat. Yemen was equally distant from the flag of Arab unification.

Lebanese officials could not help but translate Greater Syria into Lesser Lebanon. Because Lebanon had been administratively created from part of historical Syria, many Lebanese feared that Syria would use the facade of Arabism to make a territorial claim on its soil. The language of Arab nationalism contained an additional threat: because political peace in Lebanon was dependent on accommodation between the Maronite and Muslim political communities, Arabism represented a threat to the former and hence a source of political instability. In fact, even those Lebanese who identified with Arab nationalism were wary of a nationalism that would subsume them under Syrian control or would disrupt the social peace.

Egypt's initial attitude toward unification was not merely dismissive but derisive. Its pre-1930 position was famously captured by Sa'ad Zaglul, the great Egyptian nationalist: "If you add one zero to one zero, then add another zero, what will be the sum?"[71] In his view the Arab countries were zeros. As Egyptians became more attached to Arab nationalism and concerned with Palestine, however, the government began to take a greater interest in regional politics. But even then, most Egyptian officials and intellectuals feared becoming entangled in Arab politics.[72]

The Egyptian government became more active in Arab politics after it made two calculations. The first was that it was in Egypt's material interests to become more involved in Arab affairs; to become identified as a leader of Arab politics could elevate Egypt's political importance in global affairs, increase its commercial relations with the Arab east, and perhaps even further its ultimate goal of independence. Second, so long as it was going to be vulnerable to Arab issues because of Arab nationalism's growing popularity at home, it might as well control the Arab agenda rather than be controlled by it.[73] And once the Egyptian government decided to become more involved in Arab affairs, it found that it was pushing on an open door. Although some Arab leaders in the Fertile Crescent resented this upstart's long shadow, they ultimately kept such reservations private and publicly welcomed Egypt's newfound activism and leadership.[74] Many Arab nationalists viewed Egypt as a cultural center for Arabism and the Arab world's most powerful country; these nationalists had found regretful Egypt's long-standing reluctance to take a leading role in Arab affairs and thus openly embraced Egypt's change of heart, even though Egypt represented a powerful force behind a minimalist view of Arab unity.[75]

The formal and informal discussions about the future regional order reflected this divide between the maximalist and minimalist camps. The leaders of the Fertile Crescent were busy circulating various proposals for unification or federation among themselves, whereas discussions that included Egypt, Saudi Arabia, and Lebanon were modest in design. The first practical steps toward inter-Arab cooperation in fact embodied a more statist and minimalist orientation. Iraq and Saudi Arabia forged a treaty in 1936 that would have been long forgotten except that it represents one of the first efforts at inter-Arab cooperation. Later that year Egypt and Saudi Arabia commenced similar treaty discussions. Although the Arab states continued their discussions about the future regional association during the next few years, these discussions subsided and then nearly vanished as World War II neared.

Arab states began a more vigorous and serious set of conversations beginning in 1941. The catalyst was Britain's announcement that it favored some sort of institutionalized arrangement among the Arab states. In his famous Mansion House speech of May 29 British prime minister Anthony Eden declared Britain's support for any proposal that strengthened the ties among the Arab states. Britain was motivated by a desire to erase its antinationalist image, associate itself with a movement that it viewed as potentially unstoppable, and convince the Arabs that they should ally with Britain against Germany. But Eden's speech attracted little acclaim among Arab nationalists, perhaps because the Allies had lost considerable prestige in the Arab world after the fall of France and because the Arabs had lost faith in the statements of Western leaders, particularly when they were being defeated in war.[76]

But Eden's speech did encourage Iraqi prime minister Nuri al-Said to forward a Fertile Crescent plan to the British minister of state in Cairo a few months later. Never formally published, officially titled "A Note on Arab Independence and Unity with Particular Reference to Palestine," and subsequently known as the "Blue Book," it had two defining features: the formation of Greater Syria (to include Syria, Transjordan, parts of Lebanon, and Palestine), which would then form a league with Iraq, and the belief that unity should be based on the states that most resembled each other in their general political and social conditions—that is, unity should include the countries of the Fertile Crescent and exclude Egypt and Saudi Arabia. To achieve this unity, Said observed, "sacrifices of sovereignty and vested interests may have to be made."[77] Said's proposal had little immediate effect, but it did place greater political weight behind the idea of some type of association.

The next phase in the debate about the desired regional order began in 1943. Again the catalyst was Prime Minister Eden, who on February 14 offered another statement on the subject of Arab nationalism. Unlike his earlier commentary, which had little long-term effect, this time his thoughts triggered a highly involved set of discussions about the future regional order among Arab leaders.[78] Nuri al-Said suggested to Egyptian prime minister Mustafa al-Nahhas that Egypt sponsor an all-Arab conference on the future regional order. Although Said knowingly risked handing the unity talks to a known opponent of unification, he believed that Nahhas would welcome the opportunity to score some domestic political points by taking the lead on the unity talks, hoped that by bringing Egypt into the picture he might overcome the obstacle posed by Ibn Saud of Saudi Arabia, and calculated that the future of Arab unity demanded the inclusion of Egypt, the most powerful Arab state.

Nahhas picked up on Said's suggestion and on March 30, 1943, proposed that Cairo host a preparatory conference on the subject of Arab unity.[79] Nahhas had various reasons for doing so. Egypt, a latecomer to the cause of Arab nationalism and an opponent of unification, saw its role as similar to the position of the United States in the Western Hemisphere: dominating and stabilizing.[80] As the largest power, Egypt could regulate Arab affairs in ways that furthered Egypt's various interests. Nahhas also stood to gain personally by sponsoring the all-Arab conference. Because of a recent political debacle he had been labeled an opponent of Arab nationalism. To now host the first all-Arab conference would be quite a personal coup, and he made sure of it. In announcing his invitation he portrayed himself as the arbiter of different Arab proposals, scoring political points and outdueling his political rival King Faruq in the process.[81] In just a few short years Egypt had moved from the wings of Arab nationalism to become one of its leaders.

During the next several months Arab officials conducted a series of negotiations about who the Arabs were and what the regional architecture and its organizing principles should be.[82] Nahhas of Egypt and Said of Iraq opened informal discussions by addressing who the Arabs were and whether to include Egypt and the Sudan; the form and system of governance of any future federation; Greater Syria schemes and the future status of Christian and Jewish minorities; the willingness of states to renounce their sovereignty; and the potential danger of Jewish expansion within a federation that included Palestine.[83] The most important results of this discussion were that Egypt must be included in any future regional association, that unification was inconceivable and federation was politically unlikely, and that future discussions should concentrate on more practical possibilities.

The subsequent discussions among the other Arab leaders came to similar conclusions regarding unification. Saudi Arabia reiterated its opposition to any Fertile Crescent plan that was based on Iraqi leadership or, for that matter, any alterations that might leave the Hashemites advantaged.[84] The imam of Yemen followed suit.[85] Lebanon continued to stand by sovereignty. Syria, though publicly favoring federation—its parliament even adopted a formal resolution calling upon the government to work for a confederation of Arab states—also told Saudi Arabia's Ibn Saud that they were in full agreement on the need to maintain the territorial status quo.[86] Although Syrian leaders might have desired some sort of federation, they feared that it would leave them susceptible to Hashemite encroachments and recognized that the mandate system had given each part of Greater Syria its own national identity.[87]

These negotiations produced three discernible patterns that would become defining features of Arab politics for the next several decades. The first was the contradictory logics of *wataniyya* [state interests] and *qawmiyya* [Arab national interests]. Although Arab leaders had become quite comfortable with these territorial entities created by the West, Arab nationalism had a transnational component that expected Arab states to pool their separate sovereignties. Arab leaders routinely handled this tension by proclaiming their devotion to Arab unity while opposing most proposals intended to bring about unification on the grounds that they were impractical for the moment, unsalable at home, and might leave them vulnerable to unwanted outside interference.

Second, Arab leaders looked upon each other as a potential threat to their sovereignty, autonomy, and survival. Although they could hardly resist scoring some easy political points by calling for unification or federation, they viewed almost all such proposals as a Trojan horse and the deliverer of the proposal as a potential threat, because no Arab leader would advance or associate himself with a proposal that did not leave him better off and with more power.[88] The result was that although Arab leaders needed to create some regional association to satisfy the aspirations of their societies, they feared that such an association might leave them vulnerable to other Arab leaders and thus threaten their survival.

The third feature of these negotiations was the ongoing debate about the meaning of "Arab unity." Arab leaders eventually converged on a meaning that discarded the possibility of unification (at least in the near term) and allowed for a formal association that did not threaten their sovereignty and autonomy. These three related dynamics—the tension between statism and nationalism, the fear that an association would only encourage an interdependence that they viewed as a threat to their stability, and the meaning of unity—would become defining features of Arab politics for the next several decades.

After months of informal negotiations and after agreeing on a meaning of Arab unity, the Arab states gathered at the Antondiades Palace in Alexandria from September 25 through October 6, 1944, for the first formal round of negotiations. Attended by most of the major Arab leaders, although Yemen and Saudi Arabia initially were absent, the early part of the conference concerned unification and various Fertile Crescent schemes, the need for a formal organization, and what its architecture and machinery might be.[89] Not surprisingly, given the conclusions of their informal consultations, the Arab delegations quickly discarded the possibility of unification or federation and agreed to work toward a less ambitious design.[90]

Two weeks of discussions by the Preparatory Committee led to a series of resolutions that became known as the Alexandria Protocols. The protocols attended to five principal issues surrounding the future regional order: creation of the League of Arab States, which included in its constitution pacific dispute settlement, binding decisions, and inter-Arab cooperation; cooperation in social, economic, cultural, and other matters; consolidation of these ties in the future; a special resolution allowing Lebanon to retain its independence and sovereignty; and a special resolution on Palestine and the need to defend the Palestinian Arabs.[91] The protocols were signed on October 7 by all representatives except Saudi Arabia's and Yemen's. Their signatures were delayed because they did not have authorization, a sure sign of their deeply held suspicions.[92]

The protocols had something for everyone. Egyptian prime minister Nahhas could feel satisfied that he had controlled the Arab agenda and, more important, scored some political points. The Lebanese government was pleased to express its Arab orientation without sacrificing its sovereignty. The Syrian government was able to assert its independence vis-à-vis the French and move toward a greater alliance with its Arab brethren. Abdullah of Transjordan, although still waiting for Syria, had emerged as one of the elder statesmen of the conference. Iraq's Nuri al-Said, though still hoping for something resembling a Fertile Crescent orientation, believed that an important step toward inter-Arab cooperation had been taken. Saudi Arabia and Yemen, still concerned about various features of the protocols, were gratified to realize that no Fertile Crescent unity was in the offing and that Egypt also opposed federation.[93] And the general Arab public greeted the protocols with accolades and as a symbol of a more independent and grander Arab future.[94]

After six months of negotiations the Arab states met at the General Arab Conference at Za'faran Palace in Cairo on March 22, 1945, to toast the birth of the first post–World War II regional organization. At a dramatic gathering and to thunderous applause the Arab leaders signed the charter of the League of Arab States (which took effect on May 10, 1945). They celebrated their new organization with boasts of having fulfilled Arab nationalism's vision and with proclamations of their desire to strengthen the Arab political community and defend its interests. Only twenty-five years before, the colonial powers had just finished carving up the Middle East, and Arab nationalism was a minor political movement that could claim only localized pockets of support. Now the Arab states had an organization that expressed their collective Arab identity, and this organization had tremendous regionwide support.

But the charter was a greater verdict for sovereignty than it was for a more robust definition of Arabism. The Alexandria Protocols envisioned no real constitutional powers for the league. Yet even this modestly restrictive organization was too much for several of the Arab states to accept. The six months of negotiations that followed Alexandria transformed an organization whose ties were supposed to bind into one that clung to sovereignty as an organizing principle and as a defense against both potential intrusions by signatories and Arab nationalism's transnational traits.[95] Egypt, Saudi Arabia, and Lebanon, which had virtual veto power over the shape of the future organization, were at the forefront of watering down even further an already soggy organization.[96]

The weakening of the protocols in favor of the possessive sovereignty that defined the charter becomes apparent with a quick survey of their key contrasting tenets. Whereas the protocols did not prescribe any basis of inter-Arab cooperation except the goal of unity, the charter insisted on the "respect for the independence and sovereignty of these states"; whereas the protocols insisted on periodic meetings, the charter did no such thing; whereas the protocols discussed the importance of binding decisions, the charter reserved veto power for states; whereas the protocols demanded that Arab states adopt a common foreign policy, the charter insisted that each state was free to pursue its own foreign policy; whereas the charter insisted that the states respect each other's choice of a system of government, the protocols made no mention of such a possibility; whereas the protocols hinted of Arab states' yielding their sovereignty to unification, the charter insisted on the retention of their sovereignty (but did pay homage to the possibility of unification through Article 9). Finally, the Arab states debated and eventually discarded any mention of a collective security system or institutionalized military cooperation.[97] However weak the protocols might have been, the only way that these separate Arab states could exist within the same organization seemed to be to hand the charter no real powers to create only the loosest of associations. This was why Abdullah of Transjordan colorfully characterized the League of Arab States as "a sack in which seven heads have been thrust."[98]

A prevalent popular opinion at the time and the subsequent scholarly view was that the Arab League represented a vindication for statism and a vanquished Arabism. For many onlookers the league was a disappointing conclusion to a process that had begun with discussions of unification and federation. Although genuinely pleased that the Arab nation had an organization that symbolized its shared identity, many Arab nationalists criticized the charter for caring more for the interests of the regimes in power than for the aspirations of the Arab people.[99] Most scholarly commentary too has characterized the league as ineffectual and designed to be so, constructed to protect the interests of the separate Arab regimes and built to contain Arab nationalism's transnational impulses.[100] The consensus, in short, is that the Arab states erected a fairly weak organization that gave institutional expression to their identity but did not threaten their sovereignty or decrease their autonomy. Perhaps Cecil Hourani delivered the most charitable comment about the league when he remarked that it was a victory for "moderate Arab nationalism."[101]

But such opinion overlooks how the very establishment of a regional organization that baptized their shared identity—even one that had no formal constitutional powers—handed Arab states a mechanism to hold each other mutually accountable and left them increasingly vulnerable to symbolic sanctions. How so? Creation of the Arab League gave fundamental and symbolic expression to their shared Arab identity. This Arab identity, they proclaimed, was connected to Arab national interests that revolved around the shared desire to reduce foreign control, confront Zionism, and search for Arab unity.[102] Because these were Arab interests, Arab states were obligated to proceed multilaterally. They might have designed the charter to defend their sovereignty and their autonomy, but by publicly acknowledging a class of issues that properly belonged to the Arab nation, they conceded that unilateralism was a violation of the norms of Arabism and that they were mutually accountable and thus mutually constrained in these critical areas.

The Arab League thus became a forum of collective legitimation.[103] This legitimation process had a number of sides that shaped the potential opportunities and constraints on the foreign policies of Arab states. First, Arab states began to look to the league to establish their Arab credentials. An Arab leader seeking to demonstrate that he was a member in good standing would use the league as a source of symbolic capital by participating in its proceedings and by honoring its resolutions. But the other side of this opportunity was a constraint on their foreign policy activities. To be counted as a member in good standing an Arab state had to abide by the norms of Arabism. The Arab states had already conceded in practice that on certain issues they must proceed multilaterally; the construction of the league formalized this process, and whatever formal or informal decisions that evolved from their discussions would now act as a normative constraint. However much Arab states might protest and point to their sovereignty, they were far from the free agents they envisioned so long as they acknowledged and proclaimed that they were married by a shared identity.

Arab states also quickly recognized that these norms of Arabism could become an effective way to control the foreign policy of their rivals and even undermine them from within. As Arab leaders increasingly sought the symbols of Arabism to legitimate their actions and to further their domestic and foreign policy objectives, they also became increasingly constrained by whatever consensus emerged. That is, they became vulnerable to symbolic sanctioning. Even though the resolutions discussed and passed at the Arab League were nonbinding and usually failed to specify sanctions if they were violated, Arab leaders who disregarded them risked being defined as violating the norms of Arabism. Increasingly aware of this dynamic, Arab Leaders began to use the norms of Arabism to constrain their rivals' foreign policies. This largely symbolic organization had pulled them closer together and increased their mutual vulnerability and susceptibility to symbolic sanctioning.[104]

The Arab League's political effect came less through its formal constitutional structure and more through its acknowledgment that Arab states shared an Arab identity and set of critical interests; that because these interests derived from the Arab nation rather than from the territorial state, they should be pursued through multilateral rather than unilateral means; and that the league might begin to serve a legitimation function and therefore become a site to accumulate the symbols of Arabism, wield them against rivals, and control the foreign policies of other Arab states. But no matter how much the Arab states intended the league to be a defender of sovereignty and the status quo, the process that led them to its construction and their willingness to seek out the league to legitimate their foreign policies and hold their rivals accountable to the emergent norms of Arabism meant that they had institutionalized their interdependence and thus undermined their autonomy.

In less than a half century Arab nationalism, once a minor, romantic, and politically inconsequential movement, came to dominate the landscape and to imprint the debate about the desired regional order. Arab nationalism emerged because of new opportunities that came with the collapse of empires and the emergence of colonialism, new transnational networks and linkages that encouraged the populations of the region to associate and identify with one another, and the attempt by Arab leaders to wield the language of Arabism to serve their various interests, including the struggle for independence, the search for legitimacy, and the project of state building. By the close of World War II Arab nationalism was the reigning ideology of the region, the generally uncontested mode of political expression and protest.

Arabism was initially unattached to any defining political projects but soon came to be defined by the demand for independence and freedom from foreign control, the struggle against Zionism, and the desire for Arab unity. The Arab identity, then, was now connected to a concrete set of interests and practices. To be an Arab nationalist meant to fight against foreign control and Zionism and for Arab unity. The Arab League was intended to sanctify their interests in the territorial status quo and to celebrate their sovereignty, but the recognition that they were Arab states that had shared interests meant that they were now susceptible not only to domestic public opinion but Arab public opinion, were capable of seizing on key Arab issues as a source of symbolic capital, and potentially susceptible to the charge that they were acting outside the Arab consensus. Such matters would become clear during the next decade, although not over the issue of unification—something that they had successfully supplanted in favor of more conservative notions of unity—but over the norms concerning their collective position vis-à-vis Palestine and their postindependence relations with the West.

4

Securing Arabism, 1945–1955

The Arab states entered 1945 with a loose association and weak set of norms and ended a decade of debate about the desired regional order with a tighter normative fabric that more carefully and closely defined the practices that were and were not consistent with Arabism. As always, the precursor to such developments was a series of important events that unleashed a symbolic competition among Arab leaders to define the situation in ways that were consistent with their various ambitions, accumulate symbolic capital, deploy symbolic sanctions against their rivals in order to control their foreign policies, and align their policies with the norms of Arabism in fits of impression management and attempts to stave off domestic and regional sanctions. Symbolic rather than military politics and the imperatives of regime rather than state survival were responsible for tightening the normative web between Arab states and holding them more fully accountable to each other.

The events surrounding the Zionist challenge, the continuing debate about unification, and the relationship between the West and the Arab states stirred the dialogues in Arab politics. The Arab states' response to the Zionist challenge can be divided into three distinct phases: from 1945 through the fall of 1947, when they limited their involvement to various resolutions and diplomatic forays; from the fall of 1947 through May 1948, when they engaged in symbolic competition, which ultimately drove their decision to invade Palestine when the mandate expired at midnight on May 14; and from late 1948 through April 1950, when they conducted bilateral negotiations with Israel and debated whether and under what conditions they might have dealings and relations with the Jewish state. These postwar discussions culminated in the normative prohibition against making peace with Israel, codified by the League of Arab States in April 1950. For the next several decades the idea of any sort of relations with Israel became the taboo of Arab politics.

Arab nationalism had brought the Arab states to Cairo and caused them to construct a regional association with a charter that acknowledged that its force owed to its insistence that sovereignty was the cornerstone of inter-Arab politics. Still, a stratum of society, particularly in the Fertile Crescent, contended that these states were artificial entities that should erase their territorial boundaries, and some Fertile Crescent leaders gestured in this direction, if only to score some easy points and keep their rivals off balance. The decade's most promising unification effort occurred in the fall of 1949, when Iraq and Syria made unity noises. Egypt led the antiunification coalition and ingeniously dangled a collective security pact to discourage Syria from joining forces with Iraq. Thus the Arab Collective Security Pact of 1950 was born; an institutional wave at collective security, it was in fact a multilateral brace for sovereignty. Although calls for unification percolated during the next decade, unification remained relatively low on the political agenda.

The third and ultimately transformational issue pertained to the unsettled and unsettling relationship between Arab nationalism and the West. Arab nationalism of the period has been described as a "protest movement," the Arab version of anticolonialism.[1] There is much truth to this. Arab nationalism during the interwar period was largely expressed through opposition to the mandates and the 1936 treaties and the demand for full, complete, and uncompromised independence. Yet such demands did not necessarily envision autarchy or neutrality but rather a revised relationship with the West, one that secured for Arab states material and political advantages without the humiliating concessions associated with colonialism. The West was intent on stabilizing its place in the region and enlisting the Arab states for its various defense plans and containment schemes. The dramatic finish to the debate was the 1955 fight over the Baghdad Pact between Iraq and Turkey, a yearlong duel between the seasoned Nuri al-Said of Iraq and a rising Gamal Abdel Nasser of Egypt, each of whom had strategic, political, and personal reasons for his position on the pact. Nuri wanted the Arab states to accept it, whereas Nasser wanted them to reject it. Nasser won, which meant that Arab nationalism was defined by neutrality and nonalignment. The Arab states now publicly subscribed to a norm of Arabism that prohibited a close relationship with the West. The pact was the decade's transformative event because it established the prohibition against a strategic relationship with the West, launched Nasser on his pan-Arab career, and fundamentally changed the parameters of Arab politics for the next decade by shifting the ground from conservatism to radicalism. In general, the decade-long debates about the relationship of Arab nationalism and sovereignty, Zionism, and the West deposited a set of norms that increasingly made Arab states more dependent on each other for social approval, and thus susceptible to symbolic sanctions, and more closely bound together, and thus more oriented toward one another.

Palestine and Israel

The struggle in Palestine between the Zionists and the Palestinian Arabs had become a struggle between Arab nationalism and Zionism. But not because many Arab leaders viewed the Zionists as an immediate military threat. Rather, the confrontation with Zionism became a test of their Arabism. Arab officials eventually staked their prestige on Palestine not only from a sense of solidarity with the Palestinian Arabs but "also from the fact that the Arab nationalists regarded the Zionist effort in Palestine as a particularly significant test and challenge."[2] An attempt to balance their various interests alongside their desire to be seen as making a good show on Palestine eventually led them to cast their lots with a military intervention; that is, a desire to defend their images rather than the Palestinians led to the campaign. Although the military showing was designed to answer their critics at home and bolster their Arab credentials, their lackluster performances only added to the chorus of criticisms and made it politically untenable for Arab leaders, regardless of their private thoughts, to entertain relations with Israel.

THE INFECTIOUS SLIDE TOWARD WAR

From 1945 through the fall of 1947 the Arab states continued the pre-1939 pattern of policies toward Palestine in three respects. First, they wanted to make a good showing on Palestine for a complex set of reasons, including a sense of obligation; a desire to distract their populations from troubles at home; and a desire to display their commitment to Arabism to their watching publics. But Arab officials had to balance their Palestine policy with their other foreign policy interests and domestic objectives. Egypt, for instance, attempted to use Palestine to maintain and protect its leadership in Arab politics but feared that becoming too entangled might jeopardize its more immediate goal of dislodging the British from Egypt. Although Arab governments wanted to give a good accounting of themselves on Palestine, few wanted to expend scarce capital and resources, lest they jeopardize their regime's other goals and objectives or find themselves involved in a war unwanted and unjustified by strategic imperatives.

Second, the Arab League provided the perfect cover for Arab states to maintain a limited, somewhat low-cost involvement.[3] Whereas before 1945 they had used informal and somewhat ad hoc arrangements to debate the Palestine issue, after they established the Arab League, Arab states used it to respond to a series of crises in Palestine and commissions of inquiry being sent by the West and the United Nations to formulate a resolution to the conflict. Yet Arab officials used the league not only as a debating parlor but also as the principal mechanism for protecting their individual interests while promoting the image of collective involvement. Such considerations explain why the league's resolutions were long on support and concern but short on concrete action.

Third, Arab governments used Palestine to score easy political points against their rivals, and their ability to do so increased as the crisis dragged on and obtained a centrality in Arab politics. A defining feature of the Arab governments' policy on Palestine both before and after the creation of Israel was the desire to use Palestine to display their allegiance to Arabism and to call into question the credentials of a rival. For instance, at the Arab League meeting in June 1946 Iraq, motivated by domestic political concerns and an opportunity to embarrass Saudi Arabia and Egypt, urged the Arab states to censure Britain and the United States for their support of the Zionists. But Iraq knew that Egypt and Saudi Arabia would oppose any such move, which they did, and thus would suffer the inevitable political fallout, which they did.[4]

The ability of the Arab governments to preserve their images while protecting their other interests through mere resolutions became increasingly difficult after February 18, 1947, when Britain announced its decision to turn its mandate over to the UN, and in the fall of 1947, when the General Assembly began debating a two-state solution. Such developments made it more difficult for Arab states to convince their publics that mere resolutions and diplomacy exhausted their obligations. In some respects they had only themselves to blame for their societies' demands for more robust action; after all, they had been ratcheting up the visibility and centrality of the conflict by holding a series of high-level and well-publicized meetings that were nearly always followed by strongly worded resolutions with calls to action and then celebrated as providing a definitive and effective response to the crisis.[5] Now they were being asked to make good on their promises.

The Arab governments continued to resist various calls from their publics and the occasional Arab official for more military action through the early part of 1948. At a conference in Sawfat, Lebanon, in September 1947 the league's political committee clashed over whether it should implement its earlier resolutions advocating an oil embargo against the West. Saudi Arabia argued against doing so, saying it only would disadvantage the Arabs. Iraq, which would continue to use the Haifa pipeline through May 1948, attempted to embarrass Saudi Arabia by urging the immediate implementation of the embargo. No oil embargo followed. In October the Council of the Arab League voted to increase the financial assistance to the Palestinian Arabs but rejected the recommendation of the technical committee to establish a pan-Arab unified command.[6]

Once the U.N. General Assembly approved the partition plan on November 29, 1947, however, the Arab governments came under greater domestic pressure to make good on their pledges.[7] At a conference in Cairo in early December the Iraqi delegate, responding directly to domestic demands, urged the league to punish those states that supported the Zionists and to order the Arab armies into Palestine. Most Arab governments bristled at this suggestion and instead opted to double their financial assistance and expedite their military assistance.[8] Egypt was so resistant to the idea of military involvement that it abstained from the initial military discussions, and other Arab officials, most notably those from Palestine and Transjordan, feared having other Arab armies on their soil.[9] For the time being cautiously worded resolutions would be the limit of their involvement.

The Arab states were unable to slide by with resolutions alone after March 1948. With war looming, the UN's recognition of a two-state solution, the British withdrawal imminent, and the Jewish state ready to proclaim its independence, the Arab governments were being forced to take concrete action to demonstrate their commitment to Palestine and to Arabism. But even under these increasingly tense circumstances a stalemate between the Hashemite and non-Hashemite states emerged regarding the necessity of military intervention because of the absence of a strategic threat. The Hashemites hardly wanted to find their armies embroiled in a war in Palestine but were at the forefront among Arab states calling for a military response. Iraq argued forcefully for military confrontation, a stance motivated largely by domestic politics and its related desire to bolster its Arab nationalist credentials.[10] From Jordan Abdullah also demanded military intervention—but hardly because of a highly developed empathy for the Palestinians. While he was pleading with his fellow Arab statesmen to enter Palestine to confront the Zionists, behind the scenes he was conducting secret negotiations with his supposed nemesis regarding their future relations, the division of the spoils, and the conduct of the coming military campaign.[11] Although Abdullah and the Zionist leadership never initialed a formal agreement, the general understanding was that Abdullah's Arab Legion would enter Palestine under cover of a confrontation with the Zionists but that the Jordanian troops would advance only so far, leaving the Zionists with what remained.

On April 10 Abdullah unilaterally shattered the stalemate between the Arab states regarding military intervention when he announced that the Arab Legion would enter Palestine upon the expiration of the mandate to protect the Arabs and to confront the Zionists.[12] Although few Arab countries wanted to follow in his footsteps, neither did they enjoy the idea of Abdullah's becoming the patron saint of Palestine, perhaps making a grab for Arab Palestine, and calling into question their own commitments.[13] Abdullah's announcement therefore left the other Arab states scurrying to keep pace and made military intervention a near certainty. On April 12 Egypt announced that it too would send its troops to Palestine. But symbolic rather than strategic factors prodded this decision. Many Egyptian officials warned that becoming too embroiled in Palestine might undermine Egypt's central goal of ridding its soil of the British.[14] During the parliamentary debate Ismail Sidqi, a prominent Egyptian politician, argued against intervention on the grounds that Egypt's strategic interests were not at risk and that it did not have the same obligations to Palestine as did the other Arab states.[15] King Faruq overruled these and other objections because of his belief that failing to intervene would cost him dearly in prestige and leave him vulnerable to both the Muslim Brotherhood at home and King Abdullah abroad. Simply put, his domestic and regional standing depended on sending his military across the Sinai and into Palestine.[16] Despite similar reservations, most Arab states also calculated that to abstain from the military campaign would subject them to domestic disturbances.[17]

Symbolic rather than strategic considerations led the Arab states to resolve on April 16 to send their armies into Palestine once the mandate ended the following month. Few Arab leaders argued vigorously in private that the Zionists were an implacable military threat, but many readily acknowledged that failure to confront the Zionists would leave them vulnerable at home. In fact, many Arab military officials warned their governments that they might not have the military wherewithal to confront the Zionists; such military dangers, however, paled in comparison to the domestic threats that Arab leaders feared they might face should they fail to go to war.[18] After years of drawing attention to the Zionist challenge and delivering little more than vaguely worded resolutions, the Arab governments sent their militaries into Palestine in an act of impression management.

The armies of Jordan, Iraq, Syria, Egypt, and a ceremonial Saudi contingent entered Palestine as the mandate expired on May 14. But from the start their military operations were permeated and undermined by the same inter-Arab rivalries and mixture of political interests that sent them tumbling into Palestine. Although the Arab states pledged to coordinate their military operations and the irregular volunteers under the direction of the Arab League's military committee, each national army was under the direction of its government.[19] The result was confusion in the field, bickering between Arab leaders, agreement on coordinated invasion routes that were ignored during the campaign, and a generally disorganized and ineffectual military effort.[20]

Indeed, although the Arab League's plan was designed to prevent partition, Abdullah's military plans were designed to effect it.[21] Abdullah's intentions toward Palestine were often considered to be less than honorable, and there were strong hints that his army had entered Palestine not for the Palestinians but for the king's glory. Consequently, the Jordanian and Egyptian armies were as wary of each other as they were of the Israelis, and their military operations were sometimes tailored to keep an eye on each other's military positions and intentions. The Israelis were a prime beneficiary of such inter-Arab suspicions.

Nor did the Arab governments throw their military weight behind the campaign.[22] Explanations for this result vary. A halfhearted military effort was consistent with their previous concern with impression management and also reflects the belief that Arab governments did not view the new Jewish state as a military threat. Domestic politics, which accounts for why they decided to mobilize in the first place, also helps to explain their weak resolve when they did: a fear that deploying their best military contingents to Palestine might leave them vulnerable to domestic insurrection at home and the basic inability of the states to mobilize the troops required. How the Arab states conducted the military campaign mirrored the processes that led them to war.

THE POSTWAR PROHIBITION OF PEACE

The splintered way in which the Arab states fought in Palestine carried over into the postwar negotiations and armistice talks. They were in general disarray over whether, in what manner, and on what terms they should politically and diplomatically engage Israel. The backdrop to that debate and a powerful force leading to their eventual decision was the bitter legacy of and political fallout from their dismal campaign in Palestine. The loss of Palestine, which became known as *al-nakba* [the catastrophe], represented a tremendous psychological blow that rippled and ripped throughout the Arab world.

All those even remotely associated with the defeat became the target of wrath and ire. Many Arabs who once expressed concern about Palestine but were unwilling to commit resources and energies to the cause were now fully anti-Israel. If Arab leaders entered the battle because of domestic political considerations and the desire to save face, they probably did not anticipate that their shallow effort and subsequent defeat would radicalize the military and society—an outcome they had hoped to avoid by doing battle in the first place. The loss of Palestine suggested that the immediate causes of Arab weakness stemmed from irresoluteness, incompetence, corruption, and disunity and "served to confirm pre-existing beliefs about the perennial backwardness of Arab society."[23] The masses, the military, and the intelligentsia were now more opposed than ever to the regimes in power and had greater reason to indict their leadership and legitimacy. Military officials returning from Palestine, and intellectuals and the masses watching from the capitals, concluded that "the enemy is us."[24] Nasser later said that he returned from war "convinced that the real enemy was in Cairo."[25]

Although this radicalized climate meant that Arab officials wanted to carefully avoid any hint of consorting with the enemy, the immediate and practical need for a formal armistice remained; cease-fire lines had to be established and patrolled.[26] A defining subtext to the armistice negotiations, however, was whether Israel and one or more of the Arab states might build on an agreement to conclude a formal peace treaty. In fact, the armistice discussions nearly always contained the implicit and sometimes explicit expectation that a separate peace might be struck at the right price.[27] But Arab officials ultimately calculated that they would be cutting their own political throats if they negotiated a peace with Israel.

During the first few months of 1949 Egypt followed a separate negotiation path and proceeded without any reference to the Arab League or other Arab states; Egypt's unilateralism was widely rumored to be linked to peace with Israel.[28] In the end, however, Egypt concluded that any benefits that might be gained from a separate peace were not worth the substantial political costs.[29]

Syria, though it lagged behind Egypt and Jordan in the armistice talks, also flirted with a separate peace. Syria's dramatic reversal in attitude was a consequence of a military coup led by Colonel Husni Za'im in March 1949.

Za'im's decision to contemplate a permanent peace with Israel is attributable to a number of factors, including Za'im's belief that the "right" peace treaty might help establish him in Syria, the region, and global politics; the fear that the other Arab states were concluding separate agreements and would leave Syria to face a militarily superior Israel alone; the understanding that the army was the mainstay of the regime, and he was well advised to shield it from Israel; the keen interest in instituting political and economic reforms, which would be more easily accomplished if Israel were removed from the top of the agenda; and, finally, that he was strikingly free from ideological politics and outside the mainstream of Arabist sentiments.[30] Itamar Rabinovich has identified this last factor—that Za'im was out of touch with the currents of Arab public opinion—as allowing Za'im to propose a peace treaty. Still, Za'im determined that any treaty would have to come at the right price so that he could defend himself against his domestic and regional critics, as his aides constantly reminded him. Israel ultimately determined that the price, including territorial concessions of strategic water rights, was too high.[31] These negotiations had already faltered when Za'im was overthrown by a coup engineered by Colonel Sami al-Hinnawi in the fall of 1949. Significantly, the participants in the coup failed to name Israel, the armistice agreements, or the peace negotiations as among their grievances. Rabinovich has speculated that the reasons for the absence of these elements were that those involved in the coup were participants in the armistice agreements, Syria wanted to avoid needlessly escalating the conflict with Israel, and perhaps that the Syrian military and society were just not preoccupied with Israel.[32]

Jordan came closest to concluding a separate peace with Israel. "For Abdullah," wrote Avi Shlaim, "peace negotiations with Israel posed not so much a question of principle but a problem of timing."[33] Abdullah used the armistice negotiations to continue his prewar discussions about the possibility of commercial dealings, a nonaggression pact, and a peace treaty. Abdullah's desire for a peace treaty stemmed from his belief that Israel would help Jordan gain political access to the United States, the world's rising and principal power; his concern that Jerusalem would be internationalized and his belief that a peace treaty with Israel would prevent this; his desire for an outlet to the sea and expectation that trade would nurture Jordan's economic development; and his assumption that the right treaty might elevate his prestige in the Arab world. Abdullah's immediate objective, however, was to complete his annexation of the West Bank. The Jericho Congress of December 1948 was the first step in that direction, but Abdullah still sought to imbue his acquisition with the trapping of legality that would come through recognition and annexation.[34] There was little Abdullah was not prepared to sacrifice for the prize of Jerusalem and the West Bank.

Israel and Jordan neared a nonaggression pact in the early months of 1950, and to prepare for this possibility Abdullah attempted to force his council of ministers to accept the principle of commercial relations with Israel. This ultimatum produced a government crisis. On March 2 three Palestinian members of the council resigned in bitter opposition to Abdullah's plan, and soon thereafter Prime Minister Abu al-Huda also tendered his resignation. Abdullah's plans for a separate peace with Israel and annexing the West Bank now became a badly kept secret. The response from other Arab governments was swift and severe. Egypt led the charge, a stand born not only from principles but also from the fear that a separate Jordanian-Israeli peace treaty would threaten Egypt's leadership in Arab politics and harm its negotiations with Britain.[35] To halt the Jordanian-Israeli negotiations Egypt took to the airwaves and portrayed Jordan as an enemy of Arabism and Israel's coconspirator. Cairo got some timely help from a Jordanian official who had been privy to Jordanian-Israeli negotiations during the 1948 war. Jordan's private discussions were now part of the public record.[36]

Egypt's portrait of an Abdullah who was nearing a peace with Israel and annexation of the West Bank and publication of the secret negotiations had their intended effect: Abdullah was vilified throughout the region. Many recommended Jordan's expulsion from the league if Abdullah concluded a separate peace treaty or annexed the West Bank, and Syrian prime minister Khalid al-Azm threatened to close the Syrian border if Abdullah proceeded as planned. Abdullah attempted to deflect the criticism by claiming that his approach alone would solve the refugee crisis and produce a just peace. But his justification convinced few. Abdullah was swimming against the tide of Arabism and subjected to a tirade of accusations that questioned his standing as an Arab.[37]

Arab leaders gathered in Cairo for the twelfth Arab League session from March 25 through April 13, 1950, and atop the agenda was what action should be taken if Abdullah concluded a peace with Israel or annexed the West Bank. At stake, however, was not only what Abdullah might do but perhaps the future of the Arab League. Much commentary at the time focused on the Arab League's ineffectiveness in confronting the Zionist challenge, the Arab states' decision to negotiate separately rather than collectively after the war, and the appearance that now Abdullah, and perhaps others, were about to conclude a separate peace treaty with Israel. Under such circumstances, many wondered, what was the point of the league?[38]

For the next several days the Arab states jostled over how to respond to

Abdullah's challenge. Should they, as Egypt initially proposed, expel Jordan from the Arab League or offer a more measured response that communicated their anger but left the door open for Jordan to remain a member? The Arab states eventually settled on a strongly worded resolution prohibiting any separate peace. Adopted unanimously on April 1, the resolution prohibited any Arab state from negotiating or concluding "a separate peace or any political, military or economic agreement with Israel."[39] A few days later the Arab League determined that a suspected violation would be referred to the political committee to consider whether a violation had in fact occurred, that such a decision would be binding if four states agreed to the decision, and that the penalties would include severing political and diplomatic relations with the violator, closing any common borders and economic dealings, and prohibiting all financial or commercial transactions. Relations of any kind with Israel were now taboo.

Abdullah bristled at this intrusion on his foreign policy, but his ministers warned him against rebuking the league's decisions lest he invite further domestic and regional abuse, which would in turn jeopardize his ultimate goal of smooth elections on the West and East Banks—if not also his crown.[40] Abdullah therefore bowed to the barrage of Arab public opinion on the issue of a separate peace with Israel and announced that he had no such intent. As aptly observed by Moshe Sasson, one of Abdullah's Israeli negotiating partners, although Abdullah had the will to make peace, he did not have the way.[41] Abdullah bemoaned the constraints placed on him by his rivals, but he could not proceed without their approval.

Now Abdullah set his sights on his ultimate ambition of the West Bank. He wasted little time. On April 11, the day after the Arab League meeting adjourned, Jordan held elections, a precursor to Abdullah's planned annexation. Then on April 24 Abdullah announced the unification of the two banks under the Hashemite crown, citing Arab League resolutions and a plebescite on the West Bank as legalizing his actions and portraying his decision as a step toward "real union."[42] His annexation was met by widespread disapproval, charges of betrayal, calls for his expulsion from the league, and claims that he was motivated not by Arab nationalism but by territorial expansion.[43] Abdullah, nonplussed by the response, dared the other Arab leaders to mete out their punishment and even to evict him from the league.[44]

Egypt called Abdullah's bluff and pushed for expulsion, a stand informed by its desire to solidify its Arabist credentials and the assumption that the other Arab states would oppose such a severe sentence. To try to heal the rift between Egypt and Jordan and in order to formulate a compromise position, the league's political committee delayed its decision for a month. In the interim Egypt retreated from its earlier demand for expulsion, not only satisfied that its credentials were now established but also fearful that Jordan's expulsion might give Abdullah a free hand to conclude a peace treaty with Israel.[45] A compromise position was struck, and on June 12 the Council of the Arab League charged that Jordan's decision was a product of expediency dictated by the situation and that the territories should be held in trust until the liberation of all the pre-1948 territories. In the end the other Arab states resigned themselves to Jordan's annexation of the West Bank, though none ever formally acknowledged the move.[46]

Although the Arab states did not punish Abdullah for his actions, he met a harsher fate and the most violent of sanctions on July 20, 1951, when he was assassinated at the al-Aqsa mosque in Jerusalem. The assassins were clearly and decidedly punishing Abdullah for his negotiations with Israel, his annexation of the West Bank, and his betrayal of the Palestinians. Indeed, the subsequent trial revealed a web of conspiracies involving various ethnic and nationality groups in Jordan, each of which was rumored to have received significant assistance from rival Arab regimes that had designs on Jordan or wanted to check Abdullah's territorial ambitions.[47] The assassination left an indelible mark on King Abdullah's grandson, the future King Hussein, who was at the king's side when he was slain. Now it was clear that making peace with Israel risked political sanctions from the Arab League and even worse from those in the street.

Relations with Israel were now a taboo of Arab politics. This taboo emerged because of the dynamic between Arab leaders who wanted to maintain their regional and domestic standing and found Arabism and a strong stand on Palestine a useful way to do so, who used Arabism as a symbolic sanction to undermine their rivals and control their foreign policies, and who engaged in symbolic competition. These symbol-laced decisions, rather than any overarching strategic or military imperative, compelled the Arab states to enter Palestine and later to prohibit relations with Israel. Little evidence exists that the decision to intervene in Palestine was driven by strategic considerations; nor does a preponderance of evidence suggest that Arab leaders were so fearful of the Israeli military threat that they were ready to use military means to contain it. Understanding the dynamics that led Arab states to commit their forces abroad requires recognizing how Arab leaders had increasingly staked their prestige on Palestine as a way to maintain their support at home and compete with their rivals abroad for symbolic capital—and how this symbolic competition led to their symbolic entrapment, that is, drove them to intervene to maintain and manage their impressions, even though they privately feared it might undercut their other objectives.

Let me briefly expand on these points. Arab governments, though not exactly embracing the Zionists, also did not expend tremendous resources on confronting them early. Instead, they limited their involvement to the diplomatic field either because of a lack of commitment and/or fear that becoming entangled would jeopardize their other objectives. If Arab public opinion compelled them to take a stand, Arab leaders nudged each other closer to the edge of intervention as they continued to use Arabism to stabilize their positions back home and to undermine their rivals abroad. The pressure to intervene became greater as the mandate came to a close and Arab states decreed the necessity of strong action but delivered only empty resolutions. The tipping point for intervention was already reached, then, when King Abdullah declared his intent to deploy the Arab Legion to protect the Palestinian Arabs and confront the Zionists. All the other Arab states followed suit to avoid the shame of being left behind, decisions sometimes made over the outright objections of their military advisers. Symbolic rather than military politics pushed the Arab armies toward the borders of Palestine.

Although the Arab states hoped that this show of force would impress their watching publics, in fact their halfhearted efforts and subsequent defeat only encouraged nationalist fervor, increased accusations against them, and hardened the opposition to Israel. Arab officials now faced a new set of constraints as they debated how far they could go individually and collectively in dealing with Israel. Many Arab leaders contemplated making a separate peace with Israel—if the price was right. But they set the price quite high because of the constraints imposed by Arabism. Abdullah was alone in calculating that the anticipated rewards outweighed the potential damage to his reputation, but an Egyptian-led campaign easily framed his actions as an affront to Arabism. The result of the diplomatic and political outcry was the creation of the norm prohibiting a separate peace with Israel. And Abdullah, though angered by this intrusion on his foreign policy, understood that to proceed with his plans might cost him his crown. In fact, it cost him his life.

For reasons that had less to do with strategic calculations and more to do with their rivalries and fear that their Arabism would be found deficient, the Arab states established the norm prohibiting peace with Israel. As one Israeli commentator astutely noted: "Had peace depended on the conflicting interests of the Arab states, then the peace prospects would have been much brighter than they were now. However, each of the Arab states as well as the Arab League cannot free themselves from their public opinion, the fruit of their own agitation."[48] Symbolic competition had left them more vulnerable and dependent on each other for social approval and led to the norm that prohibited them from considering any relations with Israel whatsoever. This norm was now a social fact, a central tenet of Arabism, and a defining feature of their identity.

Arab Nationalism and Sovereignty

The Arab states had already vetted the question of unification during their negotiations regarding the Arab League, and their response was contained in its architecture and constitution, which reinforced the principle of sovereignty. But a body of public opinion, particularly in the Fertile Crescent, continued to champion the idea of unification and to view these states as artificial entities. Thus Iraqi and Jordanian leaders were at the forefront of expressing sentiments for unification if only to score easy political points, raise havoc, or embarrass their rivals. Iraq's interest in unification had various sources, including personal aggrandizement of the palace, domestic politics, and a desire to cast a longer shadow over Arab politics. Always ready to forward a Greater Syria plan with himself crowned king in Damascus, Abdullah had an impulse toward unification that derived from a desire to break out of his desert kingdom; a belief that the Hashemite thrones in Iraq and Transjordan should be united and that by all rights Syria also should have been Hashemite; the goal of elevating his stature in Arab politics and bolstering his domestic fortunes; the wish to fulfill his Hashemite family's longstanding goals; the concern that his heir apparent, Talal, was unfit to rule; and perhaps the dream of reconquering the Hijaz and settling an old debt with the Saudis.[49] Abdullah had more reasons than not to trumpet unification. In both the Iraqi and the Jordanian cases the unity theme derived from a mixture of regime survival and nationalism, but the Iraqis' and Jordanians' ability to use unification as a means to extend their influence or absorb new territories can be attributed only to the enabling conditions of Arabism.

Various unification proposals were floated between 1945 and 1955, but none was more credible than a Syrian-Iraqi unification proposed in the fall 1949.[50] Unification had become a more frequently mentioned goal after the Palestine war. In the debate about the causes of the loss and how to increase the power and security of the Arab world, one candidate was unification, which offered the promise of both answering the challenge posed by Israel and fulfilling a long-standing goal of Arab nationalism. Then came the first post-1945 coup in the Arab world: on March 30, 1949, Husni Za'im, chief of staff of the Syrian army, overthrew President Shukri al-Qwattli; Za'im was motivated by various reasons, including personal ambition, nationalist goals, defense of the army against charges of corruption, and maintaining the army's material privileges.[51] Until Za'im's coup Syria had been ruled by politicians and parties that originated in the National Bloc, the corpus of the nationalist movement in Syria during the interwar period. Increasingly discredited, it began to rely on the military for support; the military meanwhile was becoming increasingly disenchanted with the ruling politicians, caused in part by the government's lackluster performance in Palestine. The result was an awkward standoff and constant friction between the military and the government. Za'im's coup shattered the uneasy truce.[52]

One of Za'im's first actions was to propose that Iraq and Syria conclude a defense treaty; he was motivated largely by his desire to strengthen his hand vis-à-vis Israel at the armistice talks in Rhodes and against any domestic criticism that he was deficient on Arab nationalism.[53] Although Syria and Iraq never concluded a defense agreement, its prospect stimulated a round of discussions concerning future regional arrangements and competition among Arab states for Syria's favor.[54] Unification talk reemerged after the overthrow of Za'im by Hinnawi on August 14, 1949.[55] Soon thereafter Hinnawi recommended that Syria and Iraq unify, a proposal motivated by Arabist sentiments and fear of Israel.[56] Their negotiations proceeded cautiously through the fall. Syria's principal objections were to Iraq's monarchical form of government and Iraq's treaty commitments to Britain; republican sentiment was strong, and much of the military and society, having won Syria's independence from France, were reluctant to be associated with the Anglo-Iraqi Treaty.[57] Therefore, as a precondition for any unity agreement the Syrian National Party, among others, demanded that Iraq abrogate its alliance with Britain.[58] Because Iraq was not about to meet this demand, Syrian and Iraqi negotiators turned their attention to the possibility of a defense treaty. But the Anglo-Iraqi Treaty once again stood in the way.[59]

These obstacles notwithstanding, unification talk filled the airwaves. The debate shifted from the newspapers and the Syrian-Iraqi negotiating table to Cairo for the Arab League meeting in October 1949 at which Iraq presented the proposed union to the Council, emphasizing its consistency with Article 9 of the league's charter.[60] Jordan, a long-time proponent of unification, came to Iraq's side and said that a lesson of Palestine was the need for unity:

[The] essential subject . . . is the regional reorganization of the Middle East Arab countries. This means first and foremost lifting the frontiers that separate parts of the single homeland. Syria must be reunited in its parts in order to acquire the stability and strength to face Israel. The next logical step would be to unite Syria with Iraq in a firm and clear military, economic, and political alliance so that the two Arab forces form two jaws of the iron pincers that would close in on Israel.[61]

The Palestine war placed another arrow in the quiver of those supporting unification, even those who been negotiating with the enemy.

If the Palestine war created some momentum for unification, it did not alter the coalition arrayed against it. Egypt and Saudi Arabia expressed their doubts about the plan, and Lebanese president Camille Chamoun said that unification depended on the will of each state's population, whether it honored the Arab League Charter and whether it was inclusive rather than exclusive.[62] But no Arab official could oppose unification outright; after all, as Arab states they were publicly committed to Arab nationalism and the idea of unification. As the Iraqi newspaper *Al-Nida* wondered, how could Egypt oppose a plan that was designed to confront Israel and realize the aspirations of the Arabs?[63] To stop the drive for unification the antiunion forces would have to find another device.

Egypt attempted to defeat the plan by ingeniously proposing a collective security pact.[64] Building on nationalism, the desire for unity, a reluctance to rely on Britain for defense assistance, and fear of Israel, Egypt proposed that the Arab states construct a regional security arrangement. With this motion injected into the debate, the meeting became a contest between Iraq's unification plan—an Iraq closely tied to Britain and a plan that was restricted to Syria—and Egypt's defense plan, which would be inclusive and perhaps a better solution to Syria's defense concerns because it included Egypt, the Arab world's largest state and one that also bordered Israel.

Egypt's strategy worked. The all-Arab military agreement became the focal point of the meetings. The Arab League subsequently adopted the military plan forwarded by Egypt, which the league compared to the Atlantic Pact, and decided not to "touch the question of Iraqi-Syrian rapprochement since it is an internal affair which should not be interfered with."[65] Egypt used the idea of collective security to defeat a unification plan and to institutionalize sovereignty, and the decision by the Arab League not to formally consider the unification proposal under the guise of the principle of noninterference worked to the same end. This was not unlike the talks that had led to the creation of the Arab League. Egypt used the idea of a multi-lateral forum to frustrate Iraq and its goal of unification and then to rein-force the principle of state sovereignty and territoriality. The head of the 1949 Saudi delegation, visibly pleased with the result, endorsed the collective security plan, implicitly rejected the proposed union, and added that Saudi foreign policy is "established on an unshakable basis: the necessity of preser-vation of the independence of every Arab state."[66]

Iraq's pitch for unification had been thwarted. Visibly bitter about the league's deliberations and conclusions, Nuri al-Said characterized the mili-tary pact as a substitute for action and an attempt to block the proposed Iraqi-Syrian unification. He lamented that "nations with no ties of language or religion or history [are] joining together through pacts and treaties [that are] stronger than those between the Arab League states." He proceeded to observe that the Arab League was founded on and continued to perpetuate "chaos," citing the recent example of the lack of coordination among the Arab states in Palestine. Not only did Arab states lack a union, he argued, but they even lacked any "operative military alliance." He then issued a chal-lenge. Either

> we cooperate in a manner compatible with our Governments' responsi-bilities . . . or we lay down another charter for our League under which every Arab government will openly give up some of its rights and author-ity as an independent sovereign state. A combination of these two alter-natives is nothing but a kind of chaos which will lead us into stumbling upon one failure after another and going from bad to worse.[67]

Said dared Egypt and other Arab states to stop using institutional devices and the cloak of collectivism to preserve their independence and frustrate inter-Arab cooperation.

Most important, now Syrians who opposed unification and/or saw the Iraqi unification proposal as a mechanism to increase Syria's security against Israel grabbed onto the proposed collective security pact as a viable alterna-tive to unity with Iraq. Syrian premier Hisham al-Atasi announced that Syria would cease its negotiations with Iraq, citing public opinion that favored the republic and concerns about the Anglo-Iraqi Treaty. Army chief Sami al-Hinnawi announced that he favored the military pact and that it was essen-tial that Syria not limit its dealings with Iraq but include all Arab states.[68] And Syrian politician Faris al-Khuri stated that unification was unlikely and unnecessary and advocated moving first with a military alliance between

Syria, Lebanon, Iraq, and Jordan—the real lesson of the Palestine war.[69] And then on December 17 and 18, one day after the proponents of closer ties with Iraq had used a major political occasion—the debate about the oath of the constitution—to pledge movement toward unity, Hinnawi was overthrown by Colonel Abid Shishakli, a Syrian nationalist and critic of unification.[70] Syria's flirtation with unification was over.

The Arab League meetings further institutionalized sovereignty and led Arab states to contemplate security cooperation as a way of maintaining their independence. For the next several months the league's subcommittee considered various permutations of collective security (including a federation of sorts) but focused on an Egyptian plan, which called for unification of military commands and guarantees of security from Arab states regardless of the source of aggression; an Iraqi plan, which forwarded an "offensive-defensive plan" and specifically identified Communism and Zionism as the threats to the Arab states; and a Syrian plan, which called for a common foreign policy and a strengthening of economic relations as a consequence of a military unity.[71] The Egyptian proposal implied a continuation of Arab League practice under a new guise, whereas the Iraqi proposal represented a more demanding alliance, defined the enemies as Zionism and communism, and made Iraq the home to the pan-Arab general staff because of its proximity to the Soviet Union.[72]

The Egyptian proposal emerged victorious and provided the foundation for the Treaty of Joint Defense and Economic Cooperation Among the States of the Arab League, better known as the Arab Collective Security Pact (ACSP). The Arab states signed the pact on April 13, 1950, pledging to settle their conflicts through nonviolent means (Article 1), engage in collective defense (Article 2), and integrate their military and foreign policies (Article 5).[73] The Arab states never implemented the conditions of the treaty, which was not too shocking because Egypt had proposed the treaty as a way to block unification and not because it was a strong supporter of closer and more encumbered ties between Arab states.

But the pact left a mark on inter-Arab politics in three ways. It reinforced the collective ethos that as Arab states they had common security interests. Whereas during the preparatory talks leading to the creation of the Arab League they had considered and ultimately rejected a security element, they were now acknowledging that they had interdependent security interests. Also, the pact rejected Iraq's proposal that the Soviet Union be included as a potential threat—a geostrategic issue—and concentrated instead on Zionism, which was an identity issue. In other words, the Arab states concluded that Israel was a threat to the Arab *nation*, whereas the Soviet Union was not. Finally, the meaning and function of the treaty were not to fulfill the goals of collective security but to frustrate any unification drive and reinforce the principle of sovereignty.[74] By offering Syria a collective security pact as an alternative to unification with Iraq, Egypt successfully enticed Syrian politicians to seek their security through more conventional means. The significance of the treaty was, in short, that it urged Arab states to coordinate their security policies while honoring their sovereignty.

In the end the debate between Arab nationalism and state sovereignty was momentarily resolved in favor of sovereignty. Although on several occasions during the next few years Iraq, Syria, and Jordan again raised the banner of unification—in early 1951 Syrian premier Nazim al-Qudsi made a highly spirited call for a united Arab state, and in January 1954 Iraq proposed another Fertile Crescent scheme—these proposals were religiously sent to the Arab League, where they were tabled and quietly died at the hands of the Egyptian-led antiunification bloc.[75] Rivalry, suspicion, and regime survival, as one commentary observed, undermined any prospect for unification.[76]

Although the proponents of unification were frustrated, the idea of unification lingered and reminded Arab states of their common past, present, and future. "The Arab League," observed veteran Iraqi politician Tawfiq al-Suwaydi, "is as much a truce between [its] leaders as it is the result of the movement of Arab unity for which we older Arab patriots have worked." This truce, he continued, was far better than the alternative, which was collapse.[77] If the Arab League was not exactly empowering the unification movement, at least its hallways created a place for Arab states to congregate, express their preferences, channel their grievances, and, most important, symbolize their commitment to Arab nationalism. This process nearly guaranteed that Arab nationalism would become expressive of their national identity, and compelled "every Arab state to become 'unity-minded.'"[78]

Arab Nationalism and the West

Arab states held mixed feelings toward the West. They had good reasons for viewing the West as a source of insecurity. Britain had promised the Arabs their independence if they joined the war against the Triple Alliance in World War I and then divided the territory between itself and France. The West was an early supporter and sometime champion of the idea of a Jewish homeland in Palestine. Britain promised independence to Jordan, Iraq, and

Egypt in 1936 but delivered an arrested sovereignty through unequal treaties that preserved colonial privileges and prerogatives for Britain. For many in the region these treaties were a major part of their long-standing grievances against the West, and for many nationalists they became part of their definition of, a defining vehicle for expressing, their Arabism.

Yet Arab officials were not uniformly opposed to the West. Many Arab political elites and military officials emulated the West; after all, they were educated at European schools and trained at European military academies and saw themselves as reformers and modernizers, something on the order of Kemal Ataturk of Turkey. The West also possessed the financial and military resources that Arab governments required to bolster their regimes, undertake reforms, modernize their militaries, and confront threats like Israel. Moreover, the Arab economies were inextricably linked to the West through trade, commerce, and finance, and therefore Arab elites had a vested interest in maintaining those ties. Although Western resources might be necessary for regime maintenance and other goals, to obtain these resources on unsavory terms might trigger the threats to the regime that those resources were supposed to address.[79] Regardless of their alignment orientation, all Arab officials were highly sensitive to any association that smacked of the colonial past and insulted their nations' current status as sovereign states.[80] The West was a mixture of temptation and threat.

Britain was the West's representative in the Middle East until the early 1950s when the cold war descended on the area. Because of its financial and strategic exhaustion and because of demands from the Arab states, after World War II Britain forwarded various proposals intended to renegotiate its Middle Eastern treaties while maintaining its strategic position for reasons of pride and power.[81] Until the late 1940s the United States, though not totally comfortable with Britain's colonial past and neocolonial diction, was reluctant to become involved in the region and willing to let Britain handle the Middle Eastern account. But in the late 1940s the United States became more interested in establishing its own relations with the Arab states and forwarding its own defense proposals. The reasons for the activism by the United States were many, though they largely revolved around geostrategic considerations: the Soviets had become active in Turkey and Iran in the late 1940s, the Middle East contained tremendous oil reserves, the Arab world was strategically located on the periphery of the Soviet Union, and the United States was not wholly convinced that Britain was up to the task of protecting Western interests.[82] Although the first formal effort by the United States to enlist the Arab states in its strategic plans came in October 1951 with the proposed Middle East Command (MEC), the United States began to aggressively press its power in the region under Secretary of State John Foster Dulles, who was armed with a zero-sum view of the world and an extensive and intensive vision of containment. Although the United States and Britain might have had somewhat similar objectives—to secure the Arab states in a strategic arrangement with the West—they occasionally clashed over goals and because of the U.S. belief that it was a fresh force and untainted by a colonial past.

Various Arab governments, then, were under countervailing pressures from Britain and the United States to become part of the Western alliance system and from their societies to revise their ties to the West. Egypt held a central place in this emerging debate about the Arab states' future defense ties to the West. The West courted Egypt heavily because of its strategic position and because the other Arab states were unlikely to accept the West's strategic invitation until Egypt gave its blessing. But such approval was dependent on a successful conclusion to Egypt's highly publicized treaty revisions with Britain for control of the Suez Canal and the Sudan. Other Arab states were willing or felt compelled to await Egypt's permission and a conclusion to the treaty negotiations because they viewed the Suez Canal as a symbol of the Arab nations' continued subordination to the West.[83] In fact, the Arab League's resolutions coupled the canal negotiations to the issue of Middle Eastern defense.[84] This meant that an Arab country would find it politically risky to ally with West before successful conclusion of the canal negotiations.[85] Arab states faced the ongoing dilemma of having to "choose between the promotion of their own interests and the maintenance of Arab solidarity, which in this case, at least, served the interests of the senior sister-state."[86] Regardless of their private desires, Arab officials reluctantly waited for Egypt.

A few instances dramatize the strategic and symbolic connection between Egypt, the canal negotiations, and the unwillingness of other Arab states to join the West without Egypt's permission. When the U.S. proposed the MEC, it offered Egypt full membership and other Arab states associate status.[87] Egypt, however, would not consider the proposal until after the Anglo-Egyptian Treaty had been revised to include the transfer of the Suez Canal from the British to the Egyptians and other conditions had been met.[88] When the Arab states debated and then rejected the MEC at an Arab League meeting, they concluded that although they favored a strategic arrangement in principle, this was not the right time.[89] The MEC soon gave way to the proposed Middle East Defense Organization, but it too died quickly because of the question of treaty revision in various Arab countries and inter-Arab rivalry. Iraq, which had a long-standing desire to establish a tighter strategic relationship with the West and was critical of Egypt's Britain policy, flirted with but ultimately rejected various proposals from the West because it did not want to be viewed as undercutting Egypt's bargaining position. The Syrian public generally marched with Egypt and was against its participation in these early proposals for similar reasons.[90] The linkage between the canal negotiations and the Arab world's strategic relations to the West was a testimony not only to the diplomatic acumen of the Egyptian government but also to the centrality of Egypt in Arab life and the framing of the canal as an Arab issue.

Egypt's relationship to Arabism, and Arabism's relationship to Egypt, underwent a profound change on July 23, 1952, when King Faruq was deposed by the Free Officers in a bloodless coup. The Free Officers were hardly revolutionaries when they came to power. Their immediate goal was to secure their domestic base, and their foreign policy tenets were Egyptian, loyal to Faruq's Arabism with an emphasis on ridding Britain from Egypt, open to some sort of defense arrangement with the West under the proper conditions, and even willing to negotiate with Israel.[91] That the Free Officers were reformist rather than revolutionary accounts for why many in the Arab world gave them a lackluster reception and judged them weak on Arabism.[92]

Was Nasser a committed Arab nationalist or simply an appropriator of Arabism's language for his goals of regime survival and extending Egyptian power? There is little question that Nasser was concerned with regime survival and furthering Egyptian power. Who would expect anything less from a head of state? Yet such concerns can accommodate the possibility of Nasser as a nationalist. As someone of his generation, trained in the military, witness to British prerogatives, and a participant in the Palestine war, he possessed the experiences likely to infuse him with nationalist sentiment. Those experiences informed his desire to restore al-istiqlal al-watani [national independence], dignity, and respect to the Egyptians and the Arabs; his view that Egypt's fate and security could not be separated from those of the other Arab states; and his understanding that unity was the best method for augmenting Egyptian and Arab power.[93] Arab states, in his view, should not only assert their independence but also espouse nonalignment. His defiant and uncompromising attitude toward the West was, in short, consistent with both Egyptian and Arab nationalism. I assume that Nasser was committed to Arab nationalism, Egypt, and himself and that these commitments were not necessarily contradictory but in fact could be consistent.

But Nasser's definition of Arabism evolved over the years.[94] As Nasser prophetically and astutely put it, "It seems to me that within the Arab circle there is a role wandering aimlessly in search of a hero."[95] What he did not predict was that this role would evolve as a consequence of the interaction between the demands of regime survival, symbolic exchanges, changing circumstances, and perhaps his own self-understandings. At the outset of his political career he maintained a minimalist understanding of Arabism, advocating independence and anticolonialism.[96] Nasser came to realize the discursive power of Arabism during the struggle over the Baghdad Pact, the Soviet arms deal in the fall of 1955, and the fight over the Suez Canal. But, according to Mohamed Heikal, Nasser was unprepared for the "tidal wave of enthusiasm which swept the country and spilled over into the whole Arab world" as a result of his spirited speeches surrounding the canal negotiations.[97] As Nasser later confessed at the 1963 unity talks, he did not take seriously the idea of unification until after the 1956 Suez War.[98] Nasser's Arabism exhibited elements of concept creep.

At each moment that Nasser shaped the meaning of Arabism—from his stand against the West in 1955 and 1956 to his embracement of unification in 1958 to his leadership in organizing the Arab challenge to Israel in 1964—he did so because of a combination of reasons involving regime maintenance, security, and nationalism. Yet once he helped to define the norms associated with Arabism, he was committed to following them in order to maintain his prestige. To fulfill the role generated by Arab nationalism meant that he had to abide by its expectations even when he thought better of it. Call it a sorcerer's apprentice effect. Nasser used and cultivated Arab nationalism for his own purposes, but his creation could—and would—circumscribe and constrain his future actions. Although politicians might be distinguished by their acumen at exploiting the normative environment for ulterior purposes, they also want to be viewed as honoring those norms, lest they be accused of being duplicitous and manipulative and thus suffer a fall from grace. Nasser's desire to save face occasionally dragged him down a perilous path: the establishment of the United Arab Republic in 1958, his intervention in the republican revolt in Yemen in 1962, and his deliberate escalation of hostilities that precipitated the June 1967 Arab-Israeli War. Nasser engaged in these and other actions in order to be viewed as acting in a manner expected of someone who was an Arab nationalist. Sometimes this meant that he cursed the role that was partially of his own making.

In general, Nasser stirred the imaginations and the desires of the masses because of his vision of an Arab nation that was restored to greatness. His acts of daring, his defiance of the power of the West, were roundly cheered and celebrated throughout the region, and secured his place as the leader of Arab nationalism.[99] Through words and deeds Nasser signaled to the Western powers that the Arab world would cease to be their political backyard. But it was not only the Western powers who found his message of independence to be insurgent and troubling. Other Arab leaders who had formally and informally aligned with the West found equally, if not more, disturbing his challenges and call for revolutionary change; after all, Nasser would challenge not simply their strategic interests but their very fitness to rule. The yearlong debate over the Baghdad Pact became Nasser's dress rehearsal for the leadership role he would soon own.

BAGHDAD PACT

> 1955 was the decisive turning-point in the post-war history of the Arab world, and the Baghdad Pact was the start of it all.
> —King Hussein, *Uneasy Lies the Head*, p. 83

Few scholars or politicians would have predicted in late 1954 that a British-backed alliance between Turkey and Iraq would become the maelstrom of the Middle East. After all, most key players in the region already had some sort of strategic relationship with a Western power, generally were open to persuasion regarding the benefits of a more formal association, and subscribed to a meaning of Arab nationalism that accommodated a guarded relationship with the West. But the debate about the Baghdad Pact defied all predictions. The yearlong debate about the pact shifted the rules of the game of Arab politics away from conservatism and toward radicalism, found Iraq increasingly alienated from the currents of Arabism and Egypt at its forefront (which caused other Arab states to shift their positions in order to keep their footing), and led to a general normative prohibition against allying with the West.[100] This outcome was probably as much a surprise to Egypt's Nasser as it was to Iraq's prime minister, Nuri al-Said. It also was testimony to Nasser's deft deployment of the symbols of Arabism as he mobilized the societies across the region to support his image of an Arab nation that was unified and finally free of colonialism and its remnants.

The clash over the Baghdad Pact could be told through its two central characters, Said and Nasser. Nuri al-Said was an Arab nationalist of long standing, educated under the Ottomans, a participant in the original Arab revolt, a veteran of various tussles and conflicts with Britain in the fight for Iraqi and Arab independence, present at the creation of the League of Arab States, and a champion of various unification proposals over the years. In

Said's view being an Arab nationalist and cooperating with the West was not contradictory.[101] Although not all Iraqis shared this interpretation, he steadfastly sought a strategic tie to the West because of the conviction that such an alignment and its accompanying assistance were necessary for domestic stability, building a more powerful army, discouraging a potential encroachment by the Soviets to the north, and confronting Israel.[102] His previous attempts to forge an alliance were frustrated by domestic and/or Egyptian opposition. Iraqi nationals scrutinized any suspected association lest it compromise Arab nationalism and Iraqi sovereignty. For instance, when Iraq and Turkey signed an agreement in March 1946 that resembled a security alliance, the signing prompted widespread domestic opposition on the ground that it contradicted Iraq's obligations to the Arab League; this opposition delayed the ratification of the treaty until April 1947.[103] When U.S. Secretary of State Dulles invited Iraq to join the northern tier, his hopes were quickly dashed because, in his view, Iraqi society would not permit such an agreement.[104] Egypt too objected to Iraq's accession to a Western-led security alliance, though its opposition largely derived from its rivalry for leadership and the concern that such an alliance would weaken its bargaining position during the canal negotiations.

Nasser, though generally pro-West, and more than willing to talk to the United States because of his attraction to its capital and arms, differed from Said in a number of respects. First, Nasser was more sensitive to any agreement that hinted at Egypt's and the Arab world's subordination to the West. Nasser's nationalism came from the military barracks and emerged from a series of defeats and humiliations at the hands of Israel and the West; thus any relationship should not compromise Egypt's independence or insult the Arabs' dignity. In this respect Nasser and Said had very different conceptions of the desired strategic order.[105] Second, Said believed that the Soviets represented a threat to Iraq, whereas Nasser could see little immediate danger from them but much from Israel.[106] Third, Nasser was more insistent that the Arab states approach the West collectively and with a singular voice, lest the West attempt to divide and rule. But such a collective approach would be best handled with Nasser at the helm.[107] In general, the duel between Said and Nasser was waged between different generations of Arab nationalism and views of what sort of relationship was possible and desirable between the Arab states and the West.

The prelude to the Baghdad Pact was the declaration of the Turko-Pakistani agreement of April 1954. Although it did not include an Arab state, it did involve two Muslim states and was widely seen by the Arab states as the

West's "calling card" to the region. Egypt and Iraq took the lead in the regionwide debate about the Arab states' position on strategic relations with the West. Egypt's initial position was that any discussion was premature until the Suez Canal dispute was settled; this obstacle was overcome with the initialing of an agreement on July 27, 1954 (formally signed on October 19). Still, Nasser and Egyptian public opinion remained cool to the idea of participating in a Western-led defense arrangement. Indeed, Nasser and British minister of state Anthony Nutting held a series of talks on the subject after the signing of the Suez Canal treaty, and Nutting concluded that although Nasser might eventually warm to the idea, Egyptian society would not be ready for some time.[108]

Nuri al-Said, however, welcomed the idea of an alliance and began seeking Arab allies who would join him, or at least not block his path. With the aims of eliminating bilateral tensions, formulating a common policy in Arab-West relations, and obtaining Egypt's approval for Iraq's accession, Said initiated a series of meetings with Egypt. The first was with Interior Minister Salim Salim at the Iraqi royal resort of Sarsank in August 1954.[109] The results of the talks were inconclusive at best and generated greater misunderstandings at worst. Said subsequently claimed that he received a green light to ally with the West, although within the context of a modified Arab Collective Security Pact (ACSP), and Salim contended that he gave no such signal and insisted that Egypt would need time to overcome its long-standing suspicions of the West.[110] Said, still seeking greater clarification and assurances, had his sole meeting with Nasser in mid-September in Cairo about the Baghdad Pact.[111] While Said asserted that Iraq had special geostrategic circumstances because of its proximity to the Soviet Union, Nasser informed Said that Egypt was unlikely to join a Western alliance because of domestic opposition.[112] Although Said gained a greater appreciation for Nasser's position, evidence exists that he left Cairo with the (perhaps mistaken?) impression that he was free to pursue his dream of a Middle Eastern alliance.[113]

The Egyptian and Iraqi discussions were the prelude to the Arab foreign ministers' meeting in Cairo in December 1954, when the Arab governments hoped to hammer out some guidelines concerning their future relationship to the West and the conditions under which an Arab state might join a Western-led alliance.[114] As Nasser welcomed the delegates, he urged them to follow Egypt's example by constructing resolutions that reflected the needs of the Arab nation, pledging not to join any outside alliance, and emphasizing their reliance on the collective security pact.[115] This they did. The foreign ministers crafted two resolutions: "that no alliance should be concluded outside the fold of the Collective Arab Security Pact," and "that cooperation with the West was possible, provided that a just solution was found for Arab problems and provided the Arabs were allowed to build up their strength with gifts of arms."[116] Egypt, which had overseen the writing of the Arab League Charter with an eye toward stopping unification and preserving sovereignty and then designed the ACSP as a way to halt the discussion of Syrian-Iraqi unification in 1949, now used the ACSP to slow down Iraq's planned alliance with the West under the Baghdad Pact. Echoing the neutrality that became a hallmark of Nasser's foreign policy, the foreign ministers proclaimed that the "burden of the defense of the Arab East should fall on the states of the area alone, and that the question of putting the Collective Security Pact into effect has become timely and inevitable if the Arab States are to form a united front in political affairs and defense against any foreign danger that may threaten any or all of them."[117] The foreign ministers publicly proclaimed that they must coordinate their policies because they were Arab states.

No sooner had the meeting adjourned than rumors swirled that Iraq would sign the Baghdad Pact. That Said should so quickly and defiantly disregard the highly publicized decisions of the foreign ministers' conference is something of a curiosity, and there are more speculations than explanations: a secret agreement with Nasser recognized Iraq's special geographic circumstances and condoned Said's plan; Said's perception of the Soviet threat; Said's need for cooperation with Turkey on the Kurdish issue to maintain Iraq's internal cohesion; and Said's belief that he could survive any public outcry that was sure to follow and that other Arab states were likely to follow his lead and thereby lend him political cover.[118] Although his motives were many, Said had good reason to believe that he might be able to sell the alliance at home and to other Arab states.

Nasser responded to the rumors of a security pact by unleashing a media tirade against Iraq. His stated objections centered on the claim that any alliance would only safeguard the interests of the West and harm those of the Arab nation and that Arab states should seek neutrality and security in their unity.[119] But such an alliance also would harm Egypt's standing, leaving it isolated and perhaps facing the threat of Israel on its own.[120] Nasser's prestige was entangled as well. Nasser, observed King Hussein, "had to attack the [Baghdad] Pact if only to prevent other Arab states from joining and so diminishing his prestige."[121]

Egypt's efforts had little apparent effect, for on January 13, 1955, Iraq and Turkey announced that they soon would sign a defense agreement. In presenting his case to the Iraqi people and the Arab world Said claimed that the Baghdad Pact was consistent with the Charter of the League of Arab States and Article 51 of the U.N. Charter and that it furthered the goals of the Arab world. He further asserted that the foreign ministers had acknowledged Iraq's "special geographic position" (a reference to the Soviet Union) at their recent meeting.[122] Said used the unveiling of his planned alliance to present a series of arguments concerning why the alliance was consistent with Arabism and why Iraq's move should be emulated, not chastised.

The Arab world responded with outrage to the news, and Nasser led the battle cry. Cairo's persistent and emphatic message was that the Baghdad Pact undermined and represented a grave challenge to Arab nationalism and Arab security. The headline of one Egyptian daily proclaimed: "Iraqi Government Demolishes All Efforts to Strengthen the Arab League and Bolster the Arab Collective Security Pact."[123] The Egyptian newspaper *Al-Ahram* wrote that Nuri al-Said's actions "touched a sensitive part in the heart of Egypt and, no doubt, of five other Arab states"; by defiantly rejecting the recent resolutions of the foreign ministers who pledged to coordinate their foreign policies on alliances with non-Arab states and to make the ACSP the center of their defense positioning, Iraq's actions were a threat to the Arab family.[124] Voice of the Arabs broadcast that:

> While the Arab States are preparing to hold a meeting of their Foreign Ministers to consider and agree on the unification of their foreign policy, the consolidation of the Collective Security Pact, and the strengthening of the Arab League, the Arab World is taken unaware by a communique issued by two countries. . . . How can it be justified that Iraq took part in this communique and indeed did so on her own when the meeting is about to be held?[125]

Nasser was deftly tying the meaning of the Baghdad Pact to both the security of the Arab states and the future of Arab nationalism. Egyptian interior minister Salim, who was one of Egypt's point men in the campaign against Iraq, responded to whether sovereign Iraq had the right to enter into any treaty it wanted by saying, "Although Iraq is an independent sovereign state, she nevertheless has obligations and responsibilities toward the League of Arab States and the Arab Collective Security Pact. Is there any state, in the Atlantic Pact, for example, free to make any decisions it chooses even it be contrary to that pact?"[126] If Arab states could not honor the decisions of the most recent conference and coordinate their foreign policies before making any formal agreement with the West, Arab nationalism and the Arab League were finished.[127] In a later statement Salim drew the current challenge dramatically: "The Arab World is now standing at a crossroads: it will either be an independent and cohesive unit with its own structures and national character or else each country will pursue its own course. The latter would mean the beginning of the downfall of Arab nationhood."[128] Egypt was framing the pact as a challenge to Arab nationalism.

To try to forge a common front against Iraq and to stop the treaty from being signed, Nasser hosted the other Arab leaders from January 22 though February 6, 1955. The Arab representatives filed into Cairo publicly proclaiming their outrage at Iraq's actions but privately were less exercised, and some even contemplated following Baghdad rather than Cairo. Saudi Arabia's position was closest to Egypt's, for it feared that its traditional Hashemite rivals in Jordan and Iraq would use their newfound resources and prestige to launch another bid for Fertile Crescent unification; that is, the Hashemites threatened Saudi Arabia's external and internal stability.[129] Yemen too came out against the pact.

Syria, Lebanon, and Jordan were less appalled and somewhat approving. Syrian officials were divided over whether to join the pact. Although espousing neutralism in the early 1950s, Prime Minister Faris al-Khuri and Foreign Minister Faydi al-Atasi were both relatively pro-West and therefore somewhat attenuated in their position: although they might not sign the pact, they were unwilling to condemn Baghdad.[130] Khuri said that he could give only his personal view that Syria should not sign the pact, that Damascus might have a different mind.[131] Lebanon was neutral to the point of being slightly encouraging.[132] The Lebanese prime minister commented that he "could not see what the fuss was all about" because there was nothing new here; Iraq, after all, already had a similar agreement from its treaties of 1937 and 1948.[133]

King Hussein was publicly cool to the idea but privately in favor, a stance informed by strategic, dynastic, and symbolic concerns. As a Hashemite monarch with close political and military ties to the British, the Jordanian king was something of a natural partner and generally disposed toward signing the pact. Yet he was not oblivious to the rising tide of Arabism in Jordan and the region, believed that any joint Arab-Western defense network might be best realized by first working through the Arab League, worried that siding with Cairo's campaign against Iraq meant exacerbating the already inflamed inter-Arab tensions, and feared alienating Egypt and Syria, on which Jordan would rely in the event of an Israeli attack.[134]

Nasser attempted to convince Syria, Jordan, and Lebanon to condemn and censure Baghdad. In an early address to the heads of state he framed the pact as representing a stark alternative between an Arab nationalism based on unity and one premised on disunity: "Egypt proposes to the Arab states a foreign policy based on developing Arab unity and independent stature and offers to put all its economic, military, and moral resources at the disposal of Arab nationalism. Nuri al-Said, on the other hand, proposes a policy under which each Arab state would act alone and decide its own future, which would make it easy for the West to swallow them."[135] Later Nasser challenged his fellow Arab leaders to answer Baghdad with strong action, including the "establishment of a unified Arab army under one command along the same lines as the proposed European army."[136] The other Arab states, however, remained unconvinced.

Irritated that the other Arab leaders were not following his dictates, Nasser threatened to go to the press and suspend Egypt's relations with them.[137] Nasser's ultimatum and threatened symbolic sanctions apparently worked. Although Jordan, Syria, and Lebanon refused to follow Nasser's admonitions and directives, the conferees passed several resolutions condemning Iraq's actions, pledged not to sign the pact, and decided to send a delegation to Iraq to try to convince Said of the error of his ways. Significantly, however, the conference adjourned without issuing a final statement.[138] If the Arab governments filed out of Cairo publicly declaring their abhorrence of the pact and their unwillingness to follow Iraq's deviation from the Arab fold, in private some felt less strongly about Iraq's actions and were seriously considering signing. The fight had just begun.

Iraq and Turkey formally signed the pact on February 24. As Said unveiled the pact to a waiting and watching Arab world, he took great pains to detail what was and was not contained in it, to defend himself against Nasser's accusations, and to portray his actions as consistent with the UN, the Arab League, and Arab nationalism. Said's speech was highly defensive, reflecting a sensitivity to the charges raised by Nasser and to the public's concern that his actions had isolated Iraq from the Arab fold. To defend himself against Nasser and to reassure the public, he spent considerable time detailing various tenets of the pact and emphasizing its link to the Arab past, present, and future.[139]

Now Said and Nasser would mobilize all their energies and tools, symbolic and otherwise, to fight for the hearts, minds, and votes of the Arab world. Syria represented the first stop in the debate about the pact, which became a sign and cause of its increasingly nationalist and neutralist lean-ings.[140] Initially, many Syrian nationalists had welcomed the pact because it might generate aid, increase security against Israel, and perhaps even professionalize the military and keep it in the barracks and out of politics.[141] Syria's attitude changed slightly when Faris al-Khuri resigned and was replaced by Sabri al-Atali in early February, a change only modestly related to the pact.[142] To steel these antipact forces Egyptian minister Salim arrived in Damascus on February 26 to propose a "federal union" with a joint military command and unified foreign policies in lieu of the now-defunct collective security pact. The Syrians, however, viewed the proposal with suspicion.[143]

In his lobbying efforts Nasser got some timely and unintended help from Israel. On February 28, just four days after the signing of the pact, Israel attacked a military installation in Gaza. Nasser quickly capitalized on the assault by claiming that it was coordinated with and enabled by the Baghdad Pact.[144] Nasser found himself riding a tide of popular support as protests erupted against the pact throughout the Arab world.[145] In Syria, Israel's attack increased the domestic pressures against the pact and in favor of an alliance with Egypt as a deterrent to Israel.[146] The army was now so determined to create a defensive alliance against Israel that several Syrian military officers threatened a coup d'état unless Syria joined an alliance with Egypt.[147]

On March 6 Egypt, Syria, and Saudi Arabia pledged to create their own alliance, which they called the Tripartite Alliance; included among its provisions was a rejection of the Baghdad Pact and the strengthening of the collective Arab defense.[148] Syrian foreign minister Khalid al-Azm noted that Jordan could not join the alliance because its army was controlled by Britain and therefore was ineligible to serve in the Unified Arab Command.[149] But Azm nevertheless insisted that the pact not "exclude Iraq or preclude the possibility of member states joining the Iraq-Turkey Pact."[150] The value of the Egyptian-Syrian-Saudi alliance from the Egyptian and Saudi perspective was not its deterrent effect but its ability to stop Syria from following in Iraq's footsteps.[151]

Yet Syria's future relationship to the Baghdad Pact remained a matter of debate. The tripartite discussions continued through May 1955, though with little resolution, given that Saudi Arabia and Egypt refused to allocate 10 percent of their budgets to a unified army and to effect economic unity with Syria. Nor would they leave the door open to Iraq's participation in the pact.[152] The Syrian presidential elections of August 1955 provided another opportunity for rival Arab states to try to influence Syria's foreign ties; Saudi Arabia, Iraq, and Egypt each opposed Syrian foreign minister Azm for their own reasons, some of which had to do with the pact, and the nomination of Qwattli provided some evidence that Syria was drifting toward the Egyptian camp.[153] Many Syrian politicians, however, voiced concerns about the Tripartite Alliance and the exclusion of Iraq, a move they feared would harm Syria's political, economic, and strategic interests.[154] Such developments pushed Syria back on the fence and delayed its accession to the Tripartite Alliance.

Nasser's arms deal with Czechoslovakia on September 27 radically transformed the climate and shifted the ground toward Nasser in the fight over the pact.[155] The arms deal electrified the region, and the response was unanimously positive; editorials and government officials throughout the Arab world applauded Nasser's audacity and courage, and even King Hussein observed that he was impressed by the boldness of the move. The arms deal had several dramatic implications for Nasser's immediate and future standing and the Baghdad Pact. First, it fundamentally transformed the West's perception of Nasser; whereas before he was a nationalist who was playing hard ball, now he was a nationalist who was flirting with the Soviets. Still, the Americans refused to write him off.[156] Second, the arms deal boldly demonstrated to the Arab world that it did not have to be subservient to the West; this action, then, rendered anachronistic strategic arrangements such as the Baghdad Pact. Third, Nasser's move, though not intended for this purpose, rescued the nearly moribund Tripartite Alliance; it was signed on October 20 (an Egyptian-Saudi mutual defense pact was signed a week later).[157] The arms deal convinced many Syrian officials that, by joining Egypt, Syria could vastly increase its security through an alliance and a parallel arms deal with the Soviet Union that would also allow Syrian officials to be identified with Arab neutrality, independence, and power. Syria was now solidly in the Egyptian camp.

The final battle over the pact would be waged in and over Jordan. Hussein's initial opinion of the pact was generally positive, but through the fall no amount of outside pressure from Britain, Turkey, or Iraq could convince him that he should antagonize Egypt and Arab popular opinion by signing the pact. Hussein abandoned his position of neutrality in November because of two principal events. The first was the Egyptian-Czech arms deal, which according to Hussein, "changed everything."[158] The arms deal reignited the debate about Jordan's participation in the pact and increased both neutralist sentiments in the region and pressure from the West for Jordan to sign the pact as a countermeasure to the perceived growth of Soviet influence.[159] Second, in early November President Celal Bayar of Turkey visited Amman and told Hussein that Britain might provide the strategic assistance he needed to

expand the Arab Legion if he signed the pact. A similar message was conveyed by Lebanese leader Camille Chamoun.[160] Hussein now decided to sign
the pact.[161] In mid-November Hussein informed Britain that he would sign
the pact at the right price, replaced one prime minister who was unwilling to
steer Jordan into the arms of the West (Huda) with another who would (Said
al-Mufti), and asked Nasser not to destabilize his regime once he made his
pro-pact intentions known.

Hussein must have known that he was asking the impossible from Nasser. Emboldened by the military pact with Syria and angered that Britain had
seemingly reneged on its spring agreement to stop recruiting other Arab
states, Nasser unleashed a fierce media campaign against Jordan and framed
the pact as undermining Arab nationalism and linking any Arab state that
supported it to imperialism.[162] In the midst of an increasingly furious debate, in early December Britain sent a top military official, John Templer, to
persuade Hussein to sign the pact.[163] This highly publicized and controversial visit by a British official in the midst of Nasser's campaign against the
pact played right into Nasser's hands. Hussein, who braced himself for some
political opposition, now confronted fierce rioting. "Hundreds of thousands
of Jordanians," Hussein reflected, "listening avidly to the propaganda on
Cairo Radio, saw in Nasser a sort of mystical savior."[164]

Despite the domestic turmoil, Hussein pressed ahead with his vision of
Jordan as a member of the Baghdad Pact. The Jordanian cabinet continued
to debate whether to sign, but the cabinet fell as a result of the divisions over
the pact.[165] Hazza al-Majali became the new prime minister on December
13 and faced the difficult task of steering Jordan into the pact.[166] He was
equally unsuccessful and now faced some of the worst rioting in Jordanian
history. Demonstrators were calling for the resignation of this recently
formed government and a public pledge to cease any further discussions of
signing the pact. As Hussein later wrote, "We were virtually helpless. . . . All
hell broke loose. Riots such as we had never seen before . . . disrupted the
whole country. This time bands of fire-raisers started burning the Government buildings, private houses, foreign properties. I had no alternative but
to call out the Legion. . . . That was the end of the Jordan and the Baghdad
Pact."[167] The riots left a deep impression on the king. The streets of Amman
were solidly behind Nasser, and Hussein was nearly an outcast in his own
kingdom. After losing two prime ministers and experiencing a near civil
war in a few short weeks, Hussein, though blaming the riots on Communist
organizers and a constitutional technicality, reluctantly decided not to sign
the pact. He declared a state of emergency, the Majali government resigned,

and soon thereafter the new Jordanian government proclaimed a "no new pacts" pledge.

Hussein, reeling from the challenges to his rule, attempted to repair his stained image through various actions during the next several months. He reluctantly accepted an offer from Egypt, Syria, and Saudi Arabia to replace his British subsidy.[168] Then he dismissed John Glubb, the long-time and legendary commander of the Arab Legion. During the December riots Nasser had turned Glubb into a symbol of Jordan's ties to imperialism.[169] Recounting the events that led to his dismissal, Glubb wrote: "The King had been enthusiastically determined to enter the Baghdad Pact, and had thereby incurred the hostility of Egypt and of Jordanian extremists. The policy had failed.... To perform some act of defiance towards Britain and to dismiss me would immediately re-establish his popularity."[170] Glubb's dismissal represented Hussein's attempt to distance himself from the past and to transform the image of his army from an agent of imperialism into a representative of the Arab nation.[171] The failure of the Templer mission suggested that Britain's day in the Middle East was nearing the end, and Glubb's abrupt eviction was an unmistakable sign. The demise of the British position in Jordan was the clearest signal that Arab states would now adhere to the norm of no alliances with the West.

As Nasser predicted at the outset of the debate about the Baghdad Pact in December 1954, the Arab world had to choose between two visions of Arab nationalism and Arab politics. The pact represented a challenge not to the balance of power per se but to Arab nationalism and its contested norms by unleashing a debate among Arab states concerning what behavior was and was not proper for *Arab* states. That Said and Nasser favored rival schools cannot be disconnected from their interests in regime and state security, but neither were they wholly derivative of them. And which version would stand at the end of the debate could not have been predicted by material power alone. That Nasser's vision carried the day was not a foregone conclusion, could not be predicted from strategic or material considerations, and in fact Said could realistically calculate that regional forces would favor him and his version. Nasser was able to defeat the pact and win the debate because of some timely events—including Israel's occasional raids on Syria, Jordan, and Egypt and Britain's insistence on sending the Templer mission to Jordan in early December—but, most important, because of his ability to frame the Baghdad Pact as a violation of Arab nationalism and link it to an imperialist past and an equally divided and dependent future. Nasser's successful ability to frame the pact in this way accounts for the symbolic sanctions that ultimately convinced Arab leaders to cut their ties with the West and strengthen them with Nasser, although these were the very leaders who had every reason to maintain an alliance with the West and to oppose Nasser's growing power.

Arab leaders dueled with symbols and images and not with militaries and attempted to portray themselves as expressing and furthering the aspirations of the Arab nation and their rival as potentially injuring those interests. In the end Said's nationalism was out of step with the politics of the period, as he held the West out as a model and source of resources; Nasser offered a vision of Arab politics in which the West was and remained under suspicion and stressed that Arab states were best served by maintaining neutrality and independence. By offering a vision of the future and outlining those policies that were viewed as harming the Arab nation, Nasser shaped the contours of Arab politics and the meaning of Arab nationalism.

Egypt had forged a series of alliances with some Arab states that concurred with Nasser's brand of Arabism (Syria) and others that did not (Jordan, Lebanon, and Saudi Arabia), and the latter states chose to ally with Nasser's vision of regional life rather than risk a decline in regional standing or a domestic backlash. Egypt's ability to mobilize a fierce media campaign or engineer a coup against the Arab leaders if they signed the Baghdad Pact convinced them that they should not sign, even though this meant solidifying Nasser's brand of Arabism, which "constituted a permanent challenge to the very legitimacy of these existing states."[172] In other words, Arab leaders interpreted Nasser's growing ability to define the events of the day as a potential threat to their own regimes' survival, but to publicly oppose him would only open questions regarding their credentials and thus invite domestic challenges. Nearly damned if they did and damned if they did not, Arab leaders publicly aligned themselves with Nasser but privately looked for ways to protect themselves.

The Baghdad Pact was a transformative event in Arab politics. This was the moment that Nasser found his footing, sharpened his message, and inaugurated a decade in which he possessed the rare ability to set the political agenda for an entire region and generation. The West was now on the decline and the Soviets on the rise. The conservative Arab leaders looked anachronistic and increasingly feeble, out of step in these changing times and the radicalization of politics. But, more indelibly, the dialogue about the Baghdad Pact changed the parameters of Arab politics and redefined the practices that were consistent with Arabism. "Nasser was able to change the rules of the game," recalled a former top-ranking Jordanian official. "The Baghdad Pact reshaped the entire region."[173]

The League of Arab States was in many respects created to smother the tendencies that emerged during the course of the decade. The league's charter envisioned an association in which members were accountable to each other in name only, but they had become much more mutually vulnerable to each other since the end of World War II. By the close of 1955 Arab states were more tightly coupled than ever before, and even those leaders who wanted to ignore the norms of Arabism could hardly do so because of the political implications of such neglect. Whereas no prohibition against relations with the Jewish community existed in 1945, five years later such relations were taboo. The strategic efforts of some Fertile Crescent leaders to tap into the popular support for unification notwithstanding, a coalition of Arab states continued to defeat the move toward territorial unification. But even here the price for keeping unification at bay was forging a collective security pact that formally acknowledged that their security was interdependent. Whereas many Arab political elites felt that their future relations with the West were in need of repair and reform, the aftermath of the Baghdad Pact deposited a strong prohibition against relations with the West and a strong force for positive neutrality.

This web of normative integration was woven through symbolic competition between Arab states. Arab leaders felt little hesitation in appropriating the symbols of Arabism in their search for regime stability and regional influence, recognizing that such symbols were ripe for accumulation and highly effective in controlling the foreign policies of other Arab states because their populations more readily identified with the symbols of Arabism than with the symbols of the state. Arab leaders attempted to further their goals through symbolic exchanges and competition, and the result was a radically transformed context to Arab politics. Few Arab leaders wanted to be encumbered by the norms of Arabism, but their willingness to use the symbols of Arab nationalism in the service of their various goals nurtured that very outcome. Arab leaders were increasingly beholden to the norms that they once feared; that they were now more tightly integrated and thus found themselves more oriented toward each other was a product of their willingness to use the symbols that Arabism made available to them to maintain their standing at home and control their rivals abroad.

5

The Ascent and Descent of Arabism, 1956–1967

Nasser helped to define what counted as an Arab state in good standing, the types of norms to which it should adhere, and how those norms might relate to the desired regional order. As the leader of a new generation of Arab politicians he possessed the rare ability to shape the political agenda and challenge the rules of the game. The Baghdad Pact was only the beginning. Having successfully challenged the legitimacy of strategic alliances with the West, he would soon associate himself with Arabism's ultimate goal of unification. By February 1958 Nasser could add to his list of distinctions and titles his new position as head of the United Arab Republic, the Arab world's first unity agreement.

To what did this development owe? Certainly not to Nasser's principled commitment to unification. Nasser's pre-1958 speeches and policies contain hardly a trace of a unification spirit; in fact, he had assiduously discouraged such unification sentiments. Nor can we attribute Egypt's willingness to unify with Syria to any earlier groundswell of support for unification among the Egyptian people. Nor was there any strategic imperative that might have moved Nasser in this direction; indeed, he would gain few material advantages by attempting to govern the unruly Syrians that might not be more easily accomplished through more conventional foreign policy controls. Instead, Nasser's willingness to unify with Syria derived from symbolic entrapment. Although he privately feared that this agreement would lead nowhere good, he felt that he had no choice but to follow his words with deeds. Nasser was not only a creator of the political agenda, he was also a creature of it. As a hero who occupied a role in Arab politics, he would soon be captured by the normative expectations of that role, and to deny the role would be to deny the very fabric of his leadership.

The unification agreement that began with such promise ended in 1961 amid mutual exchanges of betrayal, name calling, and recrimination. Another round of unification fervor took hold in 1963, but its balance sheet contained one stillborn political agreement and even greater acrimony and venom. Arab leaders professed their devotion to unification while publicly denouncing the sincerity of their rivals' commitment in the most unsavory and unflattering terms. These exchanges and charges resulted in mutual suspicion and growing differentiation between the same Arab states that harped on the theme of Arab unity. Many of the same Arab officials and intellectuals who once demanded unification now began to retreat toward statism and sovereignty, to the safety and sanctity of their borders, and to assert the authenticity of their particular identities as they continued to pledge themselves to the Arab nation.

The result was that by 1964 the rules of the game in Arab politics had begun to shift toward norms of Arabism that were consistent with sovereignty. Claiming that Arabs were one family that should live under one roof had unleashed a whirlwind of turmoil, resulting in a greater willingness to embrace a version of Arab nationalism that was consistent with sovereignty and to begin to stress the legitimacy of their territorial identities. That symbolic exchanges produced this new set of normative arrangements among Arab states and encouraged states and their societies to more closely identify with the territorial status quo contrasts with the more established explanations for the demise of unification: the 1967 Arab-Israeli War and state formation. Unification had receded from the Arab agenda, and Arab states had embraced a more centrist conception of Arab nationalism before the 1967 war. Nor were long-term structural processes associated with state formation directly connected to these regional developments; symbolic exchanges that played themselves out around the dialogue about unification created a new normative environment for Arab politics.

An immediate consequence of the rivalry among the radical states over unification was the reappearance of the Arab-Israeli conflict atop the Arab agenda. Palestine, and not unification, now became the principal way that Arab states attempted to establish their credentials and challenge their rivals. The "era of summitry"—beginning in January 1964 and ending in September 1965—symbolized the move by Arab states to set aside the debate about unification, embrace sovereignty, and shift their focus to Israel. As Arab leaders increasingly used Palestine to strut their credentials and challenge those of their rivals, they became increasingly vulnerable to symbolic sanctions regarding their commitment to Arabism as defined by the Palestine conflict. For these and other reasons the era of summitry collapsed as Syria coaxed Nasser away from his two-year détente with the conservative Arab states by challenging his commitment to Palestine. Nasser took the bait, pledged his commitment to justice in Palestine, and renewed his rivalry with the conservative Arab states. Symbolic competition took hold as Syria, Egypt, and Jordan competed through words and deeds to demonstrate which was most opposed to Israel. This deadly game of outbidding and symbolic entrapment concluded with an unwanted war with Israel.

Suez, Arabism, and the West

Although the debate about the Baghdad Pact made it more difficult if not highly unlikely that Arab states (other than Iraq) would align with the West, it was not until the Suez War that the West earned in spades its insecurity-provoking reputation. In this respect much is rightly made of the Suez War. But the Suez War might be better understood as symbolizing the end of one era and the beginning of another, reinforcing tendencies and social forces already present. In any event, the story of the Suez War can be told briefly.[1] Egypt and Britain had been involved in a decadeslong struggle over control of the Suez Canal, which Britain suspected was finally settled to their mutual advantage with the Suez Canal treaty of October 1954—which gave Britain control of the canal's operations and a healthy share of its revenues.[2] Soon after the conclusion of the treaty Nasser opened discussions with the United States and the Soviet Union over which would provide him with the more generous assistance package for his planned Aswan High Dam. The Soviets and the Americans soon found themselves in a bidding war for the right to provide the assistance and to claim Nasser for their camp. These negotiations continued through the first part of 1956, when John Foster Dulles, the U.S. secretary of state, doubting Nasser's sincerity and tiring of the haggling, abruptly ended negotiations and told Nasser that his chances of getting Western assistance were virtually nil. The manner in which Dulles ended the negotiations led Nasser to conclude that the United States was intent on humiliating him; he now began to contemplate nationalizing the canal and, finding no immediate objections, determined to do just that.[3]

Nasser nationalized the canal on July 26, 1956. The speech contained some common themes, including the pronouncements that the canal was not simply Egyptian but was also a symbol of Arab independence; that Egypt was restoring not only Egyptian sovereignty over the canal but also Arab pride and power after centuries of colonialism and imperialism. The speech was vintage Nasser, using various symbols to connect Arab nationalism, Egyptian power, and him. The centrality and drama of the moment, and Nasser's mixture of joy and anxiety, were symbolized by his spontaneous outburst of laughter in the middle of his speech, a highly unusual event that represented a personal and national expression of relief and catharsis.[4] Egypt and the rest of the Arab world widely and wildly applauded Nasser and his actions. Even his regional rivals were forced to put on their best faces, acknowledge the boldness of the move, and cable their congratulations.[5] Nasser had already established himself as the new leader of Arab nationalism, and audacious acts—beginning with his opposition to the Baghdad Pact and continuing with his arms deal with the Soviets and the nationalization—only solidified his credentials.

Nasser knew that nationalizing the canal would not endear him to the West.[6] England, France, and Israel now determined that they had a common enemy in Nasser and might profitably join forces—literally. By all accounts British prime minister Anthony Eden was nearly apoplectic over the nationalization.[7] Eden—fearing that Nasser was nothing short of an Arab Hitler who had an insatiable lust for power and lived only to torment Britain and its Arab allies—believed that Nasser would listen only to force. Britain thus began to contemplate military action to recapture the canal and put Nasser in his place. France's ire against Nasser derived from his support of the Algerian rebels. Convinced that removing Nasser would deal the rebels a major blow, France now decided to accept the military, political, and diplomatic risks associated with a war against Egypt.[8] Israel had its long-standing grievances against Nasser, mainly involving Nasser's failure to end the fedayeen raids coming from the Gaza strip and his closing of the Strait of Tiran earlier that year, and Israeli prime minister David Ben-Gurion hoped that a quick strike against Egypt would cause Nasser to change his policies, open the sea lanes to Israel, and clear the fedayeen from the area.[9] Israel, France, and England each had a vendetta against Nasser and believed that a successful military campaign would change Nasser's strategic calculations, if not sever Egypt's head.

On October 29 the Israeli army swept through the Sinai and advanced on the Suez Canal. Britain and France's declaration that they were landing their troops to separate Egypt and Israel and protect the Suez Canal on behalf of the international community was the barest of covers for their military intervention.[10] France and Britain encountered little military opposition from Egypt but vocal condemnation from the international community, aggressive gestures from the Soviet Union, and, more ominously, diplomatic and economic threats from the United States. They limped home from Egypt, replaced by the first use of United Nations peacekeeping forces, and Israel hesitated but eventually retreated from the Sinai a few months later under considerable pressure from the United States.

Several consequences of the Suez War were exactly the opposite of what Britain and France had intended. Far from arresting the decline of the British Empire, Britain's militarized response only hastened it. Far from winning the West any friends, the West was now persona non grata, and the Soviet Union stepped into the power vacuum. Far from bolstering the conservative forces in the region and ending Nasser's brilliant career, the attack by the old colonial countries in concert with Israel against Arab nationalism's heart and soul only undermined the attackers, elevated Nasser's prestige, and swelled the ranks of his disciples in the Arab world.

The overall effect of the Suez War was to shift the tide of regional politics toward Nasser and his brand of Arab nationalism, completely vindicate Nasser's line that the West could not be trusted, and wholly undermine the credibility of any politician who was viewed as remotely sympathetic to the West.[11] Syria, which only a few years before had been somewhat suspicious of Nasser and sympathetic to the West, now did a full turn leftward and was firmly in Nasser's camp, strengthened its ties to the Soviets, and became the home of the most serious Communist movement in the region.[12] The spirit of unification also reappeared. Although there was some discussion of unification before the Suez War, these discussions had played a minor role in Egyptian-Syrian relations (and even in Syrian politics of the period).[13] That would now change. The Suez War catalyzed both domestic turmoil in Syria and unification fever.[14] Such developments contributed to and were exacerbated by another crisis the following summer when the United States, watching a growing radicalization of Syrian politics and growth of the Communist Party, attempted to engineer a pro-U.S. coup in Syria. Nasser responded by sending his troops outside Egypt for the first time in a symbolic show of support.[15] The demand for unification and the radicalization of regional politics took another step forward.

Saudi Arabia, which was allied with Egypt because of their common opposition to the Hashemite monarchies, now became ever more suspicious and fearful of Nasser's growing power, particularly as Nasser flirted with rewriting the regional rules of the game and Saudi Arabia found it had its own Free Officers movement. Therefore, while Saudi Arabia remained aligned with Nasser publicly, privately it began to express greater concerns about Nasser's growing power, contemplate how it could best shield itself from him, stress its Islamic credentials, and distance itself from Egypt and toward the West, though with a method and style that would retain its distance from Iraq.[16]

Lebanon faced a major political crisis as a consequence of the war because the government refused to sever relations with Britain and France. As a result, Lebanese premier Abdullah Yafi resigned, asserting that Lebanon should adopt the same responses to the crisis as the other Arab states and that its failure to do so would only arouse further suspicion of Lebanon's place in the Arab world.[17] Many Lebanese were sympathetic to Nasser's message before October 1956, and the Suez War only swelled and intensified their numbers and further weakened the credentials of conservative politicians.[18]

King Hussein, though historically aligned with the West, weathered the storm because he had demonstrated greater allegiance to Nasser during the past year. In early 1956 he had publicly refused to sign the Baghdad Pact and pledged his commitment to Nasser's concept of neutrality. And then in October he concluded a military agreement with Nasser as Arab-Israeli tensions were rising and it appeared that Israel's army was heading east and not west.[19] Hussein took the additional step of offering his services to Nasser upon hearing the news of the invasion. But Jordan's Arab credentials remained suspect so long as it remained allied with Britain. Because Hussein refused to break relations with Britain as it had with France because of the financial costs,[20] the pressures on the palace persisted. Then Jordanian prime minister Sulayman al-Nabulsi announced that Jordan would "in principle, accept the Arab grant offered by Egypt, Syria, and Saudi Arabia, in place of the Arab and British grants to the National Guard and army, respectively," and take the necessary steps to abrogate the Anglo-Jordanian agreement, an unequal treaty concluded under special circumstances and recently violated by Britain.[21] On January 19, 1957, Jordan, Syria, Saudi Arabia, and Egypt signed the Arab Solidarity Agreement in Cairo.[22] Although Hussein put on his best face in public and warmly toasted the agreement, he was less enthusiastic in private and confessed that regional and domestic pressures left him no choice.[23]

Still, Hussein was not out of the woods. Throughout 1957 he was subjected to a series of attacks from abroad. But far more disturbing and ominous were the attacks from home. Briefly, from the time of the Suez War through

April 1957 Prime Minister Nabulsi was actively attempting to bring Jordan into the nationalist camp, touching off a political crisis and struggle for political control between the king, who saw himself as the defender of Jordan's sovereignty and orientation toward the West, and a prime minister who was intent on integrating Jordan into Arab nationalism.[24] In an interview with the *New York Times* on December 15, 1956, Nabulsi proclaimed that "Jordan cannot live forever as Jordan. Jordan must be connected militarily, economically, and politically" with other Arab states.[25] Hussein ended this flirtation with Arab nationalism in April 1957 when he disbanded the cabinet, moved against an attempted coup, and took the domestic reins.[26] Although still insecure in the region and at home for the remainder of the year, Hussein retained control through domestic and regional maneuvers designed to contain his enemies and keep them off balance.

Iraq's Nuri al-Said, Britain's chief Arab ally, suffered much from the invasion, and his fate was largely sealed by the British he so favored. As tensions mounted on the Israeli-Jordanian border during the month of October, Egypt increased its media barrage against Iraq. Oddly borrowing from the title of Emile Zola's famous essay defending Captain Alfred Dreyfuss, Egyptian interior minister Salim Salim penned an article entitled "I Accuse," in which he charged that Nuri al-Said had turned his back on the Arab world, handed imperialism an entry, was a lackey of the British ambassador, and gave the Baghdad Pact its very name.[27] Iraq attempted to break out of its isolation and demonstrate its Arabist credentials by concluding an agreement with Jordan that would allow Iraqi troops to be stationed there, ostensibly to defend the Arab nation against an Israeli attack, though actually designed to shield Iraq from its regional critics.[28] Nuri al-Said's dwindling prestige virtually evaporated when Iraq's chief ally, the one to which it clung for security, invaded Egypt in concert with Israel.[29]

Nasser showed no mercy for the weak. In a speech immediately following the war Nasser recounted how the various Arab leaders had phoned to offer their troops to Egypt and the Arab nation; the lone leader not on Nasser's roll call of honor was Nuri al-Said.[30] Later Cairo criticized Iraq's "neutrality" in the war, declaring this a sure sign of imperialism's success against the Arab nation and that the Baghdad Pact represented an unsuccessful attempt to destroy the Arab countries.[31] Syria was equally merciless in its attacks on Nuri al-Said, claiming that the Baghdad Pact meant that Iraq had helped Israel and the imperialist countries to carry out their campaign against the Arab nation.[32] And just when matters could not get worse for Said, they did. On November 17 Syrian officials announced that they had uncovered a plot by

Iraq to overthrow the Syrian government and bring to power a pro-Iraqi regime. As fate would have it, the coup was planned for the very day that the Suez War began, inextricably tying Said to the invasion and Israel.[33]

Said attempted to defend himself by calling for calm and by undertaking a series of countermeasures that included severing diplomatic ties with France, reminding his listeners of Iraq's historical contributions to the Arab nation, and sending a division to Jordan.[34] This was not enough to halt the deteriorating domestic scene and to salvage his Arab credentials. So Said imposed martial law on October 31, suspended Britain's participation in the Baghdad Pact (and subsequently emphasized that it was now a true regional defense organization and something of an Islamic Pact), and adopted a more radical stance on the issue of Palestine.[35] In a lengthy address delivered on December 16 Said provided his own understanding of the Baghdad Pact and stressed his long-standing Arab credentials: "The call to Arab nationalism is not accidental to me, it is my very being."[36] The speech did little to rescue him from domestic criticism or regional estrangement.

In fact, Nasser responded with another media barrage, ridiculing Said and his Arabism that allowed him to be a handmaiden of Western imperialism.[37] In January 1957 Egypt, Saudi Arabia, Syria, and Jordan concluded the "Treaty of Arab Solidarity"; Iraq was notably absent, pointedly excluded, and now isolated from the Arab world. Although the Baghdad Pact and Nuri al-Said survived this and other episodes for the next eighteen months, the Suez War had completely undermined his position, and he could do little to resuscitate it, save distancing himself from the pact that bore his stamp and the Iraqi capital's name. What was once a source of prestige was now a lightning rod.

The Suez War shifted the ground toward Nasserism, strengthening all who were associated with radical politics and undermining all those associated with the West. Nasser's power came not from the barrel of a gun—after all, he had just been routed by Israel—but from his symbolic capital and his ability to frame the Suez War as part of a history of imperialism that had dismembered the Arab nation and continued to keep it powerless. Broadcasting his message of the threat posed by the West to the Arab nation and speaking of the need to have the conservative Arab leaders change their tune or be swept from office, Nasser mobilized the streets throughout the region and brought pressure to bear on the governments to align their policies with his. Iraq and Jordan found themselves confronting a nearly unresolvable dilemma: in private they were increasingly resolute that Nasser had to be stopped and was a greater menace as a consequence of the Suez War, but in public they found it more difficult to oppose him because of his unrivaled prestige and the soiled reputation of the West.[38] To shield themselves from criticism and from being labeled enemies of nationalism and agents of imperialism, Jordan and Iraq—particularly Jordan—attempted to portray themselves as allies of Nasser's brand of Arabism (though not necessarily of Nasser) and clamped down on domestic opposition groups. But regional radicalization was the dominant trend, leaving the Hashemites in Iraq and Jordan increasingly isolated in Arab politics and their own capitals. This radicalization of Arab politics, moreover, increasingly demanded that Arab officials not only shun associations with the West but also fulfill Arabism's highest aspiration—unification.

Arabism and the Rise and Decline of Unification

The call for unification had receded from the agenda since 1945, and the Arab states that once were its principal champions, Iraq and Jordan, were now associated with conservatism and imperialism. But unification, the summit for many Arab nationalists, became a reality when Egypt and Syria announced the creation of the United Arab Republic (UAR) on February 1, 1958. Although the architects of the federation presented it as a natural and logical development in the steady march of Arab nationalism, behind the scenes its creation was quite messy and something of a shotgun marriage.[39] That Syria and Egypt found themselves the highly reluctant partners at the altar of unification was a testimony to Syrian domestic politics, Nasser's attempt to maintain his symbolic standing, and the politics of impression management.

What possessed the Syrian leaders to get on a plane in January 1958, fly to Cairo, and offer up the Syrian state to Nasser? The triggering factors were ideology and the domestic turmoil that had been Syria's decadelong undoing and had increasingly defined its political life since 1956. The Suez War and the crisis of 1957 strengthened the Syrian Ba'ath Party, whose intellectual writings stressed the singularity of the "eternal nation" and the necessity of having this one nation united under a single state.[40] But the Communist Party was another beneficiary of this domestic turmoil; in fact, its growing popularity placed it on the verge of taking state power. The Ba'ath Party was not alone in fearing this outcome; so too did a highly conservative element within the military. By the final days of 1957 the only safe predictions for the future of Syrian politics were that the Communists were likely to take power in the near future and that Syria's unending governability crisis was not about to end.

The Ba'athists and the military turned to Nasser and the prospect of a federation with Egypt to halt the ongoing political turmoil and to keep the Communists at bay.[41] The Ba'athists surmised that they would achieve numerous domestic and ideological goals, for they would realize an ideal of unity that they probably would not accomplish through electoral means; obstruct the growing power of the Communists; have an opportunity to school Nasser in a more pristine form of Arabism; and obtain a vehicle for exporting their revolution abroad and enhancing their political prestige.[42] Simply put, having Nasser rule the Syrians seemed preferable to trying to govern themselves.[43] Few Syrian politicians could oppose the idea of union, and even the Communists had to pay lip service to this goal. "The idea of Arab unity was irresistible, and, like motherhood, no politician with any aspirations could speak against it."[44] That such a political arrangement was thinkable owed to the salience of the idea of unity in Syrian intellectual life and the perceived artificiality of the "region" of Syria.[45]

Nasser was hardly overjoyed by the Syrian proposal. Never one to trumpet the unification theme, he responded coolly to the recent unity discussions with Syria, and the Egyptian public was hardly pushing Nasser in that direction.[46] So when the Syrian leadership landed in Cairo and presented Nasser with the gift of Syria, his lack of enthusiasm came as no surprise. To unify with Syria meant to become entangled in the web of Syrian politics that had been the demise of so many. No wonder, then, that his initial response to the visiting Syrians was to tell them to get their house in order first.[47] But they persisted and insisted that this was the moment to realize a central tenet of Arab nationalism and the only way to stifle the growing power of the Communists.

Nasser confronted a dilemma that was partly of his own making. How could he, the leader of Arabism, reject the pinnacle of Arabism's aspirations? To refuse the Syrian offer would be to deny his own leadership and to turn his back on the role that he created and that bore his name. But governing Syria might be his political undoing and force him to squander resources on a losing foreign policy adventure. According to one aide to Nasser, some within Egypt's inner circle strongly advised against this entanglement, fearing that it would undermine Egypt's other political and economic interests.[48]

Impression management rather than military calculations led Nasser to accept the merger. Nasser ultimately accepted the Syrian invitation because of his calculation that he had more to lose by rejecting the unity agreement than he did by accepting the trouble that was Syrian politics. "For Nasser to refuse unity would undermine his prestige," recalled one of Nasser's political advisers from the period. "He is an Arab leader, and if he refused unification, then how can he be an Arab leader?"[49] To limit his exposure to Syrian turmoil he sought as much control over Syria's political and economic life as possible.

The Syrian leap into Nasser's arms was in fact a product not only of domestic survival but also a strong measure of symbolic entrapment and face saving. Syrian leaders had correctly predicted that Nasser would be cool to the idea of unity and therefore believed that they could make a dramatic gesture of unity that Nasser would turn down, thus solidifying their domestic credentials without actually having to surrender their sovereignty to Nasser. Clearly, they had not counted on Nasser's accepting the offer. Now the Syrians were caught. They could hardly rescind their unity offer. And once the unification drive picked up steam, Syrian leaders felt compelled to accept Nasser's control over Syrian political life, including the dissolution of the army, political parties, and most other mechanisms of social control.[50] For both the Syrians and the Egyptians, then, the road to unity was paved by symbolic interactions, attempts at impression management, and then symbolic entrapment. Such symbolic exchanges led them to accept a political agreement that both considered against their strategic interests but absolutely necessary for their symbolic standing and thus regime survival.

Egypt, which had once been unification's staunchest opponent, was now its midwife and principal champion, instantly and dramatically telescoping the idea of unification from the far and distant future into the here and now. The creation of the UAR reverberated throughout the Arab world—and Nasser made sure of it. Although Nasser was the reluctant head of the Arab world's newest political experiment, his vitriolic speeches in Cairo and Damascus betrayed not a hint of hesitation: he urged all Arabs to join the UAR in its inevitable march to unity and glory and challenged Iraq and Jordan to follow in Syria and Egypt's footsteps, for public opinion demanded it and the UAR welcomed it.[51] Yemen soon joined Nasser's bandwagon and became a member of the UAR.

The Jordanian and Iraqi governments, Hashemites who were closely tied to the British and who had long waved the banner of unity, felt the symbolic aftershocks of the UAR and the growing pressures from their societies to match unification with unification.[52] In fact, Iraq and Jordan had discussed unification as recently as late 1957 when their Arab credentials were in desperate need of repair.[53] They reconvened their unity talks now that the UAR was hanging over their heads and hurriedly concluded their own agreement, the Arab Federation, on February 14, 1958. Few mistook the Arab Federation for the UAR. The former was decidedly less ambitious than the latter and had none of the dramatic effect.[54] In his speech announcing the Arab Federation a publicly reserved Nuri al-Said immediately warned against expecting too much too soon by stressing how the federation was the beginning of unification and that the road would be long and rocky.[55] Said's sober tone reflected not only caution and conservatism but also disagreement between the two thrones, including who would head the federal army, whether the Iraqi or Jordanian military would be preeminent, and who had the authority to ratify and declare treaties.[56] The first two points concerned who would acquire authority and power, whereas the third reflected King Hussein's insistence that Jordan be exempt from now having to honor the Baghdad Pact lest he repeat past mistakes.[57]

Nasser gave a perfunctory welcome to the Arab Federation, but in no time a war of words ensued between the two rival federations.[58] Cairo declared that Arab unity without liberation from the West was sham unity, Iraq and Jordan should reject the Baghdad Pact and ties to the West, Iraq had consulted with the West and Israel before the agreement, the other members of the Baghdad Pact actively opposed Arab unity schemes, and that the Arab Federation was nothing more than another tool of the West.[59] Syrian newspapers echoed these themes and observed that the Arab Federation was "something artificial and confused . . . established for negative reasons and designed to distract the populace from the UAR."[60] In response to Nasser's claim that the Arab Federation was an entree for imperialism, a Jordanian official chided Nasser for being new to the cause of Arab nationalism and for using such unity schemes as the joint command of 1955 as a "plot to commit treachery" rather than, as Hussein viewed it, a step toward unification.[61] Although the effect of Nasser's charges on his listeners in Amman and Baghdad is unknown, the Arab public's response to the news of the Arab Federation paled in comparison to its response to the UAR. The Arab Federation's failure to erase the accusations against the monarchies would become evident in a few months.

The announcement of these federations alarmed Saudi Arabia and further destabilized Lebanon. Saudi Arabia did not look kindly on this federation mania. It had always opposed unification attempts in the past, particularly the Fertile Crescent schemes that united the Hashemite kingdoms in Iraq and Jordan. To demonstrate its opposition Saudi Arabia reportedly suspended its annual grant to Jordan and began to consider additional diplomatic and security measures to counteract these federations.[62]

Nasser and the UAR had galvanized the popular imagination in Lebanon and further destabilized an already teetering political system. The Lebanese constitution had been in dire need of reform for some time because of economic, political, and demographic changes, and although domestic forces were largely responsible for propelling the political crisis, Nasser's fingerprints also were present and complicating matters. Lebanese president Camille Chamoun, though confessing that Lebanon was "going through a difficult ordeal," blamed the UAR for "interfering in our internal affairs with the aim of effecting a radical change in our basic political policy."[63] The crisis bubbled along throughout the spring and summer with no resolution in sight. A friendless Iraq urged Chamoun to stay the course, fight Nasser, and establish a defense or political agreement between Iraq and Lebanon. Nuri al-Said then convened a meeting of the Baghdad Pact countries to discuss the crisis in Lebanon.[64] The meeting occurred in Istanbul on July 14, but Iraq's chair was empty.

The Hashemite monarchy met its demise in the early morning of July 14, 1958, when General Abd al-Karim Qasim and Colonel Abd al-Salaam Aref overthrew the Iraqi government. The royal family was murdered, and Nuri al-Said was killed while trying to escape the city. Although many factors led to the revolution, the Baghdad Pact and the general sense of Iraq's isolation from Arab politics contributed mightily.[65] As Hanna Batatu has written, "The pact not only perpetuated the undesired connection with the English and guaranteed them the privilege they had hitherto enjoyed but also entailed a severing of Arab ranks and an open taking of sides in the 'cold war.' It alienated, in other words, neutralist, nationalist, and pan-Arab opinion."[66] The Free Officers were quite clear about their distaste for the former government's opposition to Nasserism and identification with British interests. In a directive signed by the Free Officers on the eve of the July 14 coup, the party proclaimed that the future Iraqi government would henceforth "pursue an independent Arab national policy . . . convert the 'Arab Union' into an authentic union between Iraq and Jordan . . . and unite on a federal basis with the U.A.R."[67] Not all segments of Iraqi society supported this brand of Arab nationalism.[68] But they were unified in their rejection of the Baghdad Pact and its symbolic defection from the Arab fold.[69]

The Iraqi Revolution, coming on the heels of the civil unrest in Lebanon, reverberated throughout the Arab world and created the perception that revolution in the Middle East was an unstoppable tide.[70] The sound of revolution crashing throughout the Middle East rang alarms in the West and led to interventions by the United States and Britain in Lebanon and Jordan, respectively.[71] Chamoun, watching a pro-Western government fall to Nasser, feared that he would be next and took the countermeasure of invoking the Eisenhower Doctrine and inviting American troops to enter Lebanon to confront the "external communist threat."[72] American forces marched onto the beaches of Beirut on July 15, more likely to confront the dangers of sunburn than they were Communists. Significantly, the first postintervention Lebanese government moved to distance itself from Chamoun and the U.S. intervention by revoking the Eisenhower Doctrine and creating a détente with Egypt.

King Hussein was visibly shaken and angered by the demise of the Iraqi monarchy and the death of the royal family. In the heat of the moment he contemplated sending his troops into Iraq under the pretext of the authority granted him by the charter of the Arab Federation, but his aides cautioned him against such a move.[73] More isolated than ever in Arab politics and fearing that he too would fall to Nasserite forces, Hussein invited the British army to help him stabilize the situation. In his address to the nation Hussein justified his invitation on the ground that the "mercenary" agents of Communism posed a threat to Jordanian stability and true Arab nationalism. The move, he said, was "designed to enable this poor and small country to improve its economy and develop its resources and to permit its army to preserve . . . the internal front," thus allowing Jordan to fulfill its obligations to the Arab nation and to keep it "from the clutches of communism."[74] In later statements Hussein was less diplomatic and more direct in his condemnation of Egypt. It was public knowledge, he exclaimed, that Syria and Egypt had been plotting against Jordan and that the Communist overthrow in Iraq meant that the burden of the Arab Federation rested on his shoulders.[75] Hussein charged that

> Nasir's bloodthirsty disciples massacred members of the Royal family. President Nasir is the only cause of crises in the Middle East, and unless he is dealt with, these crises will continue. Nasir is the source of difficulties and disturbances in this part of the Arab world. . . . We want Nasir to know that Arab nationalism was born before he was, and that the holy march to which he referred will make tangible progress if he disappears.[76]

Nasser answered these interventions with words alone and did not dare to pick a fight with the West. Nasser predictably denied any meddling and claimed that the U.S. and British landings represented old-fashioned imperialism and an attempt to undermine Arab nationalism.[77] As the Western troops took their positions in Jordan and Lebanon, Nasser and the new

Iraqi leaders flew to Damascus and delivered a scathing attack on Lebanon and King Hussein, ridiculing them for siding with the imperialists and against the nationalists. Hussein might have felt temporarily braced by the British forces stationed throughout the country, but these Western allies only amplified his loneliness in the Arab world and played directly into Nasser's hands.

The events of 1958 inaugurated a new phase in Arab politics. Whereas in recent years Arab states had been debating their relations to the West and defining Arab nationalism as nearly tantamount to neutrality and anticolonialism, now unification became a rallying cry throughout much of the Arab world. But this was hardly a phase that Arab leaders, and particularly Nasser, had longed for. That unification now came to the fore is attributable to three central factors. The combination of domestic turmoil and Ba'athist pan-Arab ideology in Syria led the political elite to propose unification with Egypt to avoid having to rule itself and to further its ideological aspirations. That the Syrian elite would look to Egypt and Nasser, whom it had mistrusted only a few years before and whose credentials it had doubted, is a testimony to the person of Nasser, the domestic chaos of Syria, and the elites' attempt to save face at home. Further, Nasser threw caution to the wind as he calculated that he must accept the Syrian invitation to govern the ungovernable or betray his image. As one who religiously promoted himself as the leader of Arab nationalism, he could hardly reject the responsibilities that accompanied that role. Symbolic entrapment and not strategic or economic calculations led Egypt and Syria to conclude a unity agreement that they privately feared might bring little but headaches. Finally, the symbolic presence of the UAR further radicalized Arab politics and added to the grievances against the conservative regimes. The Iraqi Revolution was the most dramatic example, but the governments of Jordan, Saudi Arabia, and Lebanon all seemed distant from prevailing opinion and increasingly isolated at home and abroad. The debate about the meaning and practices associated with Arabism now entered a new phase; an Arab state in good standing, according to the radical states, worked toward unification.

Imperatives of regime survival, combined with symbolic accumulation and entrapment, set into motion a series of developments that increased normative integration and mutual orientation. But no evidence exists that this outcome was desired or planned by the key participants, demanded by unforgiving societal elements, or dictated by strategic considerations. Rather, the interactions between Arab leaders spun a web that increased their mutual orientation and thus their mutual vulnerability, and they did so because of their desire to maintain their standing and protect their image. The same symbolic interactions that brought Arab leaders to this highly undesired point would continue but in a more deadly and consuming fashion during the next several years.

DIVISIONS IN THE RADICAL CAMP

No sooner was Nasserism the dominant political force in the region than the radical regimes turned their attention to each other, though in the most destructive manner. Their highly poisonous interactions, and their willingness to expose each other's dirty laundry in the most confrontational and derisive communiqués, directly contributed to the decline of Arabism and to a growing perception that unification was unlikely in the near future—if desirable at all. In short, these highly inflammatory interactions between the leaders of the radical camp encouraged not integration but differentiation. The dynamics that had driven them forward toward unity would now cause them to reverse gear.

Iraq and Egypt soon replaced their initial exchanges of praise with a vicious feud.[78] Illustrative of this abrupt change was the fate of Colonel Abd al-Salaam Aref, one of the architects of the Iraqi Revolution and a leading Arab nationalist: three days after the revolution he was standing on a balcony in Damascus with Nasser, but three months later he was in jail in Baghdad with a death sentence imposed by his (and Nasser's) rival, Qasim.[79] Part of the reason for the chill in Egyptian-Iraqi relations derived from a split and power struggle within the Iraqi regime. Aref was a Ba'athist, member of the ruling government, and supporter of Nasser, and he championed unification with the UAR and made his sentiments publicly known as early as July 18, 1958. President Qasim, along with the large Shi'i and Kurdish minorities and the Communist Party, was less enthusiastic about unification; the president had personal reasons, whereas the Kurds and Shi'ites did not share in the Arabist fervor. The Aref-Qasim power struggle developed into a rivalry between the Ba'ath and Communist Parties, with each attempting to enlist whatever domestic, regional, and international resources it could to maintain its power base.[80]

This power struggle, with Qasim at the top and using his pulpit to challenge Nasser and silence the Ba'athists and other supporters of the Egyptian president, cast a pall over the radical camp and the entire region. The low point in UAR-Iraq relations came in March 1959 when Iraq brutally suppressed a UAR-sponsored uprising in Mosul. A month later Nasser joined with King Saud of Saudi Arabia to ask the Arab League to condemn Qasim as a Communist and for his actions in Mosul.[81] From now until the Iraqi coup of 1963, Egyptian-Iraqi relations remained bitter. But one notable consequence of this feud was that it "marked one of the first moments in the short history of pan-Arabism when it came into conflict with nation-state nationalism or particularism on a regional scale."[82] The Egyptian-Iraqi duel led the Iraqi government to repudiate Nasser's claim to regional leadership and to accentuate Iraqi particularism in relationship to Arab nationalism. This was not the first time that such themes emerged, but it foreshadowed a string of events to come in the radical camp as their brutal interactions would further the cause of statism.

The cause of unification suffered a major blow on September 28, 1961, when Syria announced its withdrawal from the UAR. The sources of the secession largely revolved around Nasser's strong hand in Syrian political and economic life.[83] But a contributing cause can be traced to the preunification period and the fundamental differences over the meaning of Arabism. Nasser's Arabism preached the interdependence of Arab security and power among sovereign Arab states, but the Syrian Ba'athists identified Arab nationalism as entailing an organic link among Arabs that demanded a singular political authority. Nasser and the Syrian Ba'athists, then, were destined for a collision course, a "long misunderstanding between them on what was meant by unity—a dialogue at cross-purposes—which only the painful union experiment brought into the open."[84]

The collapse of the UAR and the public fallout that ensued only reinforced the understanding that this unification did little to extinguish national differences. In fact, it exacerbated them. In Syria another debate emerged about its relationship to Arab nationalism and, accordingly, the Syrian national identity. Syrian politics was largely defined by different strands of Syrian and Arab nationalism, and the rise of the Ba'ath Party in the late 1950s represented a pan-Arab vision and the most powerful voice of the period. The secession and charges against Nasser, however, reinvigorated a debate about Syria's national identity. Rabinovich has described what happened:

> The experience of union with a much larger, stronger, and rather self-assertive nation-state strengthened the feeling of Syrian distinctiveness and the notion of a Syrian entity, which in early 1958 had been very weak. But this change found no overt ideological expression as no one dared challenge the doctrine of pan-Arab nationalism and unity. The proponents of Syria's renewed independence and sovereignty found themselves in the

awkward situation of having to defend their position while professing allegiance to a doctrine that denounced it.[85]

During the eighteen months between the Syrian secession of September 1961 and the Syrian coup of March 1963 the Syrian government, while clearly wrestling with the relationship between the Syrian national identity and the projects of Arabism, attempted to maintain its ideological standing by forwarding various unification schemes and occasionally drawing closer to Iraq.[86]

Nasser was ideologically and politically stunned by the demise of the unification that he never wanted. Although he likened the secession to a coup, no amount of rhetorical camouflage could undo the damage done by Syria's catalogue of charges against him.[87] Unaccustomed to being on the defensive, he moved in two different directions. The first was a hint of revisionism and a drift toward a more centrist version of Arab nationalism. In an interview with West German television a month before the Syrian secession Nasser revealed a new flexibility toward the concept of Arab unity, stressing a progressive development from "solidarity, to alliance, to total constitutional unity."[88] Shortly after the coup Nasser confidant Mohamed Heikal insisted that unions must have a real foundation, that is, be based on certain political and economic conditions, and Nasser confessed that he told the Syrians on January 15, 1958, that any constitutional union should have a five-year waiting period and should be consummated only after they have achieved an economic, military, or cultural union.[89] Although shaken by the secession, Egyptian society, always wary of Egypt's relationship to Arab nationalism and suspicious of these so-called organic links to the Fertile Crescent, "could now breathe a sigh of relief."[90] One response to the secession, then, was to revert to a more Egypt-centered view and retreat from the idea of unification and toward Nasser's original view of Arabism.

But such hints of ideological revisionism were overshadowed by ideological purification. To shield himself from the Syrian accusations and to reestablish his Arab credentials Nasser purified Egypt's Arab message. Now Mohamed Heikal published his famous essay distinguishing between Egypt as a state and Egypt as a revolution. Although as a state Egypt would conduct itself in a manner so becoming, as a revolution Egypt would go over the heads of other Arab leaders, deliver its message to the masses, and foment radical change.[91] Nasser, who once spoke of "unity of ranks" and implied that regimes of divergent orientation could cooperate to confront common external threats, now began to champion a "unity of purpose" to best further the goal of true unity and revolution.[92] In one account of the collapse of the UAR Nasser confessed that his error was to consort with Syrian conservatives and reactionaries.[93] Never again, he told his audience.

This renewed religious zeal meant trouble for Nasser's enemies at home and abroad. On the home front he moved against the bourgeoisie in a series of nationalizations ostensibly intended to further his brand of Arab socialism. On the regional front he proclaimed the necessity of maintaining ideological purity and began challenging radical and conservative governments alike. He refused to recognize the legitimacy of the Syrian government, delivered a relentless series of indictments in regard to its supposed conservatism, and more openly challenged the conservative states.[94] Soon after the secession he withdrew his troops from the Arab force protecting Kuwait because it was unseemly for the vanguard of the revolution to be stationed alongside the reactionary monarchies of Jordan and Saudi Arabia.[95]

Egyptian troops departed from one part of the Arabian Peninsula only to find themselves at war in another—Yemen. In September 1962 Imam Ahmed of Yemen died and was succeeded by his son Mohammed al-Bader. Soon thereafter Bader was overthrown by the chief of his royal guards, Abdallah al-Sallal, who formed and headed the Revolutionary Command Council (RCC). The RCC ended the imamite and the reign of the Hamid al-Din family, established the Yemen Arab Republic, and pledged loyalty to Nasser and radical Arabism. Bader made his way north, where he established the counterrevolution among local loyal tribes. The republicans, headed by Sallal, and the royalists, headed by Bader, were now involved in a bloody civil war.[96]

Saudi Arabia and Egypt soon became embroiled in the Yemen conflict. Saudi Arabia dreaded the thought of Nasser protégés gaining a foothold on the Arabian Peninsula, which the Saudis had always considered of immense strategic value, and they feared that Nasser's real agenda was the overthrow of the Saudi monarchy.[97] Nasser's decision to support the RCC had little to do with military politics and everything to do with symbolic politics. As the leader of Arab nationalism and still reeling from the Syrian secession, Nasser could hardly reject the request for aid from the RCC and was captivated by the opportunity to bolster his radical credentials.[98] As one Egyptian official of the period put it, "Nasser intervened in Yemen to recover his prestige. It is natural for a leader to try and restore himself after the failure of the UAR."[99] Nasser responded to the Syrian secession with a pinch of revisionism and a heap of ideological purification and impression management.

Nasser's regional recovery had less to do with his actions and more to do with a quick succession of coups, the first in Iraq in February and then in

Syria in March 1963. Both revolutions presented themselves as correctives to the conservatism and authoritarianism of the regimes that preceded them, and this meant above all a renewed emphasis on unification and their longing for approval from Egypt.[100] The Iraqis immediately proclaimed their desire to form a political union with Nasser.[101] Such proclamations stemmed not only from ideology but also from a desire to generate political support from the demonstrators in the streets of Baghdad who were shouting the name of Nasser.[102] The Syrian coup also brought to power a government that proclaimed its stand with Arab unity and wanted a détente with Nasser.[103] Although the new Syrian regime was not necessarily engineered or run by members of the Ba'ath Party, it did call itself a unionist government and wanted a warmer relationship with Nasser, something that the previous eighteen months suggested was imperative for domestic stability.[104] The street demonstrations in Damascus in favor of unification with Egypt in mid-March only reinforced the domestic imperative for unification; in fact, while the regime hardly warmed to the idea of its citizens' clamoring for Nasser, it could hardly break up these demonstrations.[105] Instinctually and politically, the Syrian leaders were determined to rekindle the idea of unity with Egypt; after all, they "could not allow themselves to be outbid in enthusiasm for unity."[106] In general, the popular pressures in Syria and Iraq for unification with Nasser placed their regimes in a difficult position of being on record for desiring unification but being quite fearful of giving up their power and national identities.

Nasser watched these coups and demonstrations with both satisfaction and alarm. After suffering the pain of the secession and feeling himself on the defensive for the past two years, he was visibly pleased by these coups and felt vindicated by the testimonials of praise coming from the Fertile Crescent. But he worried about being dragged into another unification scheme that he neither sought nor saw to his advantage. Indeed, all three governments approached the prospect of unity with tremendous reservations. Echoing Nasser's reservations, Mohamed Heikal cautioned that "unity of ranks is more important than unity of purpose" or "any other form of constitutional unity."[107] In his Unity Day Speech on the fifth anniversary of the establishment of the UAR Nasser proclaimed that "for us, the concept of Arab unity at present does not mean constitutional unity or paper unity. Arab unity means that we all stand against enemies, that we all meet on great occasions, that we all face enemies as one man, and that we all celebrate our victories."[108] Still, Nasser willingly accepted the public call by Syria and Iraq for unity talks because it provided him with the opportunity to erase the stain of the UAR, reassert his leadership over these radical rivals to the Arab monarchies, and point another weapon at the conservative Arab states.[109]

All three regimes approached unification with a mixture of fear and necessity; as self-proclaimed radical states that had as their governments' stated goals the erasure of the legacy of San Remo and the creation of a single state for a single nation, they could hardly sidestep the challenge. But to erase their boundaries might only leave them with greater troubles. Syria, Iraq, and Egypt laced their pledges for unification with character assassination. Syria initially and quickly proclaimed its willingness to engage in unification talks, but the regime also noted for good measure that Nasser had done his best to sabotage this form of true Arab expression.[110] Nasser was hardly outdone in this contest of recriminations, and Iraq was not far behind.

These destructive and suspicious dynamics surrounded the unity talks between the three countries. The talks had three phases: five tripartite meetings from March 14 to 16; five bilateral meetings of Syria and Egypt from March 19 to 20; and a series of bilateral and tripartite meetings from April 6 to 14. The history of these failed talks is copiously detailed in Malcolm Kerr's *The Arab Cold War*.[111] But one of their principal characteristics was that the courtship defined by mutual mistrust, suspicion, and antagonism carried over into their formal negotiations. Cairo and Damascus became champion mudslingers. During the negotiations Mohamed Heikal published an article under the now familiar title of "I Accuse!" in which he portrayed Syria as attempting to discredit Nasser and to delay unification through provocative acts.[112] Syria responded in kind.[113] These rivalries colored the proposals that each brought to the negotiating table. Nasser originally proposed a union of it and Syria for four months, and if this trial period was successful, Iraq could join. Or, Nasser offered, perhaps Iraq and Syria could unify first. But neither Iraq nor Syria enjoyed the prospect of unification without Nasser because only he could give them the legitimacy that they sought for domestic stability.[114] In the end each wanted a loose federation rather than immediate unification because Syria and Iraq feared Nasser's long arm and Nasser feared becoming engulfed in Syrian and Iraq politics.[115] "Everyone wants to show that he is for unity but without taking practical steps because of the tremendous mistrust," recalled an Egyptian official from the period.[116]

The desire to project the image of unity without making the necessary sacrifices became painfully clear soon after the announcement of the Tripartite Unity Agreement, the Declaration of Union Accord, of April 17.[117] But at first there was much rejoicing. As Egypt, Syria, and Iraq announced to the waiting Arab world the fruit of their negotiations, they stressed how this unification was an important step toward fulfilling Arabism's goals, and how the "nonliberated" states, most notably Jordan, were now living on borrowed time. Crowds swarmed the streets throughout much of the Arab world, shouting, "Nasser! Nasser!"[118] The memories of the UAR were seemingly erased if only for the moment by the promise of another unification experiment. It is worth emphasizing that Israel hardly figured in the discussion surrounding the agreement, and nearly all attention was directed at satisfying the long-standing desire for unification as the fulfillment of Arab nationalism. The crowds filled the streets and proclamations filled the airwaves as the tide of unification moved to reclaim the "nonliberated" Arab capitals and not nonliberated Palestine.

King Hussein, who reveled publicly in the demise of the UAR and gained some breathing space from the infighting in the radical camp, watched these events with great alarm. He viewed the Iraqi and Syrian coups as a sign of his encirclement.[119] The media campaign unleashed by the radical capitals justified his paranoia. One broadcast at the height of the unification discussions asked Hussein if he wanted to be a friend of the Arabs—if so, "then remove the British crown from your head and trample it under your feet. We do not think that you will do so. Then issue your royal orders to the British imperialist bases in Jordan to leave Jordan immediately."[120] The unity talks and these highly incendiary broadcasts triggered rioting in Jordan, and Hussein found himself in the uncomfortable but familiar position of being a stranger in his own capital.[121] Hussein responded in his usual manner by portraying the radical states as Communists, asserting that Arab nationalism must respect state sovereignty, and imposing strict curfews. Replying to the tendency of the radical states to classify Arab states by degrees of liberation, Jordanian official Wasfi al-Tal noted that "the Communist Party was the first to make such a classification."[122] In a later review of the principles of Jordanian foreign policy Tal insisted that "every Arab country has the right to choose the form of Government it deems suitable to its conditions."[123] These and other statements by the Jordanian government did not have their intended effect, for the announcement of the unity agreement unleashed another wave of protests. The Jordanian Parliament passed a resolution demanding unity, and it appeared as if there would be a replay of 1958, though this time without an Iraq to forge a fictitious and safe union.[124] This time, however, Hussein was rescued not by the British but by his nemeses.

The tide of unification was obstructed by the signatories to the recent unity agreement. Iraq, Syria, and Egypt hardly had a honeymoon. Immediately following the agreement the Syrian government expelled the Nasserites from its inner circle because of personal and unionist politics.[125] As the animosity raged, it became increasingly apparent that this was a marriage heading quickly toward divorce. Then, after months of political hostilities, on July 22 Nasser announced Egypt's withdrawal from the agreement and delivered a scathing attack on Damascus.[126] This would not be the end of Egypt's accusations against its ex-partners, for during the next few months it would repeat the theme that Syria and Iraq were using the cloak of Arab unity to move against their domestic opposition and to extinguish true Arabist aspirations.[127] To add insult to injury Nasser published a transcript of the failed talks as a way of demonstrating his correctness and the shallow Arabism of his rivals. Although the Syrian and Iraqi regimes accused Nasser of doctoring the transcripts, they were highly mortified by the image of their excessive deference to Nasser.

The demise of the unity agreement was a blow to Syria and Iraq. Although the Egyptian regime could survive politically without the agreement, Syria's and Iraq's domestic popularity depended on this ideological prop. To shore up their regimes both Iraq and Syria lashed out in every direction possible: they attacked Nasser and used Nasserism as a code word for conservatism, made preparations for their unification, wrapped themselves in the symbols of union among the three, and insisted that they were the true carriers of pure Arabism.[128] Significantly, the Syrian Ba'athists began to emphasize that true unity can be achieved only after a struggle by and among separate movements that reflect the residue of regional differences. Through such doctrinal maneuvering the Syrian regime attempted to justify its conflict with Nasser, distinguish its brand of Arabism, and prepare the way for a union with Iraq and without Egypt.[129] Iraq too used similar ideological devices and political instruments to deflect domestic criticism, stressing its singularity and the differences between Arab countries.[130] To recover their prestige and to satisfy the minimal expectations that might be had for two Arab nationalist parties, on October 8 Syria and Iraq announced their desire for unification of their two "regions" by beginning with a treaty of military unity. Putting aside their rivalry with Nasser in the spirit of public relations, Iraqi and Syrian officials flew to Cairo to encourage Nasser to join their compact.[131]

Nasser, though somewhat alarmed that Syria and Iraq were nearing formal unification after years of traditional Egyptian opposition to this outcome, declined to join.[132] Cairo portrayed the agreement as mere theatrics, nothing more than an attempt by both regimes to shore up their domestic situations,[133] and accused their leaders of worse:

Michel Aflaq [the leader of the Syrian Ba'ath] must have visited an ear specialist in London who has been able to restore his sense of hearing. As a result the little philosopher has heard the Arab people's curses. . . . However, London and Paris reports have said that Michel Aflaq did not meet with eye, ear, and throat specialists, but that he had met with British and French political experts interested in seeing Aflaq grow more deaf, more blind, and more dumb.[134]

Nasser was exploiting the fact that Aflaq had a first name that was hardly Arab and was phonetically tied to France; in doing so Nasser was coupling Aflaq and Syria to imperialism.[135] But his taunts only aggravated the more injurious act of not joining the unity agreement. A unity agreement without Nasser was not much to celebrate. In contrast to the tripartite agreement in April, which brought the crowd to its feet in Damascus and Baghdad and rioting in Jordan, the Iraqi-Syrian agreement was greeted by polite applause in Damascus and Baghdad and quiet in Jordan.[136]

The failure of these unity talks and the subsequent public airing of the radical laundry damaged the desirability, legitimacy, and overall appeal of unification.[137] Symbolic exchanges and symbolic competition drove several Arab leaders to toss their states into the unification ring; symbolic exchanges and competition encouraged these same leaders to retrieve them. They talked their way into a unity drive that they privately lamented but to which they were rhetorically committed. Each leader's response was to present himself as a sincere believer and his rivals as using Arabism to their own cynical and self-interested advantage. Hurling accusations at each other that they once reserved for King Hussein, they provided direct evidence for the growing sentiment that Arab leaders were using Arabism either to maintain their domestic power or to extend their regional influence.

The goal of unification had been soiled by its architects, and Arab politics now began to have a different look and texture. According to Tahseen Bashir, a Nasser spokesperson during the 1960s, the failure of the unity talks meant that unification was now "gone with the wind."[138] Many who once counted themselves among the unity faithful now began questioning the utility if not ultimate futility of pursuing unification—at least with these governments, with these means, at this time. Although many Arab leaders still mouthed the words of unification, from now on they became less quick to portray their military, political, and economic agreements as a step toward unification; indeed, the number of concrete proposals toward this end now declined precipitously. The search for the Arab community contributed to and bred hostility, rivalry, and fragmentation; consequently, Arab leaders began to conduct and orient themselves in a different mannner.

In such an environment Arab leaders began to rethink the relationship between the state and Arab unity. One immediate outcome was that Arab officials began to forward interpretations of Arab nationalism that were consistent with sovereignty and that were now well-received. King Hussein now had an easier time defending his definition of an Arab nationalism that was consistent with sovereignty and based on "equality."[139] Hussein wrote that "my own concept of Arab nationalism . . . is different from what I understand President Nasser's to be. If I interpret his aims properly, he believes that political unity and Arab nationalism are synonymous. Evidently he also believes that Arab nationalism can only be identified with a particular brand of Arab unity. I disagree. This view can only lead, as it has in the past, to more disunity." Conversely, Hussein believed that "Arab nationalism can only survive through complete equality. It is in our power to unite on all important issues, to organize in every respect and to dispel friction between us. . . . Let all this be undertaken through an active, respected Arab League, in which . . . danger of domination by any member of the family would be eliminated."[140] After the highly charged and ultimately dispiriting unity debate, this understanding of Arab nationalism now seemed less conservative and more practical. And although many Arab intellectuals and leaders who were closely associated with Nasser's version of Arab nationalism hardly embraced Hussein publicly, they did echo many of the tenets that he was espousing. Indeed, Hussein gained some support from an unlikely source—Nasser. Nasser had never championed unification, had entered into the UAR and the unity talks with suspicion and concern, and left these talks deciding to expunge unification from his concept of Arab unity.[141]

Unification in practice left a residue of particularism and growing support for a conception of Arab nationalism that was consistent with sovereignty. "The impact of the unity failures on the thinking of Arab leaders," recalled one Nasser aide, "was to shift the concept of unity to something more practical and desirable like cooperation."[142] Their own strategic and symbolic interactions moved them toward a new understanding of Arab unity, left them less vulnerable to symbolic sanctions on matters of unification because of these recent experiences, and less able to use the themes of unification for symbolic capital and as a source of symbolic sanctions. This did not exhaust the possibilities and opportunities for symbolic competition, as would become evident in the next few years. But it did mean that Arab states had begun to converge on a meaning of Arab unity that was consistent with sovereignty and that left more room to distinguish their local identities from the Arab national identities.

The Debate About Israel

Since the Suez War the Arab-Israeli conflict had taken a backseat to the acrimonious debate among Arab states about their organizing principles. But now that would change. The backdrop was Syria's attempt to reclaim its prestige after the failed unity talks. In the fall of 1963 Syria began raising the matter of Israel's plans to pump water from the Jordan River for its irrigation projects. The Arab states were on record as opposing the Israeli scheme, and Syria now had the perfect foil for embarrassing Nasser; after all, Nasser could outbid Syria on unification, but Egypt had no such leverage in the Arab-Israeli conflict.[143]

With Israel insisting that it would carry out its irrigation plan, the Arab states in opposition, and Syria chiding Nasser for being weak on Israel, the Arab-Israeli conflict careened toward a major crisis. Nasser watched with some alarm, for Syria's accusations were quite effective at painting him as a conservative, and he feared that Syria's belligerent rhetoric might cause an unwanted war. On December 16, 1963, the Cairo weekly *Rose el Youssef* published an article that claimed that "unstable" Syria, "unfriendly" Jordan, and "isolationist" Saudi Arabia were trying to stab Egypt in the back by involving it in a war with Israel.[144] The article signaled that Nasser had no intention of being manipulated into a war that was not of his choosing. But he still had to address Syria's rather pointed accusations and control its foreign policy actions lest he suffer a loss of prestige and/or find himself at war with Israel.

THE SUMMIT SYSTEM

Nasser's response was a major diplomatic and political coup: on December 23 he invited his fellow Arab leaders to come to Cairo to discuss the Arab-Israeli conflict.[145] By reaching out to all Arab states, both radical and conservative, Nasser accomplished a number of important goals. First, he could use this multilateral mechanism to quiet the Syrians while maintaining his prestige and leadership.[146] By bringing the Arab states into a multilateral framework, insisting on collectivism, and adhering to the principle of the "Arab consensus," he could better control Syria's foreign policy.[147] Second, the failed unity talks left him bloodied, and Israel provided a useful way to reclaim his leadership. Third, Israel was the perfect vehicle for forging a détente between Egypt and the conservative Arab states that he had taunted and threatened for the past decade. "Having repeatedly failed in attempts to impose his will on other Arab rulers," observed Kamal Salibi, "President Nasser was starting to present himself as no more than first among equals."[148] Fourth, finding some common ground with the conservative Arab states in general and Saudi Arabia in particular might help resolve the Yemen war and enable Nasser to shift resources from abroad to more pressing domestic issues.[149]

The era of summitry symbolized an important change in Arab politics. The growing particularism in Arab politics, partly a result of the failed integration attempts, produced a new form of organization in Arab politics: summit meetings. Whereas Arab states had been fighting each other for the past several years over whether Arab nationalism was consistent with sovereignty, now Nasser, the symbolic leader of Arabism, signaled that he was less interested in this debate, had reconciled himself to a statism of sorts (though he did not necessarily consider other Arab leaders his peers), and wanted to find some common ground. By inviting the conservative Arab states to Cairo, Nasser was conceding that coexistence should define inter-Arab politics, and coexistence was tantamount to regime survival.[150] King Hussein quickly recognized that Nasser's invitation to Cairo was not about Israel but about a new phase in Arab politics, and he enthusiastically accepted a proposal that he viewed as vindicating his interpretation of Arab nationalism.[151] Good news from Hussein's perspective meant bad news from the Syrians': this era of summitry meant isolation for Syria, which wanted neither a return to the spirit of unification nor this détente between the radical and the conservative states.[152] In general, focusing on Israel, a common threat, enabled Arab leaders to temporarily overlook their differences, represented a shift in how Arab leaders displayed their credentials and where they accumulated symbolic capital, and provided a vehicle for altering the definition of and debate about Arab nationalism and the Arab national identity.

The Arab states held three summits before the Arab-Israeli War of 1967—in January and September 1964 and in September 1965. The first two summits focused on the Arab-Israeli conflict and creating new mechanisms for furthering the collective Arab effort; the third continued that debate about the Arab states' collective response to the Israeli challenge but also spent considerable energy institutionalizing a meaning of Arab nationalism that was consistent with sovereignty. More to the point, the agenda of these summits confirmed and reinforced three related and emerging trends in inter-Arab politics: the decline of unification, the emphasis on the Arab-Israeli conflict for defining Arabism, and a move to harmonize the relationship between Arabism and sovereignty.

The decline of unification.   The theme of unification was hardly heard during these summits.[153] Although Syria and Iraq would occasionally suggest that all-Arab institutions were the wellspring of unification, the public speeches and news conferences gave little attention to unification and instead wrapped their multilateral proposals in the Arab-Israeli conflict. The lone unity agreement concluded during this period came after the second summit between the Egypt and Iraq.[154] But Iraqi president Abd al-Salaam Aref was notably reserved as he claimed that cultural and educational unity would precede economic unity, with political unity trailing behind.[155] In contrast to the region-wide enthusiasm that greeted the short-lived unification agreement between Egypt, Syria, and Iraq in 1963, the announcement of the Egypt-Iraqi union produced few accolades and much disdain. The Lebanese paper *Al-Hayat* characterized the agreement as a "personal plan" that would be difficult to implement because "the establishment of a constitutional political unity between the two countries requires the presence of two constitutions. Where are the two constitutions?" Although Nasser was wiser than he was six years earlier and recognized the difficulty of achieving unity, he could not back down because to do so "would be a worse setback than 17 April 1962 [a reference to Egyptian intervention in Yemen]. Still, if Iraq wants to orbit around Egypt, Egypt minds little so long as it does not require getting involved in Iraq like it got involved in Yemen."[156] Unification was disappearing from the political map. Few Arab leaders seemed willing to expend much energy working toward unification or even draping their policies in its rhetoric.

The emerging centrality of the Arab-Israeli conflict.   The Arab-Israeli conflict dominated the summit meetings. Israel, not unification, now became the vehicle for displaying Arab nationalist credentials. The conflict in fact now served to allocate the labels of radical and conservative. While Syria was ridiculing Nasser for turning his back on radical politics to consort with conservative Arab states, Nasser defended the conservatism of the summits by saying that "three years ago . . . there was not even talk about Palestine" and that these summits had elevated the issue to its proper place. Throughout an interview with the Egyptian newspaper *Al-Hurriyah*, Nasser insisted that the "ultimate Arab objective" was the liberation of Palestine, declining to discuss or comment on the issue of unification, which only recently had defined his foreign policy and his radicalism.[157]

But Nasser was equally insistent that any movement on the Arab-Israeli front, unlike the near carelessness that characterized his career in unification, be carefully orchestrated and prepared lest the Arab states find themselves in an unwanted war. Recall that one of Nasser's principal reasons for devising the summit system was to fashion a multilateral mechanism to control Syrian foreign policy and to ensure that its unilateralist impulses did not become the Arab states' nightmare. Nasser knew that the conservative Arab states would happily play along. King Hussein, for instance, predicted that success on the Arab-Israeli front required a slow, cautious, and careful approach; there are no shortcuts, he said, and inter-Arab differences must be settled before concrete action can be undertaken.[158] In general, the summits were a victory for Nasser, enabling him to demonstrate resolve on the Arab-Israeli front without actually confronting Israel, and to control the more spirited members.[159]

To further the collective Arab cause the Arab states created two new instruments: the Unified Arab Command (UAC), which was announced with great fanfare but had negligible influence, and the Palestinian Liberation Organization (PLO), which was expected to have little autonomy but unexpectedly transformed inter-Arab politics and the Arab-Israeli conflict.[160] Nasser was the principal architect of the Unified Arab Command, claiming that to stand resolute against the Israeli threat required "unified military action" and a joint command.[161] After considerable debate the participants approved the UAC and handed Egypt the general responsibility of organizing other Arab states' contributions.[162] The UAC remained a paper institution. A central sticking point and the subject of intense debate at the September 1964 summit concerned whether the UAC would have access to all the front-line Arab states.[163] Although Iraq and Egypt insisted that Arab states be allowed to transfer their forces from one country to another, Lebanon and Jordan were hardly excited about an all-Arab army under Nasser's direction stationed on their soil.[164] This was, after all, the same Nasser who only two years earlier had called for the removal of the Lebanese and Jordanian regimes. In the end the Arab states failed to unite and coordinate their militaries, but few of them mourned this failure.[165]

The more enduring creation of the first summit was the Palestinian Liberation Organization. Since 1948 the Arab states had ostensibly represented the Palestinians, and the Arab states had accrued much symbolic capital from that status. Nasser's ebbing popularity was a principal reason behind his decision to sponsor the PLO; he believed that being credited with the formation of a Palestinian organization would hand him much prestige and enable him to better control the tempo of the confrontation with Israel.[166] Hussein, traditionally opposed to the establishment of an all-embracing or-

ganization for the Palestinians that might claim the West Bank and authority over Jordan's Palestinian population, now consented because he wanted to
remain within the Arab consensus, believed that this threadbare organization posed little threat and was designed to keep the Arab-Israeli conflict
quiet, and might support Jordan's custodial role vis-à-vis the Palestinians.[167]
Hussein's hopes were not groundless, for the PLO was designed to be a conservative institution controlled by the Arab states: the PLO was created with
the understanding that it would not demand the unification of and would
respect the sovereignty of the Arab states. The general opinion at the summit was that, by creating the PLO but by denying it any real power, the Arab
states were communicating their readiness for action when they had nothing of the kind in mind.[168]

The Arab states had designed the PLO as a Potemkin village, but its leader,
Ahmad al-Shuqayri had greater plans. Although initially thought to be
something of a demagogue with little organizational or leadership skills, he
soon began irritating the Arab states with his rather far-reaching and ambitious proposals that were designed to hand the PLO greater resources and
freedom of action. At the second summit he demanded that the Arab states
increase their bilateral assistance and impose special taxes on such com-
modities as matches and movie tickets to help finance Palestinian activities.
The Arab states were "annoyed."[169] The third summit rejected the PLO's demand that it be allowed to recruit, train, and arm Palestinians outside the
Jordanian government's authority. This upstart organization, initially established as an instrument of the Arab states, was quickly becoming more autonomous and potentially more threatening to state sovereignty.[170] But for
the time being the PLO played the role of the dutiful client and restricted its
actions to agitating the Arab states for concrete action rather than undertaking those actions itself.

Maintaining the Arab consensus also required reinforcing the collective
stance prohibiting relations with Israel. Since the 1950 Arab League meeting
the Arab states' policy had been to not negotiate with Israel. They had observed this religiously until April 21, 1965, when Tunisian president Habib
ibn Ali Bourguiba stated that the Arabs might recognize Israel within the
boundaries of the UN partition resolution of November 29, 1947. Bourguiba went further than any Arab leader since King Abdullah in acknowledging Israel's existence, and he was doing so as Arab leaders were increasingly
using Israel to exhibit their credentials. By hinting that a peaceful settlement might be found and by suggesting that Arab states should work as
hard on the political as on the military front, Bourguiba was widely inter-

preted as taking a unilateral stand, perhaps even offering an olive branch to the Israelis.[171]

Nearly all Arab leaders quickly and roundly rebuffed Bourguiba's statement, accusing him of everything from conspiring with Israel to being a misguided fool. The Syrian delegate to the Arab summit portrayed Bourguiba as the "sick man" of the Arab world. "As a doctor," he said, "a person who was inflicted by a contagious disease should be isolated." The delegate demanded that the Arab states unequivocally declare Bourguiba's statements a "deviation from the Arab agreement" and repledge their adherence to the Arab League resolutions.[172] The PLO was equally incensed, viewing Bourguiba's statements as challenging its claim that it was the "first and last authority regarding the Palestinian question."[173] The May session of the Arab League considered Tunisia's expulsion but decided not to. The point had been made.[174]

Bourguiba, now ostracized from Arab politics, elected not to attend the next summit meeting in September in Casablanca and instead broadcast his views and the reason for his absence. Bourguiba professed that he had been unfairly and unjustifiably attacked regarding his statements on Israel. He then assailed "the mouthpieces of Cairo," accused Nasser of being committed to Arabism only so long as it served his interest and undermined his rivals', and ended with a spirited defense of sovereignty as the basis of inter-Arab relations and unity. It is worth quoting at length from various parts of the speech:

> There was not an existing Arab regime which was not abused and attacked, or whose overthrow was not attempted if it did not show submission or if it did not make an effort to escape the Egyptian orbit. . . . What Arab State has not uncovered a conspiracy engineered from Cairo? What Arab State has not sought the assistance of Egyptian teachers without regretting it and without being compelled to expel them as a result of what they have done to cause sedition and to mobilize public opinion to declare a revolution.
>
> Cairo only regards the leaders of [other] Arab countries as rulers for a time waiting to die. . . . That is why Cairo only deals with the States by regarding them as imaginary structures, semi-empty and lacking the hidden essence which generates prestige and brings forth respect. Arab rulers are regarded as either agents of imperialism or stooges of Cairo, and they cannot escape this inevitable fate.
>
> We believe that the [current] crisis of confidence has resulted from the way Egypt looks at Arab unity. The Arabs are not the only ones who are a homogenous group in culture and history. There are many groups like this

in the world. . . . Unity will not last or bear fruit unless it is established on free choice and not imposed by various kinds of pressure, suppression, and bargaining.

We therefore think that the only method of establishing co-operation between us is the method of free dialogue on the basis of mutual respect for national sovereignties.

Tunisia announces its rejection of all interference in its policy, whether that policy concerns its internal system or its external relations. It regards these spheres as the essence of sovereignty and it cannot accept any dispute on them. . . . We believe that the safest basis for cooperation among States is that each should concern itself with what concerns it and that co-operation should take place in common in common spheres.

We sincerely hope that the meeting of the Arab Kings and Heads results in affirming these basic principles on which the Arab League was established.[175]

Bourguiba's extraordinary speech represented the culmination of a decade of sentiments and sedimented resentments concerning Egypt's pan-Arabism.[176]

Dovetailing with themes of the failed unification attempts that were still fresh in everyone's minds, Bourguiba claimed that the death of pan-Arabism had come at the hands of its architects and that it should be replaced by an Arab nationalism that was consistent with sovereignty. Bourguiba's speech, then, was noteworthy in two respects: he was on the defensive because he was seen as outside the Arab consensus on the Arab-Israeli conflict and he was paying dearly for it, and he took the offensive by accusing Nasser of using Arabism to create mayhem and to insist that sovereignty govern inter-Arab relations.

The move toward sovereignty.   Whether the Arab states were moved by Bourguiba's diagnosis of the Arab condition or not, his prescription for recognizing sovereignty defined the 1965 summit's central resolutions.[177] The concluding resolutions reinforced an interpretation of Arabism that was consistent with sovereignty. Five of the six principles adopted under the theme of "strengthening Arab solidarity" referred explicitly or implicitly to the norms of sovereignty and the society of states. Point 2 pledged to "respect the sovereignty of each of the Arab states and their existing regimes in accordance with their constitutions and laws, and to refrain from interfering in their internal affairs." Point 3 vowed to "observe the principles and ethics of political asylum in accordance with the principles of international law and conventions."

Significantly, points four, five, and six were directed at using national media for good and not for ill, including a decision to "keep discussion objective and criticism constructive in dealing with Arab questions and to end the campaigns of suspicion and slander in the press, radios, and other information media." Because Arab leaders used symbolic technologies to undermine each other from within and to control each other's foreign policies, their move toward détente included an attempt to disarm those weapons that counted most: their media. Thus it was not surprising that the Arab states trumpeted as one of the summit's major accomplishments the decision to halt the media campaigns, because these campaigns "have been a fundamental sign of the disunity of Arab ranks, and not just a mere sign for they have moreover constituted an effective factor in widening the gap at every point of difference."[178] Many Arab leaders highlighted the importance of the resolutions on sovereignty and mudslinging as representing major moves toward stability and détente.[179]

The summit system symbolized and confirmed that Arab states were converging on the principle of sovereignty to organize their relations; many of its resolutions were designed to guide the foreign policies of Arab states toward sovereignty and away from unwanted intrusions in their domestic affairs. The collapse of the 1963 unification talks had encouraged Arab states to step closer to a meaning of Arab nationalism that was consistent with the territorial status quo. Unification had already run its course by late 1963 when Syria elevated the Israeli threat to embarrass Nasser because the unification issue no longer served that purpose. Nasser responded to the failure of unification by embracing a more state-centered view of Arab nationalism; he responded to Syria's challenge by devising the summit system as a multilateral control on Syrian's actions. The proposals designed to join their military forces to confront the Israeli threat carefully avoided any hint that they represented a step toward unification; the decision to try to stop the mudslinging was designed to arrest the symbolic technologies that Arab leaders feared most in their competitive interactions. But soon the summit system would collapse under the weight of its contradictions and spawn a new, and more dangerous, round of symbolic competition.

THE END OF THE ERA OF SUMMITRY AND THE SYMBOLIC DANCE TO WAR

Arab leaders were increasingly demonstrating and defining their commitment to Arabism around the Israeli threat; an implication was that they were highly vulnerable to symbolic sanctioning and sensitive to the charge that they were not doing enough for the cause of Palestine. The problem for Nasser was that the summit system was designed to encourage conservatism rather than radicalism, and his ability to maintain the system depended on the willingness of the other Arab states to play their parts. Therefore, when the era of summitry ended after two short years, its undoing was largely the result of the very forces and contradictions that had led Nasser to propose the summit system at the outset.[180]

The contradiction that proved to be the summit system's undoing was Nasser's attempt to use the summit meetings as a multilateral device to control Syria's Israeli policy and Syria's desire to use the Israeli stick to bolster its credentials and embarrass Nasser. Two events brought this tension to a breaking point. The first was an Israeli attack on May 13, 1965, on one of Syria's diverting stations. At the January 1964 summit the Arab states had resolved to establish a series of stations to divert the sources of the Jordan River in response to an Israeli plan for a large-scale diversion project. The Israelis threatened to forcibly dismantle such stations, and the Arab states resolved to meet that action collectively. A matter left unresolved by the Arab states, however, was when the host of a diverting station could act unilaterally to respond to a "minor" act of aggression and when an Israeli act would be considered "major," thus requiring that Arab states to collectively determine the proper response. The May 1965 Israeli attack magnified the contradiction between Syria's need to get the Arab states' backing to respond to Israel and the Arab states' decision that each state was responsible for responding to "minor" incidents. Syria presented its case in late May at a conference of the Arab premiers, but they rejected the plea for support. A bitter Syria subsequently launched a full-scale propaganda attack on Nasser, proclaiming that it was ready, willing, and able to confront Israel in regard to the Jordan River or any other issue but that Nasser was hiding behind the summit resolutions to avoid a war with Israel.[181]

This was exactly what Nasser was doing, but he could not very well admit it. At a meeting of Palestinian National Congress in June Nasser attempted to refute the Syrian charges by insisting that Arab states must coordinate their policies before confronting Israel.[182] A united Arab army, he said, required unified Arab action, which was difficult at the moment because of significant inter-Arab differences. As troubling as this reality was, Nasser confided, it was an improvement over the early 1960s when no Arab summit, no Arab resolutions, and no statements of concrete action existed. How should the Arabs proceed? Through revolutionary action. But, he emphasized and qualified without a hint of irony, this must be cautious and careful revolutionary action. Defending his go-slow policy against Syria's charges of weakness, Nasser raised a theme that would define his position toward the Arab-Israeli conflict for the next two years:

We must first of all have a plan. If, for example, an aggression is committed against Syria, do I attack Israel? If the case is so, then Israel can set for me the time at which to attack. Why? Just because it commits an aggression and hits one or two tractors, I am to attack Israel the second day. Is this logical and sound talk? It is we who will choose the time of the battle. It is we who will assess our position. It is we who will fight our battle.[183]

Nasser feared that the same dynamics and vulnerability to symbolic sanctions that had dragged him into an unwanted federation with Syria in 1958 might now force him into an unwanted war with Israel.[184] The Arab summits became the perfect device for sitting on Syria, but Syria might eventually engage in unilateral action that not only challenged the summit system but also threatened to call Nasser's bluff. Symbolic entrapment was an ever-present possibility.

That was exactly what happened. A coup in Syria in February 1966 brought to power the most radical regime in Syrian history, according to Patrick Seale.[185] Since the failed unity attempts the Syrian government had been engaging in various political and ideological moves designed to bolster its self-image as a sovereign independent state. It is unknown whether the Ba'ath was successful in its stab at legitimacy by posing as an equivalent and as an alternative to Nasser, but the party was able to secure its political power by controlling the army and suppressing the Nasserites. In any event, the declining appeal of the unionist idea and of Nasser's leadership meant that although Egypt's "ill will remained a source of embarrassment for the Ba'ath, it no longer posed a grave threat to its rule."[186] A more confident and radical Syria spelled bad news for Nasser.

The new regime explicitly framed past Arab summits as selling out the Arab nation and the cause of Palestine and as offering little more than feeble excuses for inaction.[187] Less beholden to the notion of an all-Arab consensus if this meant conservatism, and more interested in establishing its independence and flushing Nasser from behind the screen of multilateralism, the Syrian government pressed its point by encouraging fedayeen raids into Israel. Although Nasser feared that Syria's provocative actions might be the Arab states' undoing, he was more alarmed by this challenge to his Arab credentials. As a result, he played into Syria's strategy: he publicly sided with Syria and began attacking the conservative Arab states. This "public declaration of war" made it virtually impossible for the Arab states to convene another summit.[188] "The era of summitry ended officially when the Arab League announced on July 22 the indefinite postponement of the fourth summit (due to convene at Algiers on 5 September)." Understandably, Saudi Arabia and Jordan, the two countries that gained most from the series of summits and the suspension of ideological hostilities, were most upset by its demise.[189]

With the summit period over, Syria and Egypt now began playing a dangerous game of symbolic competition. Syria's earlier challenges had coaxed Nasser away from the multilateral mechanism that he had designed to control it, and now that Syria had drawn him out into the open, it continued to turn up the heat. Israel's actions played right into Syria's hands, for it faithfully retaliated for every fedayeen action, demonstrating that Syria was in no position to defend itself and increasing the pressure on Egypt to come to Syria's defense. While Nasser watched in horror because he feared that Syria's actions might precipitate a war with Israel, he was equally fearful of confirming Syria's charge that he was indistinguishable from the conservative Arab states and weak on Palestine. Nasser, still seeking to control Syrian policy but with the summit format no longer available, finally established diplomatic relations with the new Syrian regime and signed a joint defense agreement in November 1966.[190] The agreement, according to Egyptian general Mohamed Abdel el-Gamasy, was formed in the absence of trust and never led to any military coordination.[191] But given the apparent motivations of the Syrians and the Egyptians, the lack of military coordination reflected the nonstrategic basis of the agreement. Syria's motives, according to Samir Mutawi, were not to "revenge the injustices done to the Palestinians but in order to gain supremacy over Nasser as leader of the Arabs."[192] Motivated by a desire to control Syria's actions, Nasser had accepted the risky wager that the alliance would leave him in control of Syria rather than vice versa, and Nasser lost the bet.[193] Syria continued its provocative ways, increasing the prospect of war and forcing Nasser to keep pace with Syria's taunts or stand accused of being weak on Palestine.[194]

Jordan watched this "dangerous game of brinkmanship" anxiously, aware that it too would be forced to keep pace or suffer a loss of prestige.[195] Syria and Egypt accused Hussein of being weak on Arabism, made worse by Israel's retaliation against Jordan for the fedayeen raids. Israel launched a particularly deadly reprisal on the West Bank village of Samu on November 13, 1966. The casualties were not only a village and dozens of soldiers and civilians but also Jordan's credibility regarding its ability to defend its territory and protect the Palestinians. Always ready to embarrass Hussein, Cairo and Damascus accused him of following in his grandfather's footsteps and failing to protect the Palestinians.[196] The combination of the Israeli attack and the inflammatory broadcasts contributed to rioting among the Palestinians for several weeks; some Palestinian figures even declared the West Bank an independent Palestinian state, and the government imposed martial law to take back the streets.[197] The consequences were not only political but also strategic. The raid convinced Hussein that Israel did not differentiate between Arab states; that the raid that led to Israel's attack on Samu had originated from Syria was well known, but Israel was perceived as preferring to target the West Bank, because attacking Syria might have greater military consequences. The raid persuaded King Hussein that his credentials and Jordan's security were on the line.[198]

The first few months of 1967 were relatively quiet, but in April a series of incidents and maneuvers began between Israel and Syria that signaled that the region was spinning toward war. On April 7 a dogfight between Israel and Syria over the Golan led to the downing of several Syrian MiGs. The remainder of the month remained relatively quiet, but events escalated considerably in early May. Perhaps because of an internal crisis Syria began publishing reports of a "Zionist-reactionary plot" against Syria.[199] Attending such reports were highly dramatic and public pleas for Egypt to assist Syria and to live up to its Arab obligations. Jordan also unleashed a media campaign against Nasser, accusing him of doing little to help his brethren and allies.[200]

Suspiciously silent on these Israeli-Syrian developments, Nasser found himself increasingly pressured to take dramatic action to support his alliance partner and to maintain his credentials. Nasser was caught between the symbolic and the strategic, and he sacrificed the latter. "Nasser's concern began not with Israel but with Syria, and pointed eventually not to Sharm al-Shaikh, still less to Tel-Aviv, but to the chanceries and streets of the Arab world."[201] Jordan and Syria kept daring him to show his mettle and to stop hiding behind the UN flag, and Nasser accepted each and every dare. On May 14 he sent his army into the Sinai, and on May 22 he closed the Strait of Tiran. Nasser's military advisers cautioned him against taking such actions for fear of provoking Israel and tempting an unwanted war. But Nasser accepted such risks "as a means to end Arab opposition to him, and to maintain his popularity and high esteem in the Arab world."[202] That he took this risk can be properly attributed to his beliefs that Israel would ultimately not launch a preemptive strike, that the combined Arab forces represented a sufficient retaliatory force, and, ultimately, that his Arab credentials were at stake.

Symbolic competition also informed King Hussein's decision to cast his lot with Egypt and Syria and go to war with Israel. The Jordanian cabinet held a fierce debate about how it should position itself in the war climate.

Jordanian official Wasfi al-Tal was nearly alone in arguing against trusting Nasser, claiming that war would bring disaster to Jordan and could cost the king Jerusalem and the West Bank.[203] Few shared Tal's pessimistic appraisal of the Arab states' military capabilities. But ultimately it was Arabism that led Hussein to embark on a path that would bring him into war with Israel. The Syrian and Egyptian campaign against Hussein had been highly effective, stirring up the Jordanian population in general and the Palestinians in particular. If Jordan stayed out of the war, Hussein would have had a difficult time containing the inevitable public outcry.[204] Hussein ultimately decided that he would rather take his chances with the Israelis than he would his own population. If he went to war with Israel, the most he would lose would be the West Bank and Jerusalem, but if he stayed on the sidelines he would probably lose his crown and his country.[205]

These calculations help to explain King Hussein's somewhat curious decision to cast his lot with Egypt and Syria when he flew to Cairo and signed a joint defense pact with Egypt on May 30.[206] Hussein was now in league with the same states that had repeatedly attempted to undermine his regime over the years and in the recent past. But Hussein flew to Cairo because of symbolic rather than strategic considerations. A palace adviser explained: "To meet with Nasser may seem strange when one considers the insults and abuse which Radio Cairo had been hurling at the Hashemite throne for the past year; nonetheless, it would have been impossible for us to justify our remaining aloof from so momentous a matter which engaged the entire Arab world."[207] "If we were isolated from the mainstream of Arab politics," reflected former Prime Minister Zaid Rifai, "we would be an easy target."[208] Jordanian King Abdullah prodded Egypt into a war that it did not want in 1948, and Egypt returned the favor to Jordanian King Hussein in 1967.

Symbolic competition propelled Arab leaders to commit to policies that they thought were unwise strategically but necessary politically.[209] This was a war that few Arab military officials had prepared for or Arab leaders wanted, but it was a war that they stumbled into and got. Their private thoughts became public soon after the end of the war. Arab intellectuals and officials began linking the very dynamics that led the Arab states into this military debacle to earlier episodes that also had unwanted outcomes; as they saw it, the 1967 war was an extreme example of the ills that defined Arab politics. In such commentaries Arab political elites left little doubt that they found few strategic imperatives in their recent war with Israel, but they did find much evidence of inter-Arab symbolic exchanges and political calculations that had left them all worse off.

Arab officials and intellectuals could look back to the events since 1955 and recall a period that began with promise and assuredness and ended with a string of failures and disappointments. The years after the Baghdad Pact seemed to be one steady march toward greater integration among Arab states. By 1958 revolution was in the air, Arab nationalism appeared to be an unstoppable tide, and the demand for unification was growing. To be sure, many Arab officials privately feared these developments, which were likely to leave them more vulnerable to each other's policies and maneuverings than ever, but they found themselves under pressure from their societies and their rivals to keep up appearances. The result was that Arab nationalism appeared to be a movement whose time had come.

What halted the unstoppable tide of Arab nationalism were the same Arab leaders who proclaimed themselves its guardian. But it was not as if Arab leaders got together and constructed a new set of arrangements and institutions that secured their states against Arab nationalism. This was not to be a repeat of the developments that led to the League of Arab States. Rather, Arab officials responded to their ideological excesses by accusing each other of various crimes and insincerities, which led to a normative deficit and greater suspicion that these leaders could not foster Arabism at this time under these conditions. Unification vanished from the agenda, and Arab states more fully converged on the norms of sovereignty and accepted the territorial status quo. Palestine now became the issue on which Arab leaders established their credentials and questioned those of their rivals. The events leading to the 1967 war were only more evidence, as if any was needed, that symbolic competition could have cataclysmic consequences.

6

Sovereignty and Statism, 1967–1990

The June war delivered a defeat that only millennialists would have predicted—in six days Israel captured Jerusalem and the West Bank from Jordan, the Sinai from Egypt, and the Golan Heights from Syria. The residues of the defeat, many of which would become clearer and more dramatic with time, were public, undeniable, and touched nearly all who were in any way associated with it. Even before the war had formally ended on June 10, Nasser announced his resignation and took full responsibility. But he returned to power after throngs of Egyptians coaxed him back, unwilling to have the Israelis claim another casualty of the war. Yet there was no hiding his devastation. "I can't forget what I went through during the first few days after the war in June," Nasser would later recall. "There is no doubt that what happened in 1967 has affected us all psychologically, morally, and materially."[1] Conservative and radical leaders alike were humiliated; those who participated and those who sat on the sidelines shared in the blame and suffered the repercussions.

One immediate consequence was a new period of malaise, self-criticism, and self-doubt.[2] The Moroccan historian Abdullah Laroui and the Syrian scholar Sadeq al-Azm found in the defeat lessons for where Arab society had gone wrong and places for the possibility of renewal. For some the road had led to defeat because Arab states and societies were not radical enough—they had made too many compromises along the way. In Egypt a student movement appeared to challenge the government's credentials. The Palestinians became radicalized, and various factions, most notably George Habash's Popular Front for the Liberation of Palestine, came to the fore; many Arabs now viewed the Palestinians as the potential vanguard of the revolution, or at least the embodiment of Arab nationalism. For others the radicals were now on trial and the jury was Islam: the road to ruin had been paved by secularism, because Arab-Islamic societies had turned their backs on tradition and religion. Islamist movements, on the defensive in the region since the imposition of the mandate system, began to reassert themselves in political life. The defeat caused one and all to rethink the past, present, and future.

The 1967 Arab-Israeli War inaugurated a new chapter in the debate about the desired regional order; the debate was shaped by the decline of Arabism and the faint beat of statism. Arabism quickly became a whipping boy for the defeat. And not without good reason. Arab leaders taunted and challenged each other in the name of Arab nationalism as they beat a path toward war. Against his better judgment, all military estimates, and the belief that Syria's Arabism would lead nowhere good, Nasser undertook a series of actions that he knew risked an unwanted war. All in the name of Arabism. Fearing that he had more to lose by standing on the sidelines than by declaring war on Israel, King Hussein had flown to Cairo on the eve of war to announce his stand with Nasser and to sign a joint defense treaty. All in the name of Arabism. And Syria could be blamed for having begun the miserable episode by intentionally and publicly embarrassing Nasser by challenging his credentials. All in the name of Arabism. Arabism spurred Arab leaders to engage in escalating actions that they believed were militarily foolish but politically expedient, outbid one another to the point of an unwanted war, and divert resources from the Arab-Israeli conflict and toward inter-Arab feuds. "For the first time, Arab leadership suddenly ceased to be a plausible ambition," wrote Malcolm Kerr. "There could hardly be competition for prestige when there was no prestige remaining. The old ideological conflicts had lost their meaning."[3]

Yet if fingers were pointed in Arabism's direction, it was because many had already tired of it. By the mid-1960s pan-Arabism had lost its luster. The UAR had failed, the unification talks between Syria, Iraq, and Egypt had concluded unsuccessfully, and the various military and political agreements between these and other Arab states had come to naught. Nasser already had concluded that although Arab leadership remained a worthy cause, he would no longer champion unification. Arab societies had grown weary of these staged unity talks and moribund decrees, identifying Arabism's principal accomplishments as propaganda wars and failed unity efforts. The 1967 war was only the latest and most ruinous reminder that Arabism's promise outstripped its payoff.

Two long-term developments reinforced the verdict in favor of a more conservative orientation. The first was the regional shift in power from ideology to oil, from symbolic capital to economic capital, from the Mashreq and the heart of Arab nationalism to the Arabian Gulf and the periphery of Arab politics. Beginning soon after 1967 and solidifying after 1973, the era of revolutionaries became the era of petrodollars, famously described by Mohamed Heikal as the change from *thawra* [revolution] to *tharwa* [riches].[4] Oilmen like King Faysal had replaced revolutionaries like Gamal Abdel Nasser as the region's celebrated figures. The Gulf Arabs, who had never been as invested in Arab nationalism, supported a more statist environment and were willing to pay handsomely for it. Within a few years "the rhetoric and revolutionary nationalism of the 1950s and 1960s began to sound peculiarly out of place in the more pragmatic and businesslike atmosphere of the 1970s."[5]

The second factor that encouraged a more conservative orientation was the growth of territorial nationalism and the growing identification of citizens with their states. The constant feuding between Arab states, the failure of the UAR and the unity talks of 1963, and the 1967 war encouraged citizens, however reluctantly and halfheartedly, to transfer their loyalties, if not simply to resign themselves, to the territorial state. Such developments combined with and reinforced ongoing state-building projects intended to increase the loyalties of societies to the state and by association to the regime in power. The surprise of the post-1967 period was the longevity of many Arab regimes and the decline of unification attempts, suggesting and reflecting the ascendance of the Arab territorial state, not only because of coercion but also some semblance of legitimacy.[6] The failures of pan-Arabism and infighting among the Arab states had undermined the cause of Arabism, but the 1967 war, the rise of the Arab oil states, and the relative accomplishments of state formation projects buried it deeper.

Yet Arabism did not quite disappear. Some scholars and practitioners tend to declare the 1967 war Arabism's Waterloo. But such claims are misleading on two counts. Unification had already dropped off the political agenda by 1964; few treaties or associations established between 1964 and 1967 were draped in unification's clothing. Also, Arabism did not disappear but became defined by and expressed through the Arab-Israeli conflict. In the past, radical and conservative Arab states had been defined by their stance toward Sykes-Picot Agreement that had created the territorial divisions in the Arab world, and by their stance toward the West, but beginning in the mid-1960s those labels increasingly depended on where they stood toward Israel. Arabism still shaped how Arab states were expected to present themselves, represented a source of symbolic capital, subjected them to Arab public opinion, and held them accountable to each other, but such processes came to rest almost exclusively on the Arab-Israeli conflict.

The defining feature of the post-1967 debate concerned how Arab states should deal with the Arab-Israeli conflict. Unilaterally or collectively? Diplomatically or militarily? Piecemeal or through comprehensive solutions? Some defined Arabism as a collective, confrontational, and comprehensive approach; for others it accommodated a more flexible and supple set of practices. How far could the meaning of Arabism be stretched? What was permissible, desirable, and acceptable? After the 1967 war the Arab states quickly answered these questions with the infamous "three no's"—no negotiations, no recognition, and no peace with Israel—but reopened the debate with force and consequence after 1973 as Egypt continually tested and pushed the normative expectations of Arabism as it pertained to the Arab states' relations with Israel. With each step on the road to its peace treaty with Israel, Egyptian president Anwar Sadat continuously attempted to redefine the meaning of Arabism, and Syria and other Arab states fought him every step of the way. To be sure, how these Arab governments attempted to define and redefine the norms of Arabism was connected to their various interests, but which definition won out was not wholly dependent on their material power. Egypt found itself expelled from the Arab family, and the Arab Gulf states could do little to halt an outcome they generally wanted to avoid.

These dialogues directly contributed to a splintering of the ranks. A defining theme of the post-1967 period is the relationship between the Arab-Israeli conflict and the normative fragmentation of Arab politics. My account of the peace process, then, will not recount its details, "missed opportunities," or how Arab and Israeli bargaining styles and negotiating principles made a complicated and highly conflictual issue even more intractable and frustrating. Instead, I will focus on how the Arab states' debate about the peace process shaped the organization of Arab politics. Once Arabism became defined by the Arab-Israeli conflict, any breaking from the ranks became a threat to the very meaning of Arabism and the ties that bind. This was the threat represented by Sadat and Camp David. He insisted on negotiating with Israel with the Arab states' blessing, but that could happen only if the meaning of Arab nationalism was weakened to accommodate Egyptian national interests and to leave Egypt less accountable to other Arab states. He was successful in that quest—until Camp David. Although the Arab states responded to Camp David with a show of solidarity, this was only a show, and backstage they were engaged in infighting that questioned the foundations of Arab politics. Of course, other factors contributed to the growing fragmentation in Arab politics—after all, transformations of this sort are rarely the result of any single force—but the dialogues about the norms governing the confrontation with Israel were critical.

Khartoum and the Consecration of Sovereignty

The surest sign of the magnitude of the defeat was the collective silence of Arab leaders in the days following the 1967 war. Perhaps they were in collective mourning or simply too shellshocked to offer much of an explanation for recent events and chart a course for redemption. But as some began to sift through the damage and contemplate their next moves, they instinctively called for an Arab summit, demanding that the Arab states gather in some dramatic setting and make bold proclamations concerning the future. Nasser, among others, was cool to the idea, suggesting that conditions were not right. The failure to convene a summit then produced its own set of commentaries and interpretations. Bourguiba of Tunisia noted that the Soviets and the Americans had set aside their ideological differences to defeat Germany in World War II, so why could the Arab states not do the same?[7] Egypt's Mohamed Heikal observed that Israel, itself a product of mixed socioeconomic, ethnic, and national heritages, had managed to organize itself into a powerful military machine, and he raised the possibility that a failure to produce a unified Arab stand portended a deterioration of the Arab nation and perhaps even an Arab "civil war."[8] How is it, asked many, that the Arab states could not even convene a summit? And, if they could not perform this simple task, how would they ever coordinate their military policies? What was the meaning of Arabism in such circumstances?

Arab governments could not give a perfunctory performance because they first needed to resolve some basic differences among themselves. As embarrassing as the failure to convene a summit was, far worse would be to hold a meeting that only telescoped their animosities. The core of their divisions concerned the relationship between their past troubles and the causes of the defeat; to offer a diagnosis of how inter-Arab relations had created the conditions for the 1967 war was to offer a prescription for how inter-Arab relations should be organized to overcome the Israeli challenge. Because how Arab states had related to each other was responsible for the defeat, a new phase in the conflict that would lead to a better result required a new relationship among Arab states.

But this new relationship was premised on converging on a meaning of Arab unity. This was the debate during the summer of 1967. Iraq and Syria proposed that the reason for the defeat was a lack of unity, which they defined as integration. Iraq, for instance, called for the "organizational nonconstitutional unity among the Arab states," including a unified military and common foreign policy.[9] Syria labeled the 1967 war a "setback" and intimated that victory was premised on greater radicalism.[10] For Syria and Iraq, then, integrating the Arab ranks was the surest and fastest way to reverse the results of June.

Cairo, once willing to match Iraq and Syria word for word, hinted that it had little time for such bidding and began to offer an interpretation of the past and the future that more closely resembled its pre-1955 statements and the positions espoused by the conservative Arab states—a change directly attributable to the 1967 war. In the context of discussing how to convene the long-awaited Arab summit meeting and prepare for war with Israel, Mohamed Heikal wrote that the first principle was to relegate "social differences to the past or the future."[11] The subtext was that Nasser was no longer interested in exporting his revolution and was prepared to cooperate with all Arab states as equals. Communiqués and government-influenced editorials signaled that Cairo was retreating from its recent views on Arab nationalism and embracing a more modest and Israel-centered interpretation.

Egypt's change of doctrine was certainly influenced by the shocking outcome of the war. Nasser left little doubt that scarce resources had to be channeled toward recovering the Sinai and not toward harassing the conservative Arab states. For Nasser, according to Tahseen Bashir, the Khartoum conference became the moment of the new realism, the ascendance of realpolitik over ideology, a commitment to the status quo rather than to revolution.[12] Nasser vowed that his goal was to regain Egyptian—and not Arab—territories.[13] Although Egypt shared with Syria and Iraq an understanding that reversing the outcome of the war required a reorganization of Arab politics, Nasser was proposing their separation whereas they were demanding integration.

Jordan and Saudi Arabia insisted that a successful confrontation of Israel was premised on inter-Arab "cooperation," that is, recognizing the legitimacy of each other's states. Feeling that he had atoned for his past sins because he had stood alongside Egypt and Syria and paid the heaviest price of the three, Hussein confidently took a more assertive role in Arab politics and insisted that, first, the failed promise of unification was responsible for the current mess and, second, that Arab states needed not integration but "coordination." However, coordination was possible only if Arab leaders recognized the principle of coexistence, the existence of different "experiments" in the Arab world.[14] The Jordanian newspaper *Al-Dustur* reflected: "Co-existence is a need which we must recognize at the present stage. An attempt to force others to adopt a certain system would . . . eventually divide the Arab ranks."[15] The Egyptian reaction was different than in the past; now Cairo was echoing a similar theme of coexistence—and Amman wasted little time in giving Cairo positive reinforcement.[16]

Saudi Arabia too had been subjected to Nasser's Arabism in Yemen and made it clear that any hope of cooperating on the Arab-Israeli front was premised on resolving the Yemen war. But the war was not just an interstate struggle. It also symbolized the divisions in the Arab world and the fight over the Arab order. Saudi Arabia made its attendance at any summit contingent on ending the war in Yemen—Egypt and Saudi Arabia would have to agree on some new principles for Arab politics, and throughout the summer they attempted to negotiate a solution.[17] In general, a long-standing goal of both Jordan and Saudi Arabia was to see an interpretation of Arabism that was consistent with sovereignty accepted by the Arab states, and Egypt was now among the converted.

The military defeat had unleashed a regional debate about the meaning of Arabism, and the summer-long air clearing and name calling was essential for building a consensus. Now that Arab governments had begun to converge on an understanding of Arab unity, they could meet and consider the relationship between inter-Arab relations and the Arab-Israeli conflict. The first critical meeting came in Khartoum in early August when the Arab foreign ministers met to lay the groundwork for an Arab summit. Sudanese prime minister Muhammad Ahmad Majhub welcomed the gathering by stressing a recurring theme: the need for unity in the ranks and unified action in the shared struggle against Israel regardless of the differences between Arab states.[18] To this end the Arab foreign ministers emphasized the importance of the 1965 summit resolutions, which called on Arab states to cease their propaganda wars and to recognize the principle of noninterference.[19] The Arab states agreed to recognize each other's sovereignty and the legitimacy of the separate Arab experiments, and they furthered the prospect of cooperation by pledging that they would desist from attempts to destabilize each other from within through their medias.

Having made progress on these critical questions regarding inter-Arab relations, they turned to the matter of Israel. An early item for consideration was the Iraqi proposal to impose an oil embargo on the West for an indefinite period as a way to punish it for its support of Israel and to pressure it to pressure Israel. The other Arab oil-exporting countries dissented from the Iraqi proposal, and Kuwait offered to transfer funds to Syria, Jordan, and Egypt.[20] The Iraqi proposal became the basis for discussions at the Arab oil ministers' meeting in Baghdad a week later.[21] Saudi Arabia and Kuwait again objected to an oil embargo on the grounds that it would lead only to a loss in revenue and be interpreted by the West as a declaration of war.[22] Unable to reach a decision, the oil ministers left the matter for the Arab leaders to decide.[23] Iraq left the conference sounding the theme of integration and the necessity of economic and political unity, but it was largely alone in advocating this view.[24] Although the Arab states still had important differences of opinion regarding the next steps, they had laid the groundwork for a meeting of their heads of state.

The Arab leaders gathered in dramatic fashion for their long-awaited summit in Khartoum in the last days of August. The first order of business was to achieve a détente between Saudi Arabia and Egypt. A good omen came early when President Nasser and King Faysal embraced each other at their hotel at the beginning of the meeting on August 30, signaling that they would literally and figuratively stop shooting at each other. This they did. By the end of the conference they joyfully announced an agreement to end the Yemen war, an event touted as one of the summit's crowning achievements.

The agreement on Yemen paved the way for the summit to discuss how to organize the Arab states' activities for the next round of the Arab-Israeli conflict. The proposal for an oil embargo was the first item considered. According to a participant at Khartoum, Nasser, infuriated and dumbstruck by the proposal, exclaimed: "Who are these foreign ministers? From what countries are they? Do they not realize that we just suffered a major defeat and that we have little time for such foolishness! They are talking as if we had won the war."[25] By foolishness Nasser meant the tendency of the Arab states to propose flamboyant and dramatic gestures that looked impressive on paper but were impotent in practice; rather than an oil embargo, Nasser offered, think about how the frontline states should repair their militaries to recover the occupied territories. The Iraqi proposal died an ignoble death.

Nasser's abrupt dismissal of the Iraqi proposal reflected his postwar plans that he calculated required a less restrictive arrangement that was better able to achieve his principal objectives of rebuilding his military and recapturing the Sinai, by force if necessary. Toward that end Nasser had various choices. He rejected a military alliance, or at least an alliance that resembled those of the past. Arab states had a penchant for creating military arrangements that looked great on paper but hardly ever became operational. This was partly by design: many of these alliances had been constructed to control another Arab state's foreign policy or to keep up appearances. The recent Syrian-Egyptian treaty of 1966 represented Nasser's unsuccessful attempt to tame Syria's actions toward Israel; it was not primarily intended to coordinate Egyptian and Syrian military forces. King Hussein flew to Cairo on the eve of the war in order to become part of the Arab consensus and to satisfy his domestic and regional critics; the three countries established no effective mechanisms for coordinating their military forces or sharing intelligence information, which Hussein would later claim was partially responsible for the magnitude of the defeat. These past and recent experiences led Nasser to conclude that to continue down this particular multilateral path was to invite inaction or worse and that he needed Arab leaders' financial assistance but not their participation in decisions as he prepared to confront the Israelis.

This appraisal of the causes of past failures and what was required for redemption drove the organization of the Arab effort. The Arab states agreed that the frontline states should be compensated for their losses from the 1967 war and helped to rebuild their militaries. Specifically, the Arab oil states established a fund for Egypt and Jordan (Syria was not included in the original compensation package because it refused to attend the summit). Although the Arab states nominally agreed to use the Joint Arab Defense Council, an inter-Arab coordinating body, to mobilize and coordinate the Arab military effort, in fact they emphasized that military development and planning would be left up to the individual countries.[26] In keeping with this initial decision Arab states during the next few years transferred, coordinated, and negotiated most resources on a bilateral rather than a multilateral basis. "We have a sense of unity of purpose," recalled one observer. "But each country has to rebuild on its own; it must fend for itself."[27]

The other major decision at Khartoum concerned their collective response to the possibility of negotiations with Israel. One hopeful scenario after the war was that it would conclude in much as had the Suez War of 1956: a return to the status quo ante. But Israel would have none of that and was tying its withdrawal to a comprehensive peace and hinting that it might make some territorial modifications in addition to its earlier decision to extend Israeli sovereignty over Jerusalem. The Arab states responded to the prospect of a diplomatic, piecemeal, and bilateral settlement with the famous no's: no negotiations, no recognition, and no peace with Israel. Although some Arab states privately preferred a more flexible document if only to present a more conciliatory image to the watching world, to suggest anything short of this formula left them vulnerable to the charge of "defeatism." For the time being the Arab states had publicly committed themselves to retrieving the occupied territories at all cost and (rhetorically at least) with no concessions.

What occurred at Khartoum was the birth of a new order, that is, a reconsideration of the relationship between the Arab regional order, the norms of Arabism, and their Arab identities. Arab states determined that their ability to confront Israel was dependent on establishing some new rules of the game. The first order of business therefore was to decide what these rules would be; without much hesitation they agreed to acknowledge and work within the parameters of their separate geographies. The Arab states reiterated that sovereignty was the foundation of the Arab order; now they would tolerate various experiments. No Arab state formally denounced the idea of unification, but its lack of popularity was evident in the insistence of the vast majority of Arab states that recovering land lost to Israel was contingent on recognizing each other's sovereignty. Nasser withdrew from the cause of radicalism and dedicated himself to the task of retrieving Egyptian land and Arab dignity, symbolically consecrated when he closed down the *Sawt al-Arab* [Voice of the Arabs] radio broadcasts. The conservative Arab states, which had prayed for this moment for more than a decade, were quite willing to compensate him for doing so.

With unification fading from the Arab agenda the social purpose of the Arab state became more closely defined by the Arab-Israeli conflict, and the Arab national interest became more closely identified with the Zionist threat than ever before. The close connection between the organization of Arab politics and the organization of the Arab-Israeli conflict had been an emergent property of the Arab states system since the beginning of the summit system in 1964, but Khartoum had made the relationship explicit. Throughout the summer of 1967 and in the hallways at Khartoum Arab leaders pressed for a new chapter in the Arab-Israeli conflict that was premised on a new chapter in inter-Arab politics. Although Iraq and Syria proclaimed that this required genuine integration, theirs proved to be the minority voice and lost out to the more prevalent demand for separateness and sovereignty. The new regional order was premised on sovereignty, and Arab nationalism became more nearly defined by the struggle against Zionism.

This new pragmatism was directly related to the types of policies that Arab states entertained to mobilize Arab resources to confront Israel. Arab states defined mobilization as coordination and cooperation—not as integration. Whereas only three years before they had answered the crisis over the Jordan River with the Unified Arab Command, now they hardly discussed military integration. The Iraqi proposal for an oil embargo and Iraq's desire for political and economic unity were the last gasps of a dying era— unceremoniously dubbed foolishness by Nasser. The mechanisms that Arab states would use to mobilize the war effort reflected a growing impatience with integrated efforts and the growing allure of modest coordinated measures. From the definition of the Arab national interest to the mechanisms they would adopt to pursue that interest, Arab states clearly had negotiated a new regional order.

That Khartoum symbolized the birth of a new order was apparent on the faces of those who gained and those who lost. King Hussein offered that the Arab world was being asked to choose between two roads. The first "was to continue the negative policies which harm us most of all . . . a continuation of the old superficial policy characterized by extemporization . . . whose harmful consequences were exposed and experienced by the people. The second road began with shouldering responsibilities . . . [which] made it incumbent upon them [Arab states] to abandon outbidding."[28] The Jordanian newspaper *Al-Dustur* wrote that if the Arab world would "not tolerate the interaction of Arab experiments, we will never progress toward Arab coexistence and will never approach our basic aim—Arab unity."[29]

Others were less happy with the results. Syria knew what was coming and preferred to stay at home rather than bear witness, shouting from afar that the attempt to smooth over differences meant sacrificing Arab nationalism for a new conservatism: "This 'Arab Solidarity' in effect means to keep silent about all the abnormal internal conditions faced by the Arab people in some Arab countries. It also means to keep quiet about the suppression of every progressive voice."[30] Iraq lamented the new "realism" and "unity of ranks." President Abd al-Rahman Aref chided the conference for failing to address directly the issue of military integration or military action, give a full hearing to his proposal to reorganize the Arab military command, and consider the issue of economic integration.[31] Others also wrote of Khartoum as a selling out of Arab nationalism, as signaling the victory of conservativism over radicalism in Arab politics.

The new conservatism was shaped by Arab governments that were attempting to connect their various interests, the norms of Arabism, and the desired regional order in the context of their plans to reverse the outcome of the 1967 war. The conservative Arab states portrayed the war as the tragic result of inter-Arab rivalries and the unwillingness of the radical states to accept the legitimacy of different Arab experiments. Arab nationalism, they argued, was premised on mutual recognition of each other's sovereignty and protecting the Arab nation from the Zionist threat; honoring the former was necessary for furthering the latter. Of course, this position was related to their own interest in regime survival. For more than a decade they had attempted to use sovereignty as a normative shield against Nasser and transnational Arabism, and the 1967 war gave their position a more favorable hearing because of the growing conviction that the radical states' version of Arab nationalism was partially responsible for the disastrous loss. And so they argued with greater assertiveness for coexistence, less fearful that their position would be successfully framed as reactionary politics and more confident that it would be received as the proper path for confronting Israel. The military loss to Israel became the fodder for a normative victory against the radical Arab agenda.

Nasser adopted a more conservative orientation and supported the view that cooperation among all the Arab states was necessary for preparing for the next phase of the Arab-Israeli conflict. To be sure, Nasser's willingness to defend an order that he had recently savaged was connected to his conception of his, Egypt's, and the Arab national interests at the time. The 1967 war had been a profoundly demoralizing and dispiriting debacle, and Nasser was ready to do all he could to recoup his prestige, Egyptian land, and Arab dignity. If this meant forging a détente with the conservative Arab states and accepting their subsidies, so be it. His former radical allies chastised him for his choice of friends and for trying to bury a movement that once bore his name. This seemed a small price to pay, given the circumstances and the historic task at hand.

But Nasser's newfound orientation was not so new. He had begun to break from the radical camp a few years before, had devised the summit system for that purpose, and then was tempted back against his better judgment but with the hope of maintaining his status and taming a potentially renegade Syria. He spent the months before the June war fearful that Syria was dragging the Arab states into an unwanted war with Israel and constantly worrying how he would avoid that outcome without soiling his credentials. A process that he hoped to control soon controlled him, and he found himself going down a dangerous path because of Syria's symbolic sanctions and his symbolic entrapment. This was not an unfamiliar dynamic; after all, the destructiveness of symbolic competition was the featured outcome of the establishment of the UAR and other episodes that were masked as cooperation among radical Arab states. Now in the aftermath of the war Nasser gazed at the Israeli army on the other side of the Suez and concluded decisively that Arabism had bred self-destructive outbidding and therefore could be partly blamed for the defeat.

Nasser, far from disavowing the Arab nationalist movement with which he was so closely identified, helped to legitimate a more conservative meaning that could better accommodate his current plans. This more conservative orientation was quite familiar to him for he had originally espoused it in the early 1950s, only to renounce it later that decade in favor of a more radical orientation that brought him some prestige but also considerable suffering. But he still had to connect this conservative meaning to the times and to have these norms of Arabism legitimated collectively by his own society and other Arab states. Few obstacles obstructed him. Nasser was nearly beyond the ideological criticisms that might have wounded other Arab leaders. But equally important was that his arguments resonated with the times. Egyptian society generally accepted Nasser's new orientation because it was determined to reverse the Israeli occupation and had traditionally maintained a more state-centered understanding of Arab nationalism, which the events of recent years had reinforced.[32] And he received few arguments from other Arab leaders, most of whom either had little taste for radical causes or believed that the spirit of radicalism should be directed at Israel and not at each other. The Arab governments negotiated a regional order that tied together regime interests, the norms of Arabism, and the confrontation with Israel.

But Arabism continued to place limits on what Arab states contemplated or considered to be politically viable. As Arab leaders debated what the contours of the post-1967 order should be, they referred to a moral order that both defined their goals and constrained what was possible. Fouad Ajami nicely concluded: "Few struggles for power are ever waged without pretensions to ideological or normative stakes. The protagonists drag ideas into the game both because they take the ideas seriously and because they wish to invest their quest with moral worth and to provide a cover for what otherwise would seen to be narrow and selfish goals."[33] Although this order was shaped by regime interests, it was still defined by Arabism. Arabism shaped the interests of Arab states and the means that they would contemplate or calculate as politically feasible for pursuing those interests. Arabism, after all, continued to define Israel as a threat and continued to orient Arab states in a similar direction. An order that embraced a severe individualism, that allowed Arab states to negotiate a separate deal with Israel, was not even considered; to forward such an order would have been labeled defeatist, illegitimate, and blasphemous. Nasser refused an Israeli offer to return the whole of the Sinai in exchange for a peace agreement.[34] It was one thing to desist from bludgeoning Arab rivals but quite another to make a unilateral peace with Zionists. The Arab states pledged their three no's, which constrained their public actions regardless of their private preferences. Although the regional order consecrated at Khartoum was a far cry from the one that they had been debating only a few years earlier, it was still an Arab order. The Arab states filed out of Khartoum claiming that they had established a new Arab order that would allow them to make peace among themselves and war with the Israelis.

CHALLENGES TO THE KHARTOUM ORDER

No political order is ever fully institutionalized, self-regulating, or without need of attention and repair, and this was certainly true of the Khartoum order. Two of its central tenets concerned the socially sanctioned means by which the Arab states could confront Israel and the recognition that the inter-Arab state system was premised on sovereignty or, as viewed by those who opposed Khartoum, conservatism. Both tenets would be challenged during the next few years but defended through symbolic sanctions in the case of the challenge to the three no's and brute force in the case of the challenge to sovereignty and conservatism.

The three no's.   The Arab states left Khartoum proclaiming the sanctity of the three no's and repeating Nasser's slogan of "what was taken by force cannot be retaken but by force." But the chance remained that an Arab state might defect from this consensus. Soon after the 1967 war and continuing for the next several years various instances of real and rumored conversations involved Arab states and several intermediaries regarding the terms of a potential political settlement; U.N. Resolution 242, a deliberately ambiguous document regarding the possibility of a settlement to the Arab-Israeli conflict based on some equation of "land for peace," usually provided the basis for such discussions.

The War of Attrition of 1969 and 1970 was the pretext for a flurry of diplomatic activity. In March 1969 Nasser commenced a series of military strikes against Israeli positions on the Suez Canal for various strategic, political, and symbolic reasons; soon Israel and Egypt were involved in an escalating cycle that far exceeded the 1967 war in terms of casualties and even involved dogfights between Israel and the Soviet Union, which was playing a greater role in Egyptian defenses. Seizing on what might be an opportunity and fearing a war that might have global implications, the United States began trying to broker a cease-fire and to raise the possibility of far-ranging talks. By the fall of 1969 there were various rumors that Saudi Arabia, which was having a difficult time reconciling its commitment to the Khartoum resolutions alongside its long-standing ties to the United States and interest in reducing the Soviet presence in the region, was warmly receiving a U.S. proposal for further negotiations that resembled one previously proposed by the Soviets and rejected by Nasser. The frontline states vehemently objected to the United States–Saudi discussions and threatened to stay away from the upcoming Rabat summit until all the Arab states reaffirmed that the battlefield rather than the bargaining table was the means to retrieve Arab lands and dignities. To not renew their vows meant defecting from the consensus and being exposed to regional and domestic sanctions, and so all Arab states took the pledge. Nasser then used the Rabat summit to "excoriate the Saudis implicitly but clearly for their association with the United States," and the subtext was that even the impression of impropriety was to be forsworn.[35]

The War of Attrition provided the backdrop for another set of negotiations the next year, though this time Egypt was the truant. In the summer of 1970 U.S. Secretary of State William Rogers successfully brokered a ceasefire between Israel and Egypt. Nasser portrayed the agreement as tactical rather than as strategic but correctly predicted that other Arab officials would receive it as evidence of potential capitulation and negotiations with Israel.[36] Perhaps because they believed that Nasser might be contemplating comprehensive talks, or perhaps because it was an easy way to score some political points, Syria and Iraq painted the Rogers initiative as defeatist. The more radical elements of the PLO similarly accused Nasser of treason and of flirting with a political solution.[37] If Nasser had any thoughts of joining the peace process, he quickly discarded them after the reception given the Rogers initiative.

The dynamics surrounding the Rogers initiative testify that regardless of whether various Arab states had private doubts about the three no's, once they had publicly pledged themselves to these principles they could not deviate from them without subjecting themselves to ridicule. Even those Arab leaders who might have privately contemplated a political compromise did not hint publicly of such sentiments for fear of being placed outside the consensus: therefore even they tended to reiterate the harshest line.[38] This is not to say that a different Israeli response might not have drawn a different Arab reaction. But Arab states had to be fairly convinced of the possibility of success and an outcome that closely resembled the Khartoum resolutions before they would willingly subject themselves to the inevitable symbolic sanctions. Nasser suggested that negotiation with Israel might be possible if the Israelis gave clear assurances in advance, but outside these terms considering such a possibility was politically unthinkable. "The heart of the problem was now apparent. Both sides [Israel and Egypt] had strong reasons to sue for peace, but the taboo made direct contacts perilous for any Arab leader."[39]

The Jordanian civil war.   The most dramatic challenge to the post-1967 order occurred in Jordan in 1970 in regard to the relationship between Palestinian nationalism and Jordanian sovereignty. Because the eventual confrontation between Jordan and the PLO represented a clash between the principles of sovereignty and the personification of Arab nationalism, the symbol of Arabism was also the opponent of the new order. "The talk about the bankruptcy of traditional orders and the revolutionary nature of the masses met its test in Jordan when the Palestinians faced King Hussein's army."[40]

Palestinian-Jordanian relations traditionally were defined by mutual suspicion and hostility, born of Abdullah's annexation of the West Bank, his near peace with Israel, and his assassination in 1951. Relations between the two remained suspicious and occasionally confrontational for the next decade, and the establishment of the PLO in 1964 marked a new phase: now the Palestinians had a formal organization that might challenge the king's authority over Jordan's Palestinian population and the West Bank.

The tensions between the PLO and the Jordanian government, barely contained through the pre-1967 period, became unbridled after the war. Several factors contributed. First, the PLO established a more independent line, less willing to view the Arab states as the guardians of the Palestinian cause. This meant that the traditional rivalry between Hussein and the PLO for the hearts, minds, and loyalties of Jordan's Palestinian population became more intense after the war because the PLO's stature was on the rise and a segment of Jordan's Palestinian population was radicalized by the defeat. At the Rabat summit the Arab states endorsed the PLO as the sole representative of the Palestinians, an issue that was far from settled and would be revisited in several forms for years to come and that only publicized and intensified the conflict between Hussein and the PLO.

A second area of conflict concerned the "freedom of the Palestinian fida'i action and the method of rendering assistance to the Palestinian fida'yin."[41] Soon after the war the PLO established bases in Jordan and Syria and began launching raids into Israel. Not only did this produce the inevitable Israeli retaliation, but the establishment of these bases could, if unchecked, challenge the state's authority. The PLO and Jordan did agree that the PLO would restrict its activities to the Jordan valley and away from the major towns, but Israeli shelling of PLO encampments led the PLO to move toward the interior and the central cities. By the fall of 1969 tensions between the Jordanian authorities and the PLO were on the rise, and they were forced to revisit the question of how much "freedom" the military arm of the Palestinians should be accorded. This was not just a Jordanian issue. It was also an Arab issue: the Rabat summit of December 1969 discussed but proved unable to answer these concerns.[42]

The tensions between the PLO and Jordan escalated unchecked. Now various fedayeen groups were establishing a nearly autonomous existence, denying the authority of Jordanian law, representing themselves as an alternative to the king, and virtually creating a state within a state. While Fatah, a moderate wing of the PLO, was seeking an agreement with the Jordanian government, other factions, such as the George Habash's PFLP and Nayef Hawatmeh's Popular Democratic Front for the Liberation of Palestine, took a more confrontational line and began openly declaring, first, their opposition to the king and, second, that Jordan was Palestine. From King Hussein's view he now hosted a people who comprised a near majority, who bore him open hostility, and whose official representative had established military activities that challenged his authority. But to clamp down on the PLO risked: being accused of betraying Arabism; being branded an enemy of the Palestinians, a particularly stinging charge given their long and hostile relations; and a civil war. By June 1970 there were feverish negotiations alongside open clashes between Palestinian guerrillas and the Jordanian military. Yasir Arafat urged the PLO's splinter groups to show some restraint and to try to settle their differences through compromise.

Such negotiations and urgings had no apparent effect. In early September the PFLP hijacked a number of planes, flew them to Amman, and blew them up. This highly provocative action was a direct challenge not only to the Jordanian government but also to Arafat's leadership. "In the game of revolution," Kamal Salibi has observed, "moderation rarely carries the day," and Arafat soon sided with the radicals in order to maintain his credentials.[43] Many fedayeen began claiming that Amman would become the "Hanoi of the revolution." On September 16, in response to the fedayeen's declaration of a "people's government" in the city of Irbid, Hussein launched an offensive against the PLO. The bloody confrontation began.

Hussein defended his actions by referring to his long-standing Arab nationalist credentials and his authority to act granted by sovereignty. In a letter addressed to Nasser and broadcast over Jordanian radio, and then in a subsequent exchange between Hussein and Nasser, Hussein portrayed the PLO's actions as part of a larger conspiracy against the Jordanian people and army, both of which had sacrificed dearly for the Arab struggle.[44] Hussein took pains to note that the "survival of this country and the safety of all Arab steadfastness" dictated that he regain control over the situation; in other words, he linked stability and order in a sovereign Jordan, him at its head, and the struggle against Israel. Conversely, any party that attempted to undermine Jordan's sovereignty was a threat to the Arab cause.[45]

The response from other Arab leaders was fierce and conflicted. The sight of Arabs aiming rifles at each other when by all rights those rifles should have been directed at Israel caused tremendous anxiety and turmoil throughout the Arab world. One commentator confessed: "The Arab, following the news of the fighting between Arab brothers on the soil of Arab Jordan, is about to lose his mind."[46] "The violence was deeply disturbing to the Arab public," wrote Malcolm Kerr, "the more so because of its apparently deliberate and systematic character and because the victims were already objectives of general sympathy."[47] The conflict between Jordan and the PLO was not an internal matter but one that concerned the entire Arab nation.

No Arab leader could sit still while the Palestinians were being dealt a blow that far exceeded anything ever meted out by Israel. Yet this clash between the PLO and Jordan also provided another excellent opportunity for Arab states to demonstrate their support for the Palestinians. Iraq and Syria each threatened to intervene militarily to protect the Palestinians.[48] Iraq declared its stand with the PLO and offered to make available Iraqi troops stationed on Jordanian soil, noting that the "road to victory and the liberation of Palestine passes through Amman."[49] Ultimately, however, Iraq remained idle when the fighting heated up. Syria repeatedly referred to the "puppet Jordanian authority" and linked Jordan's "massacre" to its past and present association with U.S. interests in the region.[50] Syria then made good on its pledge to intervene on behalf of the PLO and crossed the Jordanian border on September 19. This development brought an immediate response from Israel and the United States. Israel feared that if the PLO toppled the king, Israel would have a radical enemy on its longest border; consequently, Israel threatened to intervene on behalf of Jordan if Syria continued southward. The United States, also fearing that a moderate pro-Western Arab state would fall to radical forces, pressed Israel into service. Syria retreated on September 22.[51]

Arab leaders were torn. They had a vested interest in defending the principle of sovereignty, but they also supported and sympathized with the Palestinians; to side with Hussein risked being portrayed as an enemy of the Palestinians, but to side with the PLO at this moment was to challenge a fundamental tenet of the political order. In a message that exemplified this dilemma Algerian president Hourari Boumedienne communicated to King Hussein and Yasir Arafat his full concern "for the sovereignty and independence of Jordan" and that Algeria did not want to "interfere in the internal affairs of fraternal countries" but was unable to "remain indifferent at any action whose aim is to put an end to the Palestinian Resistance."[52] To be sovereign entailed authority over domestic space, but to be an Arab nationalist meant to support the Palestinians. Hussein had the right to assert his authority, but he did not have a license to bludgeon the Palestinians.

Nasser was particularly split by the war. He was the leader of Arab nationalism, the long-standing adversary of King Hussein, and a genuine supporter of the Palestinian cause; he also had recently resigned from the radical Arab agenda and signed the Rogers initiative that the radical Arab states had labeled as defeatist. In this tug of loyalties and interests Nasser ultimately sided with Hussein. Perhaps part of the reason had to do with his rumored soft spot for Hussein because of the 1967 war; Hussein had followed through on his alliance commitments and suffered for doing so.[53] But any soft spot Nasser had for Hussein only reinforced the convergence of their strategic and political interests.[54] Both were committed to the status quo and proceeding cautiously in the next phase of the Arab-Israeli conflict. Hussein's downfall would undoubtedly introduce a more radical and less controllable entity that was rumored to be committed to a policy of *tawreet*, dragging the feet of the Arab leaders into battle, which in turn would signal a return to the pre-1967 period.[55] While reminding everyone of his unimpeachable nationalist credentials, Nasser accused Iraq and Syria of instigating the civil war (if not actually carrying it out in collusion with Israel and the United States), which only undermined the cause of Arab nationalism and played into the hands of Israel. At times Nasser hinted that the PLO was the enemy of Arab nationalism. Such messages conveyed Nasser's commitment to the status quo.

Arab states convened a summit in Cairo on September 22 to discuss how to stop the civil war in Jordan, how to curb the crisis and prevent any further foreign intervention, and "how the future status of Jordan could be defined after what has happened."[56] All sides put numerous proposals on the table. Sudanese president Gaafar Mohamad Numairi, no friend of Hussein's and critical of his offensive against the PLO, reflected the commission's principled tension between the desire to maintain Jordan's sovereignty and the commitment to the Palestinians. The issue at stake was not only a "constitutional one concerning Jordan alone," he insisted, "but is a historical and humanitarian responsibility affecting the destiny of the whole Arab nation."[57] Hussein demanded an end to the conflict that reaffirmed Jordanian sovereignty and restricted the PLO's activities to the occupied territories and the Jordan valley. "The State will exercise its full sovereignty over everyone present on its territory. All shall respect that sovereignty."[58] Although sympathetic with his demands, those at the Cairo summit also insisted that Hussein cease his offensive against the PLO. Hussein dismissed their severe criticism and veiled threats, in part because he was convinced that their words were intended for Palestinian and popular consumption.[59] The war continued.

Finally, on September 27 the PLO and Jordan signed the Cairo Agreement.[60] The Cairo conference, according to Adeed Dawisha, was a "turning point in the history of inter-Arab relations no less important than the Arab defeat of 1967. It marked the beginning of the gradual decline of the Palestinian movement as a radicalizing and destabilizing factor in Arab politics."[61] The PLO was established in 1964 as a conservative organization that was to be controlled by the other Arab states. The 1967 war, however, had radicalized and loosened the strings, leaving the PLO more determined than ever to strike out on its own and strike on its own. Such developments meant that this symbol of Arabism was also a threat to an order that had sovereignty and territorial integrity at its core. However genuine or artificial their expressions of conflicting sentiments, the Arab states supported in some cases and in others acquiesced to Jordanian sovereignty even if that meant bludgeoning the symbol of Arab nationalism. Although this tension between state sovereignty and the aims of the PLO would clash in the future, Hussein's blow to the Palestinians represented a brace for the status quo.

The Cairo agreement designed to end the civil war ultimately reproduced rather than resolved the contradictions between Hussein's claim to sovereignty and the PLO's claims to authority. Jordanian sovereignty was reaffirmed. And the PLO retained the right to establish bases in restricted areas.[62] The result was that the conditions that precipitated the civil war persisted, nearly guaranteeing another round of violence.[63] And so there was. Although the violence never attained the heights of Black September, with each succeeding crisis Hussein winnowed the PLO's territorial and political space. And with each crisis came cries of protest from around the Arab world, but with each succeeding crisis the outcry was increasingly muted. King Hussein finally evicted the PLO from Jordan in July 1972. The tensions between sovereignty and Arab nationalism were now for Lebanon to resolve—or not.

Nasser died on September 28, 1970. Although this was a "man of defeats," the Arab world had lost its leader and its pulse.[64] The last few years had not been particularly easy or distinguished ones for Nasser. In contrast to the Nasser who set the agenda of the 1950s and 1960s, and who urged the masses to unify and fulfill pan-Arabism's mission, in recent years Nasser had abandoned the cause of unification, shifted his rhetoric from the "unity of purpose" to the "unity of ranks," lost the Sinai to the Israelis, retreated from Arab socialism and resurrected the same private capitalist class he once had excoriated, accepted the Rogers initiative, and intervened to save the king of Jordan in his fight against the PLO. The Nasser of the 1970s was hardly the Nasser of the past. He had entered politics as the revolutionary who challenged the dominant order. He exited as one of its guardians.

The War of Ramadan, the Peace Process, and Constricted Arabism

As soon as the 1967 war ended, the frontline states began mobilizing their societies for war, and Arab leaders everywhere began predicting that they soon would reclaim Arab lands and dignity. Such proclamations grew increasingly stale as each year passed and the battle was nowhere nearer in sight; many began doubting that war would ever come, grumbling that they were sacrificing for nothing. But the impasse ended dramatically when Egypt and Syria launched a surprise attack on October 6, 1973, and smashed through Israeli defenses. Initial Israeli losses were quite heavy as Egypt captured part of the East Bank of the Suez and Syria landed a highly damaging blow to Israeli positions on the Golan Heights. But within a week Israel stabilized its position and soon thereafter established military dominance, establishing a presence on the West Bank of the Suez Canal, surrounding the Egyptian army on the East Bank of the canal, recapturing all the territory it initially lost to Syria, and threatening to march on Damascus. After several weeks of fighting and a near conflict between the Soviets and the Americans, the United States made Israel heel and accept a cease-fire on October 24.

The Arabs celebrated the October War. The airwaves were thick with messages of self-congratulation, testimonials to how the Arab army had demonstrated its mettle, how it had fought and defeated the supposedly superior Israeli army. The applause grew louder as the Arab oil-exporting states imposed an oil embargo on October 20, an option that they had consistently rejected but now undertook for strategic, economic, and symbolic reasons.[65] The unprecedented coordination of the Arab states' military, political, and economic resources was an impressive demonstration of Arab power and unity.

But behind the curtain of unity stood relatively modest coordination at best and the shadows of divisions at worst. Syria and Egypt had received nominal troop contributions from the other Arab states. Egyptian officials, impatient with all-Arab mechanisms, had prepared and then conducted a campaign that was designed to reclaim the Sinai and restore Egyptian pride. Syria too limited its military plans to retaking the Golan Heights and stopped its tanks from continuing toward the old Syrian-Palestinian border; through its military actions Syria conveyed that it was thinking in territorial terms.[66] Although the symbols and shadows of the war were of the pre-1967 generation, the motivations and goals of its leaders and its conservative and statist orientations were of the post-1967 period.[67]

The Arab states would now face the challenge of coordinating their postwar political and diplomatic strategies, which meant revisiting the questions that had dogged them at Khartoum—unilaterally or collectively? piecemeal or through comprehensive solutions? But the different set of circumstances hinted that they would have a more difficult time maintaining the facade of unity. Understanding the developments and dynamics that emerged during the next several years requires attention to how Arab states went into the post-1973 phase with different interests, schedules, and relationships to Arabism and thus susceptibility to symbolic sanctions. Such differences informed the pace of the post-1973 peace process.

The first issue concerns the interests and timetables of the different Arab states after the 1973 war, and here the most important players were Egypt, Jordan, Saudi Arabia, Syria, and the PLO. Sadat emerged from the 1973 war with three interdependent goals designed to restructure Egyptian politics and the country's place in global politics. He concluded that reclaiming the occupied territories would have to come through diplomatic negotiations and not through military encounters. Egypt had spent the past seven years engaged in sustained war preparation, and the best it could accomplish was a psychological victory and a dent in Israel's vaunted military superiority. Second, Egypt's economy was in shambles largely as a result of the costs of war. Sadat had little interest in dusting off Nasser's Arab socialism, and intended to welcome domestic and foreign capital. Indeed, foreign capital, in terms of technology from the West and petrodollars from the Arab Gulf states, was essential to Egypt's economic strategy because, in the words of a former finance minister, "That was where the money was."[68] The package of economic changes became known as *infitah* and represented a structural change in Egypt's economic orientation. Third, Sadat was intent on restructuring Egypt's place in regional and global politics. Egypt already had a détente with Saudi Arabia, but now Sadat intended to strengthen those ties. More dramatically, Sadat planned to end Egypt's twenty-year alliance with the Soviet Union and jump to the United States, a move that would further his goals of economic development and recovering the Sinai.

A reconsideration of Egypt's national identity and relationship to Arabism furthered and stimulated this wholesale reorientation of Egypt's domestic and foreign policy. Although domestic critics offered resistance and raised objections to Sadat's approach to Israel and withdrawal from Arabism, the growth of Egyptian nationalism cushioned his road.[69] Having sacrificed blood, money, and soil for Arabism and carried much of the burden of the Arab-Israeli conflict for decades, many Egyptians believed that they had paid their dues and that it was time to concentrate on national development. In this respect the national mood was similar to what emerged after the 1948 war: a questioning of Egypt's relationship to Arabism and an assertion of a form of Egyptian nationalism.[70] Sadat cultivated and encouraged such sentiments, for they were consistent with his foreign policy initiatives and made them politically palatable; to this end the Egyptian government developed various symbols of Egyptian nationalism that were intended to better distinguish Egypt from the other Arab states.[71] The result was a debate about the Egyptian national identity and whether Egypt was even Arab. This "dialogue of the 1970s" was a highly polemicized discussion about Egypt's relationship to Arabism and the practices constitutive of that identity.[72] Of course, these questions had no definitive answers. But the fact that these issues were up for debate meant that Sadat would be less susceptible to symbolic sanctions and might be better able to define Arabism in ways consistent with his foreign policy plans, which were geared toward recovering the Sinai and cozying up to the United States.[73]

King Hussein's position during this period was as conflicted as ever. Of paramount importance was regime survival. Such imperatives directly informed many of Hussein's actions. As the head of a country without a state-national identity and that housed a large Palestinian population, King Hussein staked much of his legitimacy on Arab nationalism. He certainly had an interest in solving the Arab-Israeli conflict if only because it was a highly destabilizing force in Jordanian politics. If at all possible, he wanted a solution that left him in control of the West Bank and Jerusalem. Therefore, although the United States and Israel counted King Hussein as a potential partner in the peace process, and although he met secretly with various Is-

raeli officials over the years and participated in various discussions with the
PLO concerning its prospects in any future Arab-Israeli negotiations and
rule over the West Bank, ultimately he turned away from anything substantive because of the fear of domestic repercussions.[74]

Saudi Arabia's post-1973 objectives were like those of the past: maintaining regional stability in the Gulf and the immediate vicinity, calming the
Arab-Israeli conflict because it encouraged Arab radicalism and Soviet involvement, and attempting to shield itself from inter-Arab squabbles. But its
newfound oil wealth changed matters, thrusting Saudi Arabia into a position
of power and preeminence in Arab politics, a position that was a mixed
blessing.[75] With such power the Saudis hoped to protect themselves from
various threats and challenges from other Arab states through checkbook
diplomacy and "political petrolism."[76] In this regard Saudi Arabia used its oil
wealth not to underwrite its hegemony but to block the attempts by others
to establish hegemony in Arab politics.[77] But Saudi Arabia's past policy of
taking a low profile on the Arab-Israeli conflict and minimizing its visibility
in inter-Arab quarrels was long gone, further eroded as Egypt withdrew
from Arab politics during the 1970s.

To further its objectives Saudi Arabia had tacit alliances with the United
States and Egypt. For several decades the Saudis had discreetly leaned on the
United States, and the decline of Arabism alongside its oil wealth made the
Saudis less apologetic and more inclined to rely on the United States. Their
alliance with Egypt was a more recent development. Saudi Arabia and Egypt
began to forge a détente in 1967, but only after the 1973 war did their relations
develop into what was frequently characterized as an "axis." Relations
warmed quickly because these two central Arab states saw the Soviet Union
as a threat to their interests and the United States as a potential force for
good, and they wanted to find a compromise solution to the Arab-Israeli
conflict. But Saudi Arabia's alliance with the United States and Egypt potentially placed it at odds with its commitment to Arabism: the United States
was still viewed as a potential menace to the region and was Israel's chief
supporter; Sadat's road to Camp David placed Saudi Arabia in the increasingly difficult position of having to choose between Egypt and Arabism.

That the tensions between Saudi Arabia's alignments and Arabism were
not greater is a testimony not only to its oil wealth and the decline of Arabism but also to Saudi Arabia's traditionally lukewarm stance toward Arabism. The Saudi government always leaned more on Islam than on Arabism
as a legitimation device, remained fearful of an Arabism that was identified

with its Hashemite rivals and radicalism, and historically had been rather distant from Arab nationalism. But Saudi Arabia was still an Arab and Islamic country, part of the Arab League, subject to Arab public opinion, and dependent on an Islam that treated Israel as an enemy to legitimate its rule. If it ventured too far from Arabism, Saudi Arabia would find itself the target of a regional and domestic backlash.

Attempting to read Syria's objectives is akin to reading tea leaves. Syrian officials consistently proclaim that Syrian and Arab interests are interchangeable: Syria is Arab, the guardian of Arab nationalism, the protector of Palestinian rights, and the first and last defense against Israeli imperialism. To be sure, such rhetoric has an instrumental side, but such rhetoric also reflects the fact that a specifically Syrian identity is only late in the making if present at all. Accordingly, much of the Syrian state's legitimacy derives from its Arabist credentials, thus fusing the relationship between domestic stability and its Arabism. As Egypt withdrew from the Arab cause after the 1973 war, Syria increasingly portrayed itself as the caretaker and defender of Arab nationalism. Syria's Arabism was clear and overdetermined.

The centrality of Arabism in Syria's political calculations—whether instrumental or genuine—meant that it was in no rush to make a deal with Israel to retrieve the Golan and was willing to use various Arab nationalist symbols, including occasional references to Greater Syria, to pursue its objectives.[78] Because its timetable was less hurried than Egypt's, and because Syria feared that its position would be weakened if other Arab states were on an accelerated schedule and open to bilateral deals, Syria's strategy was to establish a norm prohibiting separate agreements and insisting on a collective and coordinated Arab approach. Through such norms Syria could control the foreign policies of other Arab states and forestall the possibility of a breakthrough on terms other than its own.

The PLO was the other key actor of this period.[79] During this period the PLO's concerns pertained to who was authorized to represent the Palestinians at the bargaining table because Israel refused to negotiate with the PLO, whether authorizing such agents was a forbidden compromise, and whether the PLO should set preconditions (usually involving the eventual status of Jerusalem and the occupied territories) before any substantive negotiations. Also, the PLO was comprised of various groups, some of which, like Yasir Arafat's Fatah, were arguably more prone to conciliation on key issues; some of which, like Habash's PFLP, were not; and some of which were virtually indistinguishable from the Arab states that provided their financial backing.

To manage such divisions the PLO frequently settled on the lowest common denominator, that is, arguably a stance more confrontational than if majority-rule mechanisms were applied.

Further, as the sole and only legitimate representative of the Palestinians, the PLO was invested with tremendous symbolic capital and thus quite capable of wielding symbolic sanctions to control the foreign policies of other Arab states.[80] The Arab states were hardly the PLO's adoring fans—they clashed with the PLO about strategy and tactics regarding the peace process, and in important historical episodes an Arab state took on the PLO directly, including Jordan's bloodying of the PLO in 1970, Syria's intervention in Lebanon and against the PLO in 1975–76, and Egypt's signing the separate peace with Israel in 1979. But because the Arab states had said repeatedly that a comprehensive peace would best protect the rights of the Palestinians, and because the PLO was recognized as the final arbiter and protector of those rights, the PLO had near veto power over the pace and direction of the peace process and probably could bar the participation of other Arab states if it withheld its approval. This was most notable in the case of Jordan. Although King Hussein might have been willing to join the peace process, he certainly was unwilling to be viewed as negotiating on behalf of the PLO or undermining its interests. He and other Arab leaders generally felt duty bound to defer to the PLO on most matters regarding the peace process.

Four dynamics that emerged during the post-1973 period follow directly from these observations. First, Egypt pushed the normative envelope through its unilateral moves—and was fought every step of the way by Syria, Iraq, selected other Arab states, and the PLO and occasionally was censured and implicitly tolerated by the Gulf Arab states. Those who opposed Sadat resorted to symbolic sanctions, but such sanctions would work only to the extent that the potential domestic or regional censure outweighed the regime's other interests. In this regard perhaps one of Sadat's defining characteristics was that he held the other Arab states nearly in contempt and tended to shunt aside rather than accommodate Arab obligations, even if that meant suffering regional and international ostracism.[81] Second, Sadat calculated that to negotiate alongside the other Arab states had both advantages and disadvantages: Egypt obtained tremendous cachet from being the Arab world's recognized power, and its bargaining position was significantly strengthened by this role, but to proceed collectively also meant being weighed down by the lowest common denominator.[82]

The third feature flows directly from Sadat's response to the constraints and advantages offered by Arab nationalism: he attempted to amend the meaning of Arab nationalism so that it was consistent with his policies toward Israel. Simply put, Sadat challenged a meaning of Arab nationalism that rendered Arab states accountable to each other regarding nearly every aspect of their policy toward Israel. By asserting that it was his prerogative to negotiate with the Israelis for the return of the Sinai and to do so in a unilateral way, Sadat was flagrantly challenging the long-standing norms of Arabism. That he coupled such claims to the declaration that his policies were permitted by Arabism and demanded by Egyptian national interests only accentuated how he was harmonizing Arabism and Egypt's national interests to the point that they were becoming synonymous. His path, though strewn with obstacles by a coalition of Arab states that framed Sadat's policies as a betrayal of Arab nationalism and as dividing the Arab nation, remained passable until his peace treaty with Israel. At that point Egypt found that it had punched through the normative envelope and was outside of Arabism looking in.

Fourth, Egypt's path to Camp David and consistent effort to redefine Arabism not only triggered a heated debate but also encouraged fragmentation in Arab politics. Egypt sought from other Arab states greater latitude in its Israel policy, latitude that it claimed was permitted by Arabism and sovereignty but that its opponents viewed as tantamount to particularism and statism. Both Egypt and its opponents were correct. The debate about the organization of the Arab effort to confront Israel had immediate implications for the Arab countries' social relations: as they steadily weakened the norms of Arabism to accommodate Egypt's policies, they steadily promoted their own separateness and authority. Although the Arab states responded to the Egyptian-Israeli peace treaty with a show of solidarity, Egypt's eviction did little to arrest this fragmentation and, according to some observers, hastened it. The 1980s became a period defined by paralysis in Arab-Israeli politics and fragmentation in intra-Arab politics.

THE DEBATE ABOUT DISENGAGEMENT

In their first postwar meeting at the Algiers summit in December 1973, the Arab states were forced to confront the central issue of how would they handle the next round of the Arab-Israeli conflict. Would they approach Israel multilaterally or bilaterally? Was a separate peace possible? They already knew that they held different priorities and timetables, and Egypt in particular was hinting of its American and bilateral orientation. After considerable debate the Arab states advised against any separate political agreement and called upon each other to seek only a comprehensive solution based on the return of all the occupied territories and the fulfillment of Palestinian rights. The summit sanctioned Sadat and Hafiz al-Asad to continue their negotiations with Israel but instructed them not to act unilaterally on political issues that might affect a final settlement.[83]

The tension between Egypt's foreign policy plans and its relationship to Arabism came early. On January 18, 1974, Egypt and Israel concluded a disengagement agreement that resolved various issues concerning the cessation of hostilities from the last war. Syria accused Egypt of betraying the Arab cause, readying itself for unilateralism, and violating the Rabat resolutions.[84] Sadat defended the agreement on the ground that it was a military rather than a political act and said that Syria should follow suit. Saudi Arabia discretely supported Sadat and attempted to mollify the Syrians by promising that it would try to limit the scope of any future agreement.[85] Syria soon thereafter concluded its own disengagement agreement, which it emphasized was military and technical and absolutely not political. Nevertheless, the agreement represented a "psychological watershed . . . weaning it from its earlier strategy of rejectionism."[86] The Arab states also discussed a Jordanian-Israeli disengagement agreement, but then concluded that because Jordan had not been a party to the 1973 war, such an agreement would be political rather than strictly military.[87]

The next chapter in Egypt's unilateralism came in March 1975 when U.S. Secretary of State Henry Kissinger renewed his shuttle diplomacy, which signaled that side deals and separate agreements might result. To alleviate such fears and to hammer out some common understandings the principal Arab states met in Riyadh in April. They agreed on some common principles—no surrender of Arab territory, no separate peace, and no final settlement without securing Palestinian rights—that were consistent with past summit resolutions. But they could not agree on a common strategy. Syria feared that Kissinger's escapades were designed to lure Egypt away from the Arab front, an outcome that Sadat coveted but that would weaken the bargaining position of the Arab states; consequently, Syria proposed that the Arab parties go to Geneva, a multilateral negotiation forum to discuss the Arab-Israeli conflict and its resolution. Sadat, who was determined to reach a limited agreement with Israel and understood that Geneva's multilateral format represented an institutional constraint on him, insisted that they should agree on some basic principles but allow some flexibility in strategy. The Saudis again intervened on Sadat's behalf.[88] Shuttle diplomacy now swung into high gear.

The results of Kissinger's efforts were a second disengagement agreement with Israel.[89] Announced on September 1, Sinai II returned four hundred square miles of the Sinai, including the oil fields and strategic passes that are the doorways between the western and eastern parts of the Sinai; provided for a separation and limitation of forces; and included an array of provisions that practically ended the state of war between Egypt and Israel. The reaction to Sinai II was as much a fight over the future as it was over the agreement. Saudi Arabia again defended Sadat and characterized the agreement as a breakthrough and an important step toward reclaiming Arab soil and solving the Palestinian problem.[90] Indeed, it launched a particularly bitter attack on the PLO, portraying its criticisms of Sinai II as representing the "voices of Arab communists"—"hirelings" of world Communism misguidedly refusing to renounce the possibility of a political solution in favor of a military solution—and in fact as comfortable with a military solution because that "would leave the situation unresolved" and allow Israel, a socialist experiment, to exist.[91] Kuwait announced that it did not "question the right of sister Arab countries part of whose territory is under occupation to use such means as they deem suitable for the liberation of their territory, provided this does not affect the crux of the basic question, namely the Palestine question."[92] In typically tortured fashion King Hussein gave his modest approval while expressing "reservations regarding the Agreement itself," namely, the renunciation of military means, the failure to connect disengagement to other dimensions of the conflict, and the continuation of arms deliveries to Israel.[93]

Syria led the fight and attempted to mobilize Arab public opinion against Sinai II. In a speech commemorating the second anniversary of the October War President Asad accused Egypt of abandoning the military option, the principle of unanimity among the Arab ranks, the boycott of Israel (because Israel could now use the Suez Canal), and the Palestinians.[94] Later Syria denounced Egypt for dividing the Arab front and transforming the Arab-Israeli conflict into a border conflict.[95] Although Syria understood that it could do little to halt the agreement, it was intent on deterring any follow-up agreements and making it more difficult for Egypt to receive strong support from the other Arab states.[96]

Iraq also labeled Sinai II a violation of Arabism. But, as always, Iraq painted Syria as much if not more the villain. Although Egypt was withdrawing from pan-Arab causes, perhaps because of its deteriorating economy, at least it was not masking its treachery.[97] Syria also was retreating from pan-Arabism but liked to pretend otherwise through tactical gestures, such as the attempt to establish a Syrian-Palestinian joint political and military command that was intended first to extract a better bargain for itself on the Golan and second to allow Syria to control the Palestinians lest they disrupt a future deal. Syria was using the cloak of Arab cooperation to cover its betrayals.

Sadat defended his policies as consistent with Egypt's Arab obligations and commented on the current state of Arab affairs in a series of high-profile speeches addressed to the Egyptian public and the Arab world.[98] In a speech to the People's Assembly and the Arab Socialist Union he defended himself by saying that he had reclaimed Arab land without sacrificing the tenets of Arab nationalism, had never divorced the Palestinian issue and the other occupied territories from his discussions, or indicated a willingness to sign a separate peace with Israel. Then he pleaded for realism and pragmatism, saying he was attempting to deliver peace to the Palestinians through deeds and not words, and he challenged other Arab regimes to follow his lead.[99] Sadat also accused Syria of theatrics, of having prior knowledge of the disengagement and raising no objections at that time, and added, "All right, I concede that the Syrian Ba'ath Party has domestic troubles. But why drag the national (qawamiyyah) cause into these domestic troubles? We all have domestic troubles."

Sadat was attempting to frame his policies as consistent with Arabism and permitted by Egyptian sovereignty. He was "painfully frank": "I say that what concerns the Arab nation is consultation among all of us, but what concerns the Egyptian homeland is the concern of the people of this homeland, since in exercising our national (wataniyyah) sovereignty we are not burying anything with the rights of others nor do we accept anything liable to hinder the united Arab march."[100] Attempting to balance his desire to retrieve Egyptian territory within the parameters of Arabism was not easy.[101] In a wide-ranging and pointed interview Sadat defended himself through a mixture of assertive sovereignty and defensive Arabism against the charge that he had abandoned Arabism for the mere retrieval of land: Egypt had the right to follow whatever course of action would retrieve the Sinai so long as those policies were consistent with Arabism, which of course was the case.[102] That Sadat was hardly apologetic but rather contemptuous and cantankerous suggested how determined he was to go it alone if need be.[103] In any event, Sadat claimed that his retrieval of part of the Sinai through political negotiations and without the formal approval of the Arab states was consistent with Arabism; in doing so, Sinai II relaxed the norms of Arabism and created another category of actions that Sadat could take without first obtaining the approval of other Arab states.

CAMP DAVID

Those who predicted that Sinai II was a preview of coming attractions were right on the mark. In early 1977 Jimmy Carter, the newly elected American president, began to float a series of proposals to restart the stalled peace process. Much time and energy focused on reconvening Geneva, but it became painfully clear that these prenegotiations were unlikely to get the parties to the table, let alone to produce any breakthrough. Sadat, who had already tired of traveling with an entourage, began considering various ways to maneuver on his own. Although the Israeli elections brought to power Menachem Begin's Likud Party, which had a well-deserved hawkish reputation, Sadat received some encouraging responses from the new Israeli government to his diplomatic overtures. By late fall he had determined he would go to Jerusalem. The debate and speculation concerning the motives behind this highly controversial act are considerable—and include domestic political and economic pressures, Sadat's belief in diplomacy as shock therapy, that he was misinformed, and that he was clueless.[104] Whatever the reason, he flew to Jerusalem in November 1977. In a moment that was stirring if only for the drama, his speech was a masterful blend of conciliation and a challenge to Israel to do what it must for peace. By becoming the first Arab head of state to visit Israel—and controversial Jerusalem, no less—Sadat challenged all the conventions of Arab politics and bent if not snapped the many established summit resolutions.

But Sadat was not done. After nearly a year of circular negotiations between Egypt and Israel Carter invited Sadat and Begin to the presidential retreat at Camp David in September 1978 for an indefinite period of intensive and extensive closed-door negotiations. From what is described as an extraordinary and excruciating experience by all those present, the three delegations emerged exhausted but enthralled by their feat. The result was the Camp David accords, which actually were two documents: the outline of an Israeli-Egyptian peace treaty and the parameters for negotiating Palestinian autonomy on the West Bank and Gaza. Sadat had fulfilled his long-standing goal of recovering the Sinai, and the agreement on Palestinian autonomy allowed him to claim that he had not sacrificed, but rather provided an opportunity for, the Palestinians.

But even at this moment of seemingly unparalleled strategic behavior, Arabism shaped Sadat's negotiating strategy and the ultimate framework of the Camp David accords. There is little doubt that Sadat's ultimate objective was to reclaim every inch of the Sinai. But the negotiations at Camp David stalled and nearly broke down over the demand for a second framework to deal with the West Bank. Simply stated, if Camp David were to deal only with the Sinai, an agreement probably would have been concluded within a few short days. But because Sadat felt compelled for presentational purposes to be seen as not abandoning Arabism or the Palestinians, he insisted on a more demanding set of agreements that he might legitimately show to the rest of the Arab world as the real fruits of his negotiating acumen and efforts. Although he would soon find that his efforts would not shield him from the general perception that he had traded the Palestinians and abandoned Arab nationalism for the Sinai desert, the lengths to which he went to conclude an agreement with the Israelis to cover the occupied territories—and, without that agreement, he probably would have walked away from the table—are a testimony to the constraints that Arabism placed on Sadat's policies.

Sadat's trip to Jerusalem and the Camp David accords each triggered a nearly identical set of responses and debates in the Arab world about whether Egypt had violated the norms of Arabism and, if so, what Sadat's punishment should be. On each occasion Sadat attempted to defend himself by framing his actions as consistent with Arabism and permitted by Egyptian sovereignty. Upon his return from Jerusalem he told the People's Assembly that risks had to be taken for peace, he had not capitulated to Israel or betrayed the Arab nation or Palestine, and Egypt had the right to make these decision because of its sovereign status and its constant vigilance of Arab nationalism.[105] His actions were hardly traitorous, he insisted, but followed from well-established Arab principles and represented a step forward for the Palestinians and a major breakthrough now available to other Arab states. Indeed, he would sometimes assert, other Arab countries had little right to criticize Egypt, for Egypt had contributed more than any other Arab state to the Arab nation and the cause of Palestine.[106] Too bad, Egyptian officials and some media commented, that other Arab states could not appreciate what Egypt had done for the Arab nation.[107] Defensiveness also became aggressiveness. Of those who charged that he was damaging Arab unity, Sadat pointedly and sarcastically asked where this so-called unity, this vaunted solidarity, was. This unity, Sadat would lecture his listeners, was better characterized by conflict than by cooperation; look at Syria's actions in Lebanon, Iraq's meager contributions to the various Arab-Israeli wars, the ongoing disputes among the North African states, and on and on and on.[108]

The Arab states were divided over their response to Sadat's initiatives. Morocco, Oman, and the Sudan condoned and defended both his trip to Jerusalem and the Camp David accords on the grounds that they handed the Arab states an opportunity to advance their objectives in a manner consistent with Arabism and permitted by Egyptian sovereignty. The Gulf states were modestly approving and defended his right to go to Jerusalem if it achieved a breakthrough in the stalled negotiations.[109] Saudi Arabia, while noting its reservations on the questions of Jerusalem and Palestine, said that it did "not give itself the right to interfere in the private affairs of any Arab country, nor to dispute its right to restore its occupied territories through armed struggle or through peaceful efforts insofar as that does not clash with the higher Arab interests."[110] Adopting a stance similar to its position on Sinai II, Saudi Arabia wanted the benefits of Sadat's actions without having to suffer the wrath of its Arab opponents.[111] Bahrain rejected the Camp David accords on the ground that they failed to explicitly recognize the PLO. Qatar rejected them as unilateral.[112]

Jordan criticized Sadat's flight to Jerusalem and denounced Camp David on various grounds but argued for calm in order to avoid further fractures in the Arab ranks.[113] In staking out his position, Hussein avoided the inevitable regional and domestic outcry that was sure to follow if he appeared to be negotiating on behalf of the Palestinians and over the future of the occupied territories. Instead of joining the Camp David process, he reiterated both his commitment to past Arab summit resolutions and said that only the PLO was authorized to negotiate on behalf of the Palestinians. The United States, Israel, and Egypt were all disappointed by King Hussein's unequivocal rejection of Camp David because they counted on his participation if it was to have a chance. But they did not fully count on his dependence on other Arab states for regime survival and his own society for the social approval that came from being viewed as a member in good standing.

Iraq, South Yemen, Syria, Algeria, Libya, and the PLO vehemently objected to Sadat's actions, decrying them as constituting a dire threat to the Arab nation and as threatening to fragment and weaken its ranks. When Sadat flew to Damascus a few days before going to Jerusalem to get a mandate from Asad, Asad responded by telling Sadat that he was lucky not to be arrested.[114] Iraq chided that it was "idiotic irony for Sadat to describe his treasonable action as civilized behavior."[115] In response to Sadat's trip to Jerusalem these states gathered in Libya in December 1977 to formulate a common front; the other Arab states refused to attend what they understood to be a public hanging of Sadat.[116] Subsequently calling themselves the "Steadfastness States" but more commonly known as the rejectionist states, Iraq, South Yemen, Syria, Algeria, Libya, and the PLO began to meet periodically to publicize their outrage at Egypt's policies and interpretations of Arabism.[117]

After Camp David they pumped up the volume.[118] Iraq, never one to pass up an opportunity to implicate Syria, claimed that Syria was using Sadat's treasonous act as a "minesweeper on the road to treason in order to cushion Arab reactions."[119] But Iraq's outrage at Sadat was equaled by their fear that other Arab states might be tempted to follow his lead. That Sadat's actions were supported by some and not condemned outright by others indicated that he might be a bad influence. Accordingly, Iraq's messages and symbolic sanctions were directed not only at Sadat but also at those who might either follow his example or give comfort to his policies. To convincingly brand Sadat as a traitor to the Arab cause was the best way to preclude other Arab governments from following Sadat or condoning his actions.[120] Once Sadat's actions were framed in this way, it became virtually impossible for Arab states to support him without also presenting themselves as a traitor.

Camp David received a trial at the Baghdad summit of November 1–5, 1978. Baghdad and Damascus were adamant that Sadat's actions were a test of Arab solidarity as they defined it—namely, greater financial assistance to the confrontation states and ostracism of Sadat. Failing to punish Sadat for his treason would, warned Iraqi president Ahmad Hassan al-Bakr, spell the end of Arab unity and signal the Arab states' failure to live up to their pan-Arab responsibility. Indeed:

> We will not argue about the right of every ruler to act within the framework of his sovereignty in his own land. However, we cannot, under any circumstances, consider the action taken by the Egyptian head of state as merely an act of sovereignty and ignore the great truth that the struggle between the Arabs and the Zionist enemy is not a regional dispute confined to the Arab states whose territory was occupied in 1967 and not a mere territorial or border dispute or a war in defense of national sovereignty. Had this been the case, what would have happened in 1967 would not have happened. . . . Therefore, and without encroaching upon the right of any Arab ruler, we do not agree that such a ruler should arrogate himself the right to deal with such a struggle and to end it according to his own will.[121]

Bakr appropriated the message Nasser had used to ostracize Iraq's Nuri al-Said during the fight over the Baghdad Pact. And it just so happens that Iraq, symbolically hosting the summit that would oversee the expulsion of Egypt, would be a beneficiary of Egypt's departure.

There was little doubt that Sadat would be judged guilty of having violated Arabism, but suspense was considerable concerning what, if any, sanctions would be imposed. The Steadfastness States adamantly called for Egypt's expulsion from all Arab institutions and organizations, including the Arab League, and ineligibility for aid and assistance from Arab states.[122] Some even went further and argued that Egyptian citizens should not be allowed to travel to other Arab states, in effect denying Egyptian workers access to the Gulf states. Yet other Arab states were notably reserved in their willingness to punish Egypt or to expel it from Arab organizations. Saudi Arabia, which privately saw Camp David as largely consistent with its interests,[123] said that isolating Egypt, the heart and soul of the Arab nation, would be impossible, that such a policy would only harm the Arab states' interests, and that it "does not see any interest for our basic cause in diverting Arab efforts toward blaming a certain state."[124] The Kuwaiti foreign minister voiced a similar theme, and Kuwait's working paper at the Arab Foreign Ministers Conference in Baghdad hinted that Egypt should not be expelled from Arab political life.[125] Oman publicly supported the accords and urged its brethren not to isolate Egypt.[126]

Although the Gulf states had filed into the summit hoping to shield Egypt from sanctions and expulsion, they quickly reversed course under the threat of being branded as Egypt's coconspirators. Kuwait and Saudi Arabia had reiterated their soft line only a few days before at the Arab Foreign Ministers Conference, but "by the time the Baghdad Summit was convened the Saudis had come to view the pressure of the anti–Camp David forces as irresistible and had concluded that the only thing they could do was fight for an opportunity for Egypt to reconsider its course."[127] According to a former top-ranking Jordanian official, Kuwait and Saudi Arabia switched their policies because they did not want to go against the Arab consensus, a position that would have led to their ostracism.[128] To fail to condemn Egypt was to support it, to support Egypt was to place oneself squarely outside the consensus, to be outside the consensus could easily unleash unwanted domestic and regional denunciations.[129]

The results of the summit were a resounding success for the Steadfastness States and a testimony to the sting of symbolic sanctions. In the final communiqué the Arab states reaffirmed that only the PLO was authorized to negotiate for Palestinians; specified that "it is not permitted for any side to act unilaterally in solving the Palestinian question in particular and the Arab-Zionist conflict in general"; declared that resolutions of previous summit conferences maintained their moral force and that any future solution must be submitted to a summit for consideration; that Camp David violated past resolutions and occurred outside the "framework of collective Arab responsibility"; and warned that Egypt would be roundly censured and face sanctions should it not immediately rescind the accords.[130] The Arab states did not level any sanctions at this point, a concession to the Gulf Arabs, reserving such actions for when Sadat followed through on his plans.[131]

Sadat, though expecting the Steadfastness States to react harshly and to support sanctions, was visibly upset that the Gulf Arabs fell in line. He reserved some of his choicest and harshest words for them, accusing them of various crimes and of now being aligned with the Soviets and the "madman" of Libya.[132] The Gulf states responded by urging Sadat to reverse course and blaming him for bringing about his isolation in order to make a peace treaty more palatable to the Egyptian people.[133]

After a winter of negotiations Egypt and Israel signed a peace treaty on March 26, 1979. There was no denying that Egypt had challenged the very core of Arabism, had openly defied all past resolutions and the warnings of Arab states. That Egypt, the Arab world's cultural and symbolic power, had signed the separate peace made the transgression that much more serious. Many Arab newspapers and officials stressed that Israel had achieved a major victory by coaxing Egypt from the Arabs, that for Arabs to band together was now more important than ever to ensure that no one made similar gestures.[134] Newspapers and commentaries spoke of loss and betrayal.

Although the Baghdad summit had decreed automatic sanctions if Egypt signed a peace treaty, the Steadfastness States and the Arab Gulf states again clashed before their next scheduled summit at Tunis over whether such a step was necessary or productive. The Steadfastness States left little doubt that Sadat's actions should be met with unified ostracism and threatened to stay away from the summit unless the Baghdad resolutions were implemented.[135] These symbolic sanctions placed the Gulf states in a politically dangerous position, for they now appeared to be siding with Sadat and thus with Israel. Saudi Arabia was forced to chose between its Arab brethren and Egypt when it was already feeling insecure because of the Iranian Revolution. The other Gulf states felt similar pressures.[136] Consequently, they reversed course. The Tunis summit implemented a series of sanctions, including the severing of diplomatic ties, the suspension of Egypt's membership in the Arab League and other all-Arab organizations, the cessation of various economic linkages, and the transference of the headquarters of the Arab League from Cairo to Tunis.[137]

Sadat responded in characteristic fashion, reminding everyone of Egypt's past sacrifices, boasting that his efforts were generating opportunities and rewards for the Arabs, and labeling those who opposed Egypt's policies as dwarfs and ignorants who had made comparatively little contribution to Arabism.[138] Sadat gave one of his most spirited defenses of Camp David and attacks on his opponents in an April 5, 1979, address to the People's Assembly.[139] Appearing soon after the sanctions were imposed, Sadat defended Camp David and Egypt's Arab credentials, denied that this was a separate solution, and then launched a no-holds-barred attack on other Arab leaders. Other Arab states are accusing Egypt of forgetting the PLO, railed Sadat, but it was Egypt in 1976 that insisted that it be made a full member of the Arab League. In case there were doubts regarding the enemies of the Palestinians, Sadat reminded all that it was the Syrians "who slaughtered the Palestinians in Tall az-Za'tar" in Lebanon, King Hussein who "slaughtered" them in Amman in 1970, and that Iraq contributed little to the Palestinian cause or any of the Arab-Israeli wars. Rather than killing them, Sadat boasted, he got Israel to release Palestinians from its prisons and to acknowledge Palestinian claims. The Gulf states were not immune to the wrath of Sadat as he directed a hailstorm of criticism their way, guaranteeing an irrevocable break.

Egypt's defection and eviction from the Arab fold have led to considerable speculation that Sadat was determined to pursue his conception of Egyptian national interests as defined by state power and untainted by Arab nationalist concerns. Although throughout his campaign he attempted to frame his policies as consistent with Arabism, his words and deeds also laid claim to the view that as the leader of the Arab world Egypt could define Arabism any way it saw fit, and as a sovereign state Egypt was entitled to retrieve its territory and make peace with whom it wanted. It is unknown whether Sadat genuinely believed that his policies were consistent with Arabism. But strong evidence exists that he was driven by a desire to reclaim the Sinai at all costs—even if that meant domestic opposition from those who believed that Sadat's policies were an affront to Arab nationalism or were costing Egypt too much in terms of regional censure and isolation. Indeed, various Egyptian officials resigned rather than be associated with acts that they believed were strategically unwise and unprincipled, and even those Egyptian officials who remained were quite disturbed by the high price Egypt had to pay for peace.[140] Regional ostracism and domestic opposition slowed Sadat's path to implementing Camp David, but it did not block it. If Sadat found his way without the obstacles that other Arab leaders at other times might have faced, it was probably because he was particularly thick skinned when it came to Arab nationalist causes, and Egyptian society was drifting toward a more Egypt-centered view of Arab politics and thus was more receptive to his policies.

Those who opposed Sadat did so because they felt it was in their interest to do so. But such statements are tautological without some substance. Asad and the other Steadfastness leaders knew that their vocal opposition to Sadat would sell well with their societies and could enhance their regional reputations and aspirations. But why deny that these same leaders who came from the cradle of Arabism might not also be committed to various features of Arab nationalism and found in Sadat's actions a challenge that could not go unmet? If Sadat could engage in unilateral actions to the point of a separate peace with Israel, pretend that he was working for justice and the Palestinians when he was merely retrieving territory and furthering Egypt's strategic and economic interests, Arabism meant little if nothing at all. The struggle over Camp David was not only a struggle about regime interests but also about the meaning of Arabism.

Those who opposed Sadat attempted to stop him—and others from condoning his actions or following them—by deploying symbolic sanctions. From the start of Sadat's negotiations Syria and others framed them as a threat to Arab nationalism. Symbolic sanctions were most effective in the epicenter of Arab nationalism but less forceful in the hinterland; if the Gulf states were less susceptible to these sanctions, it was not simply because they had the wealth to shield themselves but also because their societies were latecomers to Arabism. But ultimately, the opposition's characterization of Sadat's policies as an affront to Arabism caused even moderate Arab leaders to tone down their support in some instances and to withhold it in others; by the time Sadat reached Camp David, even those who might have wanted to give him a tongue-lashing and nothing more yielded to the pressure and assisted in his public hanging.

Egypt paid a price for its heresy. It faced a series of sanctions that symbolically and politically excised it from the Arab body politic. Egypt was not the first Arab state to be condemned for actions that were viewed as a violation of Arab norms. The Arab states responded to the rumors of a peace treaty between King Abdullah and Israel by threatening him with a variety of sanctions, including expulsion from the Arab League. Nuri al-Said was never formally evicted from the Arab League for the Baghdad Pact, but his alliance with the West placed him outside the prevailing sentiment in Arab states. But the real penalties were not doled out to these states but to the leaders viewed as responsible for betraying Arab nationalism. King Abdullah was assassinated in 1951, in large measure because of his flirtations with the Israelis. Nuri al-Said died in July 1958 at the hands of revolutionary elements in the Iraqi military whose grievances included the Baghdad Pact and Iraq's isolation in Arab politics. Anwar Sadat was assassinated in October 1981, and his assassins accused him of a laundry list of crimes, including his close ties to the West and his peace with Israel.[141] Betraying Arab nationalism came with a price.

But the Arab response to Sadat and the Arab response to Abdullah and Nuri were different in an important way—the latter event led to a tightening of the Arab ranks, and the former event led to the opposite outcome. To stop King Abdullah in his tracks the Arab states established a prohibition against separate relations with Israel that lasted several decades. To limit the strategic alliances between Arab states and the West most Arab states signed on to Nasser's vision of positive neutrality. In each case, then, the Arab states responded to the triggering event by establishing a norm that more closely circumscribed what was considered proper conduct for Arab states.

The post-1973 debate about the next stage of the Arab-Israeli conflict and Egypt's unilateral policies fragmented the Arab ranks. On the surface Camp David represented another point at which Arab states tightened their ranks; after all, they evicted Egypt and renewed their vows of collectivism. But such surface impressions are misleading. By the late 1960s Arabism had come to be defined largely around the Zionist threat. The implication was that the group's identity and solidarity were increasingly dependent on an external threat that the group agreed to address in a collective manner; potential defections from these norms were interpreted not simply as free riding but as threatening the group's existence. Because the norms of Arabism were tied to their Arab identity, to "narrow" these norms was tantamount to weakening the Arab identity.

This scenario and development came to define the Arab debate about Sadat's policies. Sadat argued for an interpretation of Arab nationalism that could accommodate Egyptian national interests and that he claimed was consistent with sovereignty. The Steadfastness States insisted on a more restrictive definition that more closely circumscribed the activities of Arab states and predicted that a more narrow definition of Arabism would weaken their social bonds. Sadat and his critics disagreed publicly about whether his policies were consistent with Arabism, but they largely agreed that his policies were narrowing the meaning of Arabism, reducing the range of issues on which they were accountable, and bringing them closer to statism. The immediate implication was that, as Arab states discussed the demands

of Arabism, they implicated their own identities; as they defined and presented themselves, they also drew conclusions concerning how Arab politics
should be organized. Although the Arab states responded to the Egyptian-
Israeli peace treaty by evicting Egypt from the Arab fold, the dialogue among
the Arab states about Egypt's policies had reduced the scope of Arabism and
allowed for greater particularism.

Fragmentation in Arab Politics

Egypt's eviction from Arab politics gave the temporary appearance of solidarity, but it also had the unintended effect of creating a more permissive environment in Arab politics that encouraged Arab states to orient their policies in separate directions. Arab scholars and policymakers frequently
couple Egypt's departure from Arab politics with the conflict and drift that
emerged in Arab politics in the 1980s. But they do not link such changes to
the loss of Egypt's economic and military power; after all, Egypt's leadership
position in Arab politics was hardly defined by its deployment of military
sticks or economic carrots. Rather, they focus on Egypt's cultural and symbolic power, its ability to project a sense of purpose and thus to act as mag-
net in Arab politics. According to one former Jordanian official: "Egypt, as
the largest Arab country, was the center of Arabism. Imagine a family and the
father abandons them—the immediate reaction is to try and cope with the
new demands but after a while the family begins to understand that there is
no father figure who can provide guidance and consequently begin to go
their own way at the first opportunity. Arab countries now begin to go their
own way."[142] Mohamed Heikal similarly concluded that "one inevitable consequence of Egypt's surrendering her traditional role as the main modernizing and unifying Arab country was that the Arab world split up into small
political and geographical entities, busy with their own affairs and often
squabbling among themselves."[143] Egypt's path to Camp David had fragmented the Arab ranks, and its departure from Arab politics only hastened
that trend.

The very structure of Arab politics was changing. Commentaries
throughout the 1980s echoed the theme of the decline of Arab national interests and the rise of state interests, the elusive quest for Arab solidarity, and
the virtual disappearance of issues that could mobilize Arab states for collective action.[144] Time and again Arab states were consumed at the Arab
summits by the subject of the causes, consequences, and cure of their frag-

mentation. The signs of their fragmentation were everywhere, and a constant topic of conversation. But the development of subregional organizations, new patterns of inter-Arab rivalry and conflict, and the desire to institutionalize sovereignty in order to halt their rivalries best signaled and most fully contributed to that fragmentation.

SUBREGIONAL ORGANIZATIONS

A telltale sign that Arab states were moving in separate directions was the development of new organizational forms. Specifically, whereas Arab states once found that the Arab League was institution enough to accommodate and express their shared identity and interests, during the 1980s subregional organizations emerged that enabled Arab states to pursue their interests and potentially express more localized identities.[145] The Iran-Iraq War was the trigger for the Arab world's first subregional organization when Oman, Bahrain, the United Arab Emirates, Qatar, Saudi Arabia, and Kuwait created the Gulf Cooperation Council (GCC) in May 1981. These Gulf states shared a common fear that the Ayatollah Ruholla Khomeini's Islamic message might stir instability among their substantial Shi'ite populations and that the Iran-Iraq War might spill over to include them.[146] But the GCC states also drew a boundary between themselves and the other Arab states, stating that, although they were all Arabs, the GCC states shared certain historical considerations that unified them and separated them from the other Arab states.[147] The GCC states, moreover, denied that the GCC would become the stepping-stone to integration and unification; in fact, its members went some distance to explain that this association was intended to be a "realistic foundation" for cooperation.[148]

The appearance of the GCC in the context of an already troubled Arab order caused many to openly ask whether Arab summits and even the Arab League would matter in the future as Arab states found more appropriate forums to express their localized identities and interests.[149] In response to this question King Hassan of Morocco, in his capacity as the host of the 1985 summit, insisted that subregional organizations did not contradict the Arab League and in fact might even strengthen the cause of Arab unity.[150] But such hopeful rebuttals became even less plausible after Iraq, Jordan, Yemen, and Egypt formed the Arab Cooperation Council (ACC) in February 1989, and later that year Morocco, Algeria, and Tunisia founded the Arab Maghrebi Union (AMU). Now the tenor of the times turned to how to coordinate relations between the subregional organizations and between each of them and the Arab League.[151] King Hassan's once optimistic appraisal turned cautionary as he warned that "these subregional groupings must not inspire a spirit of isolation."[152] Although many Arab elites claimed that subregional groupings were broadly compatible with pan-Arab principles and the charter of the Arab League, the prevailing sentiment was that Arab states were going their separate ways because they were organizing their activities based on geography rather than shared identity.

INTER-ARAB CONFLICT

Alongside these new patterns of cooperation were new forms of conflict. Arab states were more than accustomed to rivalry and hostility. But there were important differences between the forms of rivalry that existed for much of inter-Arab politics and those that were now being detected. Whereas Arab states once proceeded on the assumption that they had a shared Arab identity that grounded them and oriented them in each other's direction, now they were openly questioning whether that shared Arab identity was enough to bring them back to the fold. And whereas Arab states once channeled their hostility and conflict through symbolic means, the evidence was growing that they were leaning toward more militarized gestures. These changes in the form of inter-Arab conflict, argued Arab officials and intellectuals, represented and contributed to the fragmentation of Arab politics.

No sooner had the Arab states pledged to respond to the heresy of Camp David with solidarity than they descended into animosity and rivalry. The 1980 Arab summit was a microcosm of these dynamics and a taste of the times to come.[153] In the summit's opening address King Hussein introduced a theme that he would recycle throughout the decade: growing divisiveness and the failure to achieve even a modicum of stability or unity were producing a "widening trend of caring for regional interests at the expense of pan-Arab interests" and creating a "revival of methods of outbidding."[154] Syrian foreign minister Abd al-Halim Khaddam summarized the overall sentiments when he said, "If we look at the map of the Arab homeland, we can hardly find two countries without conflicts. These conflicts have already erupted or are explosive. We can hardly find two countries who are not in a state of war or on the road to war."[155]

Although Arab leaders vocalized their need to rise to the challenge, their actions betrayed their words. Syria refused to attend the 1980 Arab summit, reiterated its support for Iran in its war with Arab Iraq, ridiculed the summit and King Hussein, and then moved its army toward the Jordanian border on the pretext of Jordan's covert operations in Syria (a charge Hussein first denied and then several years later confessed was correct).[156] The Arab leaders at the summit pleaded for calm and for fraternal Jordan and Iraq to find more pacific ways to settle their differences. Although a war was averted, the willingness of Syria to amass its troops on the Jordanian border invited commentators across the region to opine that Arab states were better at conflict than they were at cooperation. Egyptian foreign affairs minister Boutros Boutros-Ghali could only gloat from the sidelines: "Cairo cannot help feeling some satisfaction at seeing the Arab world, which expelled Egypt from its midst, being torn apart."[157]

The remainder of the decade percolated with the theme of dissension; it seemed as if every failure to cooperate and every instance of conflict was transformed into a symbol of the Arab states' disintegration. The 1981 summit, the briefest in history, led to a flurry of postmortems that saw dissension as a sign of the deteriorating state of Arab politics.[158] The following year the Arab states failed to confront the Israeli invasion of Lebanon.[159] At the 1985 Arab summit in Rabat, King Hassan said that a central agenda item was "the situation prevailing in the Arab nation and the need to clear them of everything that might tarnish that atmosphere."[160] In his opening speech Hassan noted how the states of the European Economic Community, which do not even have a common language, are able to come to agreement on major issues, convene meetings with "a smile and look happy," are the powerful, "arm us with the most modern weapons," and discuss issues with responsibility to resolve common interests.[161] Echoing Hassan's theme, King Hussein lamented that it was impossible for the Arab nation to make progress when "there is disintegration instead of congregation, regionalism instead of pan-Arab solidarity, plotting instead of harmony, hegemony instead of fraternalization, destruction instead of construction, and the placing of obstacles instead of their removal."[162]

Arab officials had good reasons to take every opportunity to claim that their conflicts were signs of their disintegration: the conflicts between Arab states were more numerous than ever before, and militarized conflicts too were multiplying.[163] Between 1949 and 1967 Arab states had roughly ten militarized disputes (three of those coming in the Maghreb); they had nineteen militarized disputes between 1967 and 1989. That is, the twenty-two years since 1967 produced nearly twice as many militarized disputes as had the nineteen years before 1967. Not only were there more militarized conflicts than ever but the cause of these conflicts increasingly was territorial grievances and the desire for strategic influence rather than strictly domestic factors such as a spillover of a internal conflict or the attempt by a regime to increase its popularity by manufacturing or playing up an external grievance. According to Malik Mufti, the Arab states were increasingly demonstrating "their willingness . . . to justify the pursuit of national interest through military means."[164] This was a dramatic turnaround from previous years when Arab officials almost always used Arab nationalist precepts to justify and legitimate their foreign policies.

These two factors—more inter-Arab disputes were militarized than ever before, and more of these disputes derived from realpolitik impulses—led Arab officials and intellectuals to claim that these conflicts represented and caused their growing statism, particularism, and fragmentation. Arab states were no stranger to conflict, they commented at the time, but conflict in the past had always unfolded amid the assumption that they had a shared set of interests because of their shared Arab identity. This shared identity and interests had always brought them back home even in the worst of times. But perhaps no more. Indeed, the more likely that Arab states were to contemplate the use of force to settle their grievances, the more likely Arab officials and societies were to consider other Arab states a potential threat. From such developments sprang further doubts that their shared identity handed them shared interests. No longer debating or dwelling on various proposals for economic or political integration, the summit meetings of the 1980s concerned resolving differences and healing wounds. Even during their darkest days of the 1950s and 1960s Arab states never coupled their conflict to impending disintegration. Not so anymore.

SOVEREIGNTY

To try to orient each other's foreign policies in a more constructive manner Arab states once again addressed the rules that should govern their relations. This discussion focused on a familiar arrangement: sovereignty. But a change marked how sovereignty was being discussed and advanced in this debate about the desired regional order. Previously, Arab states gravitated toward sovereignty to dampen Arab nationalism and the tendency of Arab leaders to use Arabism as an instrument for symbolic sanctioning; now few Arab leaders viewed Arab nationalism in the same light, and more were interested in institutionalizing sovereignty in order to limit their conflicts. Arab states once forwarded pan-Arab ideals as the inspiration for cooperation; now they were looking to base their cooperation on norms that were indistinguishable from those of international society. Arab states once insisted they had shared interests because of their shared identity; now they were hinting that proximity and geography were better and more realistic rationales for inter-Arab coordination. Arab states once were looked to sovereignty to defend their individuality against Arabism; now they were looking to sovereignty to preserve their Arabism against unbridled individualism.

The draft protocol regulating joint Arab action that was discussed at the 1985 Arab summit exemplifies the remedies that Arab states sought for their ailments. The protocol specified that "each Arab country will pledge to respect the system of rule in other Arab countries, not to interfere in the domestic affairs of other Arab countries, and refrain from assisting any elements that act against the sovereignty, independence, and safety of the territory of any other Arab country."[165] In addition to other clauses concerning the peaceful settlement of disputes, the draft protocol "obliges the member-states not to permit the establishment of foreign military bases and not to grant any military facilities or any foreign military presence in their territories," to withhold support from any foreign country at war with another Arab country, and to refrain from interfering in Palestinian affairs and proposing a separate agreement on the Palestine issue. Echoes of past Arab nationalist principles carried over into these proposals, but the central points that animated their debate revolved around the desire to use sovereignty to better protect their territoriality and perhaps to provide the basis for cooperation.

No one was a more active or outspoken advocate on these issues than King Hussein. Throughout the Arab summits of the 1980 he made the importance of sovereignty a routine feature of his speeches. According to Taher al-Masri, a former prime minister of Jordan, behind this move were various Arabist and self-interested reasons.[166] Without an agreement on the basic rules of the game Arab politics would only fragment further. In other words, absent some general norms to guide their relations in ways that might encourage cooperation, Arab states were likely to orient their policies in disconnected directions. Moreover, Jordan's location—at the center of the Arab world and containing a large Palestinian population that blurred the boundaries between Jordan and other Arab countries—gave it a keen interest in establishing such an order.[167] When pressed to address why King Hussein was now pushing sovereignty when these same "destabilizing" conditions were present during the 1960s, Masri responded without hesitation: "This is because the era of Arab nationalism is over. Now that nationalism has declined, we can begin to emphasize sovereignty without being accused of being opposed to Arab nationalism." According to another former top-ranking Jordanian official, "There are new rules of the game. There is a general under-standing that Arab nationalism had created only turmoil and instability." So, he continued, Jordanians were much more interested in sovereignty, and the decline of Arab nationalism allowed King Hussein to make the pitch even more strenuously and successfully than in the past.[168]

By the end of the decade the Arab states had healed some wounds—Egypt had returned to the fold in 1987, the bloody Iran-Iraq War had finally ended—but they were still discussing their rules of the game. At the 1989 Arab summit in Casablanca King Hussein commented on the relationship between the individual national securities of the separate Arab states and the desire for unity in the context of Palestine. His speech is worth quoting at length, for it dramatizes the ongoing debate and tension between acting col-lectively and individually with regard to Palestine and how statism was creeping into regional life:

> On the one hand, the problem has an Arab aspect concerned with the Arab order and with inter-Arab relations within the framework of our re-gional institution. On the other hand, there is the aspect of relations with others, of our conflicts, and of cooperation with others. . . .
>
> A decision must be made. Sooner or later, the ambiguity must be re-solved. We simply cannot continue to oscillate between the two concepts without a thorough examination or proper clarification. If the question is purely one pertaining to individual states, then Jordan's problem becomes quite simple, in essence not exceeding the occupation of a few square kilo-meters of Jordanian territory in Wadi Arabah and the northern segment of the Jordanian valley. . . . The question then becomes: If the Palestine question pertains to individual states, why should Jordan, Syria, and Lebanon continue to sustain a situation of protracted attrition? Why should they sit and wait? And in whose interest is this situation? If on the other hand, the question is a pan-Arab one, as indeed it is, where are our collective efforts and pan-Arab commitment?
>
> What breaks the heart and calls for sorrow and concern is that the Arab League, the oldest regional organization in this world since World War Two and the one having the most components of cohesion, devel-opment, and survival, has sunk into disarray at a time when the world is moving toward regional blocs, multilateral institutional cooperation and integration between resources and capabilities in the search for a comprehensive development and entrenchment of the pillars of region-al security. Where is the common Arab market? Where is the Collective Arab Defense Pact?[169]

The problem, according to Hussein, was that although the rhetorical rules reflected a hope for pan-Arab aspirations, Arab states increasingly adhered to alternative principles. Such gaps were causing confusion and conflict.

What was the ultimate cause of the present state of disarray in Arab politics? Hussein bluntly noted that individualism dominated:

> First, the obstacle lies in bilateral differences, which usually grow out of political disagreement and occasionally lead to punishing the peoples of the two concerned countries. . . . Second, another problem is a narrow pan-Arab vision resulting from the preoccupation of each Arab state with its own development, security, and defense concerns. . . . It has also resulted in diminished concern for and demotion of pan-Arab issues to the lowest level of state priority, except in cases of a directly perceived connection between a particular state and an outside threat. Third, the unjustified exaggeration in the implementation of the principle of profit and loss in dealing with pan-Arab issues.[170]

Arab states were now evaluating their policies based on state rather than Arab national interests and were likely to be more stingy when asked to contribute to Arab national concerns.

Using his country's first appearance at an Arab summit since 1978, Egyptian president Hosni Mubarak forwarded the "pillars of Arab solidarity," which were nearly identical to the norms of international society and sovereignty:

> First, to arrive at an agreed-on formula for peace. . . . Second, to define for ourselves an active role in the process of international detente. . . . Third, we should agree on a realistic meaning for Arab solidarity, which we will be committed to in order to reach an understanding and agreement of views on the principle and its practical applications in the Arab reality, regardless of any differences in views or in policies.
>
> Fourth, we should be strictly committed to the principle of noninterference in the internal affairs of each other, because the people of each country knows [sic] better than others what realizes their own interests and are more capable of defining their path at the internal level. It is unfeasible that we be enthusiastic in proposing this principle in the sphere of international relations only to be incapable of honoring it and consolidating it in our narrower pan-Arab sphere in which there are common interests unavailable in the wider international circles.
>
> Fifth, this is connected to . . . the basic fact . . . that governs the motion

of history a great deal—that the many opinions and efforts are inevitable necessities that we cannot do without. The law of life calls for diversity. We cannot change this law.

Sixth, in the coming period we will have to direct a great deal of . . . attention to laying down agreed-on practical policies that may lead to more economic, cultural, and political cooperation . . . inside the Arab homeland. . . . [We must also consider] the question of . . . the relationships between the Arab groups . . . and the relationship between them and the Arab League.[171]

Egypt's comeback speech urged the repair of inter-Arab relations by finding some common norms that rested on sovereignty. Such sovereignty was coupled with the understanding that these were separate Arab states that might have separate interests because "the people of each country know better."

At the close of the 1980s the debate about the desired regional order still focused on the relationship between the Arab state and Arabism. But this debate departed sharply from the one that occurred only two decades before. Whereas Arab states once debated different versions of Arab unity, how to effect collective action on matters of Arab national interest, and how their sovereignty was circumscribed because of the norms of Arab nationalism, now they focused on how to contain their conflicts and openly debated whether they had any reason to orient their actions toward each other except strictly material grounds or for only the most immediate threats. As one Cairo newspaper observed, Egypt now believed that no single Arab country could shoulder the responsibility for the Arab nation and establish a "single center of power" and that Arab unity was based on coordination of common interests that were largely limited to economic ties. "The nature of the Arab objective is now different."[172]

If the "Arab objective" was different, it was different because the structure of Arab politics had changed. Arabism no longer represented the defining source of the Arab states' identity, shaped their interests and strategies, or moved them to act collectively. Arab states still presented themselves as "Arab," but they also were acknowledging their separate and distinct personalities that had potentially separate and distinct interests. Arab states still talked about Arab national interests and debated a set of norms tied to their Arab identity, but these interests and norms almost exclusively revolved around the subject of Palestine; the other interests and norms discussed at the summits and in various protocols were identical to those of international society. Arab states still focused on the relationship between Arab nation-

alism and sovereignty, but whereas they once considered how to institutionalize sovereignty to circumscribe the transnational effects of Arabism, now
they were looking to sovereignty to limit their conflicts and save some semblance of Arab nationalism and we-feeling. The debate about the desired regional order, the relationship between the Arab states' identities, the norms
that bound them together had shifted dramatically since the late 1960s because of the decline of Arabism and the rise of statism.

No single factor contributed to this outcome. Reductionism is to be avoided when searching for the ingredients of macrohistorical change. Geostrategic forces contributed to the decline of Arabism. The 1967 war was a cataclysmic event and certainly caused Arab states to recalculate their strategic
policies and to become more self-reliant and less interested in multilateral
posturing. Egypt, the most powerful Arab country, threw its weight behind
the conservative agenda in part because it was intent on reclaiming Egyptian
soil and Arab dignity. The emergence of petropolitics and the growing power
of the Arab Gulf states, which had always been on the periphery of Arab nationalism, supported a more statist orientation. But strategic factors and systemic changes are a poor predictor of the foreign policies adopted by Arab
states and why they moved from integration to fragmentation. It was not the
distribution of power but their own interactions that led Arab states to move
away from the radical agenda before 1967. Conceivably, Arab states could have
responded to the 1967 war by tightening their alliance; other states at other
moments have responded to a rise in an external threat by coming closer together. If Arab states responded to the defeat by deciding to move further
apart, it was because of their collective interpretations of how their past
strategic and symbolic interactions in the name of Arab unity had created
their current plight. Many Arab leaders were noting that the same global and
regional developments that seemed to be encouraging other areas to rush
into regional cooperation in the late 1980s were not leaving a similar mark on
the Arab states' dispositions; indeed, they were taking such developments as
a cue to distance themselves from one another even further.

Domestic changes in general and state formation in particular also contributed to a growing statism. Virtually all Arab states pledged their devotion
to Arab nationalism while pursuing state-building projects intended to encourage their citizens to identify with the capital city and not transnational
Arabism. State formation spurred a revolution in identities that encouraged
Arab states to express new sets of interests; as Arab societies more closely
identified with the territorial state, Arab leaders were less fearful of the symbolic sanctions unleashed by other Arab governments. Although evidence

exists that state formation in the context of Arab politics is associated with a decline in the desire for transnational projects and inter-Arab cooperation in the l980s, Arab scholars and officials were noting that state formation per se was open ended with regard to international outcomes and transnational obligations as they claimed that hardening of the Arab state would provide a solid foundation for inter-Arab cooperation. After all, they frequently noted, the European states—states that were strong and legitimate on any scale—were integrating at an unprecedented rate. Systemic and domestic forces played a role in the growing territorialism and statism that increasingly defined the regional order, but the existence of both systemic and domestic factors does not directly point to integration or fragmentation.

How Arab leaders played the game of Arab politics led to the widely observed fragmentation. Years of symbolic competition and outright conflict had created growing differentiation between Arab states. Unceasing inter-Arab rivalry had encouraged citizens, and even partisans of Arab nationalism, to make their peace with the state. That inter-Arab interactions and conflicts encouraged differentiation was already evident from their unity experiments of the mid-1960s; each failed unity attempt had led Arab states to stress their separate personality in relationship to the Arab nation. The symbolic competition that immediately preceded the 1967 war, and then the collective interpretation of the causes of the failures of past Arab efforts, further institutionalized sovereignty and statism.

The Arab states' debate over the peace process shaped the organization of Arab politics in general and led to a more centrist version of Arabism in particular. Khartoum was the first and most dramatic instance of this relationship. To reverse the outcome of the 1967 war Arab states concluded that they must construct a new regional order that would allow them to make peace with each other and war with Israel. Sadat's post-1973 policies led to a narrowing of the meaning of Arab nationalism as it reduced the Arab states' mutual accountability on a host of issues and legitimated their autonomy according to their special circumstances. The Egyptian-Israeli Peace Treaty represented a short-lived moment when the other Arab states overcame their differences of opinion over Sadat's policies to agree that he had gone too far and was stretching the meaning of Arabism to the point where it was meaningless. Soon after they collectively delivered their guilty verdict on Sadat's policies, the Arab states returned to their conflicts with renewed ferocity.

During the 1980s the Arab states proclaimed that they must tighten their ranks, all the while engaging in new forms of inter-Arab organization and conflict that were both a cause and a consequence of their growing fragmentation. Having lost their patience with pan-Arab forums, Arab states began to drift toward more localized associations that were interpreted as a challenge to Arab nationalism and based on more narrowly-defined state interests. More worrisome for those still longing for inter-Arab cooperation was the new pattern in inter-Arab conflict. At the 1989 summit King Hussein discursively linked the presence of severe bilateral differences to the emergence of a narrow pan-Arab path that focuses on the individual Arab state, nearly ignoring developments that occur in other Arab states. This record of conflict, King Hussein suggested, had left Arab states less committed to each other and more willing to evaluate policies on more narrow self-interested terms. If Arab states could not learn to cooperate after decades of attempts, and if conflict rather than cooperation was the sole legacy of such attempts, then perhaps Arabs states should go their own way.

Arabism had narrowed considerably as a consequence of the dialogue over the peace process, their longstanding bilateral disputes, and the near absence of awe-inspiring acts of inter-Arab cooperation. Simply stated, the very structure of Arab politics had altered considerably since 1967. Now Arab states were no longer as desirous of the social approval that they gained from participating in Arab activities and contributing to Arab causes, as interested in competing for symbolic capital because its value had depreciated considerably, as susceptible to symbolic sanctions because their societies were less easily mobilized except for the most dramatic and subversive actions, and less oriented toward each other. The changes in the very structure of Arab politics were there for all to see and for Arab leaders to fret publicly about at their summit meetings, evident in their new patterns of association and in their forms of conflict and cooperation.

By the late 1980s the Arab states were searching for rules of the game that would arrest their unbridled fragmentation and reinstate some political force behind their shared Arab identity. Years of rivalry and conflict had steadily relaxed the meaning of Arabism and made it more consistent with statism. Faced with a situation of their own making, Arab states now were seeking to contain their ever-present potential for conflict by establishing some rules of the game that were virtually synonymous with international society and premised on the recognition that, although Arab states were a single family, the members of the family had separate personalities. Unless Arab states were able to find some common ground, Arab scholars and officials warned, then they had to seriously question their future.

7

The End of the Arab States System? Arab Politics Since the Gulf War

The Iraqi invasion of Kuwait and the subsequent U.S.-led campaign to restore Kuwaiti sovereignty set off a chain reaction of fragmentation in the Arab world. From the moment Iraqi troops rolled into Kuwait on August 2, 1990, government officials and commentators spoke gravely about the future Arab states system. No sooner did the war officially end on March 1, 1990, than those same voices talked about the need for, but unlikelihood of, Arab reconciliation. Arab reconciliation was a polite way of describing what was unrelenting fragmentation, a splintering of the Arab family. Some Arab governments argued that the end of the cold war and the Gulf War demanded a tightening of the ranks; unfortunately, the leader of this camp, Iraq, had just invaded Kuwait. After the war the conversation was dominated by pleas to alter their conduct, free themselves of sentimentality, and base their policies on "realism." The retreat to the state was unmistakable.

Their post–Gulf War policies paralleled such talk. Arabism had encouraged Arab leaders to coordinate and harmonize their policies, sometimes against their better judgment and personal preferences, but now their collective acknowledgment of Arabism's dysfunctional qualities led to a wholesale contemplation of new policies based on "interests" and realism. Although none denied the ideal of Arab unity or surrendered its membership in the Arab League, Arab states began contemplating alliances that were once taboo, to imagine the construction of regional organizations that might supersede the Arab League, and even to reconsider the boundaries of the region. The Gulf War had unleashed a tidal wave of inquiry concerning what remained of Arabism.

That Arabism rather than Kuwait was the longer-term casualty of the Iraqi invasion is testimony to Arabism's already frail condition, the result of years of inter-Arab squabbles. As Arab leaders and commentators singled out the cause of their present condition, they directed their attention to a legacy of hostility seemingly sponsored and permitted by Arabism. Saddam Hussein's invasion of Kuwait was only the ultimate and most heinous of such actions occurring between Arab states. Consider Hosni Mubarak's explanation of why the Arab states were delayed in congregating to discuss their response to the Iraqi invasion:

> Our problem in the Arab nation is that if you express your opinion, and this opinion is different from someone else's, you are considered an enemy. In other words, if someone expresses an opinion that is different from mine, we become enemies. There are different opinions throughout the world. But the principle of difference of opinion is not a basis for enmity. Brother, I tell you my opinion, and you tell me yours. I tell you: Beware, you are an Arab state. Your affairs are of interest to me. I care that your country should not be overthrown. I care about your country's standard of living. I care about peace in the area. When I express my opinion, this should not provide a basis for you to say that Egypt is hostile.[1]

Mubarak's statement can be read as a sweeping indictment of Arab politics over the decades and a microcosm of the processes that led to the decline of Arabism. In many respects the Gulf War was the proverbial straw that broke the camel's back. Regardless of whether the Gulf War is best considered a cause or a pretext for existing attitudes, the war represented the most recent and most shocking violence done in the name of Arab solidarity. Because Arabism seemingly brokered only hostility and suspicions, Arab officials began to publicly confess their exhaustion from its demands and its unfulfilled promises. According to one Jordanian official, because of Iraq's invasion "even Jordan feels liberated. There are no external forces that can dictate to us what we can and should do."[2]

All this suggests the end of the Arab states system. By "Arab politics" I have meant the existence of certain core issues—the Arab-Israeli conflict, autonomy from the West, and unity among Arab states—that are expressive of the Arab political identity, that help to define the Arab state's interests and the legitimate means to pursue those interests. A dominant concern of the 1990s has been the need for Arab reconciliation, the possibility and timing of Israel's integration into the region, and even the possibility of closing the

Arab League. To be sure, Israel's place in the region remains in dispute pending a final treaty with the Palestinians, but the retreat on these "Arab" issues as they directly pertain to inter-Arab action has been impressive, calling into question the organization—indeed, the existence—of Arab politics. This conversation was produced by the insult of Iraq's invasion of Kuwait, the indifference that marked the 1980s, and decades of an Arabism whose most memorable contributions were injury and rivalry.

The Gulf War

The history of the Gulf War has been chronicled exhaustively, and I need to discuss only some basic features.[3] Catching a second wind after the conclusion of the Iran-Iraq War, beginning in 1990 Saddam Hussein engaged in a series of highly aggressive actions that caused considerable alarm inside and outside the region. He hinted at using nuclear weapons against Israel and proclaimed at a February 23 meeting of the Arab Cooperation Council that the Arab states—with Iraq at its helm—should take a more aggressive posture in global politics. U.S. distraction by the fallout from the end of the cold war was providing an opening, he surmised. Saddam Hussein attempted to rally Arab states around him by stating that Arab power would promote (his version of) regional peace and by issuing thinly veiled threats against Israel.[4] At the all-Arab summit in Baghdad that year Saddam Hussein warned his audience that the end of the cold war was bad news for the Arabs. Israel was growing in strength because of Soviet Jewish immigration to the West Bank, and its patron, the United States, was more powerful than ever. Indeed, the United States no longer had to work through Israel to control the region, for the retirement of the Soviet Union from the Middle East meant that the United States was free to impose a regional hegemony. Some might rejoice at the end of the cold war, cautioned the Iraqi leader, but its demise spells bad times for the Arabs.

Much speculation concerned the motives behind these inflammatory statements and policies so soon after the end of the Iran-Iraq War and while Saddam Hussein was in the midst of postwar reconstruction. Most explanations centered on Saddam Hussein's need to consolidate his power at home and on his bid for leadership in the Arab world. But the twins drives of consolidation and leadership were founded on a more basic desire to arrest Iraq's economic crisis. Iraq had accumulated substantial debts during the Iran-Iraq War, and a major economic imperative was to increase the capital available for postwar reconstruction. Saddam Hussein identified two options, increasing revenue from oil exports and persuading Iraq's largest lenders to extend debt forgiveness. Both options would require cooperation from the neighboring Gulf states, which helped set the quotas on oil production and owned a fair percentage of Iraq's outstanding debts. The Gulf states were hesitant to oblige Iraq on either course of action, and Iraq soon focused its grievances and allegations against Kuwait, which it accused of not appreciating that Iraq had incurred its war debt in defense of all Arabs in general and Kuwait in particular, of siphoning oil from the al-Rumaylah field that bridged their two countries, and of attempting to wage a war against Iraq through economic means. Soon Iraq and Kuwait were engulfed in a minor crisis.[5]

The Iraq-Kuwait confrontation escalated throughout July 1990, with various Arab leaders attempting to determine the price of a peaceful conclusion.[6] A flurry of Arab mediation and a highly controversial discussion between the United States and Iraq concerning what the United States was prepared to do if Saddam Hussein invaded Kuwait had little demonstrable effect. Iraqi forces overran Kuwait on August 2. *Al-Ahram*'s headline, "The Arabs' Blackest Day," reflected the prevailing reaction in the Arab world.[7] The international community also was outraged by this unprecedented bid to swallow another sovereign state whole, an act made doubly outrageous in the prevailing opinion that the post–cold war order would be kinder and gentler. The U.N. Security Council quickly convened during the next few days and adopted a series of resolutions (660, 661, and 662) roundly condemning the invasion, demanding an immediate retreat, imposing economic sanctions, and hinting of more robust measures if Saddam Hussein did not heed the Security Council's warning.

The Arab states were not nearly as quick to respond. Although they issued individual statements condemning the invasion and urging Saddam Hussein to reverse course, the Arab states did not immediately convene an emergency summit to issue a collectively determined response.[8] Their failure to do so was something of an embarrassment, making them look dazed and confused, as they were well aware that the rest of the world was waiting for the Arab states to act boldly and collectively.[9] Explaining why the Arabs still had not convened to discuss the crisis a full week after the invasion, Mubarak observed on August 8 that "no one wanted an expanded Arab summit, because the Arabs, by nature, prefer to talk in small groups. At Arab summits, we trade accusations and curses without reaching any results. Therefore, we find that we do not want to meet at Arab summits." Later he added: "The UN Security Council beat us to a decision, as though we were not Arab and the Arabs were a motionless corpse who could not move, speak up, or react to an invasion of a state by another Arab state. They must have said that we were scared. The worst accusations were levelled at us, and you must have heard them."[10] The invasion brought not only a crisis within the family but also unleashed anxieties among many Arab states as they imagined themselves as "others" saw them.[11]

During these first days many Arab states insisted that the crisis be kept "in the family" and that they be allowed to find an "Arab solution." Most proposals offered by Arab states were designed to enable Iraq to save face, which meant winning some key concessions from Kuwait in exchange for a complete or partial retreat. The urgency with which they insisted on an Arab solution revealed a widespread fear among Arab states that the internationalization of the conflict, that is, involvement by the West, would make a solution that much more complicated and elusive—and increase the damage already done to Arab politics. The Iraqi invasion, in this reading, was not simply a border dispute between two sovereign states but an unprecedented act by one Arab state against another. An often-heard view was that the invasion endangered all Arab institutions and groupings, with the possibility that Arab politics would suffer a greater setback than it had from the 1967 war.[12] To involve the West would only compound an already devastating situation; it was bad enough that an Arab state had invaded another. It would be far worse if Western intervention became part of the equation.

After considerable delay and much (somewhat) quiet diplomacy, the Arab states held their much anticipated emergency meeting in Cairo on August 9. Although the summit ostensibly was designed to create an environment that might encourage Iraq to soften its hardening position, few predicted that it would be a success. The outbreak of a food fight between the Iraqi and Kuwaiti delegations, appropriately started by Iraq, only symbolized the unlikelihood of resolving the crisis.[13] By most accounts the formal proceedings were only slightly more constructive. The inter-Arab divisions became clearer and went on the record when the summit put to a vote a series of resolutions that condemned the Iraqi invasion and demanded an unconditional withdrawal.[14]

Twelve Arab states voted for the resolution. Although the reasons for doing so were many—including economic and strategic considerations, a fear that Iraq might become too militarily and economically powerful, and in Mubarak's case a sense of personal outrage that Saddam Hussein had lied to the Egyptian leader about Iraqi intentions—nearly all justified their vote on the basis of the present and future of the Arab regional order. A sense of foreboding—concern that if the Arab states could not settle the conflict among themselves, Arab politics would be radically and permanently altered—permeated the proceedings. Mubarak captured such sentiments at a news conference at the opening of the summit when he stressed the various principles and norms that were at stake and shattered by Iraq's invasion. These included the need to preserve a concept of pan-Arab security, which had been part of recent summit discussions at Rabat and Baghdad and was premised on sovereignty, noninterference, and the pledge to settle disputes without force.[15] At stake, in short, were the rules of the game of Arab politics. If Iraq's invasion was permitted to stand, Arab politics would have a dim future indeed.

Those who opposed the resolution also made clear that theirs was a principled stand informed by Arabism. Algeria and Yemen abstained, Jordan, the PLO, Sudan, and Mauritania expressed reservations, and Tunisia did not attend the summit. Although none publicly embraced the Iraqi invasion per se, all were widely interpreted as giving comfort to Iraq because they consistently clamored for an Arab solution at all costs and refused to be associated with a Western intervention under any circumstances.[16] But behind these pan-Arab considerations were ulterior motives. The PLO's (mis)calculation that its road to statehood might go through Baghdad was one it would later regret. King Hussein, though opposing the invasion, justified his defiance of the growing international show of support for Kuwait by saying that the problem should, and would most easily, be settled by Arab states. There is little doubt, however, that domestic considerations propelled the king's stance. With Palestinians a majority of his population and an economy dependent on trade with Iraq, King Hussein calculated that he had more to fear by angering Jordanian society than he did by defying the growing international coalition against Iraq.[17]

Saudi Arabia, Egypt, and Syria formed the eventual backbone of the Arab coalition aligned against Saddam Hussein and provided the bulk of the Arab forces in the U.S.-led coalition.[18] They might have contributed their troops to the cause for their individual "vital interests."[19] But they were potentially vulnerable to the charge of collaborating with the West against another Arab and Muslim state. Saddam Hussein attempted to exploit that vulnerability by drawing upon a reservoir of resentments against the West and the economic divisions in the Arab world to attempt to mobilize the Arab streets on his side and thus destabilize his Arab opponents from within.[20] Specifically, he portrayed the Western buildup against Iraq as a modern-day San Remo and called for the liberation of the holy sites in Mecca and Medina from a Western-allied Saudi Arabia. In doing so he linked his actions to long-standing popular causes and grievances against the West, portrayed other Arab leaders as allies with the West against fundamental Arab and Islamic interests, and was able to play into anxieties concerning foreign control of the Arab world that had been heightened by the end of the cold war and the perception of unbridled U.S. power.[21] Arab leaders took seriously his threat to destabilize them from within through symbolic means; they tightened security, discouraged public demonstrations, and unleashed their spokesmen to justify their actions as consistent with an Arabism that Saddam Hussein had defamed. Egyptian leaders attempted to defend their actions and defuse Saddam Hussein's destructive plea that the Arabs set fire to their leaders, and even Syrian officials spelled out why the Israeli occupation and the Iraqi invasion were not comparable events.[22]

The crisis continued through the fall and came to a dramatic conclusion with a series of high-level meetings between the United States and Iraq in Geneva in early January. When these meetings produced their predicted failure, the United States carried out its threat to start the military phase of the war. On January 16 the American-led coalition unleashed a relentless and devastating air campaign against Iraq, which continued for the next several weeks. The ground campaign began on February 24 and ended one hundred hours later on February 28. Kuwait's sovereignty was successfully restored amid much celebration in Kuwait City and elsewhere. Operation Desert Storm was a military success.

But there was comparably little public cheering throughout the Arab world.[23] The affair had been emotional and heart-wrenching for Arabs on both sides of the coalition. The Iraqi invasion of Kuwait represented an unprecedented breach in Arab politics. And the decision by many Arab states to align with the West in a war against fraternal Iraq was, for many, equally blasphemous. These impious acts committed in the name of Arabism created a series of immeasurable divisions in Arab politics. So great was the damage, according to many, that all thoughts of repair should be summarily dismissed for the time being. Boilerplate statements regarding the need for "Arab reconciliation" were eclipsed by a flurry of commentaries that described in unusually candid and hostile terms the fissures and fragmentation in Arab politics. King Fahd of Saudi Arabia, for instance, portrayed a huge rift in the Arab world, one that was created by the willingness of many Arab actors to implicitly or explicitly condone Iraq's invasion of Kuwait for economic reasons.[24] On the other side of the aisle were cries that the decision by the Arab states to join the coalition against Iraq was a conspiratorial act that gave the West the opportunity to impose a hegemony over the region. Although disagreement about who was to blame for these events was considerable, agreement was widespread that these events had created fragmentation.

Arab nationalism was already in a highly weakened state before the war, and the Gulf War only hastened its demise. As Jordanian journalist Fahd al-Fanek put it, "The Gulf War was Arabism's bullet of mercy."[25] Shaykh Zayid of the United Arab Emirates observed that "the Arab nation's split and fragmentation existed before the Gulf War, but this war has aggravated and deepened this split."[26] In the recent past Arab leaders had portrayed Arab unity as around the corner and usually left Arab summit meetings declaring their solidarity. The Iraqi invasion, however, provided them with an opportunity to come clean, to declare that Arabism had been sickly before the invasion and may have been dealt a mortal blow by the war. As if to punctuate their divisions and unwillingness to go through canned performances and rituals, the Arab states refused to hold a perfunctory Arab summit after the Gulf War. All calls for an all-Arab gathering were quickly dismissed. The first sign that Arab states might be ready for some sort of reconciliation did not come until late December 1995 when Saudi Arabia, Syria, and Egypt convened a "tripartite" summit. The purpose of the summit, according to the Arab League's secretary-general, was to go back to the drawing board to discuss "higher Arab interests," "a unified position on the peace challenge," and "regional cooperation and its limits."[27] Such agendas scarcely resembled those of old.

The weakened state of Arabism, coupled with the Gulf War, inaugurated a new chapter in the debate about the Arab order, one unlike any other. Rather than Arab unity, Arab leaders now publicly wondered whether and when "Arab reconciliation" might occur. Instead of a turn to Arabism, Arab leaders now urged the dismissal of policies based on "emotion" and "sentiment" in favor of policies founded on "realism."[28] These publicized perceptions of fragmentation alongside the demand for realism are testimonials to the decline in Arabism and the rise of interests that no longer flowed from a shared identity. Ideally, I would offer survey research, public opinion polls, and other sorts of attitudinal measures to ascertain the declining weight of Arabism. However, such measures do not exist. But indirect evidence of the decline of Arabism is suggested by the reorganization of the Arab-Israeli conflict and the contemplation of Israel's integration into the region, new security arrangements and alliances, the reconsideration of the boundaries of the region as exemplified by the controversial concept of "Middle Easternism," and the debate about the future of the League of Arab States and the region's other organizations. These developments spell not only the further fragmentation of Arab politics but also the potential demise of the Arab states system.

The Reorganization of Arab-Israeli Politics

Most expectations were that the Arab-Israeli conflict would receive renewed attention after the Gulf War, and such predictions came to pass. During the war Saddam Hussein had justified the invasion as a step in his grand plan to focus world attention on Palestine. Although few in the international coalition supported this attempted linkage, U.S. President George Bush tried to placate and strengthen his Arab allies by asserting that he would use the diplomatic capital generated by the Gulf War to obtain progress on the Arab-Israeli front, and the U.S. State Department posited that the conditions for a breakthrough were now ripe.[29] Bush successfully followed through on his pledge. Using various carrots and sticks, he pushed and prodded Israel and the Arab states to gather in Madrid in late October 1991 to reconsider their present and future relations. But some Arab states did not have to be prodded. According to former Jordanian ambassador Adnan Abu Odeh, many Arabs jumped at the chance to come to Madrid and rid themselves of their pan-Arab commitments.[30] Others were less enthusiastic; Syria and Israel were present reluctantly and made their reluctance known in their opening speeches. But they were there. Israel was especially piqued by the composition of the Palestinian delegation, blessed by the PLO and comprised of many members who hailed from Greater Jerusalem. But the PLO-sanctioned delegation was at an international conference with Israel, and the Israeli delegation was forced to listen to its grievances and proposals. For Palestinian leader Faysal al-Husaini this was Madrid's true accomplishment.[31]

The Madrid talks represented a major turning point in the organization of the Arab-Israeli conflict. Before Madrid the Arab states, with the exception of Egypt, had adhered to the norm that Arab states should move in lockstep and collectively and avoid any bilateral discussions outside a comprehensive peace. Madrid, however, marked a subtle but important departure from this modus operandi. Although still insisting on coordinating their ranks and rejecting the idea of establishing relations with Israel before signing a comprehensive agreement, the post-Madrid talks continued in two different institutional forums. The first were bilateral talks between Israel and the frontline states. The second were multilateral talks regarding develop-ment, refugees, security, water, and the environment.[32] Many Arab states in-sisted that the "fruits" of the multilateral talks should be denied until after progress on the bilateral front, but most Arab states participated, however halfheartedly, and they made some progress on technical and environmen-tal matters.[33] Although it was easy to dismiss these talks because of their fail-ure to produce any tangible breakthrough, their very existence was taken by the participants as breakthrough enough. The Arab-Israeli conflict was being transformed from an ideological contest into an interstate conflict, and this transformation was altering its very organization.

The absence of a genuine breakthrough on the Palestinian-Israeli front, however, was a brake on the bilateral and multilateral cooperation between the Arab states and Israel. Many core Arab states were quite angered by Yasir Arafat's support of Saddam Hussein during the Gulf War, and in the imme-diate postwar period they were signaling that they had tired of his shenani-gans, were willing to punish him for his actions, and were more open than ever to a radical transformation of the Arab-Israeli conflict. But they were unwilling to move toward Israel in a public or far-reaching manner until there was movement in the Palestinian-Israeli negotiations because the Arab states feared being charged with defecting from the Arab consensus and weakening the PLO's bargaining position.

That breakthrough was unlikely so long as Yitzhak Shamir remained the Israeli prime minister. The June 1992 Israeli elections, however, rejected Shamir, a hawk who championed the idea of "Greater Israel," in favor of Yitzhak Rabin, who campaigned on the idea of security within constricted borders. Soon thereafter Israel and the PLO signed the Declaration of Prin-ciples on September 13, 1993, in which both parties formally recognized each other's existence and established the parameters for continued negotiations and the settlement of the conflict. The very existence of Israeli-Palestinian negotiations, once completely unthinkable, served further notice of the fun-damental reorganization of the Arab-Israeli conflict.

The changes that were taking place in Israeli-Palestinian and Israeli-Arab relations also reflected a decline in the Arab states' perception of the Israeli threat. This decline was spurred by several developments, though none more important than the radical change in Israeli foreign policy that occurred with the 1992 election of Rabin as prime minister and the subsequent push by Foreign Minister Peres to jumpstart the peace process. Arab states now began to downgrade their perception of the Israeli threat. This change had the additional effect of reinforcing the fragmentation of Arab politics. At a

1994 Arab League meeting, the foreign ministers noted that, although Israel had been the Arab nation's staunchest enemy for fifty years, from now on each country would identify its own enemy.[34] For years Arab states had proceeded on the assumption that their shared Arab identity generated a common definition of what threatened their interests; the decision to allow each country to determine its own enemy was a nod to the belief that statist and geopolitical interests were now central to each Arab state's definition of that threat. According to Egyptian foreign ministry official Nabil Fahmy, the decline of the Israeli threat gave the Arab states less reason to hang together: "It makes sense that we are now going more our own way now that the Israeli threat is gone. The Arab-Israeli conflict brought together Arabs into political institutions," but because the conflict has been transformed it is only natural that Arab states should move in different directions.[35] Theoretically speaking, identity (self) is defined in relationship to a relevant "other," and that other is frequently viewed as a threat.[36] Accordingly, a self-identified group will tend to construct organizations to mobilize group action against a shared threat. The converse is also likely. In this instance the decline of Arabism altered how Arab states organized themselves to confront Israel, and the perceived decline of the Israeli threat in turn relaxed the impulse for coordination and cooperation. From such developments came a reorganization of the Arab-Israeli conflict.

Now that there were productive Israeli-Palestinian negotiations and a decline in the perception of the Israeli threat, Arab officials felt freer to contemplate diplomatic, commercial and economic relations with Israel. Beginning before but becoming a dominant theme after the signing of the Declaration of Principles, the Arab world debated Israel's "normalization," that is, the pace and extent of its integration into the region. Israel and the Arab states began to explore issues of common interests, achieved progress in the multilateral talks, and held an economic summit in Casablanca in October 1994 (with annual conferences each year thereafter).[37] The boycott by Arab states of companies that do business with Israel began to crumble in late 1994. Israeli officials were now routinely meeting with leaders from Oman, Qatar, Morocco, and Tunisia. That Arab states have a collective investment in the peace process and Israel's eventual normalization was demonstrated time and again, most dramatically at the "Peacemakers Conference" in Sharm al-Sheikh in March 1996 after the wave of terrorist attacks in Israel. Even Syria, which routinely insisted that it carried the flame of Arab nationalism, no longer made a Syrian-Israeli peace treaty conditional on a Palestinian state.[38] In general, Arab states began to intimate that their individual interests were dependent on a resolution to the Arab-Israeli conflict and began to move in ways that encouraged that resolution and to consider how collaboration and cooperation with Israel might be to their mutual benefit. That Arab states might begin to move in this direction, however, was enabled by the decline of Arabism.

The Jordanian-Israeli peace treaty of October 26, 1994, was the extreme illustration of this new climate, the elevation of state over Arab national interests, and the related willingness to consider relations with Israel now that the PLO was doing the same. As King Hussein defended the treaty, he made gestures toward Arabism but also aggressively asserted Jordan's interests. "It is meaningless and unjustified to say that Jordan should stand by idly until all the issues are resolved, after which Jordan can address its own issues," King Hussein commented. "Had this happened, no one would have cared about Jordan's state of affairs. . . . Having regained our rights, our objective is now to build Jordan, enable its sons to lead a decent life."[39] Hussein was clearly separating Jordanian from Arab interests. The treaty underscored that state officials felt less beholden to traditional Arab stands and less susceptible to symbolic sanctions of old.

But the debate about the treaty in Jordan also communicated to all who cared to listen that establishing relations with Israel was not uncontroversial. Many Jordanians resented and objected to the treaty: this was a "Hashemite peace," representing the interests of the palace and not the people; the king had gone too far, too fast, and should have waited for a final settlement to the Palestinian conflict; a peace treaty was acceptable, but relations were an entirely different matter; and many Islamic organizations protested any ties whatsoever with Israel.[40] Such opposition did not deter the palace, as it proceeded to conclude a series of agreements with Israel that included cooperation in commerce and tourism, contemplated unification of the airports and the electrical grids of the towns of Eilat and Aqaba, and even considered the servicing and upgrading of Jordanian F-16s by Israel Aircraft Industries.[41]

The reaction to the treaty suggests that although Arab heads of state are willing to contemplate relations with Israel on the ground that it furthers the state's interests, their societies are not always of the same opinion. Developments in Jordan are not unique. Nabil Fahmy said that a major reason that Egypt remains attentive to the Palestinian issue is that it affects Egyptian domestic politics. Because of the "communications revolution" what transpires in Palestine has an immediate effect on Egyptian society. Therefore, he continued, "for us to have a calm constituency in Egypt, we need peace for Egypt—not for pan-Arabism. Peace is in Egypt's national interest."[42] Even when Arab officials discuss their Palestine policy, they explicitly link its transnational character, its influence on domestic politics, and its subsequent impact on their foreign policy.

That Palestine remains a powerful symbol of Arabism limits what is permissible and expected of Arab states. No Arab leader mimicked King Hussein's complete embrace of Israel; Arab leaders preferred to keep their relations and contacts low key, and even then they frequently came under criticism from other Arab states for giving Israel the "fruits of peace before the facts of peace." Such concerns informed the debate about the "rush" to normalization.[43] Most Arab states cautioned against premature relations with Israel before peace was an accomplished fact; in a famous exchange Egyptian foreign minister Amr Musa accused King Hussein of "scurrying" to the Israelis.

One stated reason Arab states insisted on a united position was to better the Palestinians' bargaining position. But many Arab states also worried that their own negotiating position was being undermined by these individual moves toward Israel.[44] Arab states had always held out "recognition" as the ultimate prize that Israel would gain; it was a potent bargaining chip available to Arab states. But if Arab states were "scurrying" to conclude relations, the value of that chip was being reduced. Lebanese prime minister Rafia al-Hariri, for instance, said that the race for normalization was coming at Lebanon's expense.[45] Syria's demand that the Arab states decelerate the pace of normalization owed to its fear that its bargaining position was being weakened.[46] Opponents of the economic summits in Casablanca in October 1994 and in Amman in October 1995 raised similar objections.[47] In this respect Arab states were engaged in a strategy reminiscent of the Arab states' treaty negotiations with the Western powers in the pre-1955 period: they were attempting to use the symbols of Arabism to control the foreign policies of other Arab states in order to increase their own bargaining leverage.

The continuing strength of Arabism in unifying the Arab ranks on Palestine was particularly noticeable in the aftermath of the election of Binyamin Netanyahu as the prime minister of Israel in late May 1996. Netanyahu campaigned on his opposition to Oslo and the negotiations with Syria, and his victory catalyzed the Arab states to convene their first summit since the Gulf War in June 1996 in Cairo. The Arab states had previously tried to organize a summit for a variety of reasons, most notably to formulate the Arab response to Israel's bombing of Lebanon in 1992 and again in early 1996, but these developments could not force them into the same room. However, the possibility that the new Israeli government might derail the peace process—a process in which they had an individual and collective investment—caused the Arab states to convene a summit and to pass a series of resolutions that expressed their collective resolve to monitor the peace process closely and to make any normalization of relations dependent on Israel's adhering to the spirit and the letter of the Oslo accords. This development was significant in a number of respects: it was the first collective statement by the Arab governments on the peace process; even Arab states—namely, Jordan, which was not necessarily enamored with having its Israel policy held hostage to collective Arab policies—hardly wanted to be portrayed as defecting from the Arab consensus; and however much Arab states might have come to accept Israel's presence in the region, a strong suspicion lingers, and it can unify the Arab ranks.

The events since Netanyahu's election provide vivid testimony to the dependence of Arab-Israeli cooperation on progress in Palestinian-Israeli negotiations and the lack of progress in the latter to put a chill in Arab-Israeli relations and encourage Arab states to meet on a regular basis to try to coordinate their Israel policy. The violent clashes between Israel and the Palestinians in September 1996, and the controversy involving the Israeli government's planned expansion of settlements surrounding Jerusalem at Har Homah, the failure of the Israeli government to keep to the timetable for the redeployment of Israeli troops on the West Bank—these and other events have not only further paralyzed the peace process but also frozen Israel-Arab cooperation and helped to unify the Arab ranks.

In general, the reorganization of the Arab-Israeli conflict reflected a shift from Arabism to realism, from an ideological to an interstate struggle. The Israeli-PLO negotiations continued to set the pace—few Arab states were willing to conclude a far-reaching agreement without progress on the Palestinian front, and many Arab societies remained cool to the idea of close relations with Israel in any event. But the tenor of the debate had shifted radically in a brief period: whereas only a few years earlier Arab states had debated how they should confront Israel, now the question was the pace and pulse of Israel's integration into the region. As one editorial lamented, "The paradox of the negotiations between the Arabs and Israel are more acceptable—and maybe successful—than the Arabs' negotiations with one another. And the enmity with Israel has begun to drop to low levels, compared with inter-Arab hostilities. The negotiations with it over the demarcation of its border are much easier than negotiations among Gulf states, on that grounds that Israel is more acceptable."[48] Arab states seemed to have an easier time sitting down with Israel than they did with each other, reflecting a dramatic decline in Arabism and the rise of statism.

The Changing Security Order

These changes in the Arab-Israeli conflict parallel a change that has occurred in inter-Arab security relations since 1990. There are two critical features here, both of which reflect the declining salience of Arabism and the explicit articulation that Arab states view each other as security threats: the first is the candid coupling of security and sovereignty; the second is the demise of pan-Arab security concepts and the emergence of new security alliances and ties that once were viewed as violating the norms of Arabism.

The Arab states' security discussions and preferred security arrangements are emblematic of the emphasis they place on sovereignty. As soon as Iraq was dislodged from Kuwait, Arab states turned to the issue of what security arrangements they should establish to discourage a repetition of this bloody encounter and foster regional security. At the forefront of many discussions was the need to reaffirm that sovereignty underpins the Arab order. The weight of pre–Gulf War opinion favored sovereignty as the basis of regional order, and the Gulf War only intensified such sentiments. During the Gulf War this took the form of the defense of Kuwaiti sovereignty and the refusal to intervene in Iraq during the war lest such an action lead to Iraq's dismemberment (among several reasons). After the Gulf War the importance of sovereignty imprinted the Damascus Declaration, the first post–Gulf War security agreement. Under the declaration, announced in March 1991 as a pan-Arab security arrangement, the Gulf states, Syria, and Egypt pledged further strategic and military cooperation, with an understanding that Syria and Egypt would be well compensated for their military commitments and troops.[50] Despite the surface rhetoric of the desirability of pan-Arab security and the ongoing conferences and meetings, the declaration has had little operational value.[51] But the intended value of the declaration, according to Abdullah Bishara, former secretary-general of the Gulf Cooperation Council (GCC), was its recognition of the legitimacy of the Arab states' borders, the right of each state to arrange its own security, and each state's exclusive claim to its resources—that is, its sovereignty and exclusivity.[52] Coming on the heels of Iraq's denial of Kuwaiti sovereignty and the claim that Gulf oil belonged to all Arabs, the GCC states held sovereignty and security as indistinguishable and insisted on institutionalizing sovereignty as the basis of inter-Arab relations. An impressive number of statements during and after the Gulf War centered on the necessity of sovereignty as the basis of the Arab order.

The fate of the Damascus Declaration highlighted the collapse of the concept of Arab national security. Since the establishment of the Arab Collective

Security Pact in 1950, Arab states had paid homage to the concept of Arab national security, and it served as a focal point for discussions. Although the concept and its institutionalized expressions had little operational value, the pact did guide many security discussions of the pre-1990 period. The Gulf War all but silenced such talk. For some the Gulf War was such a shock that the concept collapsed. For others, according to former Jordanian ambassador Abu Odeh, the Gulf War provided a convenient pretext for burying a concept that they had long ago considered more debilitating than useful.[53] Whether the Gulf War was cause or pretext, little sustained attempt has been made to resuscitate the concept of pan-Arab security arrangements.

In lieu of pan-Arab possibilities Arab states now began to contemplate alternative regional arrangements, many of which broke some long-standing taboos. Consider the activities of the GCC states. Eschewing notions of cooperative security that were supposedly the foundation of the GCC, and quickly discarding the Damascus Declaration, which was the sole vestige of any notion of Arab security, the Gulf states quickly demonstrated that they had greater faith in the United States and the West than they did in each other. They provided the United States with access for military bases and concluded stockpiling and over-the-horizon agreements.[54] Simply put, whereas once the Gulf states had kept their association with the United States subterranean (if they acknowledged it at all) and did so because they anticipated domestic political repercussions from an alliance with the West, now they were more openly embracing such an arrangement. Arab leaders who once avoided any alliance with the West for fear of inciting instability no longer had the same fears.[55] This outcome nearly reversed the independent security stance that the Gulf states carefully cultivated after their independence beginning in the 1960s and resembled the Western protectorate that dominated much of the area's pre-independence history.

In general, any notions of Arab collective security lay in ruins after the Gulf War as Arab states began emphasizing individual over Arab security and began demonstrating a strong preference for bilateral security pacts with Western states.[56] The apparent consensus was that Arabism had long outlived its usefulness, that the region should sober up and embrace sovereignty, and that Arab states should be allowed, within reason, to consort with whom they wanted.[57] Normative fragmentation and the declining political salience of the Arab national identity produced a change in regional security patterns. Except for the all-but-defunct Damascus Declaration, concerted attempts to rekindle anything resembling an all-Arab security arrangement were few.[58]

The Future Arab Order

The decline of Arabism imprinted not only the region's security arrangements but also the debate about the very boundaries of the region, what if anything remains of an Arab order, and Israel's place in the region. Such discussions, in short, implicate the more fundamental issue: what remains of the Arab states system? In recent years numerous conferences, newspapers, and articles in the Arab world have considered this theme.[59] A conference at Cairo's Al-Ahram Center in late 1994 was dedicated to the necessity of Arab reconciliation and maintaining some semblance of an Arab order. The Lebanese-based journal *Al-Mustqbal al-Arabi* [The Arab Future] has been consumed with the general issue of what remains of the Arab order, and does an "Arab" state exist? What is the social purpose of the Arab state? Do Arab states have distinct interests? And if not, is it defensible to talk about an Arab national identity that has political consequences?

The highly charged discussion over the concept of "Middle Easternism" is a useful vehicle for entering into this debate. The term became current after the Madrid talks of 1991 and largely originated with Egyptian intellectuals and policymakers. Middle Easternism is best understood as embodying a number of tenets. It begins with an implicit and sometimes explicit belief that pan-Arabism's promise was misspent or misapplied, and in either case pan-Arabism is an inappropriate guide for reconstructing the post–Gulf War order. Instead, the future order should be founded on a realistic understanding of state interests. After all, the problem with past pan-Arab arrangements was that they looked great on paper but diverged from what Arab states were prepared to contribute or implement; the Arab League and other institutional expressions of Arab nationalism were founded on sentiment and emotions and not on interests.

These state interests, however, concern a desire not only for sovereignty but also for economic, environmental, and security cooperation designed to enhance the peace and prosperity for each Arab state. According to Nabil Fahmy, Egypt's foreign policy must begin with a recognition of its interests, which are primarily economic: "We have to think about region building . . . where our economic interests reside. . . . As we build these institutions we must recognize that we are building them on our interests. Too often we have built them without the solid political foundations, and then these institutions came to naught." Fahmy emphasized the language of interests and juxtaposed the new Middle Eastern order, founded on interests and thus capable of having practical consequences, with the Arab order, which was based on identity and generated little more than some modest political coordination.[60] In many respects Fahmy's view is reminiscent of the Egypt-first discourse that defined Egyptian foreign policy before 1948 and since Sadat; in other respects his view is less unique to Egypt and more representative of contemporary political discourse and practice in the Arab world.

But these interests are not necessarily exclusive to Arab states. In fact, because non-Arab states might share these basic interests, and because the ability of Arab states to further their interests might depend on reaching agreement and cooperating with these non-Arab states, the future regional order should embrace Arab and non-Arab states, including Turkey, Iran, and, most controversially, Israel. Those who champion Middle Easternism are at the forefront of suggesting various ways in which Israel might become integrated into the region's future security, economic, and political institutions. Such proposals are based on a reading of the state's interests and the understanding that individual self-interest is premised on collective action among the region's states, not just Arab states. Lotfi el-Khuli, a well-known Egyptian journalist and author of the best-selling and highly controversial book *Arabiyya, Aywa. Wa al-Sharq al-Awsat, Kathaleka* [Arab, Yes—And Middle Eastern, Too], observed:

> There are two schools of thought in the Arab world. The first is Middle Easternism. The view here is that this is an American-Israeli project to try and conquer the region and is against pan-Arabism. Consequently, these people want to see a rebuilt Arab order, to build on the Arab economic market passed at the 1964 [Arab] summit and to confront Israeli hegemony. They are against the peace process and see Israeli imperialism. They have been educated to see Israel as the "other" which is why the peace with Israel is such a shock. . . . The second view sees no contradiction between a rebuilt Arab order and a new Middle East.[61]

Khuli stressed how a Middle Eastern system that includes Israel still permits pan-Arab arrangements that are expressive of an Arab identity,

Those who champion Middle Easternism continue to foresee a role for all-Arab organizations and institutions, but their emphasis on Middle Eastern arrangements on issues of central importance leaves them open to the criticism that they are attempting to bury Arabism. According to Nassaf Hitti, an adviser to the secretary-general of the Arab League, Middle Easternism is viewed as an alternative to, if not a denial of, pan-Arabism.[62] In this respect those who oppose Middle Easternism accuse its proponents of attempting to extinguish the Arab identity and of opening the door to Israeli domination; at stake is "whether Israel will be merely a Jewish Quarter in an Arab city or will become like the British East India Company, which ruled the Indo-Pakistani subcontinent."[63] Syrian information minister Muhammad Salman pledged Syria's resistance to all efforts to "replace Arabism in the region with Middle Easternism," which is attempting to reduce the Arab identity and replace it with an Israeli hegemony.[64] Opponents of Middle Easternism are tapping into long-standing fears of the West and Israel.

Part of the controversy surrounding the concept of Middle Easternism stems from its close association with former Israel prime minister Peres's concept of the "New Middle East."[65] Peres offered his grand plans for the Middle East based on his reading of contemporary European politics. Not only does he hope that the Middle East's future will duplicate Europe's past—where modest experiments in cooperation snowballed into greater interdependence and institution building—but his vision is premised on erasing the cognitive boundaries between Israel and the Arab states, resulting in a Middle East that no longer distinguishes national, religious, and ethnic identities, where borders are open for commercial transactions and exchanges of peoples, and transnational relations provide the underpinnings for peace and prosperity.

Peres's concept unleashed two principal fears among many Arabs. The first is of Israeli hegemony. Not all trusted Peres's vision of the future Middle East or believe that it is attainable or even desirable. Many feared that Peres's vision of peace, prosperity, and equality is nothing more than a cover for Israeli control of the region and, by association, U.S. control. Such fears were particularly noticeable when considering Israel's future economic relationships. When Peres spoke the language of interdependence, many Arabs heard a future of dependence. Such interpretations were reinforced by Peres's highly publicized statements at the 1994 Casablanca economic summit that, in the future regional division of labor, Israel contributes the technology and know-how, while the Arab world offers vast markets, cheap labor, and ready capital.[66] In this reading Israel is poised to become the regional core, whereas the Arab states will become the periphery. The underlying fear is that Israel stands to conquer through market power what it could not through military power.[67] A second concern was that Peres's concept of the New Middle East spelled the end of Arabism. In a series of interviews with former and current Jordanian officials in September 1995, a running theme on the issue of the New Middle East was that Israel was attempting to douse what little remained of the Arab identity. As one former top-ranking official put it, "Israel is now trying to rid Arabism from the Arab states."[68] To embrace the Middle East means to deny Arabism. If Arabism were alive and well, Peres's proposals would have evoked laughter and outright dismissal; it is a testimony to the times that they were taken seriously and evoked such fears.

The debate about the boundaries of the region, the future regional order, and what remains of the Arab order have imprinted the discussion surrounding the future of the Arab League.[69] The record of the Arab League is, to be charitable, disappointing. But these recent developments in regional politics, coupled with the league's dismal history, led to an open debate concerning its future, if any. The commemoration of the Arab League's fiftieth anniversary in March 1995 left many openly wondering whether and why the league should celebrate its centennial.

According to Ahmed Yousef Ahmed, director of the Institute of the Arab League, Arab states fall into three camps regarding the future of the Arab League. In one camp are those who envision the Arab League subsumed under a Middle Eastern order for all intents and purposes. King Hassan of Morocco and perhaps King Hussein, alongside some other Arab intellectuals, are in this camp. A second view is that the Arabs should adhere to pan-Arabism and reject the concept of Middle Easternism, which is little more than attempted Israeli hegemony. Syria, Yemen, Libya, and Lebanon are included here. The third view, represented by Egypt, Saudi Arabia, the PLO, and Algeria, takes an intermediary position, desiring new Middle Eastern arrangements while retaining a semblance of Arabism. In Ahmed's view, those in the second and third camps are using the Arab League as a tactical device; those in the second camp are attempting to defeat developments that they fear might hurt their foreign policy interests, and those in the third camp believe that the Arab League provides a useful device for increasing their individual bargaining position by maintaining a collective Arab posture.

Although those who support the league might do so for tactical reasons, there is little doubt that the league represents an identity-expressive function that few Arabs want to see disappear. Consider the outcry that greeted Peres's suggestion that Israel become a member of the League of Arab States. In a well-publicized chance encounter between Peres and Arab League secretary-general Esmet Abdel-Meguid at the Casablanca economic summit in 1994, Peres asked Abdel-Meguid, "And when will we be joining the Arab League?" Somewhat surprised by the question, Abdel-Meguid retorted, "The day you decide to speak Arabic."[70] Undaunted, Peres continued to suggest that Israel

be part of the Arab League; the nearly uniform Arab reaction was indigna-
tion and suggestions that Israel was only attempting to "humiliate" the
Arabs.[71] The Egyptian ambassador to Israel, Muhammed Bassouni, a supporter of normalization, came close to portraying the future Arab League as
little more than a cultural parlor, with higher profile and more central issues
handled through bilateral and multilateral channels, but he bristled at
Peres's suggestion that Israel be allowed to join the Arab League, characterizing the request as insulting and offensive.[72] In general, those who oppose
Middle Easternism and the New Middle East, and even many why support
normalization, have rallied around the Arab League. As one league official
put it, "Peres became the greatest friend of the Arab League."[73] For many the
Arab League is a last-ditch defense of the Arab identity.

At present Arab states find themselves largely torn between identity and
interests, reflected in the types of organizations and associations that are
proposed and constructed. This has been a steady development since the
early 1980s. The GCC, the Arab world's first subregional organization, was
founded in 1981, later joined by the Arab Maghrebi Union (AMU) and the
Arab Cooperation Council (ACC). The move toward subregional organizations reflected the growing salience of localized identities and interests relative to "pan" sentiments. After the Gulf War Arab states began to imagine and
organize themselves into alternative and cross-cutting regional groupings
that included Arab and non-Arab states; the multilateral talks, the plan for
the Organization for Security and Cooperation of the Middle East, the Damascus Declaration, and the Barcelona talks of November 1995 that involved
the Arab states of the Mediterranean and Europe; the possibility of a common market of Arab states and non-Arab states; and so on. The common denominator of these conferences, standing committees, and fledgling organizations is that they are based on states that share interests. But in this context
to follow interests means to bracket identities and the long-standing demand for all-Arab associations, generating the fear that an Arab order is a
thing of the past. The language of interests now rivals the language of identity in justifying and considering the post–Gulf War regional organizations.

The centrality of pan-Arab organizations for mobilizing the sentiments,
actions, and interests of Arab states has steadily relaxed. In the beginning was
the Arab League, the central location for expressing and organizing political
action. But today the Arab League has many rivals, and its agenda has narrowed considerably. On the occasion of the league's fiftieth anniversary
Mubarak reviewed the history of the league and divided it according to four
phases: in the 1940s and 1950s its goal was to "deepen our distinguished iden-

tity" and to "liquidate all forms of foreign control"; in the 1960s the goal was to strive for social justice and a unified Arab society; in the 1970s and 1980s the goal was liberation of the occupied lands, formulation of a common front on the Arab-Israeli conflict, and assertion of "control over our natural resources"; and since 1992 the goal has concerned the attempt to find justice in Palestine.[74] Arabism, in this reading, has been steadily narrowed to the question of Palestine because the Arab state's other, and more central, interests are now handled through other mechanisms and institutions.

The steady demise of pan-Arab organizations suggests a decline in the centrality of the Arab identity. "On the whole, men move most easily from those groups or systems where effective and affective commitment, and identification with common symbols which evoke and sustain commitment, is low."[75] A withering of a shared Arab identity is likely to produce a shift in the definition of the group, the attributes that are required to become a member of the region's organizations, and the relationship between the region's organization and the identities of its members. Whereas Arab states once handled many of their most important foreign policy issues in the confines of the Arab League and other all-Arab institutions, the decay of Arabism and the rise of statism have produced a decline in the centrality of the Arab League, consideration of new regional organizations that do not use identity as a criterion for membership, and a proliferation of organizations and institutions that are reflective of state interests and designed to overcome collective action problems and handle functional issues.

The contemporary debate about the regional order raises the possibility of the end of the Arab states system. What were once considered Arab interests—unity, fear of foreign control and the West, and the Arab-Israeli conflict—have receded from view. The debate about unity once pitted the advocates of unification against those who envisioned inter-Arab cooperation based on sovereignty. But this debate ended decades ago and was decisively decided in favor of the latter camp. And even now considerable concern exists that inter-Arab cooperation is not only elusive but also secondary, yielding to realism and statism.

Fear of the West and foreign control remain. In aftermath of the Gulf War and alongside America's "unipolar moment" many asked whether the destruction of Iraq, the Arab world's largest military and industrial power, was not part of a conspiracy to keep the Arab world weak and vulnerable to the West. The West remains a source of suspicion, not completely groundless given the long history of imperial tentacles, the ubiquitous power of the oil companies, and the West's occasional attempt to overthrow Arab regimes. The West looms large in the Arab imagination as a source of threat, and developments since the collapse of the cold war and the Gulf War have not assuaged such fears. Such fears derive not only from Arabism but also from Islam, which tends to view the West as a corrupting influence when it is not actively attempting to undermine either Islamic regimes or Islamic movements. Although some variants of political Islam and Arabism envision the possibility of cooperation with the West, both are unified by a fear of the West. Such cultural artifacts notwithstanding, most Arab states have responded to the end of the cold war and the Gulf War by tightening their relations with the West rather than their own ranks.

Although the question of Palestine continues to reverberate throughout the region and to inspire inter-Arab coordination, the organization of the conflict has altered radically and permitted a growing if grudging acceptance of Israel's place in the region. Indeed, Arab states appear to be more relaxed and interested in doing business with Israel than they are with each other. But within limits. The election of Netanyahu as Israeli prime minister and the stalled peace process vividly demonstrated that Palestine remains a concern that no Arab leader can ignore; thus it has tremendous mobilizing capacity. Whether because of a genuine concern for the plight of the Palestinians or because of the fear of symbolic sanctions, the Arab states have proceeded cautiously when considering relations with Israel on the ground that the "fruits of peace should not come before the facts of peace."

The sweeping changes that have occurred in inter-Arab politics, the decline of the Arab political community, and the hardening of the Arab states have led to a diminished responsiveness to core Arab concerns.[76] As Arab states imagine a regional order, it is virtually indistinguishable from what is broadly understood as the basic tenets of international society. Mubarak proposed the Charter of Arab Honor in 1995 and a new Arab order, which call for "rearranging pan-Arab objectives" largely founded on ridding the region of unconventional weapons, furthering economic cooperation, forwarding an Arab cultural renaissance, and achieving Arab reconciliation based on sovereignty.[77] Mubarak is essentially asking Arab states to renew their vows to the original charter of the League of Arab States, because the Charter of Arab Honor, according to the Arab League secretary-general, was designed to "prevent the emergence of destructive differences in the future, to ensure that any dispute is contained in a way that does not allow the situation to explode as seen before, and to get all members of the Arab family to adopt a position that leads to settling the dispute and preventing its aggravation."[78] Inter-Arab politics more closely resembles the politics of other regions. None of this means the "end of Arabism" or denies the possibility that Arab societies might be mobilized to confront issues that flow from their collective identity, sense of the past and historical injustices, and vision of a shared future.[79] The social processes and political interactions that were responsible for creating a tighter normative fabric and incentives for mutual orientation among Arab states could re-emerge. But for the moment and the foreseeable future Arabism no longer provides the rules of the game of regional politics.

8

The Making and Unmaking of Arab Politics

Arab states and societies have been involved in an ongoing debate about the desired regional order, imagining different possibilities for the future as they contemplated their present circumstances and reevaluated the past. As Arab states negotiated their response to the fundamental challenges of the day, as they strategically and symbolically jousted to establish those norms that would guard their interests, they also defined who they were, delineated the actions that were permissible and comprehensible, and generated a map of possible worlds. But these negotiations and dialogues have left a contemporary map that is far different from the one that existed decades ago. Arab states created a world of their own making and unmaking.

This narrative, organized as it is around dialogues in regional order, represents a decided alternative to the more familiar and accepted realist interpretation of Arab politics. The realist narrative begins with the presumption of anarchy and proceeds to examine how states attempt to maximize or maintain their security or power while constrained by the international distribution of power. This realist narrative leads to a consideration of different sorts of international events and processes, including the rise and decline of state power, the creation and dissolution of alliances, and the causes and consequences of wars. By importing these enduring themes to the study of Arab politics, realist-inspired accounts have aspired to demonstrate how the same concepts and theories that provide leverage over other regions and periods can be of equal value in evaluating Arab politics. In doing so they have thankfully corrected the unfortunate but all too frequently held insinuation that the region is driven by "irrational" forces that have their roots in its culture, religion, and ideology. But these realist-inspired frameworks come at a cost: they have generally shoehorned the history of Arab politics into the boxes provided by realism and ignored the social foundations of inter-Arab politics. The result is that although the region looks more familiar to many students of international politics, it looks exotic to students of the region.

My constructivist interpretation of inter-Arab politics is intended to capture what makes Arab politics distinctive and what makes it familiar. Arabism and not anarchy, I have argued, informs the debate about the desired regional order, the social, strategic, and symbolic interactions that unfold between Arab states that in turn are responsible for the changing norms of Arabism and ultimately normative fragmentation. But to claim that Arabism is part of the structure of regional politics is not to encourage a return to the idiographic or to assert that the region can be understood only in terms of categories that are specific to the region. Far from it. Arab politics has a social foundation that is culturally distinctive yet theoretically recognizable. Arabism will not exist anywhere except where an Arab identity exists, but how Arabism played itself out, or rather was played out, in inter-Arab politics is comprehensible from a broader framework. In short, this constructivist approach offers a set of analytic categories that attempt to approach Arab politics on its own terms while recognizing that Arab politics is intelligible from macrohistorical concepts and categories.[1]

But this is a two-way street. The history of Arab politics can contribute to contemporary debates in international politics. The recognition that debates about the desired regional order also implicate the identities of the members, the prominence of symbolic exchanges, and how these interactions sustained and transformed the fabric of the group are not unique to Arab politics. They exist within most group settings. They may be more prominent, or at least more easily identifiable, in Arab politics for what may be historically specific reasons, but their prominence helps illuminate some features of global politics that have largely been ignored by scholars of international politics. By building a theoretical bridge between the history of Arab politics and theories of international politics, my modestly ambitious goal is to suggest how international relations theory can help us to better understand the making and unmaking of Arab politics and how its making and unmaking can help scholars of international relations theory think more analytically and creatively about global politics. This final chapter speaks to these twin themes.

The Game of Arab Politics

How Arab leaders played the game of Arab politics depended on the nature of that game. The pattern of inter-Arab interactions during a dialogue was defined by the underlying normative structure, in this instance Arabism and sovereignty, which shaped the Arab states' identities, interests, strategic interaction, and technologies of power. That Arabism and not anarchy defines the structure of Arab politics is consistent with the claim that international politics is comprised of both social and material elements.[2] This structure, moreover, is a source of identities and the interests of the actors.[3] Actors are not weightless. They are social and historical beings, and their identities and interests are produced by a historical and institutional context.

Arab politics is Arab because of Arabism. Chapter 3 described the historical processes that generated Arabism and constructed the categories of Arab states with an accompanying set of interests. Intellectual movements, a series of political shocks, and competitive rivalries between Arab leaders and their societies created a set of concerns that came to be defined as Arab national interests. The West's segmentation of the Arab nation into separate territories generated the fledgling demand for unification; Britain's and France's hold over these states established an Arab nationalism that became associated with anticolonialism and independence; and the Zionist movement made Palestine a defining Arab national concern. By the mid-1940s the Arab political identity was a chief category for political identification, mobilization, and organization. From then on Arab states routinely proclaimed themselves and identified each other as representatives of the Arab nation, vowed to follow its interests, and were obligated to follow its norms. The normative structure shaped by Arabism, then, is a source of identity and interests and contains the socially determined norms that restrict and guide what is considered to acceptable play.

Although Arab leaders and other social movements were responsible for creating and reproducing Arabism, it was in many respects external to them, a constraint on and potential aid to their objectives. Arab nationalism constrained Arab governments, circumscribing what was politically viable. Yet Arabism was not only a constraint. It also represented a resource that the Arab governments could use for other ends. Nasser might have believed that he was good for Arab nationalism, but he also knew that Arab nationalism could be good for him. Arab leaders, in short, simultaneously felt the weight of these normative expectations and manipulated them for ulterior purposes. Arabism could be a constraint one moment and an instrument the next.

Arabism was not unique in this regard; the normative expectations that accompany social roles generally display this double-edged property.

Arab nationalism constituted, constrained, and could be a resource available for the pursuit of an Arab government's various interests. Because Arabism was a source of identity, Arab leaders could be expected to genuinely care about those issues identified as matters of concern to the Arab nation. But Arab leaders had another and arguably more immediate and pressing concern: regime survival. Still, the quest for regime survival quickly became entangled with the regionwide expectation that as Arab leaders they were expected to protect the Arab nation. Most Arab leaders went to extraordinary lengths to be identified with the symbols of Arabism because it was instrumental to their other objectives. They pursued a strategy of symbolic accumulation, in short, because these symbols could be exchanged for other highly valued objectives.[4] If Arab governments competed for regional leadership, they did so in part because they could exchange such titles for political capital at home and financial and military concessions from abroad. Soon after gaining power Nasser realized that his bargaining leverage vis-à-vis the West would increase dramatically if he was identified as the "leader" of the Arabs. So Nasser did all he could to promote this image, and with title in hand he attempted to extract more strategic and financial rents from the West. After the 1970s Saudi Arabia exchanged economic capital for symbolic capital as it shipped petrodollars to the confrontation states in order to solidify its credentials as an Arab power in good standing.

Arab leaders pursued both private and socially determined interests. As Arabs they were likely to closely identify with Arab national concerns; as leaders they were likely to closely identify with regime survival. And as Arab leaders they were likely to portray and fashion their policies in ways consistent with the norms of Arabism because doing so was instrumental for regime survival. The attempt, then, was to blend the sociological and the economic actor. Sociological actors are social creatures; the institutions in which they are embedded can be a source of identities, interests, and meaningful behavior. But sociological actors can also resemble economic actors: they can be calculating and cunning creatures, acting purposefully upon the world in creative and artful ways that are intended to achieve their various objectives under a set of constraints.[5] Therefore, rather than commit to an oversocialized view of state action and presume that Arab leaders internalized the norms of the group, I allowed for the possibility that Arab leaders were genuinely committed to Arab nationalism but emphasized the incentives that encouraged them to adhere to these public interests. Arabism was instrumental for achieving their private pursuits. Individuals usually act from a mixture of motives, sometimes because of self-interest and sometimes because of self-understanding, and both private and public interests are likely to lead to action. Arab leaders are social and purposeful beings, and the alloy of sociological and economic models generates a richer and more accurate understanding of their practices.

The Pattern of Strategic Interaction

The game of Arab politics generated certain patterns in the strategic interactions among Arab states. But because actors will not mindlessly follow a "logic" imposed by the structure in which they are embedded, the object is to identify enduring patterns that are linked to the underlying structure while allowing for creative, imaginative, and skillful use of these norms by the actors in different ways from one game to the next. Therefore, the intent is not to explain any one move but to consider how these rules of the game generated certain enduring patterns. I organize these patterns around three defining themes: the overall objective of the game, which was to promote a definition of the situation; the symbolic technologies used to try to promote a definition of the situation and to control the foreign policies of other Arab states; and the endgame, the (temporary) closure to the dialogue.

THE OBJECTIVE OF THE GAME OF ARAB POLITICS

A dialogue commenced when an event or development occurred that caused Arab States to debate the desired regional order. During these dialogues Arab governments competed to determine whether a norm properly applied to a situation, to fix the meaning of the events of the day, and to stabilize a norm. Arab governments did so because they recognized that their various domestic and foreign policy interests would be shaped and constrained by the norm that was established or revised by the dialogue. In this way, their overall objective during a dialogue was to create a definition of the situation that could sustain an interpretation of Arabism that was consistent with their various interests.

Because these dialogues revolved around issues that concerned the entire Arab nation and were connected to their shared Arab identity, they were withdrawn from the domain of private choice and calculations and subjected to a public reasoning process that constantly referred to the wider Arab nation. Issues that concerned how an Arab state was to conduct its relations with Israel, the West, and the wider Arab political community were categorized as "Arab" and thus had to be collectively legitimated through justifications that referred to the expectation and aspirations of the Arab political community. Arab states were therefore accountable to one another on these issues and obligated to have their actions formally or informally legitimated collectively. Although Arab leaders generally viewed this legitimation process as an unwanted intrusion on their foreign policy, they nevertheless submitted to this process because to do otherwise was to invite domestic and regional retribution. And as Arab states argued for a particular course of action or interpretation of Arabism, they almost always did so by claiming how it was consistent with previous interpretations of Arabism and the goals of the Arab nation. Arab states competed through the discourse of community and not the discourse of the territorial state to define the meaning of events.

The very fact that Arab leaders were competing to define the meaning of events highlights that they did not have an objective meaning but were made meaningful by Arab leaders who attempted to invest them with historical relevance, to use Arabism to guide their actions in ways that would favor their regime's interests. Arab leaders used three distinct frames that derived from Arab nationalism to organize experience and mobilize action: injustice, insecurity, and cultural renaissance. Anwar Sadat attempted to frame Camp David as a major step toward finding justice in Palestine. Hafiz al-Asad offered a counterframe of injustice and insecurity and portrayed Camp David as illegitimate, divisive, and blasphemous. Although these alternative frames might have derived from rival interpretations of Arab nationalism, it just so happened that they almost always were consistent with the respective regimes' interests. Nasser framed the Baghdad Pact as another instance of Western imperialism; it was not coincidental that this frame aided Egypt's strategic and political interests. Nuri al-Said countered that the pact furthered Arab nationalism, was justified by Iraqi sovereignty, and necessary because of geopolitical pressures emanating from the north. Every frame had a counterframe. Arab nationalism, though, was the source of these frames, situated Arab states within a comparable set of interdependent social roles, and demanded collective action.

These frames derived from and were embedded in a story line that concerned and helped to reproduce the Arab political community. By situating an event within a frame that derived from Arab nationalism, Arab states tied it to other events and thus invested it with symbolic meaning and emotional content. Moreover, the connection of the present to the past was a fundamental feature of the organization of historical time; temporality is organized around events, turning points that are made meaningful by their placement within the context of a community that has some understanding of its origins and its life history.[6] Finally, communities produce narratives about themselves through events that have a common resonance and historical meaning. According to David Carr, "a community exists wherever a narrative account exists of a we which has continuous existence through its experiences and activities."[7] The 1948 war. The 1967 war. These events were lived and experienced as a collective we. The 1948 war involved not only the expulsion of the Palestinians but a crisis for all Arabs, collectively referred to as *al-nakba*. The 1967 war was not experienced by Jordanians only as a disaster for Jordan, though it certainly was, but also as a tragedy for the Arabs. These events were communal because of their reference to the we and not because of their magnitude or their scale. Such events, in other words, constitute collective experiences, implicate all those who are recognized as members of the community, and are situated alongside other temporally and sequentially configured events that have a similar communal reference.[8] Therefore, as Arab states and societies debated the event under discussion, they were producing a narrative about who they were and establishing the boundaries of the community; reminding themselves of the historical linkage of the past, the present, and some imagined future; and defining these events as symbols of the community.

SYMBOLIC TECHNOLOGIES AND EXCHANGES

Arab leaders generally used symbolic and not military technologies to control the foreign policy of their rivals. Of course, they occasionally engaged in saber rattling and then some.[9] Syria and Jordan not only exchanged witty retorts but also contemplated overthrowing each other's governments, sometimes through covert and sometimes through overt means. Iraq invaded Kuwait. But a notable feature of this survey of inter-Arab conflicts, and particularly those conflicts before the 1970s, was how rare military threats were in comparison to symbolic threats.[10]

Why was symbolic politics so prominent in Arab politics? Perhaps Arab states did not possess the military and economic technologies of influence. But this explanation falls short for two reasons. Arab states accumulated the military means to confront Israel, military capacities that they could just as easily have aimed at each other. Yet if Arab states did not possess the military technologies, from the standpoint of realist theory—which presumes that a high-threat environment should lead to militarized responses—this is anomalous in itself. Although the Middle East is routinely celebrated as a high-conflict environment, Arab states nonetheless abstained from arms racing. Indeed, little evidence exists that alliances Arab states formed against each other were driven by military threats.[11]

The prominence of symbolic competition is more directly attributable to the normative structure of Arab politics. The "thicker" the normative environment is—that is, the more embedded its actors are in a network of relations invested with symbolic content and a source of identity—the more dependent they will be on each other for social approval. This dependence on social approval in turn increases their susceptibility to normative suasion and symbolic sanctions. If Arab politics was symbolic politics, it was because Arab states were embedded in a shared normative order in which they were mutually dependent for social approval.

The more general point is that the group's social fabric can be expected to imprint its patterns of conflict, competition, and conflict regulation.[12] International relations theory has generally focused on economic and military means of influence, reflective of a preference for treating the international system as comprised of states embedded in a nearly normless environment and whose interests are defined by wealth and security. But if the international environment is recognized as having a social character, if states are conceptualized as involved in patterns of relations that can confer social standing or moral censure, and if scholars are willing to concede that state officials desire social approval, states can be persuaded and embarrassed into submission through symbolic and diplomatic means.[13]

The key concept here is symbolic sanctioning: the attempt by one actor to influence the actions of another by deploying the symbols of the community. Arab leaders deployed symbolic sanctions, symbols that derived from the Arab political community, to control each other's foreign policies by raising the costs of a particular action. For Nasser to connect the Baghdad Pact to the mandate system meant drawing historical lines between imperialism, the proposed pact, and the continuing division of the Arab nation; in doing so he escalated the political costs for any Arab leader who contemplated following Iraq. During the 1980s the Steadfastness States discouraged other Arab leaders from flirting with a diplomatic settlement with Israel by calling it "Camp David."

Three factors made symbolic sanctioning effective and possible. One necessary condition was that actors were embedded in a shared normative order that left them mutually susceptible and dependent on each other for dignity, honor, and approval. The care that Arab leaders took to guard their images reflected a more generalized desire for social approval; such desires steered them away from crudely self-interested behavior and encouraged them to contribute to the maintenance and collective goals of the group. Second, Arab leaders sought such approval not only from each other but also—and ultimately—from their societies. The effectiveness of symbolic sanctions, in short, depended on the anticipated or accomplished mobilization of Arab societies in order to raise the political costs of a particular course of action. This presupposes that these separate Arab societies identified with the symbols of the Arab political community and the frame that was being deployed by another Arab leader, again pointing to their embeddedness in a common normative structure.

A third ingredient necessary for symbolic sanctioning was that Arab states possess the technologies of communication.[14] Not all Arab states were equally capable of being part of symbolic exchanges because not all had access to the technology required. Consider the following description of the "transmitter" gap between Jordan and Egypt before the 1967 war:

> The Jordanian propaganda machine, compared with Egyptian, Syrian, and PLO machines, was small and ineffective. Egypt was broadcasting from Radio Cairo, from *Sawt al-Arab*, and from many other stations, with wave lengths reaching nearly every part of the globe, while the Jordanians had a small radio station. And the Egyptian press reached everywhere in the Arab world. The Jordanian press reached nowhere.[15]

Because the principal means of competition and control were symbolic and communicative, Arab leaders were particularly attentive to the gaps in technologies that would make them competent and effective players. Accordingly, they were much more troubled by their inability to project their media into each other's terrain than they were by their inability to project their military power. For this reason Arab leaders signaled their willingness to reduce their level of hostility through mutual media disarmament, as they did during the era of summitry.

The historical analysis suggests five ways that Arab leaders anticipated and realized the sting of symbolic sanctions. First, Arab leaders exhibited role-taking behavior; that is, they saw themselves as they imagined others saw them and therefore attempted to conform to those expectations because of self-image and self-interest. At various moments Arab leaders contemplated but ultimately shied away from a course of action because they did not want to leave themselves vulnerable politically. Second, because few formal mechanisms of political expression and protest were not controlled by the state, societal preferences were voiced through ad hoc demonstrations in the streets and on the airwaves.

Third, Arab leaders who were deploying symbolic sanctions did not leave mobilization to the power of the spoken word: frequently, they bought a coterie of politicians and rabble-rousers in other Arab capitals that the leaders could call upon at the proper moment to raise havoc and public opinion in their favor. Collective mobilization is rarely a spontaneous affair, and political elites were actively engineering it. The "struggle" for Syria involved other Arab states that were buying and influencing Syrian politicians and military officials, and Jordanian political parties and social movements frequently had strong ties to other Arab states. In such a context party politics was indistinguishable from Arab politics. Fourth, symbolic sanctions were part of intragovernmental competition and the calculus of regime stability and power. Arab leaders were frequently kept "honest" because they always had a domestic political rival—often controlled or aided by the military—who was ready to capitalize on a violation of a norm in order to bring down the government in power or to cause mayhem.

Finally, the effectiveness of the symbolic sanction depended on the credibility of the deliverer. Arab leaders frequently reminded their listeners that their credentials were unblemished and beyond reproach. During the debate about the Baghdad Pact Nuri al-Said constantly reminded the Iraqi people that he was the veteran Arab nationalist and Nasser was the upstart. To this day King Hussein parades his historical and ancestral ties to the leaders of the Great Arab Revolt. Ultimately, however, the credibility of an Arab leader depended on how Arab societies judged his past behavior. Nasser was unsurpassed in this regard. All else being equal, a phrase he uttered was more credible than the same phrase delivered by any other Arab leader at the time or since. By all accounts, part of Nasser's success came from his charisma and ability to use the language of the street in a way that transcended the territorially segmented Arab societies. But charisma was not enough. His credibility increased after he undertook a string of bold acts— including his opposition to the Baghdad Pact, his consignment of Soviet weapons, and his nationalization of the Suez Canal—that surpassed anything ever done in the name of Arab nationalism. No Arab leader could match his reputation in part because no Arab leader had ever accumulated such a record. Although historical and geographic variations occurred, as a general rule Arab states were susceptible to symbolic sanctions in proportion to their dependence on each other for social approval, the degree to which their populations were stirred by the symbols of Arabism as it pertained to the matter of the day and were mobilized around it, and the credibility of the deliver of the message.

Symbolic sanctioning could feed into symbolic competition. Arab leaders often wanted to demonstrate that their credentials were unimpeachable and those of their rival were suspect. Sometimes such boasting and swaggering was more a nuisance than an actual threat, but at other moments such public displays became challenges that had to be answered. This could generate a dangerous game of brinksmanship that carried substantial rewards but equally substantial risks; after all, Arab governments might have cared about the issue at hand and enjoyed the prestige that accompanied such displays, but these frequently were not enough to cause them to sacrifice other highly valued objectives. This escalating process was a high-wire act, with Arab leaders challenging each other to step farther away from the ledge and sometimes to perform without a net.

Symbolic competition typically ceased in one of three ways. The first was the development of an alliance or institution designed to halt the bidding process and save face. Nasser created the summit system in 1964 to wrest control of Syria's unilateral impulses with regard to Israel and to maintain his standing. In late 1966 he signed a defense treaty with Syria for much the same purpose. These were institutional expressions of impression management, designed to keep the Arab states from backing themselves into a corner and having to follow an unwanted course of action.

Second, Arab states often began the dialogue with a more "flexible" interpretation of the norm under discussion, but a competitive bidding process not only repaired but frequently tightened it. The Baghdad Pact began as a general discussion of when Arab states could enter into alliances with the West and ended with their near prohibition. The inter-Arab discussions regarding the termination of the mandate in Palestine began with few Arab leaders who wanted to expend many resources on the matter but ended with a military intervention; the negotiations that preceded the war contained the seeds of a political solution, but symbolic competition and the desire to maintain public face led to the norm prohibiting a separate peace with Israel. Strong hints exist that several Arab leaders believed that Khartoum's "three no's" were either unwise or unnecessary, but they could hardly make their objections public without being ostracized and called defeatist. The desire to save face and to manage their impressions could lead them to publicly pledge a course of action that they privately rued.

Finally, symbolic competition might devolve into symbolic entrapment, as when an Arab leader had his bluff called and was forced to take action in order to save face. Entrapment's renowned episode was the 1967 war. During the mid-1960s Nasser maintained a strong verbal stand against Israel while cautioning that moderation was important, lest the Arabs find themselves in an unwanted war. By the spring of 1967, however, Israel and Syria were engaged in a spiraling number of skirmishes, and Nasser found himself under pressure to show his resolve. That he did. But Nasser was less concerned with Israel's military power than he was with Arab public opinion, and he knowingly flirted with the former in order to impress the latter. Soon Nasser found himself locked into a course of action that delivered the war he privately feared. Symbolic entrapment also claimed King Hussein. After mercilessly daring Nasser to adopt this risky course of action, Hussein found himself in a similar predicament, forced to declare war on Israel lest his own society declare war on him. Symbolic entrapment also shaped the dynamics leading to the creation of the UAR. Neither the Syrian Ba'ath nor Nasser was enamored of the idea of a union, but once they put their credentials on the line, they felt pressured to proceed with a scheme that each privately predicted would be a disaster.

THE ENDGAME

Strictly speaking, the debate about the desired regional order never ended. Rather, there was a temporary pause, or a lull in the conversation, once Arab states repaired or transformed the norm under discussion. Erving Goffman likened this to moral pacification, a decision to drop the matter at hand and get on with life—for the moment. Arab leaders generally welcomed such moments with testimonials to how they had banded together, successfully addressed the challenge of the day, and demonstrated their unwavering commitment to Arab nationalism. But at other times an Arab leader on the losing end of the dialogue lashed out at the other Arab states; Anwar Sadat received the news that Egypt had been expelled from the Arab League because of Camp David by publicly calling the leaders of the Gulf Arab states dwarfs who ruled nameless pockets of sand. In addition to these expressions of self-congratulations and sour grapes, three important developments accompanied the end of a dialogue: the creation of power, establishment or tightening of alliances and institutions, and accomplishment of solidarity and cooperation.

But before considering these developments, it is important to emphasize that the outcome of the debate about the desired regional order could rarely be properly reduced to the preferences of the most powerful states. These symbolic and strategic exchanges were informed by earlier dialogues, riddled with self-interest, justified with reference to and constituted by moral considerations, connected to public and community-wide aspirations, vetted through a public reasoning process, and checkered with power. The informal desire to proceed on the basis of consensus, moreover, handed other Arab states and nonstate actors a say in the decision. As such, even a modest coalition of less powerful Arab states could veto or severely complicate the policies sought by a coalition of stronger states. The most powerful Arab states frequently found themselves frustrated and unable to achieve their preferences—and certainly not without an exhaustive and sometimes highly costly public debate that had only the vaguest relationship to state power.

Consider the following examples. Egypt, the military giant of the Arab world, started down the path to the Camp David accords, supported by Saudi Arabia, the economic giant of the Arab world. But Egypt found the road impeded by normative restrictions erected by a coalition of weaker Arab states. In the end Saudi Arabia decided that although it privately supported Sadat it could not do so publicly, and Sadat could not change the norms to accommodate his policies. Thus he found himself on the outside of Arab politics looking in. Or consider the PLO's role in Arab politics. Although the PLO did not have the material, economic, and organizational power that comes with being a sovereign state, the organization was invested with symbolic capital because it was recognized as the legitimate and sole representative of the Palestinian people. Such symbolic capital handed it tremendous leverage over the policies of Arab states, and few dared to get ahead of what the PLO was willing to accept on matters concerning Israel. Nasser's preference before meeting with the Syrians in 1958 was to tell them to clean up their own house; Egypt's military power could not save him from agreeing to a misbegotten union with a much weaker and internally divided Syria. The 1967 war was followed by a summer of debate about the meaning of the defeat. Some Arab intellectuals and officials argued that the problem was too little Arab nationalism and too much conservatism; now was the time for real Arab unity. Others argued for a more centrist conception of nationalism that accommodated the existing Arab states. The outcome was not unrelated to state power, but neither was it determined by it. Power was always a factor in these debates, but such power was mediated and defined by Arabism and a process of public contestation that referred to the existing normative order and pointed to community aspirations.

Power. Arab states competed to define the events of the day and to establish the norms of Arabism because doing so would further their interests and could act as a mechanism of social control over the foreign policies of other

Arab states. Investing the situation with a particular meaning constituted an important source of power for Arab states because it oriented and constrained social action. Actors struggle over the power and the right to impose a legitimate vision of the world because doing so helps to construct social reality as much as it expresses it.[16] Nasser's brilliance and power derived not from Egypt's military capability, for what little he use he made of it was hardly awe inspiring. Rather, he is remembered for his ability to define the events of the day. E. H. Carr similarly claimed that the power over opinion is one of three forms of power. To mobilize the masses on behalf of foreign policy requires that the public be educated to identify with the state and its goals. To be able to sway public opinion in other countries constitutes an important foreign policy weapon; it also presupposes that these opinions are founded on international rather than strictly national ideas and aspirations.[17]

Power also was bound up with symbolic exchanges, giving rise to hierarchy and segmentation. This is akin to what Peter Blau has called the "paradox of social integration": the qualities that make an individual especially valuable as a group member "also constitute a threat to the rest" because those qualities can represent a claim to status and thus a threat to other members of the group. Group members may respond in several different ways—pretend that they are not easily impressed, compete for a similar social status, or belittle each other.[18] Various Arab leaders were forever attempting to prove their credentials by taking a commanding role on Arab issues. Although such leadership can help to overcome collective action problems and thus represent a useful contribution from the vantage point of the group, such contributions might force an individual Arab leader to engage in action that he privately opposes and place him in a subordinate position vis-à-vis the provider of the good. Furthermore, because Arab leaders wanted the social approval and legitimation of others, they were mutually susceptible and hence influenced by them. But some actors' approval matters more than others.' Nasser's blessing, for example, was as sought after as his censure was feared because he was viewed as the personification and guardian of Arab nationalism. Arab leaders needed each other for social approval and thus had common interests, but they also had conflicting interests because of the inevitable status differentials that resulted from these exchanges. Nasser's standing made him both a formidable ally and a threat.

In general, because power is bound up with the production of symbols, political struggles are frequently expressed through symbolic struggles.[19] As scholars of international relations continue to consider the different forms and instruments of power, they should give due consideration to how states use symbolic and normative means to define the situation in ways that orient and constrain action. Because symbols can orient action, shape identities, and draw boundaries, they are expressions of power and midwives of hierarchy.

Alliances and institutions.   Sometimes dialogues ended with the establishment or strengthening of an Arab institution or inter-Arab alliance. But these institutions and alliances had their origins in and operated according to principles that depart from the traditional view of international relations theory. According to neoliberal institutionalism, states construct institutions in order to further their shared interests and to overcome problems associated with interdependent choice.[20] According to realism, states seek alliances primarily to enhance their capabilities through combination with others, which helps to deter a potential aggressor and avoid an unwanted war, to prepare for a successful war if deterrence fails, or more generally to increase one's influence in a high-threat environment or maintain a balance of power in the system.[21] Although some Arab institutions and alliances followed a neoliberal or neorealist logic, their defining attributes derived from symbolic politics—specifically, their expressive role, their function as a symbolic means of social control and as an instrument of impression management.

Many Arab organizations were symbolically tied to the Arab identity and thus served an expressive function.[22] The establishment of the Arab League was celebrated as a confirmation of Arab nationalism's existence and vitality. The recent and heated debate about its future—and particularly then–prime minister Shimon Peres's suggestion that Israel be admitted as a member—revealed a loyalty and identification to the organization less for its material contributions than for its expressive foundations. Create other regional arrangements that include Israel, asserted many Arab officials and intellectuals, but keep the Arab League Arab.

Arab states constructed inter-Arab alliances and institutions as a mechanism of social control and as a response to a normative rather than a military challenge. The Arab League provided few formal or constitutional constraints on Arab states that were distinguishable from Dumbarton Oaks; indeed, the majority of the Arab states were keen to use it to protect their sovereignty from an Arabism that demanded unification. But Arab states later used the Arab League to display their allegiances, to hold each other mutually accountable, and as a mechanism of social control. Several famous alliances were designed to control the foreign policy of another Arab state. In 1950 Egypt proposed the Arab Collective Security Pact, not for the stated purpose of coordinating and integrating the Arab states' military forces to confront a shared threat but to halt the possibility of Syrian-Iraqi unification. Egypt and Saudi Arabia used the Arab League to defend the principle of sovereignty and to contain the drive for unification. Nasser proposed a string of alliances in the mid-1950s designed to control the foreign policies of other Arab states and to ostracize Iraq—not to balance against Iraq's or any other Arab state's military power.

Many Arab alliances were bound up with impression management and presentational politics.[23] Because the inter-Arab threat derived from symbolic rather than military politics, Arab leaders constructed security institutions that had a comparable function. Arab states routinely joined alliances, but they frequently did so to maintain their image as an Arab state in good standing.[24] King Hussein joined the 1956 Treaty of Arab Solidarity to repair his image as an Arab nationalist even though—and actually because—it meant siding with the same Nasser who had made his life a living nightmare the month before. Normative considerations generally drove these alliances and institutions, so Arab states frequently felt considerable pressure to ally with the very state that presented a normative threat, lest they deliberately choose to be portrayed as outside the consensus. Call this bandwagoning behavior, though in these instances power that was the source of attraction and fear derived from normative and not material considerations.

Given that these alliances and institutions were frequently designed for presentational purposes and to control the actions of other Arab leaders, it should come as little surprise that they have accumulated a dismal record of furthering collective Arab causes. Generally that was not their primary function. Arab governments feared the interdependence that these institutions were ostensibly designed to promote. Their interest in regime survival told them to pledge allegiance to Arab unity and its organizational expressions, but those interests also warned them against anything more than a surface commitment. Because these states were highly permeable and had no domestic basis for legitimacy, they feared encouraging outside interventions that might undermine regime stability. This was not unfounded paranoia. All too often an Arab leader who sounded the call of Arab unity was attempting to control the foreign policy of another Arab state or destabilize it from within. The occasional unity calls by Jordan and Iraq frequently played havoc with Syrian domestic politics. The UAR was the extreme but classic example of what might happen if Arab states took their Arab unity too seriously. Consequently, although Arab officials recognized the symbolic advantages to be gained from pursuing inter-Arab cooperation, their political instincts told them to preserve their autonomy at all costs. The result was the continuing creation of organizations and alliances that had presentational, control, and symbolic functions and were never really intended to achieve their explicitly stated objectives of economic and military cooperation.

Moreover, Arab states might have welcomed a genuine show of inter-Arab cooperation, but they also worried—and this was particularly so from 1945 to the mid-1960s—that any major breakthrough might generate further expectations among their societies that Arab states should now push for political unification, leaving them more vulnerable than ever and perhaps even expected to surrender their territorial basis of power. In the context of Arab nationalism cooperation and interdependence could be discursively linked to Arab unity—and few Arab states wanted to encourage such sentiments.

In general, the results of these numerous experiments in regional institution building were dismal if evaluated from the vantage point of their public proclamations; if judged from the private and regime-sustaining intentions of their creators, however, they were remarkably successful. The imperatives of regime survival in the context of Arab nationalism explain the creation and impotence of these organizations and alliances.

Solidarity and cooperation.   Arab states have sustained solidarity with the norms of Arabism, particularly in regard to Israel. But most studies of Arab politics tend to overlook this cooperation for four reasons: the notoriety of inter-Arab conflict; the impressive failure of integration efforts; the constant berating by Arab nationalists of Arab governments for failing to fulfill Arabism's demands—the nationalists pray for more cooperation than is ever delivered; and models of international politics that begin with a given set of state interests predict much less solidarity than is actually accomplished. These historical patterns and structural models might help get a handle on conflict, but they do not explain the accumulated record of Arab solidarity.

How do we account for Arab solidarity and the remarkable compliance with the norms of Arabism? One possibility is that Arab states internalized and felt a degree of commitment to the group's norms. Actors, in other words, are not only seekers of immediate gratification but also agents of moral purpose. International relations theorists generally dismiss such possibilities because of a commitment to methodological individualism, a belief that anarchy penalizes any hint of transnational obligations, and the methodological difficulty of tracing the causal significance of identity toward that end. But Arabism—not anarchy—was a source of state identity, interests, and strategies, creating the real possibility that Arab leaders might exhibit a responsibility to Arab issues. And although it is difficult to demonstrate empirically that a state actor has internalized norms that are linked to conceptions of self, the converse is also true—it is often asserted rather than empirically substantiated that an actor's actions are driven by expedience and narrow self-interest and not by a sense of obligation that derives from mutual identification. Is it so incredible that Arab leaders might actually be committed to Arab nationalism?

My conclusion, however, suggests that although Arab leaders felt an obligation to these Arab issues, the primary mechanisms for keeping them honest were the entanglement of private and public preferences, the presence of symbolic sanctions, and the desire for social approval. This view in fact shares much with the more conventional way of representing compliance: actors abide by societal norms because the costs attached to any violation outweigh any potential benefit, and because third-party monitors, who can detect whether a violation has occurred, are present.[25] Considerable evidence exists that Arab leaders complied with the group's norms because of the anticipation or the application of symbolic sanctions that could jeopardize their various goals. Often these sanctions were left unspecified in terms of who would do the sanctioning and what the exact sanctions would be. Indeed, the ultimate punishment came not from other states but from their own societies. Sadat, Nuri al-Said, and King Abdullah knowingly transgressed a norm of Arabism and subsequently found themselves sanctioned in a permanent way.

But at other times Arab states formalized these sanctions in Arab summits and Arab League resolutions; such formalization occurred when an Arab state threatened to unilaterally and defiantly violate a long-standing norm of Arab politics. Arab states portrayed these violations as representing a cancer that had to be isolated and expunged from the Arab body politic. For instance, when Sadat signed a separate peace with Israel and when King Abdullah was flirting with the idea, Arab states communicated the penalties for such heresy. The primary sanction on such occasions was the threat of expulsion from the organizations of, and the severing of all ties with, other Arab states. Nasser made it clear that Iraq was not an acceptable member in any inter-Arab security arrangement because of the Baghdad Pact. To ensure compliance with that norm, moreover, Arab states meted out sanctions to those Arab states that gave comfort to the violator; in the language of Robert Axelrod, these were metanorms.[26] For another Arab state to give comfort to Egypt at the time of Camp David was to willingly expose itself to the same accusations and repercussions directed at Egypt.

Thus Arab leaders brought about solidarity and compliance through their sense of self and desire for social approval. This was about identity and interests. Actors will be both self-interested and abide by certain standards and codes of conduct because they want to be viewed as a moral agent and maintain the presentation of self, if only for strategic purposes. Thus the normative structure of Arabism operated as an enforcement mechanism as it shaped the ends and the means that Arab leaders could pursue.[27] We do not have to submit to an oversocialized view of actors to recognize that they will adhere to societal norms for a variety of reasons, including consistency with their identity and material interests.[28] In general, the norms served to orient Arab states in the same direction, generated the expectation of some modest policy coordination, and left Arab leaders dependent on each other for social approval and thus susceptible to the sanctions that became the cornerstone of cooperation and norm compliance.[29]

In sum, as Arab states debated the desired regional order, they exhibited centrifugal and centripetal tendencies, a dance of conflict and cooperation that corresponded to a rhythm of individuation and identification. The same Arabism that compelled them to work in concert and to identify with each other also represented a source of conflict and competition. This constructivist reading of Arab politics, then, runs counter to the standard treatment of conflict in two principal respects: in contrast to the belief that anarchy is the one true source of conflict, I have noted how Arabism provided a structural incentive for competition and conflict; in contrast to the implicit belief that a shared identity and norms are bound up with cooperation, I have continually stressed how identity and norms can be a source of conflict and that all social relationships transpire within a normative framework and exhibit elements of conflict. Arab states have impressively reproduced and maintained the group identity that they privately found so threatening and a source of conflict and did so because of a sense of self and a sense of survival.

An additional feature of this endgame points to a larger issue: the debate about the desired regional order implicated the definition of the game. Dialogues were, in effect, moments when Arab states reconsidered the Arab state's identity, the norms that were expressive of that identity, and how those norms defined the Arab order. To recognize orders as negotiated is to remain attentive to the social, strategic, and symbolic interactions that sustain and transform them.[30] In this way Arab states were debating, creating, and sustaining the structure in which they were embedded. The norms of Arabism were not "concrete girders constraining action but, instead, [were] media through which action [became] possible, and which action itself reproduces and transforms."[31] Arabism was not merely a constraint on their action but also a creation of their actions. Arabism was not simply external to Arab states but also was the mechanism of communication, reproduced and instantiated through their practices. The regional order in which Arab states were embedded was not a permanent fixture but was an accomplishment, repaired and transformed by them through their interactions.

A Narrative of Arab Politics

The history of international and regional politics can always be told in several ways. Different narratives have different ways of organizing history, rendering events intelligible and influential, and connecting them to generate an identifiable pattern. My narrative organizes the history of Arab politics according to dialogues about the desired regional order. Events are made meaningful in this broader narrative, and the pattern of these events generates a story line that concerns the changing debate about the desired regional order. I chose events because they revealed some enduring themes of Arab politics and because they were consequential for its development. As Arab states negotiated the desired regional order, they paused to reconsider their relationship to one another. Sometimes they sustained their relations, but at other times they transformed them. Sometimes these transformations brought them closer together, but at other times it pushed them further apart. But understanding the changing fabric of Arab politics requires a more detailed consideration of these seminal events in Arab politics.

NORMATIVE FRAGMENTATION

I identified five distinct periods in inter-Arab politics defined by different themes regarding the relationship between Arab nationalism and the Arab state. The first period examined the historical evolution of the Arab states system and the inaugural debate about the enduring questions of Arab politics—who the members of the political community are, what its interests are, and what norms should regulate their relations. Beginning in the late nineteenth century in response to the breakdown of the old order that resulted from the demise of the Ottoman Empire, the emergence of nationalism, and the spread of the world economy, individuals in the Fertile Crescent were forced to reconsider their political identity, how they wanted to live with one another—who constituted the political community.[32] Modernity and imperialism, in other words, provided an impetus for Arabs to "discover" their common identity and destiny and to suggest that a meaningful response to these economic, cultural, and political dislocations required collective action on an expansive scale and under the banner of Arab nationalism. But the central debate between Arab states and societies centered on the (evolving) meaning of Arab nationalism in relationship to their (expected) status as sovereign states. This issue was provisionally addressed in the talks leading to the Arab League and led to a blueprint that inscribed a possessive sovereignty that kept at bay the most demanding and constraining features of Arabism. Sovereignty before Arabism, read the jury at the Arab League.

The second period occurred between 1945 and 1955 and was defined by the creation of more restrictive set of norms that increased the mutual accountability of the Arab states. This was not necessarily by design but through a process of symbolic competition. The prospect of a Syrian-Iraqi union led Egypt to dangle the Arab Collective Security Pact (ACSP) as a way of derailing the union in favor of an all-Arab security system. Although the ACSP had little operational effect, it did strengthen the view that the security of Arab states was interdependent and left them mutually accountable. Such matters reemerged during the debate about the Arab states' relationship to the West. Almost all Arab states had some sort of political or financial tie to the West and wanted to see it continue in the future, though under more favorable conditions. But their debates about the Baghdad Pact led to general acceptance of Nasser's concept of positive neutrality. The Baghdad Pact did more than favor Nasser's view of alliances with the West—it also marked the passage to a more radical version of Arab nationalism, with Nasser as its unchallenged leader. By the beginning of 1956, then, Arab states were more mutually accountable to each other than ever before.

The third period began with the 1956 Suez War, ended with the 1967 war, and was defined by the rise and decline of the clash between the state and the nation, symbolized by the rise and decline of unification on the political agenda. But perhaps entrapment in the name of Arabism better characterizes the period. Egypt and Syria found that they had a shotgun marriage, but they possessed the guns, in the name of the UAR. Once was not enough, and so in 1963 they added Iraq to the mix and constructed a unity agreement that was even briefer and created more bitterness. As consequence, Syria, Iraq, and Egypt began to stress their diversity within unity. A direct outcome of the failures of 1963 was the Arab summit system, the détente between the radical and conservative Arab states that also represented a move to institutionalize a more centrist reading of Arab nationalism. But this détente was not long lasting. Significantly, the issue that divided them was not unification but the Arab-Israeli conflict. Soon Arab states were involved in a heated debate about their Israel policy, inviting symbolic competition and eventually entrapment in the form of the 1967 war. A decade's experiences of symbolic competition and entrapment created a movement in favor of a more centrist version of Arab nationalism that was more consistent with state sovereignty and better able to accommodate the Arab states' separate identities.

The theme of the post-1967 period was the relationship between the debate about the organization of the Arab-Israeli conflict and the emergent statism in Arab politics. One effect of the 1967 war was to encourage Arab states to more fully converge on the norms of sovereignty to organize their relations in order to reverse Israel's victory. This new arrangement had its apparent payoff in the victory of the Arab states in the 1973 war. But such successes provided another moment for Arab states to revisit the relationship between the Arab-Israeli conflict and the meaning of Arab nationalism. By relaxing the norms of Arabism so that it could accommodate Sadat's desire to retrieve the Sinai, his path to Camp David created an environment more favorable to statism. The Arab states responded to the heresy of Camp David by isolating Egypt and proclaiming their solidarity, but the 1980s continued the trend of fragmentation and division. By the late 1980s the norms of Arab politics were nearly indistinguishable from those of international society, save a founding concern with Israel, and Arab states looked to sovereignty to rescue themselves from each other.

The Iraqi invasion of Kuwait stirred the most recent debate about the desired regional order: what was, is, and will become of Arab politics. Whereas the earlier dialogues about regional order assumed that as Arab states they had shared interests that demanded collective mobilization, the Gulf War, coming on the heels of rising statism, sovereignty, a centrist definition of Arab nationalism, and political Islam, led Arab states to look for alternative mechanisms to further their interests. These alternative mechanisms in turn raised the issue of what remained of the Arab states system. The language of Arab nationalism can still be heard as Arabs continue to confront the fundamental changes in international and domestic politics within a new context—that of Arab *sovereign* states responding to perceived common challenges. In this way the continued existence of an Arab identity that serves as a bridge between Arab states, and the awareness by Arab governments of the permeability of their borders to cultural forces, preserves a nominal desire for policy coordination. This is particularly so when Arab states perceive themselves to be assailed by non-Arab forces. But there is no mistaking the current order for those of decades past.

This changing debate about the desired regional order elevates the current condition of normative fragmentation: Arab states are no longer as pressed toward mutual orientation because of underlying shared values and interests. At the outset of the Arab states system Arab nationalism was a defining source of the Arab state's interests, encouraged Arab states to actively consider how they could further their interests, and generated the strong expectation that Arab states would foster close economic, cultural, and security ties to further their shared interests and deepen the sense of community. Although Arab governments were frequently resistant parties to these cultural assumptions and expectations, they generally honored them—even as they manipulated them—through word and deed.

But the existence of normative fragmentation has steadily replaced this search for normative integration. Inter-Arab solidarity has declined in the past few decades. However elusive and tortured the inter-Arab contest over the norms that should govern their relations might have been, at least it proceeded on the assumption that they should work to further their collective projects that derived from their shared identity. But now Arab states express grave reservations concerning the feasibility or even desirability of such collective projects, are no longer as dependent on each other for social approval, as active in coordinating their relations, or as oriented in each other's direction. Arab states are now actively debating the relative merits of "Mediterraneanism," "Middle Easternism," and a "new Arab order," punctuating how they are imagining themselves in new ways and orienting themselves in new directions.

This theme of normative fragmentation is quite familiar to students of Arab politics. "The end of pan-Arabism," the debate about Middle Easternism, and the shift from the language of *qawmiyya* [national identity] to *wataniyya* [state identities] represent different ways that scholars and policy makers package what can be understood as normative fragmentation. Sometimes these labels are offered as a lament, and sometimes they are offered with a sigh of relief, but in either case there is general agreement that the structure of Arab politics has changed remarkably over the years, and such changes can be best understood at the level of identity politics.

Accordingly, how scholars and policy makers categorize the change that has occurred in Arab politics is decidedly closer to constructivism than it is to realism. Neorealism examines a change in the structure by examining shifts in the distribution of material power, viewing norms and rules as dependent on that distribution and holding constant the identities and interests of the states that are constrained by that structure.[33] But students of the region implicitly reject such formulations in favor of a characterization of structural change that is bound up with identity politics. In making these observations, they are favoring a constructivist claim that a theoretical connection exists between the regional order, the practices of states, and their identities.[34]

The change in the structure of Arab politics and the normative fragmentation are detectable in three related areas: state identities, the norms that are constitutive of those identities, and the convergence on sovereignty to organize their relations. Scholars and practitioners generally agree that Arabism has declined. Although accounts differ regarding the motivating force for the revolution in identities and loyalties, they concur almost uniformly that state discourses and practices are reflective of a rise in statist identities and a decline in Arab national identities. This does not mean that statist identities are hegemonic and have captured the hearts and minds of Arab citizens; after all, religious, sectarian, and ethnic divisions and challenges to the state's authority do exist. But there is little doubt that the Arab political identity has lost ground to these other identifications, and this is particularly so in the domain of the state's foreign policy, where Arabism has become overshadowed by statism in recent years.[35]

The rise of statist and the decline of Arab national identities are reflected in a change in the institutions and organizations that Arab states construct to pursue their interests. Whereas Arab states once handled many of their most important foreign policy issues in the confines of the Arab League and other all-Arab institutions, the decay of Arabism and the rise of statism have produced a decline in the centrality of the Arab League, a consideration of new regional organizations that do not use identity as a criterion for membership, and a proliferation of organizations and institutions that are reflective of state interests and designed to overcome collective action problems. A particularly propitious moment came after the 1967 war. Before that war Arab officials reflexively pointed to the idea of military integration and coordination when considering the means to confront Israel; after the 1967 war, however, they shifted to bilateral arrangements that stressed financial assistance and little else. The shift in the organization of security reflected an emerging belief that the best way to pursue inter-Arab goals was through more statist designs. But part of the reason was that the 1967 war provided a subtle but important shift in the Arab-Israeli conflict from an ideological to a territorial conflict.

The change in the formal organization of Arab politics became more apparent after 1980 and again after 1990. The establishment of the Gulf Cooperation Council (GCC) at the beginning of the 1980s and of the Arab Maghrebi Union (AMU) and Arab Cooperation Council (ACC) at the end of the decade provided further evidence of declining Arabism and emerging statism. Since the Gulf War the Middle East has seen an explosion of different regional organizations that are unapologetically offered as furthering state interests irrespective of their Arab identities. Although Arab states still wave at the importance of all-Arab organizations to pursue their interests, they are emphasizing alternative arrangements that include non-Arab states for the first time; the current consideration of the Mediterranean region and Middle Easternism highlight such considerations. Indeed, in this context there arguably is an inverse correlation between the strength of Arabism and the prospects for strong regional organizations; that is, as Arabism has declined, Arab states have been more inclined to consider a prominent role for regional organizations because they have now agreed on some fundamental rules of the game and interdependence no longer appears as regime threatening. In general, a withering of the Arab identity produced a shift in the definition of the group, the attributes that are required to become a member of the region's organizations, and the relationship between the region's organizations and the identities of its members.

The changing state identities also are reflective of the changing definition of the threat. Historically, Arab states have been concerned with non-Arab entities defined as a source of insecurity to the Arab nation. Simply stated, the Arab identity and threat construction are connected.[36] Most prominent here are the West and Israel. Although the Arab states still view both suspiciously, particularly Israel, many Arab states now have alliances with the West and have been contemplating Israel's "normalization" in the region in ways that include new sorts of security ties that were once unthinkable. Perhaps the surest barometer of the emergence of statist identities is Israel's unprecedented integration into the region; the decline of the Arab political community, the hardening of the Arab states, and a diminished responsiveness to core Arab concerns mean that Israel is more fully recognized as a legitimate member of the region.[37] In general, the declining salience of the Arab national identity and the rise of statist identities contributed to a declining salience of the Israeli threat.

The norms that constitute Arab politics and that orient the actions of Arab states have also changed. During the first decades of the Arab states system Palestine, the West, and unification were central issues that animated Arab politics. All three retain some prominence in contemporary debates, but unification has dropped off the political agenda, the fear of the West is less connected to Arab nationalism than it is to political Islam, and Israel alone still registers a strong reaction. The decreased centrality and scope of Arabism are evident in the diminished ferocity of symbolic competition, which suggests that state-based identities are better able to compete with Arab national identities for citizens' political loyalties. Conversely, Arab states are no longer as susceptible to symbolic sanctions—this is particularly evident in the Arab states' fragmented approach to Israel's place in the region, suggesting again the declining salience of the Arab national identity relative to other identifications. Those Arab states that have moved to carefully and cautiously integrate Israel into the region have done so despite the protests by Syria and others, providing indirect evidence that the symbolic sanctions that once proved so effective no longer are because other Arab states are no longer as desirous of social approval from each other, their populations are no longer as stirred by these symbols, and the deliverers of these symbols are no longer as credible. Following Pierre Bourdieu's observation that different forms of capital are reflective of different structures, the declining value of symbolic capital relative to other forms of capital suggests a shift in the structure of politics.

Evidence that the structure of Arab politics has changed is also reflected by the Arab states' convergence on sovereignty to organize their relations. The Arab states system has moved from state versus nation and the acrimonious debate about the region's organizing principles to the simultaneous existence of separate sovereign states, a centrist conception of Arab nationalism that is consistent with sovereignty, and the establishment of relatively stable expectations and shared norms to govern inter-Arab relations. Arab states have been navigating between the sometimes contradictory expectations of sovereignty and Arab nationalism, or, more precisely, the meaning of sovereignty in relationship to a meaning of Arab nationalism. Arab governments in this respect had to negotiate between two roles as they performed on the regional stage. As representatives of sovereign states, they had a strong interest in defending the territorial and sovereign basis of their authority and power and recognizing the norms of sovereignty. But as *Arab* states they were expected to defend the Arab national interests, to pursue Arab unity that at the least undermined their autonomy and at the most instructed them to cede their sovereignty to a single Arab state, and to deny sovereignty's distinction between the domestic and the international.

For much of the pre-1970 period Arab states had a difficult time establishing a stable set of normative expectations because of the simultaneous presence of sovereignty and Arab nationalism that provided contradictory incentives and normative expectations. If the theme of state versus nation dominated the divisive debate about regional order through the 1960s, since then it has quieted and apparently settled on sovereignty.[38] Arab states have exhibited a greater willingness to recognize each other's sovereignty and honor the principle of noninterference as the basis of their relations. At one level, then, sovereignty is a focal point that has allowed Arab states to further their interests and to better handle contingencies.[39] But this particular focal point also implicated their state identities. As Arab states converged on sovereignty to organize their relations, they reconsidered the Arab state's identity, which was bound up with the declining salience of the Arab identity.

Some scholars and practitioners of Arab politics portray this outcome as the "new realism," suggesting that Arab states are now practicing their politics in ways that mimic how scholars of international relations understand international politics. But this "realist" conclusion would be erroneous for several reasons. This is a regional order that is secured not only through force but also through the establishment of relatively stable normative expectations that revolve around sovereignty. Arab leaders have had a never-ending series of discussions to get them to this point, discussions that labor to secure this outcome and to infuse it with legitimacy. In fact, this environment now looks more like an "anarchical (Arab) society" than it does a "new realism."[40] Further, to claim that the Arab states system has moved from Arabism to realism is to advance the proposition that the Arab states have gone from a social world to an asocial world. Although Arab nationalism has declined, a normless environment does not, indeed cannot, exist, and Arab states still dwell within a normative structure—even if it is one that legitimates the discourse of state interests. In other words, this might be a normative structure that legitimates and fosters the discourse of state interests, but, as Emile Durkheim noted a century ago, even a society that is seemingly comprised of atomized actors contains both a set of relations that continue to exist outside the momentary exchange and a set of social rules that legitimate those practices.[41] Although Arab nationalism no longer informs inter-Arab politics the way that it once did, and although this evolving states system has been characterized as realist by many policy makers because Arab states are favoring the language of state interests over Arab national interests, the discourse of state interests is an emergent rather than a taken-for-granted property of Arab states. State interests are being legitimated with reference to a normative order, and the regional order is still secured through negotiation and not military coercion alone.

This narrative of Arab politics tells the story of normative fragmentation. Arab states began by nominally professing the desire to deepen their sense of community and coordinate their political, economic, and security relations. Although highly wary of a too-close association, their initial interactions increased their dependence on and orientation toward each other. This drift toward normative integration halted abruptly in the mid-1960s and slowly yielded to a dynamic that generated fragmentation. The change in the desired regional order was detectable not only by what Arab leaders said but, more important, by what they did. Because of the decline of Arab national identity and the rise of statist identities, Arab states began constructing new foreign policies, organizing themselves according to new groupings, and orienting themselves in new directions. By following these dialogues about the desired regional order, we have been able to chart the ebbs and flows of the Arab states system.

DIALOGUES AND THE CHANGING GAME OF ARAB POLITICS

How Arab leaders played the game of Arab politics transformed that game. Although the structure in which they were embedded constrained what they could do, they acted upon and were capable of transforming the norms that defined the structure in which they were embedded.[42] Structures leave a great deal of slack that can be capitalized on—or not—by actors who can work creatively, imaginatively, skillfully, and strategically to defy the structures that supposedly determine their actions.[43] To understand how the Arab states' interactions transformed the normative structure requires a detailed consideration of events, that is, the "structuring of social action in time."[44] The events examined were unique to the extent that the conjunction of factors that produced them was unlikely to be replicated, but my interest in them was not to understand their details but to gain leverage over their relationship to the structure of Arab politics. These events were the sinews of regional order and group identity.

Sometimes their social, strategic, and symbolic interactions led to outcomes that more clearly proscribed their behavior, as was the case for many of the pre-1965 events, but events since have precipitated normative fragmentation. That their encounters led them in this direction is somewhat paradoxical. After all, they began every encounter with the assumption that because of their common past and common fate they had to coordinate their actions. But these cultural touch points also were principal reasons that these encounters were laden with suspicion and that their interactions deposited animosity and created the foundations for fragmentation. How so? Recall that Arab leaders looked upon Arab nationalism as savior and as threat: it was a source of symbolic capital and a resource of domestic stability, but it also allowed—indeed, invited—other Arab leaders to engage in predatory and regime-threatening behavior. Rare was the encounter that Arab leaders did not approach guardedly. As Goffman understood, performing on the public stage is always a risky proposition because one must put one's self on the line; such performances are made doubly disconcerting by the fear that other actors might alter the script in midscene.

Because of the mutual suspicions that permeated their every encounter, Arab leaders engaged in various practices that were designed to protect themselves from unwanted encroachments and interventions. But these same practices intentionally and unintentionally encouraged their fragmentation. One such practice was to construct a grammar of Arabism that accommodated itself to and highlighted regional and local differences.[45] To deter the symbolic tentacles of others, Arab governments frequently stressed the theme of diversity within unity and that, while they were members of the same family, they should be allowed some latitude because of their separate circumstances and geographies. This discourse was particularly visible when an Arab state was proposing a policy that departed from the prevailing consensus. Nuri al-Said claimed that the Baghdad Pact was permitted by Arabism and necessitated by Iraq's geostrategic location. King Hussein sounded the theme of the legitimacy of the separate Arab experiments as he welcomed the British troops into Jordan to deter the tide of Nasserism from claiming another victim. Sadat continuously stressed that Egypt's negotiations with Israel were consistent with Arabism and permitted by sovereignty, emphasizing that Arab states should not be accountable on all Arab issues because each had special circumstances that exempted it from the prevailing consensus. No Arab leader rejected the legitimacy of Arab nationalism outright, but many attempted to limit Arab nationalism's claims on their behavior by stressing their individual circumstances and separate features.

Alongside these defensive positionings, Arab leaders portrayed each other as threats. Such depictions were particularly pronounced during symbolic competition. "Our problem in the Arab nation," reflected Hosni Mubarak, "is that if you express your opinion, and this opinion is different from someone else's, you are considered an enemy."[46] There were good reasons for this tendency. During a dialogue Arab governments vied to establish the norms of Arabism because it was bound up with power and regime interests. To do so successfully, however, required persuading others that one's message was consistent with Arabism, whereas another's was a betrayal. But Arab governments frequently attempted to discredit the message by discrediting the messenger. To shield themselves from such attacks Arab governments would emphasize the unblemished character of their own credentials and the tarnished reputation of their rivals.' Such displays of enmity and rivalry undermined the prognosis for unity.

Their mutual suspicions were equally evident in their unwillingness to establish effective and functional all-Arab institutions. Their failure to do so soon discredited the idea of joint Arab action and encouraged Arab states and societies to pursue other means to achieve interests that were increasingly defined in statist terms. The search for interdependence and integration was a state-led affair, but those doing the leading were fearful of the unity they were proposing because it represented a potential threat to their autonomy, if not their sovereignty. As such, the promise of integration that began on cultural foundations was never followed by the material elements that would create a greater incentive for deepening the transnational networks of association. Arab nationalism began as a romantic movement that asserted the primacy of language and history as the bedrock of shared identification. It was an imagined community in the truest sense of the concept. But marrying this identification with material and political interests depended on the policies of the same Arab leaders who privately feared that integration would further erode their autonomy and only leave them more fully exposed to the predatory behavior of other Arab governments.

But even when Arab states did act collectively and did establish inter-Arab alliances and institutions, the results frequently reinforced a desire for separateness, not solidarity. Recall that many of these inter-Arab institutions and alliances were driven by a desire to save face and to control the foreign policy of a rival, that is, not necessarily to obtain collective Arab action. The result was that their accomplishments fell far short of their public rhetoric, causing Arab leaders and Arabism to suffer a normative deficit. The Arab Collective Security Pact, the Unified Arab Command, and other arrangements were welcomed with high hopes and euphoric rhetoric but rarely were implemented. A chain of these impotent inter-Arab arrangements decreased the demand for them and increased the acceptability of unilateral arrangements. The most dramatic move in this direction occurred in response to the 1967 war. Convinced that if he waited for a collective Arab effort, he would probably wait forever, Nasser led a move to jettison the multilateralism of the past and move toward more selective groupings. The move away from all-Arab arrangements became a defining feature of the 1980s, embodied in the emergence of subregional organizations that was attributed to a decline in the Arab identity and a "return to geography."[47] These unfulfilled promises led Arab societies to make their peace and identify more closely with the state. These failed promises also took their toll on the sensitivity among Arab societies to all-Arab issues. As dramatically demonstrated by the relatively muted response by the Arab states to the beginning of the intifada, by the end of the 1980s the Palestine conflict no longer resonated with Arab societies the way that it once did, a result not simply of fatigue but also of decreased sensitivity after years of instrumental appropriation.[48]

But even when the Arab states did contribute to their collective causes, their mutual suspicions hindered their efforts to coordinate their actions, and subsequently contributed to their fragmentation. The UAR and the 1963 unity agreement were defined and undermined by mutual suspicions, and their collapse triggered a vindictive period of name calling that included highly vocalized claims regarding the legitimacy and authenticity of the separate states. The disappearance of unification from the Arab agenda after 1963 had everything to do with how Arab states and societies reevaluated the prognosis for unification, deciding that unification was unlikely to breed anything other than hostility. King Hussein accused Egypt of supplying him with faulty intelligence information during the 1967 war that directly contributed to the loss of Jerusalem and the West Bank. Because of such experiences, Hussein subsequently claimed, Jordan should follow a more Jordan-centered policy that better distinguished between Arab and Jordanian interests. Even the pinnacle of inter-Arab collective action, the 1973 War of Ramadan, was laced with mutual suspicions that shaped the Arab states' generally uncoordinated military plans and the postwar political phase. After these and other fatal encounters Arab states stressed first how Arab unity was premised on the recognition of their diversity and second that, although they were members of the same family, their individual personalities and identities had to be respected and protected.

Arab states conducted themselves during a dialogue in ways intended to preserve domestic stability, and they pursued their various interests in the context of an Arab nationalism that placed unwanted restrictions on their activities and invited encroachments from other Arab states. To manage the tensions endemic in a situation in which they were expected to associate with the same movement that posed a potential danger, Arab states took evasive action that intentionally and unintentionally encouraged Arab societies to more fully identify with the territorial state and to draw distinctions and differences between Arab states. Arab states began each and every encounter with testimonies to their shared identity and their common fate. And then they proceeded to engage in policies and practices designed to protect them from the predations of other Arab leaders and to construct norms that bettered their standing. These new norms slowly privileged their separate identities and thus stressed their differences. Arab states sustained a pattern of interactions that eroded their shared fabric, created new identities, and oriented them in new directions.

But certain encounters and episodes represented historical turning points, moments of punctuated equilibrium when Arab states decisively turned toward new and separate directions. To understand how these events contributed to normative fragmentation requires an appreciation for how they were sequentially and causally connected, how Arab states charted a course of action after subjectively and strategically describing and situating the particular event in relationship to earlier events.[49] A decisive moment came after the failed 1963 unity agreements. But this moment was a testimony not only to the events of 1963 but also to the failure of the UAR in 1961 and the growing belief that unity as political unification was a breeding ground for rivalry. To protect themselves from the consequences of their failures Egypt, Syria, and Iraq began to stress the authenticity of the territorial state. The string of failures and confrontations surrounding the goal of unification, moreover, led Nasser to invent the summit system, to move away from the idea of unification, and to make (a temporary) peace with the conservative Arab states. The significance of the 1963 unity talks lies in how Arab states perceived those talks in relationship to past and present circumstances and in how the talks propelled Nasser in directions that moved him away from the idea of integration.

The 1967 war represented another such turning point. But to understand why the war led Arab states to conclude that their confrontation of Israel depended on their converging on sovereignty in inter-Arab relations requires an appreciation for how the Arab states understood the 1967 war in relationship to what had proceeded it. The return of the "Arab cold war" after the collapse of the summit system in 1964, and the subsequent symbolic competition among Arab states that was held partially responsible for the defeat, convinced most Arab states that Arabism had encouraged them to react to each other in the most destructive ways. Accordingly, they agreed to rechannel their energies away from each other and at Israel, and this required their convergence on a meaning of Arabism that was consistent with their separate sovereignties and the legitimacy of their separate "experiments."

Egypt's path to Camp David represented a similar turning point of considerably longer duration. Sadat claimed that his negotiations with Israel were permitted by sovereignty and consistent with Arabism, though this required him to relax the meaning of Arabism so that it left him less accountable to the other Arab states. For most of the 1970s he was relatively successful. However, Sadat's visit to Jerusalem represented shock therapy for both the Israelis and the Arabs, forcing both to revise their understanding of Egypt's place in Arab politics. His astounding journey demonstrated how imaginative and skillful actors can defy the constraints that supposedly shackle them. The rejectionist states successfully framed Camp David as antithetical to Arabism and thus discouraged other Arab states from following Sadat, but the long-term consequences of Sadat's policies were to relax the meaning of Arabism and encourage Arab states to orient themselves in new directions.

And, finally, there was the Iraqi invasion of Kuwait. The sight of one Arab state swallowing another Arab state whole in the name of Arab nationalism encouraged Arab states to orient themselves in new directions. This was the lesson of the Gulf War—Arab states had already tired of Arabism and could confidently assert, as they could not before, that policies taken in the name of Arab nationalism had contributed to more defeats than victories. The Gulf War, in other words, was understood and situated alongside other events that were similarly interpreted as miserable encounters registered in the name of Arabism. Given such realities, many Arab leaders argued, it was time to become more "realistic," which was tantamount to privileging the discourse of state interests over Arab national interests.

The unity talks, the 1967 war, the Camp David process, and the Iraqi invasion of Kuwait were historical turning points, causing the region's inhabitants to reconsider who they were, with whom they wanted to associate, and according to what norms. These events were like ice crystallizing in a cracking edifice, pushing Arab states further apart and leading them to stress their separate identities and interests. But they charted this course after situating that event in relationship to their actively, strategically, and collectively interpreted history and as a guide for their future directions. Arab states looked forward after understanding where they were in relationship to an imagined past.

Arabism encouraged Arab states to pursue both identification and individuation, but how they played the game of Arab politics, itself a product of their interest in regime survival, led to estrangement rather than collaboration, difference rather than fraternity, fragmentation rather than integration. Strategic and symbolic interaction was responsible for creating new and separate identities, roles, and interests that encouraged Arab leaders to adhere to the norms of sovereignty and to privilege the discourse of state interests over Arab national interests. Years of such interactions in the context of challenges that were supposed to unite them produced a regional order in which they stressed their growing diversity within unity and looked to sovereignty to rescue them from their worst hostilities. What began as a romantic movement at the beginning of this century has nearly returned to its original form at its end.

Arab states created a world of their own making and unmaking. As they discussed their collective response to the events of the day, they reconsidered their identities, roles they might assume, and eventual worlds. For most of this century Arab states were oriented toward each other, a movement that produced a rich mixture of conflict and cooperation. But the Arab world today is a far cry from the one that was demanded and desired only a few decades ago; the conflict that once marked the region has receded, but so too have the forms of desired and realized cooperation. Such historical developments are a testimony to the politics of identity and regime survival as Arab states negotiated the regional order.

Notes

Preface

1. Albert Hourani, "How Should We Write the History of the Middle East?" *International Journal of Middle Eastern Studies* 23, no. 1 (February 1991): 133.

1. A Narrative of Arab Politics

1. See, for instance, John Mearsheimer "The False Promise of Institutions," *International Security* 19, no. 3 (1995): 5–49; Kenneth Waltz, *Theory of International Politics* (Reading, Mass.: Addison-Wesley, 1979); David Baldwin, ed., *Neorealism and Neoliberalism* (New York: Columbia University Press, 1993); Benjamin Frankel, "Restating the Realist Case: An Introduction," in B. Frankel, ed., *Realism: Restatements and Renewal*, pp. 3–14 (New York: Frank Cass, 1997).

2. See Stephen Walt, *The Origins of Alliances* (Ithaca, N.Y.: Cornell University Press, 1987); Shibley Telhami, *Power and Leadership in International Bargaining: The Path to the Camp David Accords* (New York: Columbia University Press, 1990); Yair Evron and Yaacov Bar-Siman-Tov, "Coalitions in the Arab World," *Jerusalem Journal of International Relations* 1 (Winter 1975): 71–108; Alan Taylor, *The Arab Balance of Power System* (Syracuse, N.Y.: Syracuse University Press, 1982); Roger Owen, *State, Power, and Politics in the Making of the Modern Middle East* (New York: Routledge, 1992), pp. 90–92; P. J. Vatikiotis, *Conflict in the Middle East* (London: Allen and Unwin, 1971), pp. 18–22, 92, and *Arab and Regional Politics in the Middle East* (New York: St. Martin's, 1984); Ellie Kedourie, "The Chatham House Version," in E. Kedourie, *The Chatham House Version and Other Middle Eastern Studies*, pp. 351–94 (London: Weidenfeld and Nicolson, 1970).

3. Joseph Nye, *Understanding International Conflicts: An Introduction to Theory and History* (New York: HarperCollins, 1993), p. 147.

4. See Michael Brzoska and Thomas Ohlson, *Arms Transfers to the Third World, 1971–85* (Oxford, England: Oxford University Press for the Stockholm International Peace Research Institute, 1987).

5. Walt, *Origins of Alliances*, p. 149.

6. Associated Press, "Jordan's King, in Frank Speech, Calls '67 War a Major Blunder," *New York Times*, June 6, 1997, p. A6.

7. For the "new realism" see Bernard Lewis "Rethinking the Middle East," *Foreign Affairs* 71, no. 4 (1992): 99–119; for "maturation" see Gabriel Ben-Dor, *State and Conflict in the Middle East* (New York: Praeger, 1983); for geography see Ghassan Salame, "Inter-Arab Politics: The Return to Geography," in W. Quandt, ed., *The Middle East: Ten Years After Camp David*, pp. 319–56 (Washington, D.C.: Brookings Institution, 1988); for pan-Arabism see Fouad Ajami, "The End of Pan-Arabism," *Foreign Affairs* 57, no. 5 (Winter 1977–78): 355–73; for fragmentation see George Corm, *Fragmentation of the Middle East: The Last Thirty Years* (London: Hutchinson, 1983); for Middle Easternism see Mohammed Sid-Ahmed, "The Arab League and the Arab State," *Al-Ahram Weekly*, April 6–12, 1995, p. 8; and for *qawmiyya* see Ghassan Salame, " 'Strong' and 'Weak' States: A Qualified Return to the *Muqaddimah*," in G. Luciani, ed., *The Arab State*, pp. 29–64 (Berkeley: University of California Press, 1990).

8. Regarding the failed unity talks see Walt, *Origins of Alliances*, p. 87; Vatikiotis elevates the 1967 Arab-Israeli War in *Conflict in the Middle East*, chap. 5; and Telhami argues for the swing in power in *Power and Leadership*, pp. 94–104.

9. Little evidence exists that the superpowers were responsible for the decline of pan-Arabism and the rise of statism or that the end of the cold war is responsible for the "new realism" in Arab politics. The overwhelming evidence is that the superpowers accommodated themselves to, accentuated, and mitigated already present inter-Arab dynamics. See Fouad Ajami, *The Arab Predicament: Arab Political Thought and Practice Since 1967* (New York: Cambridge University Press, 1981); L. Carl Brown, *International Politics of the Middle East* (Princeton, N.J.: Princeton University Press, 1984); Paul Noble, "The Arab System: Opportunities, Constraints, and Pressures," in B. Korany and A. Dessouki, eds., *The Foreign Policies of Arab States*, pp. 41–78 (Boulder, Colo.: Westview, 1984); Walt, *Origins of Alliances*, p. 158; Yezid Sayigh and Avi Shlaim, eds., *The Cold War and the Middle East* (New York: Oxford University Press, 1997); Basam Tibi, *Conflict and War in the Middle East, 1967–91* (New York: St. Martin's Press, 1993), chaps. 2 and 3.

10. There are some important exceptions. Prominent are those that begin with domestic rather than systemic politics to understand how Arab politics is shaped by states whose lack of legitimacy forces them to use Arabism as an ideological prop. See Michael Hudson, *Arab Politics: The Search for Legitimacy* (New Haven, Conn.: Yale University Press, 1977); F. Gregory Gause III, "Sovereignty, Statecraft, and Stability in the Middle East," *Journal of International Affairs* 45, no. 2 (Winter 1992): 441–67; Paul

Noble, Rex Brynen, and Baghat Korany, "Conclusion: The Changing Regional Security Environment," in B. Korany, P. Noble, and R. Brynen, eds., *The Many Faces of National Security in the Arab World*, pp. 275–302 (New York: St. Martin's, 1993); Avraham Sela, *The Decline of the Arab-Israeli Conflict: Middle East Politics and the Quest for Regional Order* (Albany: State University of New York Press, 1997). Laurie Brand, in *Jordan's Inter-Arab Relations* (New York: Columbia University Press, 1995), looks at "budget security." Baghat Korany and Ali Hillal Dessouki ("The Global System and Arab Foreign Policies," in Korany and Dessouki, *Foreign Policies of Arab States*, pp. 19–39) offer a framework that forwards the centrality of Arabism but accept many core realist assumptions and ultimately point to the dominance of realism.

11. Constructivism is not a research program that is organized around the attempt to explain a particular outcome—for instance, neoliberal institutionalism's concern with the "cooperation question" and realism's focus on the "problem of war"; rather, it attempts to understand how agents and structures are involved in a process of mutual creation and reproduction—that is, how *structure* broadly defined shapes the nature of the agents and their capacities, how their interaction is constrained by that structure, and how their interaction serves to either reproduce or transform that structure. See Nicholas Onuf, *World of Our Own Making* (Columbia: University of South Carolina Press, 1989); Alexander Wendt, *Social Theory of International Politics* (New York: Cambridge University Press, forthcoming); Emanuel Adler, "Seizing the Middle Ground: Constructivism in World Politics," *European Journal of International Relations* 3, no. 3 (September 1997): 319–63; Peter Katzenstein, ed., *The Culture of National Security: Norms and Identity in World Politics* (New York: Columbia University Press, 1996).

12. For sociological statements that inform this conception of order, see Dennis Wrong, *The Problem of Order* (New York: Free Press, 1994), p. 38; Erving Goffman, "The Interaction Order," *American Sociological Review* 48, no. 1 (February 1983): 1–17; Peter Berger and Thomas Luckmann, *The Social Construction of Reality* (New York: Anchor, 1967); Jeffrey Alexander, *Twenty Lectures* (New York: Columbia University Press, 1987), chap. 1; Onuf, *World of Our Making*.

13. This interactional theme has its roots in the works of George Simmel, *Conflict and the Web of Group Affiliations* (New York: Free Press, 1955), and "Group Expansion and the Development of Individuality," in D. Levine, ed., *On Individuality and Social Forms*, pp. 351–93 (Chicago: University of Chicago Press, 1971); George Herbert Mead, *Mind, Self, and Society* (Chicago: University of Chicago Press, 1934); and Erving Goffman, *Strategic Interaction* (Philadelphia: University of Pennsylvania Press, 1969). For other sociological treatises see Anselm Strauss, *Negotiations* (San Francisco: Jossey-Bass, 1978); Barry Barnes, *The Elements of Social Theory* (Princeton, N.J.: Princeton University Press, 1996); Mustafa Emirbayer, "Manifesto for a Relational Sociology," *American Journal of Sociology* 103, no. 2 (September 1997): 281–317; Paul Hare and Herbert Blumberg, eds., *Dramaturgical Analysis of Social Interaction* (New York: Praeger, 1988).

14. I am modifying Erving Goffman's concept. He observed a dialogue when some offense to the group's norms compels actors to address not only the nature of the offense but also their "own role and the role of the other participants in a system of control through which corrective action can be handled reasonably." *Relations in Public* (New York: HarperBooks, 1971), p. 120.

15. That norms are created by and through interactions is a long-honored tradition in sociological research in a wide variety of fields. See Deirdre Boden, "The World as It Happens: Ethnomethodology and Conversational Analysis," in G. Ritzer, ed., *Frontiers of Social Theory*, pp. 185–213 (New York: Columbia University Press, 1990); Harold Garfinkel, *Studies in Ethnomethodology* (Englewood Cliffs, N.J.: Prentice-Hall, 1967); William Gamson, *Talking Politics* (New York: Cambridge University Press, 1992); Berger and Luckmann, *Social Construction of Reality*; Nicos Mouzelis, "The Interaction Order and the Micro-Macro Distinction," *Sociological Theory* 10, no. 1 (Spring 1991): 127.

16. Strategic interaction can be understood as a "level of analysis" in its own right. See Goffman, "Interaction Order"; David Lake and Robert Powell, "Strategic Choice and International Relations," in D. Lake and R. Powell, *Strategic Choice and International Relations* (Princeton, N.J.: Princeton University Press, forthcoming); Wendt, *Social Theory*, chap. 4; Randall Collins, "On the Microfoundations of Macrosociology," *American Journal of Sociology* 86, no. 5 (March 1981): 984–1014; Jonathan Turner, *A Theory of Social Interaction* (Palo Alto, Calif.: Stanford University Press, 1988); Barry Buzan, "The Levels of Analysis Problem Reconsidered," in K. Booth and S. Smith, eds., *International Relations Theory Today*, pp. 198–216 (College Station: Pennsylvania State University Press, 1995).

17. For game-theoretic treatments of international politics see Thomas Schelling, *The Strategy of Conflict* (Cambridge, Mass.: Harvard University Press, 1980); Lake and Powell, "Strategic Choice"; James Morrow, *Game Theory for Political Scientists* (Princeton, N.J.: Princeton University Press, 1994).

18. See Taylor, *Arab Balance of Power*; Walt, *Origins of Alliances*; Telhami, *Power and Leadership*.

19. Clement Henry Moore, "On Theory and Practice Among the Arabs," *World Politics* 24, no. 1 (October 1971): 106–26.

20. On the importance of distinguishing between state and regime survival, see Noble, Brynen, and Korany, "Conclusion"; Mohammad Ayoob, *Third World Security Predicament* (Boulder, Colo.: Lynne Reinner, 1994); Michael Barnett and Jack Levy, "The Domestic Sources of Alignments and Alliances," *International Organization* 45, no. 3 (Summer 1991): 369–96.

21. See Robert Jervis, *The Logic of Images in International Relations* (New York: Columbia University Press, 1970), for a classic statement that builds on the work of Goffman to generate similar observations.

22. Ann Swidler, "Culture in Action: Symbols in Strategies," *American Sociological Review* 51, no. 2 (April 1986): 273.

23. For rationalist approaches see Baldwin, *Neorealism and Neoliberalism*; Michael Hechter, *Principles of Group Solidarity* (Berkeley: University of California Press, 1987); James Coleman, *The Foundations of Social Theory* (Cambridge, Mass.: Harvard University Press, 1990).

24. Also see Andrew Abbott, "Sequences of Social Events: Concepts and Methods for the Analysis of Order in Social Processes," *Historical Methods* 16, no. 4 (Fall 1983): 129–46, and "From Causes to Events: Notes on Narrative Positivism," *Sociological Methods and Research* 20, no. 4 (May 1992): 428–55; Larry Griffin, "Temporality, Events, and Explanation in Historical Sociology," *Sociological Methods and Research* 20, no. 4 (May 1992): 403–27; William Sewall, "Three Temporalities: Toward an Eventful Sociology," in T. McDonald, ed., *The Historic Turn in the Human Sciences*, pp. 245–80 (Ann Arbor: University of Michigan Press, 1996).

25. A second domestic-centered explanation examines the rise and decline of domestic coalitions that support Arab nationalist goals. Sometimes domestic support is linked to class orientation; notably, the lower and middle classes are more accepting of Arabism's goals, whereas the upper classes are more conservative and supportive of the territorial status quo. In other cases domestic support is connected to generational politics, as, for instance, a younger generation that leans toward radicalism. But this literature has generally focused on the rise and not the decline of Arab nationalism. On class politics see Hanna Batatu, *The Old Social Classes and the Revolutionary Movements of Iraq* (Princeton, N.J.: Princeton University Press, 1978); Philip Khoury, *Syria and the French Mandate* (Princeton, N.J.: Princeton University Press, 1987); C. Ernest Dawn, "The Origins of Arab Nationalism," in R. Khalidi et al., eds., *The Origins of Arab Nationalism*, pp. viii–xix (New York: Columbia University Press, 1991); Nazih Ayubi, *Overstating the Arab State* (London: I. B. Taurus, 1995). On generational politics see Paul Salem, *Bitter Legacy: Ideology and Politics in the Arab World* (Syracuse, N.Y.: Syracuse University Press, 1994); Manfred Halperin, *The Politics of Social Change in the Middle East and North Africa* (Princeton, N.J.: Princeton University Press, 1963).

26. See Sela, *Decline of the Arab-Israeli Conflict*; Malik Mufti, *Sovereign Creations: Pan-Arabism and Political Order in Syria and Iraq* (Ithaca, N.Y.: Cornell University Press, 1996); Gause, "Sovereignty, Statecraft, and Stability"; Noble, Brynen, and Korany, "Conclusion"; Rex Brynen, "Palestine and the Arab State System: Permeability, State Consolidation, and the Intifada," *Canadian Journal of Political Science* 24, no. 3 (September 1991): 606; Amatzia Baram, "Territorial Nationalism in the Middle East," *Middle Eastern Studies* 26, no. 4 (October 1990): 425–48; Albert Hourani, *A History of the Arab Peoples* (Cambridge, Mass.: Harvard University Press, 1991), p. 448.

27. Giacomo Luciani and Ghassan Salame, "The Politics of Arab Integration," in Luciani, *The Arab State*, p. 398.

28. For discussions of narrative analysis see Lawrence Stone, "The Revival of the Narrative: Reflections on a New Old History," in L. Stone, *The Past and the Present Revisited*, pp. 74–93 (London: Routledge and Kegan Paul, 1981); Hayden White, *Metahis-*

J

tory (Baltimore, Md.: Johns Hopkins University Press, 1973); William Sewall, "Introduction: Narratives and Social Identities," *Social Science History* 16, no. 4 (Winter 1992): 479–88; Jerome Bruner, "The Narrative Construction of Reality," *Critical Inquiry* 18, no. 1 (1991): 1–21; Alex Callinicos, *Theories and Narratives* (Durham, N.C.: Duke University Press, 1995), chap. 2.

29. Mohamed Heikal, *Secret Channels* (London: HarperCollins, 1996). Ali Hillal Dessouki similarly argues that these were the defining Arab issues. "The New Arab Political Order: Implications for the 1980s," in M. Kerr and E. Yassin, eds., *Rich and Poor States in the Middle East: Egypt and the New Arab Order* (Boulder, Colo.: Westview, 1982), p. 322.

30. See Sewall, "Three Temporalities"; Abbott, "Sequences of Social Events," and "From Causes to Events"; Hendrik Spruyt, *The Sovereign State and Its Competitors: An Analysis of Systems Change* (Princeton, N.J.: Princeton University Press, 1994); Stephen Jay Gould, *Wonderful Life: The Burgess Shale and the Nature of History* (New York: Norton, 1988); Kathleen Thelen and Sven Steinmo, "Historical Institutionalism in Comparative Politics," in S. Steinmo, K. Thelen, and F. Longstreth, eds., *Structuring Politics: Historical Institutionalism in Comparative Analysis*, pp. 1–32 (New York: Cambridge University Press, 1992); Stephen Krasner, "Sovereignty: An Institutional Perspective," *Comparative Political Studies* 21, no. 1 (April 1988): 66–94.

31. For the rise of political Islam see Dale Eickelman and James Piscatori, *Muslim Politics* (Princeton, N.J.: Princeton University Press, 1996).

32. Shirin Fathi, *Jordan: An Invented Nation?* (Hamburg: Deutsches Orient-Institut, 1994), p. 228; Eickelman and Piscatori, *Muslim Politics*; John Esposito, *Islam and Politics*, 3d ed. (Syracuse, N.Y.: Syracuse University Press, 1986).

2. The Game of Arab Politics

1. Erving Goffman, *Strategic Interaction* (Philadelphia: University of Pennsylvania Press, 1969), pp. 100–101.

2. Martin Hollis, *The Philosophy of Social Science: An Introduction* (New York: Cambridge University Press, 1994), p. 159. Also see Pierre Bourdieu and Loic Wacquant, *An Invitation to Reflexive Sociology* (Chicago: University of Chicago Press, 1992), pp. 98–100.

3. Hollis, *Philosophy of Social Science*, p. 159–60. Also see Martin Hollis, *The Cunning of Reason* (New York: Cambridge University Press, 1988), p. 140; Goffman, *Strategic Interaction*, p. 113; K. M. Fierke, "Multiple Identities, Interfacing Games: The Social Construction of Western Action in Bosnia," *European Journal of International Relations* 2, no. 4 (1996): 470–71; Roger Hurwitz, "Strategic and Social Fictions in the Prisoner's Dilemma," in J. Der Derian and M. Shapiro, eds., *International/Intertextual Relations: Postmodern Readings of World Politics*, pp. 113–34 (New York: Lexington, 1989); Aaron Wildavsky, "Indispensable Framework or Just Another Ide-

ology? Prisoner's Dilemma as an Antihierarchical Game," *Rationality and Society* 4, no. 1 (1992): 8–23.

4. A tenet of social interaction and social exchange models is that the social structure in which actors find themselves will shape the strategic interaction that follows. See Peter Blau, *Exchange and Power in Social Life* (New Brunswick, N.J.: Transaction, 1992), p. ix; Linda Molm, *Coercive Power in Social Exchange* (New York: Cambridge University Press, 1997), pp. 11–13.

5. On the importance of ascertaining the identity of the players before trying the game, see Goffman, *Strategic Interaction*; Frederick Frey, "The Problem of Actor Designation in Political Analysis," *Comparative Political Studies* 17, no. 2 (January 1985): 127–52; Nicos Mouzelis, *Sociological Theory: What Went Wrong?* (New York: Routledge, 1995), p. 37; Wildavsky, "Indispensable Framework."

6. Jeffrey Alexander, *Twenty Lectures* (New York: Columbia University Press, 1987), p. 170; Barry Barnes, *The Elements of Social Theory* (Princeton, N.J.: Princeton University Press, 1996), p. 14.

7. Anthony Giddens, *The Constitution of Society* (Berkeley: University of California Press, 1984), p. 288.

8. Structures contain normative and material elements, which drive complex overlying rules or schemas—that is, they have "generalizable procedures applied in the enactment/reproduction of social life," and human and nonhuman resources. William Sewall, "A Theory of Structure: Duality, Agency, and Transformation," *American Journal of Sociology* 98, no. 1 (July 1992): 8.

9. For the concept of roles see Peter Berger and Thomas Luckmann, *The Social Construction of Reality* (New York: Anchor, 1967), pp. 72–74; Sheldon Stryker, *Symbolic Interactionism: A Social Structural Perspective* (Reading, Mass.: Benjamin/Cummings, 1980), p. 57; Heinrich Popitz, "The Concept of Social Role as an Element of Sociological Theory," in J. A. Jackson, ed., *Roles* (London: Cambridge University Press, 1972), pp. 16–17; Ralf Dahrendorf, "Homo Sociologicus," in R. Dahrendorf, *Essays in the Theory of Society*, pp. 15–25 (Palo Alto, Calif.: Stanford University Press, 1968); Erving Goffman, *The Presentation of Self in Everyday Life* (New York: Anchor, 1959); Hollis, *Philosophy of Social Science*, chap. 8.

10. See Dennis Wrong, *The Problem of Order* (New York: Free Press, 1994), p. 46; J. R. Landis, *Sociology: Concepts and Characteristics* (Belmont, Calif.: Wadsworth, 1971), p. 288; Kent Bach, "Analytic Social Philosophy: Basic Concepts," *Journal of the Theory of Social Behavior* 5, no. 2 (October 1975): 196.

11. Barnes, *Elements of Social Theory*, p. 55.

12. For this distinction see Hollis, *Cunning of Reason*, pp. 137–41, and *Philosophy of Social Science*, pp. 152–53; Brian Fay, *Contemporary Philosophy of Social Sciences* (New York: Basil Blackwell, 1996), pp. 65–67; John Heritage, "Ethnomethodology," in A. Giddens and J. Turner, eds., *Social Theory Today* (Palo Alto, Calif.: Stanford University Press, 1987), pp. 240–48; Ron Jepperson, Alexander Wendt, and Peter Katzenstein, "Norms, Identity, and Culture in National Security," in P. Katzenstein, ed., *The*

Culture of National Security: Norms and Identity in World Politics, pp. 33–75 (New York: Columbia University Press, 1987).

13. Tom Burns, *Erving Goffman* (New York: Routledge, 1992), p. 40.

14. In this respect Arab states experienced "role conflict," a situation in which actors occupy more than one social role, which confers contradictory behavioral expectations. "Such expectations may call for incompatible performances; they may require that one hold two norms or values which logically call for opposing behaviors; or they may demand that one role necessitates the expenditure of time and energy such that it is difficult or impossible to carry out the obligations of another role." Stryker, *Symbolic Interactionism*, p. 73. Also see Hollis, *Philosophy of Social Science*, chap. 8; Ralph Turner, "The Role and the Person," *American Journal of Sociology* 84, no. 1 (July 1978): 1–23. In this view Arab states were expected to reconcile the potentially contradictory expectations of Arabism and sovereignty. For this argument see Michael Barnett, "Institutions, Roles, and Disorder: The Case of the Arab States System," *International Studies Quarterly* 37 (September 1993): 271–96.

15. John Ruggie, "Continuity and Transformation in the World Polity," in R. Keohane, ed., *Neorealism and Its Critics* (New York: Columbia University Press, 1986), p. 145.

16. See Alexander Wendt, "Anarchy Is What States Make of It: Anarchy and the Social Construction of Power Politics," *International Organization* 46, no. 2 (Spring 1992): 391–426; Hedley Bull, *The Anarchical Society* (New York: Macmillan, 1977); Thomas Biersteker and Cynthia Weber, "The Social Construction of State Sovereignty," in T. Biersteker and C. Weber, eds., *State Sovereignty as Social Construct*, pp. 1–21 (New York: Cambridge University Press, 1996); Robert Jackson and Carl Rosberg, "Why Africa's Weak States Persist: The Empirical and Juridical in Statehood," *World Politics* 35, no. 1 (October 1982): 1–24.

17. Identities are social—shaped by the actor's interaction with and relationship to others; the process of interacting and participating within an institutional context, which the actor ascribes to a particular identity, takes on a conception of one's self in relationship to another. George Herbert Mead, *Mind, Self, and Society* (Chicago: University of Chicago Press, 1934). On national and state identities that build on this definition, see Alexander Wendt, *Social Theory of International Politics* (New York: Cambridge University Press, forthcoming). On corporate identities see Mary Douglas, *How Institutions Think* (Syracuse, N.Y.: Syracuse University Press, 1986); David Kertzer, *Ritual, Politics, and Power* (New Haven, Conn.: Yale University Press, 1988), pp. 17–19.

18. In *The Arab States and the Palestine Conflict* (Syracuse, N.Y.: Syracuse University Press, 1981) Barry Rubin similarly argues that Arabism shaped the definition of state interests. On identities as the basis of interests see Mark Granovetter, "Problems of Explanation in Economic Sociology," in N. Nohria and R. Eccles, eds., *Networks and Organizations: Structure, Form, and Action*, pp. 25–56 (Cambridge, Mass.: Harvard Business School Press, 1995).

19. Walid Khalidi, "Thinking the Unthinkable: A Sovereign Palestinian State," *Foreign Affairs* 56, no. 4 (July 1978): 696.

20. Kamal Salibi, *A House of Many Mansions: The History of Modern Lebanon Reconsidered* (Berkeley: University of California Press, 1988), p. 55.

21. Fay, *Contemporary Philosophy*, p. 65.

22. Also see Nicos Mouzelis, "The Interaction Order and the Micro-Macro Distinction," *Sociological Theory* 10, no. 1 (Spring 1991): 126; Hollis, *Cunning of Reason* and *Philosophy of Social Science*; Stryker, *Symbolic Interactionism*; Peter Berger, *Invitation to Sociology* (New York: Anchor, 1963), pp. 135–36; Donald Searing, "Roles, Rules, and Rationality in the New Institutionalism," *American Political Science Review* 85, no. 4 (December 1991): 1239–60.

23. Goffman, *Presentation of Self*, p. 251.

24. Also see Erving Goffman, "The Interaction Order," *American Sociological Review* 48, no. 1 (February 1983): 5–7; Randall Collins, "On the Microfoundations of Macrosociology," *American Journal of Sociology* 86, no. 5 (March 1981): 984–1014; Blau, *Exchange and Power*, chap. 3.

25. For a more general argument regarding how the logic of regime survival imprints the state's foreign and domestic policies, see Mohammad Ayoob, *Third World Security Predicament* (Boulder, Colo.: Lynne Reinner, 1994); Christopher Clapham, *Africa and the International System: The Politics of State Survival* (New York: Cambridge University Press, 1996).

26. Adnan Abu Odeh, interview by author, Washington, D.C., April 2, 1996.

27. Michael Hudson, *Arab Politics: The Search for Legitimacy* (New Haven, Conn.: Yale University Press, 1977).

28. Nazih Ayubi, *Overstating the Arab State* (London: I. B. Taurus, 1995).

29. For similar analytic points see Blau, *Exchange and Power*; Amartya Sen, "Rational Fools: A Critique of the Behavioral Foundations of Economic Theory," *Philosophy and Public Affairs* 6 (Summer 1977): 317–44; Timur Kuran, "Private and Public Preferences," *Economics and Philosophy* 6 (1990): 1–26.

30. Scholars from a variety of disciplines and theoretical dispositions have considered how the resources that are valued and exchanged may be cultural or symbolic. See Marcel Mauss, *The Gift: Forms and Functions of Exchange in Archaic Societies* (New York: Norton, 1967); Marshall Sahlins, *Culture and Practical Reason* (Chicago: University of Chicago Press, 1976), chap. 5; Karen Cook, Jodi O'Brien, and Peter Kollock, "Exchange Theory: A Blueprint for Structure and Process," in G. Ritzer, ed., *Frontiers of Social Theory* (New York: Columbia University Press, 1990), p. 169; Pierre Bourdieu and Loic Wacquant, *An Invitation to Reflexive Sociology* (Chicago: University of Chicago Press, 1992); Blau, *Exchange and Power*, p. 132; Karen Cook, ed., *Social Exchange Theory* (Beverly Hills, Calif.: Sage, 1986); Randall Collins, "Conflict Theory and the Advance of Macrohistorical Sociology," in Ritzer, *Frontiers of Social Theory*, pp. 69–87; Mouzelis, *Sociological Theory*, pp. 143–45; Molm, *Coercive Power*, p. 15.

31. Arab politics is not unique here, for state elites in the context of newly developing societies have tended to use symbols for nation building. See Christopher Clapham, *Third World Politics* (Madison: University of Wisconsin, 1985); Clifford Geertz, "After the Revolution: The Fate of Nationalism in the New States," in C. Geertz, *The Interpretation of Cultures*, pp. 193–234 (New York: Basic Books, 1973).

32. Mead, *Mind, Self, and Society*; Anselm Strauss, *Negotiations* (San Francisco: Jossey-Bass, 1978), p. 215; Barnes, *Elements of Social Theory*, p. 58, and *The Nature of Power* (Cambridge, Mass.: Polity, 1988). For various discussions and definitions of the "problem of order," see Talcott Parsons, *The Structure of Social Action* (New York: Free Press, 1968), pp. 89–91; Wrong, *Problem of Order*, chap. 3; Alexander, *Twenty Lectures*, chap. 1; John Rhoads, *Critical Issues in Social Theory* (College Station: Pennsylvania State University Press, 1991), chap. 5; Max Weber, *Economy and Society* (Berkeley: University of California Press, 1978), p. 31.

33. Barnes, *Elements of Social Theory*, p. 55.

34. Stewart Clegg called this "strategic agency." "Power and Institutions in Organization Theory," in J. Hassard and M. Parker, eds., *Toward a New Theory of Organizations* (New York: Routledge, 1994), p. 36.

35. Goffman, *Presentation of Self*, pp. 8–14.

36. Ann Swidler, "Culture in Action: Symbols in Strategies," *American Sociological Review* 51, no. 2 (April 1986): 273–86.

37. George Simmel, *Conflict and the Web of Group Affiliations* (New York: Free Press, 1955), chap. 2; Marc Howard Ross, *Culture of Conflict* (New Haven, Conn.: Yale University Press, 1993); Blau, *Power and Exchange*; Molm, *Coercive Power*.

38. For a general statement see Friedrich Kratochwil, *Norms, Rules, and Decisions* (New York: Cambridge University Press, 1989), p. 11.

39. As Martha Finnemore notes, "Normative claims become powerful and prevail by being persuasive; being persuasive means grounding claims in existing norms in ways that emphasize normative congruence and coherence." *National Interests in International Society* (Ithaca, N.Y.: Cornell University Press, 1996), p. 141.

40. Erving Goffman, *Frame Analysis* (Cambridge, Mass.: Harvard University Press, 1974), p. 21; Murray Edelman, *Constructing the Political Spectacle* (Chicago: University of Chicago Press, 1988); Jonathan Turner, *A Theory of Social Interaction* (Palo Alto, Calif.: Stanford University Press, 1988), pp. 108–13. Also see David Snow and Robert Benford, "Master Frames and Cycles of Protest," in A. Morris and C. Mueller, eds., *Frontiers in Social Movement Theory* (New Haven, Conn.: Yale University Press, 1992), p. 138; David Snow et al., "Frame Alignment Processes, Micromobilization, and Movement Participation," *American Sociological Review* 51, no. 3 (August 1986): 464; Morris and Mueller, *Frontiers in Social Movement Theory*.

41. Mayer N. Zald, "Culture, Ideology, and Strategic Framing," in D. McAdam, J. McCarthy, and M. Zald, eds., *Comparative Perspective on Social Movements: Political Opportunities, Mobilizing Structures, and Cultural Framing* (New York: Cambridge University Press, 1996), p. 262.

42. Donald Schön and Martin Rein, *Frame Reflection: Toward the Resolution of Intractable Policy Controversies* (New York: Basic Books, 1994), p. 29.

43. Doug McAdam, John McCarthy, and Mayer Zald, "Introduction," in McAdam, McCarthy, and Zald, *Comparative Perspective on Social Movements*, p. 6.

44. Sidney Tarrow, *Power in Movement* (New York: Cambridge University Press, 1994), p. 119. Also see Swidler, "Culture in Action"; Jean Cohen, "Strategy or Identity: New Theoretical Paradigms and Contemporary Social Movements," *Social Research* 52, no. 4 (Winter 1985): 663–716.

45. Jerome Bruner, *Actual Minds, Possible Worlds* (Cambridge, Mass.: Harvard University Press, 1986), p. 66. Also see Scott Hunt, Robert Benford, and David Snow, "Identity Fields: Framing Processes and the Social Construction of Movement Identities," in E. Larana, H. Johnston, and J. Gusfield, eds., *New Social Movements: From Ideology to Identity* (Philadelphia: Temple University Press, 1995), pp. 190, 193, 198.

46. Tarrow, *Power in Movement*, pp. 122–23; William Gamson, *Talking Politics* (New York: Cambridge University Press, 1992), chap. 3.

47. On symbols and historical movements and social organization see Sherry Ortner, "Theory in Anthropology Since the 1960s," *Comparative Study of Society and History* 26, no. 1 (January 1984): 126–66; Zdzislaw Mach, *Symbols, Conflict, and Identity* (New York: State University of New York Press, 1994); A. P. Cohen, *The Symbolic Construction of Community* (New York: Tavistock, 1985); Kertzer, *Ritual, Politics, and Power*.

48. Kertzer, *Ritual, Politics, and Power*; Hunt, Bedford, and Snow, "Identity Fields," p. 195.

49. Mach, *Symbols, Conflict, and Identity*, p. 36; Robert Benford and Scott Hunt, "Dramaturgy and Social Movements: The Social Construction and Communication of Power," *Sociological Inquiry* 62, no. 1 (February 1992): 36–55.

50. Cohen, *Symbolic Construction of Community*; David Kertzer, *Politics and Symbols* (New Haven, Conn.: Yale University Press, 1996); Dale Eickelman and James Piscatori, *Muslim Politics* (Princeton, N.J.: Princeton University Press, 1996), chap. 1; Pierre Bourdieu, *Language and Symbolic Power* (Chicago: University of Chicago Press, 1994).

51. Mach, *Symbols, Conflict, and Identity*, p. 37.

52. Barnes, *Elements of Social Theory*, pp. 77–78; also see Michael Hechter, *Principles of Group Solidarity* (Berkeley: University of California Press, 1987), p. 157.

53. Tarrow, *Power in Movement*, p. 123.

54. Amin Hewedy, interview by author, Cairo, March 16, 1996.

55. Mohamed Heikal, *The Cairo Documents* (New York: Doubleday, 1973), quoted in Marc Lynch, *Contested Identity and Security: The International Politics of Jordanian Identity* (New York: Columbia University Press, forcoming).

56. Mead, *Mind, Self, and Society*.

57. Benjamin Most and Harvey Starr, "International Relations Theory, Foreign Policy Substitutability, and 'Nice' Laws," *World Politics* 36, no. 3 (April 1984): 383–406.

58. Stated more formally, the "more *dependent* a member is on the group (that is, the more costly it is to leave the group in terms of opportunities foregone), the greater the tax that the member will be prepared to bear for a given joint good." Hechter, *Principles of Group Solidarity*, p. 10; emphasis in original.

59. Samir Mutawi, "The Jordanian Response," in R. Parker, ed., *The Six-Day War: A Retrospective* (Gainesville, Fla.: University Press of Florida, 1996), p. 179.

60. Goffman, *Presentation of Self*.

61. Joel Brockner and Jeffrey Rubin, *Entrapment in Escalating Conflicts: A Social Psychological Analysis* (New York: Springer-Verlag, 1985), chap. 6, p. 5.

62. For general statements on the relationship between identity and collective action, see Craig Calhoun, "Problem of Identity in Collective Action," in J. Huber, ed., *Micro-Macro Linkages in Collective Action*, pp. 51–75 (Beverly Hills, Calif.: Sage, 1991); Alexander Wendt, "Collective Identity Formation and the International State," *American Political Science Review* 88, 2 (June 1994): 384–96; Morris and Mueller, *Frontiers in Social Movement Theory*.

63. According to Barnes, "sanctioning the collective good may or may not effect its enactment, depending upon the individual sacrifice required and the power and the coherence of the sanctioning." *Elements of Social Theory*, p. 84.

64. Goffman, "Interactive Order," pp. 5–7.

65. William Sewall, "Three Temporalities: Toward an Eventful Sociology," in T. McDonald, ed., *The Historic Turn in the Human Sciences*, pp. 245–80 (Ann Arbor: University of Michigan Press, 1996); Andrew Abbott, "Sequences of Social Events: Concepts and Methods for the Analysis of Order in Social Processes," *Historical Methods* 16, no. 4 (Fall 1983): 129–46; Peter Burke, "Identity Processes and Social Stress," *American Sociological Review* 56, no. 4 (December 1991): 836–49. On interaction and new roles, identities, and interests, see Wendt, "Anarchy Is What States Make of It," pp. 406–407; George McCall and J. L. Simmons, *Identities and Interactions* (New York: Free Press, 1978); Nicholas Abercrombie, "Knowledge, Order, and Human Autonomy," in J. Hunter and S. Ainlay, eds., *Making Sense of Modern Times: Peter Berger and the Vision of Interpretive Sociology* (New York: RKP, 1986), pp. 18–19; Turner, *Theory of Social Interaction*.

66. Mead, *Mind, Self, and Society*, p. 309.

67. William Connolly, *Identity/Difference* (Ithaca, N.Y.: Cornell University Press, 1991).

68. Clement Henry Moore, "On Theory and Practice Among the Arabs," *World Politics* 24, no. 1 (October 1971): 106–26; Fouad Ajami, "The End of Pan-Arabism," *Foreign Affairs* 57, no. 5 (Winter 1978–79): 355–73.

69. Giacomo Luciani and Ghassan Salame, "The Politics of Arab Integration," in G. Luciani, ed., *The Arab State*, (Berkeley: University of California Press, 1990), p. 398. State formation can occur through myriad activities and processes, but figuring centrally in the comparative politics and the Middle Eastern literatures are material incentives, the presence of external threats, and the manipulation of symbols.

On economic and political developments see F. Gregory Gause III, "Sovereignty, Statecraft, and Stability in the Middle East," *Journal of International Affairs* 45, no. 2 (Winter 1992): 460; Malik Mufti, *Sovereign Creations: Pan-Arabism and Political Order in Syria and Iraq* (Ithaca, N.Y.: Cornell University Press, 1996). See Eric Davis, "State Building in Iraq in the Iran-Iraq War and the Gulf Crisis," in M. Midlarsky, ed., *The Internationalization of Communal Strife*, pp. 69–92 (London: Routledge and Kegan Paul, 1992), for the relationship between war and Iraqi nation building. On symbols see Eric Davis and Nicolas Gavrielides, ed., *Statecraft in the Middle East: Oil, Historical Memory, and Popular Culture* (Miami: Florida International University Press, 1991); Samir al-Khalil, *The Monument: Art, Vulgarity, and Responsibility in Iraq* (Berkeley: University of California Press, 1991); Neil Asher Silberman, *Between Past and Present: Archeology, Ideology, and Nationalism in the Modern Middle East* (New York: Holt, 1989); Roger Owen, *State, Power, and Politics in the Making of the Modern Middle East* (New York: Routledge, 1992), p. 92; Amatzia Baram, "Territorial Nationalism in the Middle East," *Middle Eastern Studies* 26, no. 4 (October 1990): 426–27.

3. The Creation of "Arab" Politics, 1920–1945

1. Kamal Salibi, *A House of Many Mansions: The History of Modern Lebanon Reconsidered* (Berkeley: University of California Press, 1988), p. 38.

2. Kemal Karpat, "The Ottoman Ethnic and Confessional Legacy in the Middle East," in M. Esman and I. Rabinovich, eds., *Ethnicity, Pluralism, and the State in the Middle East*, pp. 35–53 (Ithaca, N.Y.: Cornell University Press, 1988); Albert Hourani, *A History of the Arab Peoples* (Cambridge, Mass.: Harvard University Press, 1991); Peter Mansfield, *The Ottoman Empire and Its Successors* (New York: St. Martin's, 1973).

3. For good overviews of Arab nationalism, see A. A. Duri, *The Historical Formation of the Arab Nation* (New York: Croom Helm, 1987); Bassam Tibi, *Arab Nationalism* (New York: St. Martin's, 1981); C. Ernest Dawn, "The Origins of Arab Nationalism," in R. Khalidi et al., eds., *The Origins of Arab Nationalism*, pp. viii–xix (New York: Columbia University Press, 1991); Rashid Khalidi, "Arab Nationalism: Historical Problems in the Literature," *American Historical Review* 96, no. 5 (December 1991): 1363–73; R. Khalidi et al., *Origins of Arab Nationalism*; Martin Kramer, "Arab Nationalism: Mistaken Identity," *Daedelus* 122, no. 3 (Summer 1993): 171–206; Israel Gershoni, "Rethinking the Formation of Arab Nationalism in the Middle East, 1920–45: Old and New Narratives," in Jankowski and Gershoni, *Rethinking Nationalism*, pp. 3–25.

4. Duri, *Historical Formation of the Arab Nation*, p. 232; Tibi, *Arab Nationalism*, p. 16; Philip Khoury, *Urban Notables and Arab Nationalism: The Politics of Damascus, 1860–1920* (New York: Cambridge University Press, 1983), pp. 58–59, 67.

5. Philip Khoury, *Syria and the French Mandate* (Princeton, N.J.: Princeton University Press, 1987), p. 6.

6. A. Hourani, *History of the Arab Peoples*, p. 316.

7. Mary Wilson, *King Abdullah, Britain, and the Making of Jordan* (New York: Cambridge University Press, 1988), p. 26.

8. Khoury, *Urban Notables and Arab Nationalism*, p. 78; Ahmed M. Gomaa, *The Foundation of the League of Arab States* (London: Longman, 1977), p. 3.

9. Wm. Roger Louis, "The Era of the Mandates System and the Non-European World," in H. Bull and A. Watson, eds., *The Expansion of International Society*, pp. 201–13 (New York: Oxford University Press, 1984). See David Fromkin, *A Peace to End All Peace: The Fall of the Ottoman Empire and the Rise of the Modern Middle East* (New York: Holt, 1989), for a detailed study of the period.

10. For various statements on Islam's relationship to Arabism see Yehoshua Porath, *In Search of Arab Unity* (London: Frank Cass, 1986), p. 151; Ernest Gellner, *Nations and Nationalism* (Ithaca, N.Y.: Cornell University Press, 1983), p. 41; Tibi, *Arab Nationalism*; Albert Hourani, "Middle Eastern Nationalism Yesterday and Today," in A. Hourani, *The Emergence of the Modern Middle East* (New York: Macmillan, 1981), pp. 186–87; Khoury, *Urban Notables and Arab Nationalism*, pp. 98–99; Salibi, *House of Many Mansions*, pp. 41–43; Malcolm Kerr, "Arab Society and the West," in P. Seale, ed., *The Shaping of an Arab Statesman: Abd al-Hamid Sharaf and the Modern Arab World*, pp. 209–224 (New York: Quartet, 1983).

11. Barry Rubin, *The Arab States and the Palestine Conflict* (Syracuse, N.Y.: Syracuse University Press, 1981), p. 41.

12. A. Hourani, *History of the Arab Peoples*, p. 339; also see Porath, *In Search of Arab Unity*, chap. 3.

13. Muhammad Muslih, *The Origins of Palestinian Nationalism* (New York: Columbia University Press, 1988), pp. 4–5.

14. Khoury, *Syria and the French Mandate*, pp. 221–22; Porath, *In Search of Arab Unity*, p. 159.

15. Khoury, *Syria and the French Mandate*, pp. 221–22; Ilya Harik, "Origins of the Arab States System," in G. Luciani, ed., *The Arab State* (Berkeley: University of California Press, 1990), pp. 17–21. As the new borders and the economy led by colonialism funneled economic activities, moreover, unity's attraction waned and weakened. Khoury, *Syria and the French Mandate*, p. 284.

16. Joseph Kostiner, *The Making of Saudi Arabia, 1916–38: From Chieftaincy to Monarchical State* (New York: Oxford University Press, 1993); P. J. Vatikiotis, *Conflict in the Middle East* (London: Allen and Unwin, 1971), p. 99.

17. Salibi, *House of Many Mansions*, p. 32.

18. Ibid., pp. 185–86.

19. Porath, *In Search of Arab Unity*, pp. 150–59; Gomaa, *Foundation of the League*, p. 31; Israel Gershoni and James Jankowski, *The Search for Egyptian Nationhood* (New York: Oxford University Press, 1987).

20. Quoted in Anwar Chejne, "Egyptian Attitudes Toward Pan-Arabism," *Middle East Journal* 11, no. 3 (Summer 1957): 253.

21. Ibid., p. 258. On Egypt's national identity also see Patrick Seale, *The Struggle for Syria* (New Haven, Conn.: Yale University Press, 1986), p. 17; Porath, *In Search of Arab Unity*, pp. 150–59; Nissim Rejwan, *Nasserite Ideology: Its Exponents and Critics* (New York: Wiley, 1974), chap. 4.

22. Derek Hopwood, *Syria: 1945–86* (Boston: Unwin Hyman, 1988), p. 1; Hanna Batatu, *The Old Social Classes and the Revolutionary Movements of Iraq* (Princeton, N.J.: Princeton University Press, 1978), p. 13; Wilson, *King Abdullah*; Malik Mufti, *Sovereign Creations: Pan-Arabism and Political Order in Syria and Iraq* (Ithaca, N.Y.: Cornell University Press, 1996), chaps. 2 and 3.

23. Clifford Geertz, "Politics of Meaning," in C. Geertz, *The Interpretation of Cultures* (New York: Basic Books, 1973), p. 315.

24. Avi Shlaim, *Collusion Across the Jordan: King Abdullah, the Zionist Movement, and the Partition of Palestine* (New York: Columbia University Press, 1988), p. 26; Khoury, *Urban Notables and Arab Nationalism*, pp. 79–81; Khoury, *Syria and the French Mandate*, pp. 40–41; Hopwood, *Syria*, pp. 21–22; Zeine Zeine, *The Struggle for Arab Independence: Western Diplomacy and the Rise and Fall of Faisal's Kingdom in Syria* (Beirut: Khayat's, 1960).

25. Daniel Pipes, *Greater Syria: History of an Ambition* (New York: Oxford University Press, 1990).

26. Khoury, *Syria and the French Mandate*, pp. 205, 217.

27. Liora Lukitz, *Iraq: The Search for National Identity* (London: Frank Cass, 1995), p. 74.

28. Batatu, *Old Social Classes*, pp. 22–23.

29. Ibid., p. 25; Lukitz, *Iraq*.

30. Lukitz, *Iraq*, pp. 90, 110–14; Mohammad Tarbush, *The Role of the Military in Politics: A Case Study of Iraq to 1941* (Boston: Kegan Paul, 1982); Reeva Simon, "The Imposition of Nationalism on a Non-Nation State: The Case of Iraq During the Interwar Period, 1921–41," in Jankowski and Gershoni, *Rethinking Nationalism*, pp. 87–105 (New York: Columbia University Press, 1997). Indeed, Sati al-Hursi, an intellectual giant in the development of Arab nationalist thought, was briefly involved in Iraq's education policy and used his government position to advance a curriculum that emphasized Iraq's Arab roots and links. See Lukitz, *Iraq*, pp. 110–14.

31. Tarbush, *Role of the Military*, chaps. 6 and 7. See Gomaa, *Foundation of the League*, pp. 17–23, on the growth of Arabism in Iraq during the 1930s.

32. Porath, *In Search of Arab Unity*, p. 3.

33. Wilson, *King Abdullah*; Shirin Fathi, *Jordan: An Invented Nation?* (Hamburg: Deutsches Orient-Institut, 1994); Aqil Hyder Hasan Abidi, *Jordan: A Political Study, 1948–57* (New York: Asia Publishing, 1965), chap. 1.

34. Fathi, *Jordan*, p. 99.

35. Some scholars claim that Britain and France devised the mandate system as a

way to divide an increasingly unified and powerful pan-Arab movement. See George Antonius, *The Arab Awakening* (New York: Capricorn, 1965), pp. 248–49; Salibi, *House of Many Mansions*, p. 39.See Majjid Khadduri, "Toward an Arab Union: The League of Arab States," *American Political Science Review* 40, no. 1 (February 1946): p. 90; and Khoury, *Syria and the French Mandate*, p. 57, on the specific instance of France's decision to create Lebanon from Syria. Although less inclined to argue that this was Britain and France's intention, other scholars also suggest that the establishment of the mandate system represented an institutional constraint on pan-Arab mobilization. See Wilson, *King Abdullah,* p. 90; Antonius, *Arab Awakening*, pp. 100, 325–26; J. P. Sharma, *The Arab Mind: A Study of Egypt, Arab Unity, and the World* (Dehli: H. K. Publishers, 1990). p. 18.

36. Khoury, *Syria and the French Mandate*, p. 485; Lukitz, *Iraq*.

37. Bruce Maddy-Weitzman, *The Crystallization of the Arab State System* (Syracuse, N.Y.: Syracuse University Press, 1993), p. 31.

38. Michael Eppel, *The Palestine Conflict and the History of Modern Iraq* (London: Frank Cass, 1994); Khoury, *Syria and the French Mandate*; Israel Gershoni and James Jankowski, *Redefining the Egyptian Nation, 1930–45* (New York: Cambridge University Press, 1995).

39. Palestinian Arab leaders had to determine whether to associate with Arab nationalism, the movement for a Greater Syria, or the struggle for statehood. For some of the younger Palestinian Arabs the idea of a Greater Syria offered them immediate protection from the Zionists and the British; for the older leaders, however, Greater Syria spelled domination by Syrian political and economic elites. Because of a confluence of forces Palestinian Arabs largely and eventually viewed the struggle in more particularistic terms and attempted to encourage identification with and support of their struggle from other Arab states through the linkages of Arabism. See Muslih, *Origins of Palestinian Nationalism*; Rubin, *Arab States and the Palestine Conflict*, p. 23; Eppel, *Palestine Conflict*, p. 27; Gabriel Ben-Dor, "Nationalism Without Sovereignty and Nationalism with Multiple Sovereignties: The Palestinians and Inter-Arab Relations," in G. Ben-Dor, ed., *Palestinians and the Middle East Conflict* (Forest Grove, Ore.: Turtle Dove, 1979), p. 150; Anne Mosley Lesch, "The Palestine Arab Nationalist Movement Under the Mandate," in W. Quandt, F. Jabber, and A. Mosley Lesch, *The Politics of Palestinian Nationalism* (Berkeley: University of California, 1973), pp. 22–24.

40. Batatu, *Old Social Classes*, pp. 298–99; Gomaa, *Foundation of the League*, pp. 32–33.

41. On the strike see Charles Smith, *Palestine and the Arab-Israeli Conflict*, 2d ed. (New York: St. Martin's, 1992), pp. 94–101; Baruch Kimmerling and Joel Migdal, *The Palestinians* (New York: Free Press, 1993), chap. 4; Rashid Khalidi, *Palestinian Identity: The Construction of Modern National Consciousness* (New York: Columbia University Press, 1997).

42. Porath, *In Search of Arab Unity*, p. 162; Gomaa, *Foundation of the League*, p. 7.

43. Khoury, *Syria and the French Mandate*, pp. 535, 542.

44. Maddy-Weitzman, *Crystallization of the Arab State System*, p. 9; Rubin, *Arab States and the Palestine Conflict*, p. 68; Khoury, *Syria and the French Mandate*, pp. 553–55.

45. Rubin, *Arab States and the Palestine Conflict*, p. 77; Eppel, *Palestine Conflict*, chaps. 3 and 5. Indeed, because of Iraq's early independence in 1930 and membership in the League of Nations in 1932, the palace and the political elite viewed themselves as having a special obligation on Arab matters; that Iraq had some economic interests in Palestine only reinforced the interest in being involved. See Rubin, *Arab States and the Palestine Conflict*, pp. 54, 56; Eppel, *Palestine Conflict*, pp. 45–46.

46. Khoury, *Syria and the French Mandate*, pp. 535, 544.

47. Ibid., p. 535.

48. Rubin, *Arab States and the Palestine Conflict*, p. 100.

49. Porath, *In Search of Arab Unity*, pp. 163–65.

50. Itamar Rabinovich, "Egypt and the Palestine Question Before and After the Revolution," in S. Shamir, ed., *Egypt: From Monarchy to Republic* (Boulder: Westview, 1995), p. 326; Porath, *In Search of Arab Unity*, pp. 154–55.

51. Rabinovich, "Egypt and the Palestine Question," p. 326. Also see Seale, *Struggle for Syria*, pp. 19, 20–21; Gershoni and Jankowski, *Redefining the Egyptian Nation*, chap. 5.

52. Khoury, *Syria and the French Mandate*, p. 535; also see Ali Abdel Rahman Rahmy, *The Egyptian Policy in the Arab World* (Washington, D.C.: University Press of America, 1983), p. 15.

53. Gomaa, *Foundation of the League*, pp. 37–39; Thomas Mayer, "Egypt and the 1936 Arab Revolt in Palestine," *Journal of Contemporary History* 19, no. 2 (April 1984): 275–87.

54. Porath, *In Search of Arab Unity*, p. 158.

55. James Jankowski, "Zionism and the Jews in Egyptian Nationalist Opinion, 1920–39," in A. Cohen and G. Baer, eds., *Egypt and Palestine*, pp. 315–31 (New York: St. Martins, 1984).

56. Seale, *Struggle for Syria*, p. 20; Rahmy, *Egyptian Policy in the Arab World*, pp. 16–18.

57. Gomaa, *Foundation of the League*, p. 8.

58. Rubin, *Arab States and the Palestine Conflict*, p. 97.

59. Maddy-Weitzman, *Crystallization of the Arab State System*, p. 9; Gomaa, *Foundation of the League*, p. 80.

60. Khoury, *Syria and the French Mandate*, p. 554; Gomaa, *Foundation of the League*, p. 45.

61. Seale, *Struggle for Syria*, p. 1; also see Wilson, *King Abdullah*, pp. 129, 140.

62. Porath, *In Search of Arab Unity*, p. 189.

63. Gomaa, *Foundation of the League*, p. 114.

64. Porath, *In Search of Arab Unity*, pp. 151, 160–62; Maddy-Weitzman, *Crystallization of the Arab State System*.

65. Porath, *In Search of Arab Unity*, p. 56; Maddy-Weitzman, *Crystallization of the Arab State System*, p. 15; Khoury, *Syria and the French Mandate*.

66. Porath, *In Search of Arab Unity*, p. 3.

67. Ibid., p. 36; Wilson, *King Abdullah*, pp. 135–40; Ron Pundik, *The Struggle for Sovereignty: Relations Between Great Britain and Jordan, 1946–51* (Cambridge, Mass.: Basil Blackwell, 1994), pp. 37–39.

68. Porath, *In Search of Arab Unity*, chap. 1.

69. The idea of unification also gained some support in response to the ongoing crisis in Palestine. See Porath, *In Search of Arab Unity*, chap. 2; Gomaa, *Foundation of the League,* chap. 2. Various Arab leaders and British officials toyed with the notion of halting the crisis by absorbing Palestine into a unified Arab state, and various Fertile Crescent leaders encouraged such thoughts as a way of increasing their domestic fortunes and symbolic capital.

70. Nadav Safran, *Saudi Arabia: The Ceaseless Quest for Security* (Ithaca, N.Y.: Cornell University Press, 1988); Porath, *In Search of Arab Unity*, p. 38; Mohammad Iqbal Ansari, *The Arab League, 1945–55* (Aligarh, Pakistan: Aligarh Muslim University, 1968), p. 22; Maddy-Weitzman, *Crystallization of the Arab State System*, p. 8.

71. Quoted in Chejne, "Egyptian Attitudes on Pan-Arabism," p. 253.

72. Gomaa, *Foundation of the League*, pp. 49, 50–51.

73. Eran Lerman, "A Revolution Prefigured: Foreign Policy Orientation in the Postwar Years," in Shamir, *Egypt*, pp. 291–92. Economic elites, particularly those that were part of the Bank Misr group, also calculated that they might profit from greater exchange with the Mashreq. Porath, *In Search of Arab Unity*, pp. 155, 188. Egypt's centrality in Arab circles increased during World War II because it became the hub of the Middle Eastern Supply Centre, Britain's supply organization for the region during the war, and corresponding political and economic linkages to other parts of the Arab world. Cecil Hourani, "The Arab League in Perspective," *Middle East Journal* 1, no. 2 (April 1947): 129.

74. Porath, *In Search of Arab Unity*, p. 314.

75. Ansari, *Arab League*, p. 13; Seale, *Struggle for Syria*, p. 23; C. Hourani, "Arab League in Perspective," p. 129.

76. Ansari, *Arab League*, p. 11; Porath, *In Search of Arab Unity*, p. 194; Maddy-Weitzman, *Crystallization of the Arab State System*, pp. 11–12; Gomaa, *Foundation of the League*, pp. 99–101.

77. Cited in C. Hourani, "Arab League in Perspective," p. 128. Also see Seale, *Struggle for Syria*, pp. 11–12; Porath, *In Search of Arab Unity*, pp. 51–53; Maddy-Weitzman, *Crystallization of the Arab State System*, p. 12; Gomaa, *Foundation of the League*, pp. 69–71.

78. Porath, *In Search of Arab Unity*, pp. 248–50.

79. Ibid., pp. 54, 258; Wilson, *King Abdullah*, pp. 142–43; Tawfig Hasou, *The Struggle for the Arab World: Egypt's Nasser and the Arab League* (Boston: Routledge and Kegan Paul, 1985), pp. 6–10.

80. Maddy-Weitzman, *Crystallization of the Arab State System*, p. 14.

81. Gomaa, *Foundation of the League*, pp. 160–61.

82. Ansari, *Arab League*, pp. 15–20.

83. Gomaa, *Foundation of the League*, p. 165.

84. Ibid., p. 174.

85. Ibid., p. 187.

86. Porath, *In Search of Arab Unity*, pp. 266–67, 272. See Ansari, *Arab League*, pp. 12–14, for other proposals of the pre-1945 period.

87. Gomaa, *Foundation of the League*, pp. 180, 181, 183; Porath, *In Search of Arab Unity*, p. 312.

88. Wilson, *King Abdullah*, pp. 143–44.

89. Ansari, *Arab League*, p. 25.

90. Gomaa, *Foundation of the League*, p. 219.

91. Ansari, *Arab League*, pp. 28–30; Porath, *In Search of Arab Unity*, pp. 278–83.

92. Ansari, *Arab League*, pp. 23–25.

93. Gomaa, *Foundation of the League*, pp. 226–35.

94. Ibid., p. 232.

95. Ansari, *Arab League*, chap. 2; C. Hourani, "Arab League in Perspective," pp. 131–32; T. R. Little, "The Arab League: A Reassessment," *Middle East Journal* 10, no. 2 (Spring 1956): 140–41; Baghat Korany, "The Dialectics of Inter-Arab Relations, 1967–87," in Y. Lukacs and A. Battah, eds., *The Arab-Israeli Conflict: Two Decades of Change* (Boulder, Colo.: Westview, 1988), p. 165.

96. Porath, *In Search of Arab Unity*, pp. 285, 286.

97. Gomaa, *Foundation of the League*, p. 240.

98. Cited in Gomaa, *Foundation of the League*, p. 265.

99. Ibid., pp. 260–62; Maddy-Weitzman, *Crystallization of the Arab State System*, p. 20. There is controversy over who was behind the establishment of the Arab League and for what ends, with views ranging from a British to an Egyptian plot. For a sampling of the debate see Lerman, "A Revolution Prefigured," pp. 290–91; Porath, *In Search of Arab Unity*, pp. 307–11; Maddy-Weitzman, *Crystallization of the Arab State System*, p. 10; Ellie Kedourie, "The Chatham House Version," in E. Kedourie, *The Chatham House Version and Other Middle-Eastern Studies*, pp. 315–94 (London: Weidenfeld and Nicolson, 1970).

100. Alan Taylor, *The Arab Balance of Power System* (Syracuse, N.Y.: Syracuse University Press, 1982); Robert McDonald, *The League of Arab States: A Study in the Dynamics of Regional Organization* (Princeton, N.J.: Princeton University Press, 1965).

101. C. Hourani, "Arab League in Perspective," p. 134.

102. According to a columnist for the *Jerusalem Post*, Arab states had three principal concerns: "Palestine: unity and defiance; the outside world: unity and hope; home politics of the Arab countries where dynastic and economic rivalries are still unsolved: circumspection." *Jerusalem Post*, March 25, 1945; cited in Gomaa, *Foundation of the League*, p. 264.

103. Inis Claude, "Collective Legitimization as a Political Function of the United Nations," *International Organization* 20, no. 3 (Summer 1966): 368–74.

104. Maddy-Weitzman, *Crystallization of the Arab State System*, p. 21.

4. Securing Arabism, 1945–1955

1. Leonard Binder, "Nasserism: The Protest Movement in the Middle East," in M. Kaplan, ed., *The Revolution in World Politics*, pp. 152–74 (New York: Wiley, 1962).

2. Itamar Rabinovich, *The Road Not Taken* (New York: Oxford University Press, 1991), p. 3. Also see Issa Khalaf, *Politics in Palestine: Arab Factionalism and Social Disintegration, 1939–48* (Albany: State University of New York Press, 1993), p. 163.

3. See Mohammad Iqbal Ansari, *The Arab League, 1945–55* (Aligarh, Pakistan: Aligarh Muslim University, 1968), pp. 63–74, and Leila Kadi, *Arab Summit Conferences and the Palestine Problem, 1936–50, 1964–66* (Beirut: PLO Research Center, 1966), for a review of the Arab League's decisions on Palestine.

4. Bruce Maddy-Weitzman, *The Crystallization of the Arab State System* (Syracuse, N.Y.: Syracuse University Press, 1993), p. 36; Michael Eppel, *The Palestine Conflict and the History of Modern Iraq* (London: Frank Cass, 1994), pp. 154–56.

5. Rabinovich, *Road Not Taken*, pp. 15–16; Eppel, *Palestine Conflict*, p. 193.

6. Kadi, *Arab Summit Conferences*, pp. 52–54.

7. Ibid., p. 55.

8. Ibid., p. 56; Eppel, *Palestine Conflict*, pp. 156, 171–72, 178–79.

9. Maddy-Weitzman, *Crystallization of the Arab State System*, p. 50; Philip Mattar, *The Mufti of Jerusalem* (New York: Columbia University Press, 1988).

10. Maddy-Weitzman, *Crystallization of the Arab State System*, p. 57; Eppel, *Palestine Conflict*, pp. 181–83.

11. Rabinovich, *Road Not Taken*, pp. 44–45; Avi Shlaim, *Collusion Across the Jordan: King Abdullah, the Zionist Movement, and the Partition of Palestine* (New York: Columbia University Press, 1988); Aqil Hyder Hasan Abidi, *Jordan: A Political Study, 1948–57* (New York: Asia Publishing, 1965), pp. 26–39.

12. Abdullah was the lone Arab leader who was willing to entertain partition, leading other Arab states to be suspicious of his motivations. Shlaim, *Collusion Across the Jordan*, pp. 95–104.

13. Ibid., pp. 128–29, 167; Maddy-Weitzman, *Crystallization of the Arab State System*, p. 51. Because of the belief that Abdullah was about to invade Palestine to further his territorial objectives, on April 12 the league passed an Egypt-sponsored resolution that insisted that any land acquired should be turned over to an Arab League committee and the Palestinian Arabs. Martin Sicker, *Between Hashemites and Zionists: The Struggle for Palestine, 1908–88* (New York: Holmes and Meier, 1989), p. 103.

14. Mohamed Heikal, *Cutting the Lion's Tail: Suez Through Egyptian Eyes* (New York: Arbor House, 1987), p. 16.

15. Rabinovich, *Road Not Taken*, pp. 170–71.

16. Maddy-Weitzman, *Crystallization of the Arab State System*, p. 61; Rabinovich, *Road Not Taken*, p. 171; Adel M. Sabit, *A King Betrayed: The Ill-Fated Reign of Farouk of Egypt* (New York: Quartet, 1989), p. 165; Shlaim, *Collusion Across the Jordan*, p. 173.

17. Patrick Seale, *The Struggle for Syria* (New Haven, Conn.: Yale University Press, 1986), pp. 34–35; Eppel, *Palestine Conflict*, pp. 183–85.

18. Kadi, *Arab Summit Conferences*, p. 85.

19. Shlaim, *Collusion Across the Jordan*, pp. 172–73, 197–201; Mary Wilson, *King Abdullah, Britain, and the Making of Jordan* (New York: Cambridge University Press, 1988), p. 173.

20. Mohamed Heikal, *Secret Channels* (London: HarperCollins, 1996), p. 78.

21. Shlaim, *Collusion Across the Jordan*, p. 202.

22. Maddy-Weitzman, *Crystallization of the Arab State System*, pp. 66–69; Shlaim, *Collusion Across the Jordan*, pp. 196–205.

23. Kadi, *Arab Summit Conferences*, p. 85.

24. Rabinovich, *Road Not Taken*, p. 19.

25. Heikal, *Cutting the Lion's Tail*, p. 17. In Egypt the loss of Palestine led to renewed debate about its national identity, a withdrawal from Arab politics, and even some demands for withdrawal from the Arab League. See Ali Abdel Rahman Rahmy, *The Egyptian Policy in the Arab World* (Washington, D.C.: University Press of America, 1983), p. 20; Ghada Hashem Talhami, *Palestine and Egyptian National Identity* (New York: Praeger, 1992), pp. 62–66; Anwar Chejne, "Egyptian Attitudes Toward Pan-Arabism," *Middle East Journal* 11, no. 3 (Summer 1957): 260.

26. The armistice negotiations were conducted bilaterally, mediated by the U.N.'s Ralph Bunche, and resulted in four separate agreements in 1949. A principal reason that the armistice agreements were concluded at all was Bunche's dogged determination and insistence that the Arabs negotiate on an individual rather than collective basis, which encouraged them to serve their own particularistic interests. Rabinovich, *Road Not Taken*, pp. 16–17.

27. Israeli officials were somewhat optimistic that the Arab governments would reconcile themselves to the Jewish state. Rabinovich, *Road Not Taken*, pp. 4–5. Indeed, previous contacts between Israel, Jordan, and Egypt had led some Israelis to contemplate a "Ligue Orientale" to include Israel and the other Arab states and render the Arab League moribund. Maddy-Weitzman, *Crystallization of the Arab State System*, p. 89.

28. Maddy-Weitzman, *Crystallization of the Arab State System*, pp. 101–103.

29. Rabinovich, *Road Not Taken*, p. 154.

30. Ibid., chap. 3. Also see Moshe Maoz, *Syria and Israel: From War to Peacemaking* (Oxford, England: Clarendon, 1995), pp. 20–26.

31. Rabinovich, *Road Not Taken*.

32. Ibid., pp. 107–108.

33. Shlaim, *Collusion Across the Jordan*, p. 359.

34. Ibid., pp. 359–60; Rabinovich, *Road Not Taken*, pp. 118–19.

35. Rabinovich, *Road Not Taken*, p. 153; Shlaim, *Collusion Across the Jordan*, p. 552.

36. "Al-Tal Requests Trial of Jordan Rulers," *Al-Misri*, Damascus, March 28, 1950, cited in *Foreign Broadcast Information Service* (hereafter *FBIS*), no. 63, March 29, 1950, PP6–7.

37. Rabinovich, *Road Not Taken*, pp. 139–41.

38. "League's Future Hangs on Cairo Session," Tunis, in Arabic, March 26, 1950, cited in *FBIS*, no. 60, March 28, 1950, PP3. Jordan initially refused to attend the meetings, citing a hostile Egyptian press and Egypt's failure to honor the previously brokered understanding between Egypt and Jordan that Egypt was to become the caretaker of Gaza and Jordan the guardian of the West Bank. Soon thereafter, however, Jordan determined that it would lose more by staying away from the league meetings than by going to Cairo and facing a hostile crowd. "Amman States Position on Arab League," Jerusalem (Jordan), March 28, 1950, cited in *FBIS*, no. 63, March 29, 1950, PP1.

39. "Arab League's Resolution," Beirut, March 30, 1950, cited in *FBIS*, no. 63, March 31, 1950, PP14. Also see Egyptian Home Service, "League Approves Defense, Economic Pact," Cairo, April 14, 1950, cited in *FBIS*, no. 74, April 17, 1950, PP1.

40. Shlaim, *Collusion Across the Jordan*, pp. 554–55; Maddy-Weitzman, *Crystallization of the Arab State System*, pp. 130–35; Rabinovich, *Road Not Taken*, pp. 148–9; Abidi, *Jordan* pp. 77–78.

41. Rabinovich, *Road Not Taken*, p. 147.

42. "Jordan Announces Official Annexation," Jerusalem (Jordan), April 24, 1950, cited in *FBIS*, no. 80, April 25, 1950, PP9. Also see Abidi, *Jordan*, pp. 75–76; Shlaim, *Collusion Across the Jordan*, p. 558.

43. Egyptian Home Service, "Abdullah's Real Motive Held Expansion," Cairo, April 24, 1950, cited in *FBIS*, no. 81, April 26, 1950, PP10; "Syria States Case Against Annexation," Damascus, April 22, 1950, cited in *FBIS*, no. 79, April 24, 1950, PP1–4.

44. "Abdullah Scorns League," April 22, 1950, cited in *FBIS*, no. 79, April 24, 1950, PP5. Also see Sicker, *Between Hashemites and Zionists*, p. 108.

45. Maddy-Weitzman, *Crystallization of the Arab State System*, pp. 138–41.

46. However, evidence exists that King Faruq and King Abdullah made a backroom deal—that Abdullah would abandon his search for a separate peace with Israel in exchange for being allowed to annex the West Bank. See Rabinovich, *Road Not Taken*, p. 184.

47. Robert Satloff, *From Abdullah to Hussein: Jordan in Transition* (New York: Oxford University Press, 1994), pp. 30–32.

48. Herzl Berger, "Arabs Refusal to Negotiate Explained," Jerusalem (Israel), April 7, 1950, cited in *FBIS*, no. 70, April 11, 1950, PP5.

49. Satloff, *From Abdullah to Hussein*, pp. 19–20; Maddy-Weitzman, *Crystallization of the Arab State System*, p. 41; Wilson, *King Abdullah*; Rabinovich, *Road Not Taken*, p. 5.

50. For instance, in March 1946 on the occasion of the first Parliament and again in the fall of 1946 and early 1947 King Abdullah raised the idea of a Greater Syria, which would include Lebanon, Syria, and Transjordan. See Seale, *Struggle for Syria*, p. 13; Shlaim, *Collusion Across the Jordan*, pp. 85–86; Wilson, *King Abdullah,* pp. 157–60. This debate, like others that would transpire for the next decade, ended at the Arab League. Meeting in late November 1946, the Arab states agreed to honor each others' sovereignty and to cease all discussion of the Greater Syria proposal. Maddy-Weitzman, *Crystallization of the Arab State System*, p. 39. In April 1947 Jordan and Iraq were rumored to be preparing a draft unification agreement but ultimately signed only an alliance. See Seale, *Struggle for Syria*, p. 14; Sharq al-Adna, "Iraq and Transjordan Sign Alliance," April 14, 1947, cited in *FBIS*, no. 37, April 15, 1947, II1. In the fall of 1947 Abdullah once again raised the idea of Greater Syria, though his timing (the U.N. was debating Palestine) caused many Arab states to publicly ponder whether a link existed between Abdullah's proposals and British and Zionist interests in the region. Maddy-Weitzman, *Crystallization of the Arab State System*, p. 42.

51. Maddy-Weitzman, *Crystallization of the Arab State System*, p. 105; Rabinovich, *Road Not Taken*, pp. 93–96.

52. Rabinovich, *Road Not Taken*, p. 19; Gordon Torrey, *Syrian Politics and the Military, 1945–58.* (Columbus: Ohio State University Press, 1964), p. 137

53. Maddy-Weitzman, *Crystallization of the Arab State System*, p. 107: Torrey, *Syrian Politics and the Military*, pp. 134–35; Seale, *Struggle for Syria*, p. 48.

54. Malik Mufti, *Sovereign Creations: Pan-Arabism and Political Order in Syria and Iraq* (Ithaca, N.Y.: Cornell University Press, 1996), pp. 51–52. Egypt and Iraq had a tendency to play out their rivalries on Syrian soil, each buying Syrian politicians and competing for advantage in Syrian politics. Cairo and Baghdad tried to break this dynamic by drafting an agreement in December 1949 that pledged them to respect Syria's political integrity. The Iraqi architects of the agreement, who also pledged to help Syria forge a proper constitution that would facilitate stability, were accused of being weak on Egypt and had to resign as a consequence. Eli Podeh, *The Quest for Hegemony in the Arab World: The Struggle over the Baghdad Pact* (New York: E. J. Brill, 1995), p. 82.

55. See Seale, *Struggle for Syria*, pp. 47–56, for a discussion of these talks.

56. Torrey, *Syrian Politics and the Military*, pp. 153–54; Seale, *Struggle for Syria*, pp. 77–83.

57. Malcolm Kerr, *The Arab Cold War* (New York: Oxford University Press, 1970), p. 3; Seale, *Struggle for Syria*, pp. 15, 79–81.

58. "Syrian Party Calls for Union with Iraq," Tel Aviv and Baghdad, September 29, 1949, cited in *FBIS*, no. 189, September 30, 1949, PP1.

59. Maddy-Weitzman, *Crystallization of the Arab State System*, pp. 115–18.

60. "Iraq Press Comments on Council, Union," *Al-Nida,* Baghdad, October 19, 1949, cited in *FBIS*, no. 203, October 20, 1949, PP2.

61. "Al-Huda Says Iraq, Jordan Agree," Beirut, October 17, 1949, cited in *FBIS*, no.

201, October 18, 1949, PP1. Also see "Unity Is Solution to Arab Problems," Jerusalem (Jordan), September 23, 1949, cited in *FBIS*, no. 186, September 26, 1949, PP9.

62. "Shamoun States Arab Unity Conditions," Damascus, September 7, 1949, cited in *FBIS*, no. 173, September 8, 1949, PP1. Lebanon expressed its reservations about the plan, including that it not intrude on Lebanon's sovereignty, not impose any military or financial obligations, and that it facilitate economic relations. "Lebanese Reservations," Jerusalem (Jordan), November 6, 1949, cited in *FBIS*, no. 212, November 7, 1949, PP4–5.

63. "Egypt Blamed for Anti-Union Campaign," Baghdad, October 20, 1949, cited in *FBIS*, no. 204, October 21, 1949, PP4.

64. Egypt also submitted a memorandum asking the Syrian government to reject the proposed agreement until after the elections because it did not represent its people. "Arab Political Discussions Cancelled," Tel Aviv, September 18, 1949, cited in *FBIS*, no. 181, September 20, 1949, PP12.

65. Sharq al-Adna, "Committee Adopts Military Plan," October 23, 1949, cited in *FBIS*, no, 205, October 24, 1949, PP1–2. For the text see Sharq al-Adna, "Clauses of the Arab Security Pact Revealed," October 29, 1949, cited in *FBIS*, no. 209, October 31, 1949, PP1–2. Also see Seale, *Struggle for Syria*, pp. 90–91; Podeh, *Quest for Hegemony*, p. 46.

66. Egyptian Home Service, "Yusuf Yassin Favors Egyptian Proposal," Cairo, October 25, 1949, cited in *FBIS*, no. 207, October 26, 1949, PP4. See also Egyptian Home Service, "Saudi Arabia Defines Attitude on Syria," Cairo, December 24, 1949, cited in *FBIS*, no. 248, December 27, 1949, PP9.

67. "Nuri: League Chaos Causes Problems," Beirut, October 24, 1949, cited in *FBIS*, no. 206, October 25, 1949, PP1–3.

68. "Syria Tells Iraq Union Impossible Now," Beirut, in Arabic to London and the Near East, December 8, 1949, cited in *FBIS*, no. 237, December 9, 1949, PP4; "Hannawi Thinks Security Plan Essential," Beirut, in Arabic, October 28, 1949, cited in *FBIS*, no. 209, October 31, 1949, PP4. Other reports, however, stated that the army was divided. See Egyptian Home Service, "Syrian Army Divided on Iraqi Union," Cairo, November 7, 1949, cited in *FBIS*, no. 215, November 8, 1949, PP7.

69. Egyptian Home Service, "Faris al-Khuri Speaks on Arab Unity," September 21, 1949, cited in *FBIS*, no. 184, September 23, 1949, PP4. Also see "Al-Khuri Says Defense Alliance Needed," Jerusalem (Jordan), October 26, 1949, cited in *FBIS*, no. 208, October 27, 1949, PP3.

70. Seale, *Struggle for Syria*, pp. 84–85, 124; Maddy-Weitzman, *Crystallization of the Arab State System*, p. 124; Rabinovich, *Road Not Taken*, p. 20.

71. "Subcommittee to Sift Security Plans," various sources, November 17, 1949, cited in *FBIS*, no. 223, November 18, 1949, PP2–3.

72. "Real Unity for Arabs Held Unthinkable," radio series "What Happens in Arab Countries," Tel Aviv, in Hebrew, November 30, 1949, cited in *FBIS*, no. 233, December 5, 1949, PP9.

73. See Seale, *Struggle for Syria*, pp. 90–91, for a discussion of the events leading to the pact. See Alan Taylor, *The Arab Balance of Power System* (Syracuse, N.Y.: Syracuse University Press, 1982), pp. 125–27, for the text.

74. Jordan, which refused to become an original member of the Arab Collective Security Pact because of Egypt's refusal to recognize the legitimacy of Abdullah's annexation of the West Bank, became a member in January 1952 when Prime Minister Abu al-Huda determined that "while the Pact can do no good, it can do no serious harm." Cited in Satloff, *From Abdullah to Hussein*, p. 45.

75. "Al-Qudsi Proposes a United Arab State," Damascus, in Arabic, January 26, 1951, cited in *FBIS*, no. 24, January 30, 1951, NN1–7. Also see Ansari, *Arab League*, p. 96. For Iraq's various political and economic motives concerning these unification moves, see Eberhard Kienle, "The Limits of Fertile Crescent Unity: Iraqi Policies Toward Syria Since 1945," in D. Hopwood, H. Ishaw, and T. Koszinowski, eds., *Iraq: Power and Society* (New York: Oxford University Press, 1993), pp. 361–63.

76. "League Committee Hears Arab Union Plan," Cairo, January 12, 1954, cited in *FBIS*, no. 8, January 13, 1954, MM1.

77. Cited in Maddy-Weitzman, *Crystallization of the Arab State System*, p. 54.

78. Ansari, *Arab League*, p. 123.

79. See Abidi, *Jordan*, pp. 122–23, for a survey of the positions of the individual Arab governments concerning relations with the West.

80. For instance, when Jordan achieved its independence on March 22, 1946, many in the region perceived the accompanying treaty as maintaining Britain's colonial privileges and therefore representing independence in name only. This resulted in various attacks from Arab circles; Syria symbolically closed its border with Jordan for a day, and other Arab states withheld their immediate recognition. Maddy-Weitzman, *Crystallization of the Arab State System*, p. 31.

81. Seale, *Struggle for Syria*, pp. 186–92.

82. Wm. Roger Louis, *British Empire in the Middle East, 1945–51: Arab Nationalism, the United States, and Postwar Imperialism* (New York: Oxford University Press, 1984).

83. J. C. Hurewitz, "The Historical Context," in W. R. Louis and R. Owen, eds., *Suez 1956: The Crisis and Its Consequences* (New York: Oxford University Press, 1989), p. 25.

84. Ansari, *Arab League*, p. 54.

85. See Podeh, *Quest for Hegemony*, and Faiz Abu-Jaber, "The Egyptian Revolution and Middle East Defense: 1952–55," *Middle East Forum* 45, no. 4 (December 1969): 25–56, for discussions of the question of Middle Eastern defense from 1952 through 1955.

86. Rabinovich, *Road Not Taken*, p. 17.

87. Podeh, *Quest for Hegemony*, pp. 50–51; Rabinovich, *Road Not Taken*, p. 193.

88. Egyptian Home Service, "Salah al-Din Interviewed by U.S. News," Cairo, October 10, 1951, cited in *FBIS*, no. 203, October 11, 1951, NN1–5; Egyptian Home Service,

"Arab Nations Confer on Defense Plan," Cairo, October 14, 1951, cited in *FBIS*, no. 205, October 15, 1951, NN1.

89. "Arab States Outline League's Policy," Beirut, November 14, 1951, cited in *FBIS*, no. 227, November 15, 1951, NN4. Syria and Saudi Arabia, however, were piqued that Egypt unilaterally rejected this proposal without first consulting the other Arab states; indeed, the Syrian paper *Al-Jil al-Jadid* reported that Syria and Saudi Arabia interpreted Egypt's decision as signaling that "each Arab country must work out its own policy in light of its own interests." "Syria Scores Egypt Defense Stand," Paris, October 17, 1951, cited in *FBIS*, no. 208, October 18, 1951, NN2.

90. Seale, *Struggle for Syria*, p. 111.

91. On sympathy for an alliance, Amin Hewedy, interview by author, Cairo; Anthony Nutting, *Nasser* (London: Constable, 1972), p. 74. On relations with Israel see Mark Tessler, *A History of the Israeli-Palestinian Conflict* (Bloomington: Indiana University Press, 1995), pp. 338–39.

92. Rashid Khalidi, "Consequences of the Suez Crisis in the Arab World," in Louis and Owen, *Suez 1956*, p. 377; Seale, *Struggle for Syria*, p. 168; Uriel Dann, *King Hussein and the Challenge of Arab Radicalism: Jordan, 1955–67* (New York: Oxford University Press, 1989), p. 24.

93. Anonymous source, interview by author, Cairo, Egypt; Gamal Abdel Nasser, *Philosophy of the Revolution* (Buffalo, N.Y.: Smith, Keynes, and Marshall, 1959), pp. 28–29; Seale, *Struggle for Syria*, pp. 193–94; Taylor, *Arab Balance of Power*, p. 30; Ali Hillal Dessouki, "Nasser and the Struggle for Independence," in Louis and Owen, *Suez 1956*, p. 32; Malcolm Kerr, "Regional Arab Politics and the Conflict with Israel," in P. Hammond and S. Alexander, eds., *Political Dynamics in the Middle East* (New York: American Elsevier), pp. 39–41. For an attempt to sort out the authenticity of Nasser's commitment to Arabism, see P. J. Vatikiotis, *Nasser and His Generation* (New York: St. Martin's: 1978), pp. 225–34.

94. See Anouar Abdel-Malek, *Egypt: Military Society* (New York: Random House, 1968), chaps. 6 and 7; Adeed Dawisha, *Egypt in the Arab World: Elements of a Foreign Policy* (New York: Wiley, 1976); James Jankowski, "Arab Nationalism in 'Nasserism' and Egyptian State Policy, 1952–58," in J. Jankowski and J. Gershoni, eds., *Rethinking Nationalism in the Arab Middle East*, pp. 150–68 (New York: Columbia University Press, 1997).

95. Nasser, *Philosophy of the Revolution*, p. 87;

96. Binder, "Nasserism"; Rahmy, *Egyptian Policy in the Arab World*, p. 31.

97. Heikal, *Cutting the Lion's Tail*, p. 32.

98. Kerr, *Arab Cold War*, p. 32. In fact, the Egyptian Constitution of January 16, 1956, only belatedly asserts that Egypt is part of the Arab nation and notes Egypt's integral relationship to the Arab nation. See Abdel-Malek, *Egypt*, p. 253; Chejne, "Egyptian Attitudes Toward Pan-Arabism," pp. 265–66.

99. His dramatic effect on the region was attributable not only to the fact that he "had the right message at the right time" but also to his charisma and ability to speak

in colloquial terms that transcended local dialects, rather than the classical Arabic preferred by most Arab leaders. Moreover, he carried his message through a new medium—radio—with his *Sawt al-Arab* (Voice of the Arabs) broadcasts, which allowed him to go over the heads of other Arab leaders and speak directly to the masses. That Nasser was broadcasting from Cairo, the heart of the Arab nation's culture, learning, and power, meant that his message carried more appeal than if, for instance, he had been in Beirut or Baghdad.

100. For an explicit discussion of the Baghdad Pact and the development of the norm-prohibiting alliances with the West see Michael Barnett, "Identity and Alliances in the Middle East," in P. Katzenstein, ed., *The Culture of National Security: Norms and Identity in World Politics* (New York: Columbia University Press), pp. 415–22.

101. Podeh, *Quest for Hegemony*, p. 33.

102. Seale, *Struggle for Syria*, p. 200.

103. Maddy-Weitzman, *Crystallization of the Arab State System*, pp. 28–29; Eppel, *Palestine Conflict*, pp. 174–76.

104. Podeh, *Quest for Hegemony*, p. 69.

105. Kerr, "Regional Arab Politics," p. 43.

106. Heikal, *Cutting the Lion's Tail*, p. 39.

107. Podeh, *Quest for Hegemony*, p. 33.

108. Ibid., p. 96.

109. Ibid., pp. 83–87; Seale, *Struggle for Syria*, pp. 204–205.

110. Podeh, *Quest for Hegemony*, pp. 83–87.

111. Ibid., pp. 87–90; Seale, *Struggle for Syria*, pp. 206–208.

112. Podeh, *Quest for Hegemony*, p. 88; Heikal, *Cutting the Lion's Tail*, pp. 53, 57; Torrey, *Syrian Politics and the Military*, p. 272.

113. Podeh, *Quest for Hegemony*, p. 90.

114. These regional discussions about the West's overtures had domestic implications; for instance, they were a major topic of the Syrian elections in September 1954. Seale, *Struggle for Syria*, p. 164.

115. Egyptian Home Service, "Egypt to Depend on Arab Defense Pact," Cairo, December 10, 1954, cited in *FBIS*, no. 239, December 10, 1954, A1.

116. Seale, *Struggle for Syria*, p. 211. Also see Podeh, *Quest for Hegemony*, pp. 98–99.

117. Egyptian Home Service, "Middle East Defense Talks Discussed," Cairo, December 7, 1954, cited in *FBIS*, no. 237, December 8, 1954, A2.

118. On the secret agreement see Podeh, *Quest for Hegemony*, pp. 89, 99. On the Soviet threat see Albert Hourani, *A History of the Arab Peoples* (Cambridge, Mass.: Harvard University Press, 1991), p. 363 and Heikal, *Cutting the Lion's Tail*, pp. 53, 57. On the Kurdish issue see Seale, *Struggle for Syria*, pp. 199–201. On the likelihood that other states would follow Iraq, see Kerr, *Arab Cold War*, p. 4, and Heikal, *Cutting the Lion's Tail*, p. 54.

119. Podeh, *Quest for Hegemony*, p. 66.

120. Ibid., p. 111; Fawaz Gerges, *The Superpowers and the Middle East: Regional and International Politics, 1955–67* (Boulder, Colo.: Westview, 1994), p. 25; Dessouki, "Nasser and the Struggle for Independence," p. 36.

121. King Hussein, *Uneasy Lies the Head* (London: Heineman, 1962), p. 84.

122. Iraqi Home Service, "Iraq Reaffirms Adherence to Arab League," Baghdad, January 18, 1955, cited in *FBIS*, no. 13, January 19, 1955, A5. See also Iraqi Home Service, "Iraq to Sign Defense Pact with Turkey," Baghdad, January 13, 1955, cited in *FBIS*, no. 9, January 13, 1951, A2; Iraqi Home Service, "Iraq Denies Disagreement on Pact," Baghdad, January 21, 1955, cited in *FBIS*, no. 16, January 24, 1955, A10. In a later attempt to defend himself against the criticism of having violated the norms of Arabism, Nuri al-Said claimed that Egypt had prior knowledge of and consented to Iraq's alliance with Turkey. Iraqi Home Service, "Premier Reviews Defense Talks with Egypt," Baghdad, February 6, 1955, cited in *FBIS*, no. 26, February 7, 1955, A6–10.

123. *FBIS—Middle East–South Asia* (hereafter *FBIS-MES*), January 14, 1955, A1–2.

124. Egyptian Home Service, "Press Criticizes Turkish-Iraq Accord," Cairo, January 14, 1944, cited in *FBIS*, no. 10, January 14, 1955, A2.

125. *Al-Ahram*, Cairo, January 13, 1955, cited in *FBIS-MES*, January 14, 1955, A4.

126. Egyptian Home Service, "Salim Answers Questions," Cairo, January 16, 1955, cited in *FBIS-MES*, no. 11, January 17, 1955, A7.

127. Muhammad Khalil, *The Arab States and the Arab League: A Documentary Record*, vol. 2 (Beirut: Khayat's, 1962), pp. 229–30; Egyptian Home Service, "Arab Premiers Called to Discuss Iraqi Action," Cairo, January 16, 1955, cited in *FBIS*, no. 11, January 17, 1955, A1–2; Egyptian Home Service, "Iraq Action Endangers Arab Nationalism," Cairo, January 17, 1955, cited in *FBIS*, no. 12, January 18, 1955, A1; Egyptian Home Service, "Iraqi Moves Seen as a Plot Against Arab Unity," Cairo, January 18, 1955, cited in *FBIS*, no. 13, January 19, 1955, A2.

128. Quoted in Khalil, *Arab States*, vol. 2, pp. 236–37.

129. Egyptian Home Service, "Amir Faysal's Statement," Cairo, January 22, 1955, cited in *FBIS*, no. 16, January 24, 1955, A5; Nadav Safran, *Saudi Arabia: The Ceaseless Quest for Security* (Ithaca, N.Y.: Cornell University Press, 1988), pp. 78–79; Gerges, *Superpowers and the Middle East*, p. 25; Podeh, *Quest for Hegemony*, pp. 193, 206.

130. Seale, *Struggle for Syria*, p. 101; Gerges, *Superpowers and the Middle East*, p. 28; Torrey, *Syrian Politics and the Military*, pp. 194–96, 273–74; "Communique Issued by the Syrian Foreign Minister, Faidi al-Atassi, on Syrian Policy at the Arab League Conference," cited in Khalil, *Arab States*, vol. 1, pp. 237–38.

131. Heikal, *Cutting the Lion's Tail*, p. 56–58.

132. Egyptian Home Service, "Khuri Again Rejects Foreign Alliances," Cairo, January 21, 1955, cited in *FBIS*, no. 16, January 24, 1955, A3; Podeh, *Quest for Hegemony*, pp. 105–106.

133. Heikal, *Cutting the Lion's Tail*, pp. 56–58.

134. Satloff, *From Abdullah to Hussein*, pp. 105, 185; Dann, *King Hussein*, p. 25. Hussein claims to have warned Turkish prime minister Adnan Menderes that to

sign an agreement with one Arab country alone and without consultation would "be disastrous." He continues: "When the formation of the Baghdad Pact was announced the Arab world was stunned. The immediate reaction—whether it was correct or not is immaterial—was that Britain . . . had 'got at' Iraq." *Uneasy Lies the Head*, p. 84.

135. Egyptian Home Service, "Press Comment," Cairo, February 7, 1955, cited in *FBIS*, no. 26, February 7, 1955, A2.

136. Sharq al-Adna, "Nasser Presents Joint Defense Plan," Limassol, Cyprus, January 26, 1955, cited in *FBIS-MES*, no. 18, January 26, 1955, A1.

137. Heikal, *Cutting the Lion's Tail*, pp. 56–58.

138. The delegation was unsuccessful in its attempt to convince Nuri al-Said not to sign the pact. Salim Salim later recalled how Nuri al-Said greeted the delegation by proclaiming, "I am no longer one of you. I have become a Zionist; I have no relationship with the Arabs any more." Egyptian Home Service, "Salim Reports on Meeting with Nuri," Cairo, February 9, 1955, cited in *FBIS*, no. 28, February 9, 1955, A1.

139. Iraqi Home Service, "Premier Reports on Pact with Turkey," Baghdad, February 26, 1955, cited in *FBIS*, no. 40, February 28, 1955, A3–5; Waldemar Gallman, *Iraq Under General Nuri: My Recollections of Nuri al-Said* (Baltimore, Md.: Johns Hopkins University Press, 1964), p. 72; Podeh, *Quest for Hegemony*, p. 124.

140. Seale, *Struggle for Syria*, chap. 17.

141. Torrey, *Syrian Politics and the Military*, p. 270.

142. Gerges, *Superpowers and the Middle East*, pp. 28–29; Torrey, *Syrian Politics and the Military*, pp. 273–76.

143. Seale, *Struggle for Syria*, p. 223.

144. Voice of the Arabs, "Israeli Attack the Result of Turko-Iraqi Pact," Cairo, March 1, 1955, cited in *FBIS*, no. 41, March 2, 1955, A3–4.

145. The Bandung conference took place during the debate about the pact in mid-April. Its spirited rhetoric of anticolonialism, independence, and rejection of alliances with the West had a major influence on Nasser as he became more insistent on the importance of neutrality. Podeh convincingly argues that the conference reinforced Nasser's understanding of the logical connection between neutrality and Arab nationalism, that nationalism could be best served through a policy of neutrality. *Quest for Hegemony*, p. 149. Also see Georgiana Stevens, "Arab Neutralism and Bandung," *Middle East Journal* 11, no. 2 (Spring 1957): 139–52.

146. Egyptian Home Service, "Syria Supports United Army Plan," Cairo, February 28, 1955, cited in *FBIS*, no. 40, March 1, 1955, A1–2; Podeh, *Quest for Hegemony*, p. 129; Seale, *Struggle for Syria*, pp. 130–31.

147. Podeh, *Quest for Hegemony*, p. 144.

148. Torrey, *Syrian Politics and the Military*, pp. 279–80; Podeh, *Quest for Hegemony*, p. 129; "Communique on Talks Between Egypt, Syria, and Saudi Arabia," cited in Khalil, *Arab States*, vol. 2, p. 240; "Three Arab States Sign New Alliance," Damas-

cus, March 6, 1955, cited in *FBIS*, no. 45, March 7, 1955, A1–3. Soon thereafter Yemen announced its support for the alliance. "Yemen Announces Support of New Arab Pact," Damascus, March 10, 1955, cited in *FBIS*, no. 48, March 11, 1955, A7.

149. "Azm Comments on New Arab Alliance," Damascus, March 10, 1955, cited in *FBIS*, no. 49, March 11, 1955, A7.

150. Quoted in Podeh, *Quest for Hegemony*, p. 144.

151. Seale, *Struggle for Syria*, pp. 224–25.

152. Podeh, *Quest for Hegemony*, p. 156.

153. Ibid., p. 162.

154. Ibid., pp. 132–33.

155. Seale, *Struggle for Syria*, pp. 233–34. In his speech unveiling the dramatic arms deal Nasser emphasized his inconclusive negotiations for arms with the West and his desire to fulfill a defining principle of the Egyptian revolution: a strong national army. Egyptian Home Service, "Nasir Reveals Arms Contract with Czechs," Cairo, September 27, 1955, cited in *FBIS*, no. 189, September 28, 1955, A1–5.

156. Heikal, *Cutting the Lion's Tail*, p. 83.

157. See Gerges, *Superpowers and the Middle East*, p. 48; Heikal, *Cutting the Lion's Tail*, p. 89; Podeh, *Quest for Hegemony*, p. 166; Dann, *King Hussein*, p. 24. See Podeh, *Quest for Hegemony*, p. 165, for an outline of the agreement.

158. Hussein, *Uneasy Lies the Head*, p. 106.

159. Heikal, *Cutting the Lion's Tail*, p. 88. Also see Satloff, *From Abdullah to Hussein*, p. 100.

160. Hussein, *Uneasy Lies the Head*, pp. 89–90; Podeh, *Quest for Hegemony*, p. 178.

161. James Lunt, *Hussein of Jordan* (London: Macmillan, 1989), p. 22.

162. Heikal, *Cutting the Lion's Tail*, pp. 88–89; Podeh, *Quest for Hegemony*, pp. 181, 191–92.

163. Egyptian Home Service, "Imperialist Plot in Jordan Revealed," Cairo, December 14, 1955, cited in *FBIS*, no. 243, December 15, 1955, A1–3; Voice of the Arabs, " 'Voice of Arabs' Attacks Baghdad Pact," Cairo, December 22, 1955, cited in *FBIS*, no. 249, December 23, 1955, A1–2; Dann, *King Hussein*, p. 27.

164. Hussein, *Uneasy Lies the Head*, p. 88.

165. Podeh, *Quest for Hegemony*, p. 185.

166. In a later statement on the pact Majali said that he supported it because he believed that it would reward Jordan for its obligations to the Anglo-Iraqi Treaty; that the pact would curtail the duration of the treaty to four years; that Jordan would receive economic aid; that regardless of whether Jordan joined the pact, it was still morally bound to it because of the Anglo-Iraqi Treaty; and that Jordan had little choice because the army was controlled by Britain. Cited in Abidi, *Jordan*, p. 128.

167. Hussein, *Uneasy Lies the Head*, pp. 92–93.

168. Satloff, *From Abdullah to Hussein*, p. 133; Podeh, *Quest for Hegemony*, pp. 187–88.

169. Salibi, *Modern History of Jordan*, p. 189.

170. John Glubb, *A Soldier with the Arabs* (London: Hodder and Stoughton, 1957), pp. 425–26.

171. See P. J. Vatikiotis, *Politics and the Military in Jordan: 1921–57* (London: Frank Cass, 1967), p. 124; Satloff, *From Abdullah to Hussein*, chap. 8; Dann, *King Hussein*, p. 31; A. Hourani, *History of the Arab Peoples*, p. 363; J. C. Hurewitz, *Middle East Politics: The Military Dimension* (Boulder, Colo.: Westview, 1982), pp. 318–19: Salibi, *Modern History of Jordan*, p. 189.

172. Podeh, *Quest for Hegemony*, p. 35.

173. Anonymous source, interview by author, Amman, Jordan.

5. The Ascent and Descent of Arabism, 1956–1967

1. For overviews of the Suez War see Wm. Roger Louis and Roger Owen, eds., *Suez 1956: The Crisis and Its Consequences* (New York: Oxford University Press, 1989); Mohamed Heikal, *Cutting the Lion's Tail: Suez Through Egyptian Eyes* (New York: Arbor House, 1987); J. C. Hurewitz, "The Historical Context," in Louis and Owen, *Suez 1956,* pp. 19–29.

2. Louis and Owen, *Suez 1956.*

3. Heikal, *Cutting the Lion's Tail*; Ali Hillal Dessouki, "Nasser and the Struggle for Independence," in Louis and Owen, *Suez 1956*, p. 38.

4. George Corm, *Fragmentation of the Middle East: The Last Thirty Years* (London: Hutchinson, 1983), p. 35.

5. Robert Satloff, *From Abdullah to Hussein: Jordan in Transition* (New York: Oxford University Press, 1994), p. 151; Tawfig Hasou, *The Struggle for the Arab World: Egypt's Nasser and the Arab League* (Boston: Routledge and Kegan Paul, 1985), pp. 36–37.

6. Eden received the news of the nationalization when he was having dinner with King Faysal and Nuri al-Said in London. Eden and Said were equally horrified, with Said urging Eden to strike at Egypt immediately and hard. Heikal, *Cutting the Lion's Tail*, p. 130. Saudi Arabia and Syria were not completely pleased with Nasser's nationalizations, for both feared repercussions and were bitter about not being forewarned. Ibid., pp. 133–34, 156–57.

7. For British motivations see Patrick Seale, *The Struggle for Syria* (New Haven, Conn.: Yale University Press, 1986), pp. 248–49; Keith Kyle, "Britain and the Suez Crisis, 1955–56," in Louis and Owen, *Suez 1956*, pp. 103–31.

8. Maurice Vaisse, "France and the Suez Crisis, 1955–56," in Louis and Owen, *Suez 1956*, pp. 131–44.

9. Johnathan Shimshoni, *Israel and Conventional Deterrence: Border Wars from 1953 to 1970* (Ithaca, N.Y.: Cornell University Press, 1993); Benny Morris, *Israel's Border Wars* (New York: Oxford University Press, 1993).

10. Heikal, *Cutting the Lion's Tail*, p. 179, and Amin Hewedy, "Nasser and the Cri-

sis of 1956," in Owen and Louis, *Suez 1956*, p. 169, write that Nasser dismissed the possibility of French and British collusion with Israel because it would only undermine the West's influence and its allies in the region.

11. Malcolm Kerr, *The Arab Cold War* (New York: Oxford University Press, 1970), p. 4; Gordon Torrey, *Syrian Politics and the Military, 1945–58* (Columbus: Ohio State University Press, 1964), p. 323; Ali Abdel Rahman Rahmy, *The Egyptian Policy in the Arab World* (Washington, D.C.: University Press of America, 1983), p. 52.

12. Torrey, *Syrian Politics*, p. 323; Seale, *Struggle for Syria*, p. 262.

13. Many Syrian pan-Arabists had viewed the 1955 alliance with Egypt as the first step toward union; in July 1956 Prime Minister Hashim Atali announced a committee to study the matter, and Syria initiated serious follow-up discussions. Torrey, *Syrian Politics*, pp. 331–32.

14. Seale, *Struggle for Syria*, chap. 21; Fawaz Gerges, *The Superpowers and the Middle East: Regional and International Politics, 1955–67* (Boulder, Colo.: Westview, 1994), p. 85.

15. On the 1957 crisis see Torrey, *Syrian Politics*, pp. 361–65; Gerges, *Superpowers and the Middle East*, p. 87.

16. Eli Podeh, *The Quest for Arab Hegemony in the Arab World: The Struggle over the Baghdad Pact* (New York: E. J. Brill, 1995), pp. 206, 209.

17. Middle East News Agency (hereafter MENA), "Outgoing Ministers' Statement," November 18, 1956, cited in *Summary of World Broadcasts*, November 20, 1956, p. 5.

18. Rashid Khalidi, "Consequences of the Suez Crisis in the Arab World," in Louis and Owen, *Suez 1956*, p. 385.

19. Morris, *Israel's Border Wars*, chap. 12. Hussein accepted a security arrangement that he had previously rejected largely because of electoral and domestic considerations. Uriel Dann, *King Hussein and the Challenge of Arab Radicalism: Jordan, 1955–67* (New York: Oxford University Press, 1989), p. 37.

20. Satloff, *From Abdullah to Hussein*, p. 156.

21. Amman Home Service, "Sulaiman al-Nabulsi's Policy Statement," November 27, 1956, cited in *Summary of World Broadcasts*, November 29, 1956, pp. 7–10. Also see Torrey, *Syrian Politics*, p. 300.

22. "Treaty of Solidarity Between Jordan, Syria, Saudi Arabia, and Egypt: The Accord on Jordan," cited in Muhammad Khalil, *The Arab States and the Arab League: A Documentary Record*, vol. 2 (Beirut: Khayat's, 1962), pp. 287–89.

23. Satloff, *From Abdullah to Hussein*, p. 159; Dann, *King Hussein*, p. 43.

24. Dann, *King Hussein*, chap. 3; Gerges, *Superpowers and the Middle East*, p. 82.

25. Cited in Dann, *King Hussein*, p. 45; also see Aqil Hyder Hasan Abidi, *Jordan: A Political Study, 1948–57* (New York: Asia Publishing, 1965), pp. 148–49.

26. Dann, *King Hussein*, chap. 4.

27. Cited in Anouar Abdel-Malek, *Egypt: Military Society* (New York: Random House, 1968), p. 282.

28. "Comment on the Iraqi-Jordanian Agreement," Baghdad, October 16, 1956, cited in *Summary of World Broadcasts*, October 18, 1956, pp. 6–7.

29. Khalidi, "Consequences of the Suez Crisis," p. 383.

30. See Cairo Home Service, "Gamal abd al-Nasir's Speech of 9.11.56 at Al-Azhar Mosque," November 9, 1956, cited in *Summary of World Broadcasts*, November 11, 1956, pp. 5–15.

31. Ahmed Said, "Cairo on Arab Neutralism," "Voice of the Arabs," November 12, 1956, cited in *Summary of World Broadcasts*, November 16, 1956, p. 8; Cairo Home Service, "Ahmed Sa'id on Baghdad Pact," November 27, 1956, cited in *Summary of World Broadcasts*, November 29, 1956, pp. 1–2.

32. Damascus Home Service, "Radio Attacks on Nuri al-Said," November 24, 1956, cited in *Summary of World Broadcasts*, November 27, 1956, pp. 10–12.

33. For discussions of the bungled coup see Khalidi, "Consequences of the Suez Crisis," pp. 382–83; Podeh, *Quest for Arab Hegemony*, pp. 217–18; Torrey, *Syrian Politics*, p. 324; Seale, *Struggle for Syria*, chap. 20. See Torrey, *Syrian Politics*, pp. 329–30, for the trials in January and February 1957.

34. Baghdad Home Service, "Criticism of Syrian 'Sabotage' of the Pipeline," November 14, 1956, cited in *Summary of World Broadcasts*, November 16, 1956, pp. 5–7.

35. Podeh, *Quest for Arab Hegemony*, pp. 214–15.

36. Quoted in Podeh, *Quest for Arab Hegemony*, p. 220.

37. "Egyptian Government's Reply to Prime Minister's Nuri As-Said's Radio Speech of December 16, 1956," cited in Khalil, *Arab States and the Arab League*, vol. 2, pp. 279–86.

38. Heikal, *Cutting the Lion's Tail*, p. 216.

39. For an excellent treatment of events leading to the unity agreement, see Malik Mufti, *Sovereign Creations: Pan-Arabism and Political Order in Syria and Iraq* (Ithaca, N.Y.: Cornell University Press, 1996), chap. 6. Also see Torrey, *Syrian Politics*, pp. 374–81; Seale, *Struggle for Syria*, chap. 22.

40. Itamar Rabinovich, *Syria Under the Ba'ath, 1963–66* (New York: Halstead, 1972), pp. 9–10. For overviews of the Ba'ath Party and its ideology see Kerr, *Arab Cold War*, pp. 7–8; Seale, *Struggle for Syria*, pp. 153–58; Rabinovich, *Syria Under the Ba'ath*, pp. 6–11.

41. Rabinovich, *Syria Under the Ba'ath*, p. 15.

42. Seale, *Struggle for Syria*, p. 311; Kerr, *Arab Cold War*, pp. 12, 15; Rabinovich, *Syria Under the Ba'ath*, p. 13; Hanna Batatu, *The Old Social Classes and the Revolutionary Movements of Iraq* (Princeton, N.J.: Princeton University Press, 1978), p. 815.

43. Kerr, *Arab Cold War*, p. 11; Seale, *Struggle for Syria*, p. 321.

44. Torrey, *Syrian Politics*, p. 377; also see Seale, *Struggle for Syria*, p. 158.

45. For the relationship between identity and the "imagined" Arab community enabling the possibility of unity as a conceptual category, see Eberhard Kienle, "Arab Unity Schemes Revisited: Interest, Identity, and Policy in Syria and Egypt," *International Journal of Middle Eastern Studies* 27 (1995): 53–71.

46. Abdel-Malek, *Egypt*, p. 256; also see Seale, *Struggle for Syria*, p. 314.

47. Kerr, *Arab Cold War*, p. 11.

48. Anonymous source, interview by author, Cairo, Egypt.

49. Ibid.

50. Mufti, *Sovereign Creations*, p. 90–92; Rabinovich, *Syria Under the Ba'ath*, p. 15; Seale, *Struggle for Syria*, pp. 321–24. See Kerr, *Arab Cold War*, chap. 1, and Rabinovich, *Syria Under the Ba'ath*, pp. 16–25, for a discussion of the rise and fall of the UAR.

51. MENA, "Haykal's Reply to Fadil al-Jamili on Arab Union," March 9, 1958, cited in *Summary of World Broadcasts*, March 10, 1958, p. 2. Also see Damascus Home Service, "Amir al-Badr's Speech on Union with the Yemen," March 8, 1958, cited in *Summary of World Broadcasts*, March 10, 1958, p. 11. For the text of the agreement see Cairo Home Service, "Convention Establishing the United Arab States," March 8, 1958, cited in *Summary of World Broadcasts*, March 10, 1958, pp. 9–11.

52. Damascus accused Saudi Arabia of hiring agents to overthrow the Syrian government and to stop the tide of Arabism and unity. See "Bill of Indictment in the 'Saudi Plot' Case," Damascus, March 29, 1958, cited in *Summary of World Broadcasts*, April 1, 1958, pp. 3–25.

53. These initial negotiations included Saudi Arabia. But the Saudis, fearing too close an association with their Hashemite rivals who were linked to the West, made Iraq's withdrawal from the Baghdad Pact a condition for its participation. Podeh, *Quest for Arab Hegemony*, pp. 221, 238.

54. "Iraqi Jordanian Union Communique," Baghdad, in Arabic, February 14, 1958, cited in *Summary of World Broadcasts*, February 16, 1958, p. 6. For the text of the agreement see "Iraqi-Jordanian Agreement on the Arab Union," Baghdad, in Arabic, February 14, 1958, cited in *Summary of World Broadcasts*, pp. 7–8. Also see Mufti, *Sovereign Creations*, pp. 102–108 for a discussion of the federation.

55. "Nuri as-Sa'id on the Arab Federation," Baghdad, in Arabic, May 19, 1958, cited in *Summary of World Broadcasts*, May 21, 1958, pp. 7–8.

56. MENA, " 'Ash-Shab Report of Iraqi-Jordanian Disputes," April 8, 1958, cited in *Summary of World Broadcasts*, April 10, 1958, pp. 8–9.

57. Podeh, *Quest for Arab Hegemony*, p. 194; also see Dann, *King Hussein*, chap. 6.

58. "Cairo Press Comment on the Iraqi-Jordanian Union," March 15, 1958, cited in *Summary of World Broadcasts*, March 17, 1958, pp. 1–5.

59. Cairo Home Service, "*Al-Akhbar* on the Baghdad Pact's Opposition to the Egyptian-Syrian Union," January 23, 1958, and "*Ash-Shab* on the Baghdad Pact's Anti-Arab Ties, January 24, 1958, cited in *Summary of World Broadcasts*, January 26, 1958, pp. 1–3. Also see Cairo Home Service, "Cairo Radio Comment on Arab Unity," February 16, 1958, cited in *Summary of World Broadcasts*, March 18, 1958, pp. 1–3.

60. "Cairo and Damascus Press Comment on the Arab Federation," February 18, 1958, cited in *Summary of World Broadcasts*, February 20, 1958, pp. 4–6.

61. "Jordanian Statement on Abd an-Nasir's CBS Interview," Ramallah, in Arabic, April 8, 1958, cited in *Summary of World Broadcasts*, April 10, 1958, pp. 4–8.

62. MENA, "*Al-Ahram* on Developments in Saudi Arabia," April 8, 1958, cited in *Summary of World Broadcasts*, April 10, 1958, p. 3.

63. "President Sham'un's Press Statement," Beirut, May 21, 1958, cited in *Summary of World Broadcasts*, May 23, 1958, p. 10. See Damascus Home Service, "Abd an-Nasir's Speeches to Lebanese in Damascus," February 28, 1958, cited in *Summary of World Broadcasts*, March 1, 1958, pp. 7–12. Also see Gerges, *Superpowers and the Middle East*, pp. 104–105.

64. Gerges, *Superpowers and the Middle East*, p. 112.

65. Ibid., p. 113; Batatu, *Old Social Classes*, pp. 801–804.

66. Batatu, *Old Social Classes*, p. 679.

67. Ibid., p. 804.

68. Ibid., p. 817; Majid Khadduri, *Independent Iraq: A Study in Iraqi Politics Since 1932* (New York: Oxford University Press, 1960), pp. 307–309; Abdul-Salaam Yousif, "The Struggle for Cultural Hegemony During the Iraqi Revolution," in R. Fernea and W. Louis, eds., *The Iraqi Revolution of 1958: The Old Social Classes Revisited*, pp. 172–96 (New York: I. B. Tauris, 1991).

69. Cairo was a bit premature in celebrating that the need to rename the Baghdad Pact because it was unwelcome in Baghdad. Cairo Home Service, "*Al-Ahram* on the Baghdad Pact," July 27, 1958, cited in *Summary of World Broadcasts*, July 29, 1958, p. 2. Although one of the Free Officers' first acts was to suspend Iraq's participation in future pact security meetings, Iraq did not formally withdraw until March 1959. Still, the new Iraqi regime left little doubt that Iraq would now follow a different foreign policy orientation and had unabashedly embraced Nasser and his brand of Arabism, symbolized by an agreement in which the Iraqis pledged to honor the Joint Defense Pact, a thinly veiled rejection of the Baghdad Pact. Cairo Home Service, "The UAR-Iraqi Agreement," July 19, 1958, cited in *Summary of World Broadcasts*, July 21, 1958, p. 12.

70. Rashid Khalidi, "The Impact of the Iraqi Revolution on the Arab World," in Fernea and Louis, *Iraqi Revolution of 1958*, pp. 106–17.

71. The Americans entered via the Eisenhower Doctrine. Unveiled on January 5, 1957, the doctrine represented another effort by the United States to construct a workable containment policy in the Middle East and to replace Britain's post-Baghdad decline. The doctrine offered $200 million in economic and military assistance to any states determined to maintain their "national independence," although the core of the policy was congressional authorization to use U.S. military authority to deter any armed aggression by international Communism. The Eisenhower Doctrine was highly reminiscent of the Baghdad Pact in its ability to split the Arab world into rival camps, though it did not exactly duplicate these camps; Nasser was the head of the oppositionist grouping, joined by Syria, whereas Iraq, Saudi Arabia, Lebanon, and the North African states were all favorably disposed. See Seale, *Struggle for Syria*, pp. 285–89, for discussions of the doctrine.

72. Gerges, *Superpowers and the Middle East*, p. 116; Beirut Home Service, "Sami

as-Sulh on the U.S. action," July 16, 1958, cited in *Summary of World Broadcasts*, July 18, p. 13; Beirut Home Service, "Sami as-Sulh's Statement in reply to Adil Usayren," July 21, 1958, pp. 13–14.

73. King Hussein, *Uneasy Lies the Head* (London: Heineman, 1962), pp. 162–64; James Lunt, *Hussein of Jordan* (London: Macmillan, 1989), p. 49.

74. Amman Home Service, "King Husayn's Address to Jordanians," July 17, 1956, cited in *Summary of World Broadcasts*, July 20, 1956, pp. 10–12.

75. "King Husayn's Press Conference," Ramallah, in Arabic, July 19, 1958, cited in *Summary of World Broadcasts*, July 21, 1958, pp. 16–17.

76. Amman Home Service, "Comment on Abd an-Nasir's Speeches in Damascus," July 21, 1958, cited in *Summary of World Broadcasts*, July 23, 1958, p. 4.

77. Cairo Home Service, "Abd-Nasir on the U.S. Landing in Lebanon," July 16, 1958, cited in *Foreign Broadcast Information Service* (hereafter *FBIS*), July 18, 1958, p. 1; Cairo Home Service, "Abd-Nasir's Speech in Damascus," July 18, 1956, cited in *Summary of World Broadcasts*, July 20, 1958, pp. 2–5; Damascus Home Service, "UAR and Iraqi Speeches in Damascus," July 19, 1958, cited in *Summary of World Broadcasts*, July 21, 1958, pp. 5–12; "Comments on the U.S. and British Landings," July 17, 1958, cited in *Summary of World Broadcasts*, July 20, 1958, pp. 1–5.

78. Kerr, *Arab Cold War*, p. 17; Kamal Salibi, *The Modern History of Jordan* (London: I. B. Taurus, 1993), p. 206.

79. Kerr, *Arab Cold War*, p. 17.

80. Gerges, *Superpowers and the Middle East*, p. 127; Batatu, *Old Social Classes*, p. 815–20; Mufti, *Sovereign Creations*, pp. 113–16.

81. Kerr, *Arab Cold War*, p. 18. Nasser was in a bind in 1961 when Kuwait declared its independence and Iraq announced its intention to "reclaim" Kuwait, and the British provided protection to Kuwait. Nasser, a supporter of unity but an opponent of Iraq's actions, was now in the uncomfortable position of siding with Britain. Although he arranged to have a UAR-Saudi-Jordanian contingent replace the British, Nasser's image gained little from the exchange. Ibid., p. 20.

82. Khalidi, "Impact of the Revolution," p. 111–13.

83. See Kerr, *Arab Cold War*; Rabinovich, *Syria Under the Ba'ath*; Derek Hopwood, *Syria: 1945–86* (Boston: Unwin Hyman, 1988)., pp. 41–42; Mufti, *Sovereign Creations*, pp. 132–39.

84. Seale, *Struggle for Syria*, pp. 224–25.

85. Rabinovich, *Syria Under the Ba'ath*, p. 20.

86. Ibid. pp. 26–27, 37–38; Mufti, *Sovereign Creations*, pp. 135–39.

87. Mohamed Abdel Ghani el-Gamasy, *The October War: Memoirs of Field Marshal el-Gamasy of Egypt* (Cairo: American University of Cairo Press, 1993), pp. 16–17.

88. Cited in Abdel-Malek, *Egypt*, p. 273.

89. Ibid., p. 274; also see Samir Mutawi, *Jordan in the 1967 War* (New York: Cambridge University Press, 1987), p. 49.

90. Adbel-Malek, *Egypt*, p. 275.

91. Kerr, *Arab Cold War*, p. 2; Adeed Dawisha, *Egypt and the Arab World: Elements of a Foreign Policy* (New York: Wiley, 1976), pp. 34–36.

92. Kerr, *Arab Cold War*, pp. 29–30; Leila Kadi, *Arab Summit Conferences and the Palestine Problem, 1936–50, 1964–66* (Beirut: PLO Research Center, 1966), pp. 116–18; Hasou, *Struggle for the Arab World*, pp. 115–17.

93. Kerr, *Arab Cold War*, p. 26.

94. Rabinovich, *Syria Under the Ba'ath*, p. 20.

95. Kerr, *Arab Cold War*, p. 27.

96. See F. Gregory Gause III, *Saudi-Yemeni Relations: Domestic Structures and Foreign Influence* (New York: Columbia University Press, 1990); Kerr, *Arab Cold War*, pp. 107–109; Saeed Badeeb, *The Saudi-Egyptian Conflict over North Yemen, 1962–70* (Boulder, Colo.: Westview, 1986); Rahmy, *Egyptian Policy in the Arab World*, for discussions of Yemen.

97. Gerges, *Superpowers and the Middle East*, p. 151; Nadav Safran, *Saudi Arabia: The Ceaseless Quest for Security* (Ithaca, N.Y.: Cornell University Press, 1988).

98. Gerges, *Superpowers and the Middle East*, p. 150; Abdel-Malek, *Egypt*, p. 284.

99. Anonymous source, interview by author, Cairo, Egypt. Gamasy similarly argues that Egypt's intervention in Yemen was a response to the failure of the UAR. *October War*, p. 18.

100. See Kerr, *Arab Cold War*, pp. 40–42, on these revolutions.

101. Baghdad Home Service, "Iraqi Foreign Minister's Press Conference," February 13, 1963, cited in *Summary of World Broadcasts*, ME/1176/A/2–5, February 15, 1963; MENA, "President Arif's Statement to MENA," February 13, 1963, cited in *Summary of World Broadcasts*, ME/1176/A/1–2, February 15, 1963. Even recognizing the Iraqi regime could not be undertaken without conflict. Although both Syria and Egypt immediately recognized and welcomed the new government, a feud broke out between the two in regard to whether Egypt's recognition was true and sincere. Damascus Home Service, "Damascus Reply to Cairo on Syria's Recognition of Iraq," February 12, 1963, cited in *Summary of World Broadcasts*, ME/1175/A/2, February 14, 1963. Also see Rabinovich, *Syria Under the Ba'ath*, p. 44.

102. Rabinovich, *Syria Under the Ba'ath*, p. 61.

103. Damascus Home Service, "Statement on the Revolution in Syria," March 8, 1963, cited in *Summary of World Broadcasts*, ME/1196/A/2–3, March 10, 1963.

104. Rabinovich, *Syria Under the Ba'ath*, p. 52.

105. Amin Hewedy, interview by author, Cairo, March 17, 1996; Rabinovich, *Syria Under the Ba'ath*, p. 61; Hopwood, *Syria*, p. 45.

106. Kerr, *Arab Cold War*, pp. 46–48.

107. Cairo Home Service, "Hasanayn Heikal's Weekly Article in *Al-Ahram*," February 15, 1963, cited in *Summary of World Broadcasts*, ME/1178/A/5–7, February 17, 1963.

108. Cairo Home Service, "Abd an-Nasir's Unity Day Speech," February 21, 1963, cited in *Summary of World Broadcasts*, ME/1185/A/5, February 23, 1963.

109. Gerges, *Superpowers and the Middle East*, pp. 162–63.

110. Damascus Home Service, "Plans for Syrian Union with Iraq," February 18, 1963, cited in *Summary of World Broadcasts*, ME/1180/A/4–5, February 21, 1963.

111. Kerr, *Arab Cold War*, pp. 49–95. Also see Rabinovich, *Syria Under the Ba'ath*, pp. 59–66.

112. Cited in Abdel-Malek, *Egypt*, p. 282.

113. Kerr, *Arab Cold War*, p. 73.

114. Ibid., pp. 55–56.

115. Salibi, *Modern History of Jordan*, p. 208.

116. Anonymous source, interview by author, Cairo, Egypt, March 19, 1996.

117. See Mohammad Mehdi, "The Cairo Declaration," *Middle East Forum* 49, no. 8 (Summer 1963): 31–40, for a discussion of the agreement.

118. Salibi, *Modern History of Jordan*, p. 209.

119. Dann, *King Hussein*, pp. 119, 128.

120. "The Campaign Against King Husayn," Voice of the Arab Nation (editorial), March 20, 1963, cited in *Summary of World Broadcasts*, ME/1206/A/2, March 22, 1963.

121. Adeed Dawisha, "Jordan in the Middle East: The Art of Survival," in P. Seale, ed., *The Shaping of an Arab Statesman: Abd al-Hamid Sharaf and the Modern Arab World* (New York: Quartet, 1983), p. 64.

122. Amman Home Service, "Wasfi at-Tall's Press Conference," March 9, 1963, cited in *Summary of World Broadcasts*, ME/1197/A/6–8, March 11, 1963.

123. Amman Home Service, "Wasfi at-Tall's Statement," February 8, 1963, cited in *Summary of World Broadcasts*, ME/1171/A/7–8, February 10, 1963.

124. Lunt, *Hussein of Jordan*, p. 73; Salibi, *Modern History of Jordan*, p. 209.

125. Rabinovich, *Syria Under the Ba'ath*, pp. 63–64.

126. Ibid., p. 72.

127. Cairo Home Service, "Hasnayn Haykal's Article of 11th October," October 11, 1963, cited in *Summary of World Broadcasts*, ME/1377/A/1, October 14, 1963.

128. Corm, *Fragmentation of the Middle East*, p. 62; Kerr, *Arab Cold War*, p. 85; Rabinovich, *Syria Under the Ba'ath*, p. 67.

129. Rabinovich, *Syria Under the Ba'ath*, pp. 84, 87–88.

130. Eberhard Kienle, "The Limits of Fertile Crescent Unity: Iraqi Policies Toward Syria Since 1945," in D. Hopwood, H. Ishaw, and T. Koszinowski, eds., *Iraq: Power and Society* (New York: Oxford University Press, 1993), pp. 367–68.

131. Rabinovich, *Syria Under the Ba'ath*, p. 95; Mufti, *Sovereign Creations*, pp. 160–63, 166.

132. Kerr, *Arab Cold War*, p. 93.

133. Baghdad Home Service, "The Announcement of Syrian-Iraqi Military Unity," October 8, 1963, cited in *Summary of World Broadcasts*, ME/1374/A/2–4, October 10, 1964.

134. Cairo Home Service, "*Al-Akhbar* Article," October 9, 1963, cited in *Summary of World Broadcasts*, ME/1375/A/7–9, October 11, 1963.

135. Yemen too got into the act, as President Abdallah al-Sallal commented: "What a strange name; we are genuine Arabs, what do we have to do with Michel?" Rabinovich, *Syria Under the Ba'ath*, p. 72.

136. Dann, *King Hussein*, p. 134.

137. Corm, *Fragmentation of the Middle East*, pp. 97–98.

138. Tahseen Bashir, interview by author, Washington, D.C., April 2, 1996.

139. Amman Home Service, "King Husayn Press Conference," March 16, 1963, cited in *Summary of World Broadcasts*, ME/1203/A/2, March 18, 1963. Also see Salibi, *Modern History of Jordan*, p. 209; Kadi, *Arab Summit Conferences*, p. 89; Mutawi, *Jordan in the 1967 War*, pp. 20–21.

140. Hussein, *Uneasy Lies the Head*, pp. 74–80.

141. Kerr, *Arab Cold War*, pp. 90–91.

142. Anonymous source, interview by author.

143. Rabinovich, *Syria Under the Ba'ath*, pp. 95–96, 101.

144. Kadi, *Arab Summit Conferences*, p. 92; Kerr, *Arab Cold War*, pp. 98–99.

145. See Kerr, *Arab Cold War*, p. 98, for a discussion of the conflict over the various water schemes.

146. Mutawi, *Jordan in the 1967 War*, p. 51; anonymous source, interview by author.

147. Bashir interview.

148. Salibi, *Modern History of Jordan*, p. 211.

149. Anonymous source, interview by author, Cairo, Egypt, March 19, 1996; Kadi, *Arab Summit Conferences*, p. 94; Gerges, *Superpowers and the Middle East*, p. 166.

150. Salibi, *Modern History of Jordan*, p. 211; also see Kerr, *Arab Cold War*, p. 110.

151. Mutawi, *Jordan in the 1967 War*, p. 22.

152. Rabinovich, *Syria Under the Ba'ath*, p. 115.

153. *Summary of World Broadcasts*, ME/1958/A/4, October 11, 1965.

154. Cairo Domestic Service, "Text of UAR-Iraq Presidential Council Decisions," October 16, 1964, cited in *FBIS*, October 19, 1964, B1–2.

155. Baghdad Domestic Service, "President Surveys Measures to Achieve Unity," October 24, 1964, cited in *FBIS*, October 26, 1964, C3.

156. Jerusalem Israel Domestic Service, "*Al-Hayah* Comments on UAR-Iraq Unity Accord," October 26, 1964, cited in *FBIS*, October 28, 1964, F1. Also see Malcolm Kerr, "Regional Arab Politics and the Conflict with Israel," in P. Hammond and S. Alexander, eds., *Political Dynamics in the Middle East* (New York: American Elsevier, 1972), p. 45.

157. MENA, "Abd An-Nasir Grants Interview to *Al-Hurriyah*," Cairo, June 7, 1965, cited in *FBIS*, June 8, 1965, B1–4.

158. Amman Domestic Service, "At-Tall Reviews Arab Problems for Press," June 6, 1965, cited in *FBIS*, June 7, 1965, D1–3.

159. Cairo Domestic Service, "Arab Premiers Reject Bourguiba Proposals," May 27, 1965, cited in *FBIS*, May 28, 1965, B3.

160. See, for instance, Cairo Home Service, "*Al-Ahram* on the Summit Confer-

ence," September 8, 1964, cited in *Summary of World Broadcasts*, ME/1653/A/2, September 10, 1964; Damascus Home Service, "Syrian Comment on Conference," September 8, 1964, cited in *Summary of World Broadcasts*, ME/1653/A/2, September 10, 1964. The decision to unify forces also caused Algeria, Tunisia, Libya, and the Sudan to now sign the Arab Collective Security Pact. MENA, "Additional States to Sign Arab Defense Treaty," Cairo, September 10, 1964, cited in *FBIS*, September 11, 1964, B2.

161. Cairo Domestic Service, "Address by President Nasser," January 13, 1964, cited in *FBIS*, January 14, 1964, B2–3.

162. Cairo Domestic Service, "UAR General to Head Joint Arab Force," January 17, 1964, cited in *FBIS*, January 20, 1964, B2. See Mutawi, *Jordan in the 1967 War*, pp. 58–59, for a general discussion of the UAC; he credits a Jordanian military paper as setting it into motion.

163. Beirut RNS, "Jordan Has No Reservations About Arab Troops," June 1, 1965, cited in *FBIS*, June 2, 1965, D2; Damascus Domestic Service, "Nasir Reveals Weak Attitude Toward Syria," June 1, 1960, cited in *FBIS*, June 2, 1960, G3.

164. Cairo Domestic Service, "Working Plan Presented by UAR Gains Approval," September 9, 1964, cited in *FBIS*, September 10, 1964, B1; Beirut RNS, "Conference Reaches Accord on Military Matters," September 8, 1964, cited in *FBIS*, September 9, 1964, B1–2; Beirut Home Service, "Lebanese Views on the Stationing of Arab Troops," September 9, 1964, cited in *Summary of World Broadcasts*, ME/1654/A/3, September 11, 1964; Cairo Home Service, "Haykal on the Arab Summit," September 18, 1964, cited in *Summary of World Broadcasts*, ME/1662/A/1, September 20, 1964. Also see Mutawi, *Jordan in the 1967 War*, pp. 62–63; Beirut RNS, "Stationing of Troops in Countries Discussed," May 27, 1965, cited in *FBIS*, May 28, 1965, B9. At the second summit Jordan agreed to allow the Unified Arab Command to cross into its territory under restrictive conditions. Jordan Home Service, "Press Conference Given by Information Minister Wasfi at-Tall," September 18, 1965, cited in *Summary of World Broadcasts*, ME/1965/A/4.

165. Beirut RNS, "Delegations Admit Conference Shortcomings," May 30, 1965, cited in *FBIS*, June 1, 1965, B6.

166. Charles Smith, *Palestine and the Arab-Israeli Conflict*, 2d ed. (New York: St. Martin's, 1992), p. 186.

167. Mutawi, *Jordan in the 1967 War*, pp. 56–57; Dann, *King Hussein*, pp. 138–41; Kerr, *Arab Cold War*, p. 114.

168. On sovereignty see Helena Cobban, *The Palestinian Liberation Organization: People, Power, and Politics* (New York: Cambridge University Press, 1984), p. 195. This also helps to account for the Palestinian National Covenant's ambiguous stance vis-à-vis *wataniyya* and *qawmiyya*. Gabriel Ben-Dor, "Nationalism Without Sovereignty and Nationalism with Multiple Sovereignties: The Palestinians and Inter-Arab Relations," in G. Ben-Dor, ed., *Palestinians and the Middle East Conflict* (Forest Grove, Ore.: Turtle Dove, 1979), p. 149. On its proposed instrumental nature, see Mutawi, *Jordan in the 1967 War*, p. 57.

169. Beirut RNS, "Some Annoyed at Shuqayri Presentation on Entity," September 1, 1964, cited in *FBIS*, September 2, 1964, B1.

170. Mutawi, *Jordan in the 1967 War*, p. 66; Dann, *King Hussein*, p. 147.

171. Also see Gerges, *Superpowers and the Middle East*, p. 192.

172. Damascus Domestic Service, "Damascus Account of 27 May Meeting," May 28, 1965, cited in *FBIS*, June 1, 1965, B4.

173. "Ash-Shuqayri's Withdrawal," Cairo Voice of Palestine, May 28, 1965, cited in *FBIS*, June 1, 1965, B2.

174. Cairo Domestic Service, "Arab Premiers Reject Bourguiba Proposals," May 27, 1965, cited in *FBIS*, May 28, 1965, B3–7.

175. Tunis Home Service, "Bourguiba's Broadcast on the Arab Summit Conference," September 13, 1965, cited in *Summary of World Broadcasts*, ME/1965/A/4–9, September 14, 1965.

176. Not surprisingly, Bourguiba's comments did little to endear him to the Egyptian government. Nasser on Bourguiba: "He claims that he is a leading struggler and that he has been struggling for 30 years. If he has been struggling for 30 years it means that he started his struggle before anyone else in the Arab world and yet was the last to attain his independence. And it has not been long since the French evacuated Tunisia. This is Bouguibism." "Haykal on Prelude to Arab Summit," *Al-Ahram*, September 17, 1965, cited in *Summary of World Broadcasts*, ME/1964/A/4, September 18, 1965.

177. Damascus applauded Bourguiba's speech in general and his reference that those who act in the name of Palestine act for themselves, noting that "a number of those who speak on the Palestine issue would like to repeat what Bourguiba recently said in this connection." Damascus Radio Service, September 18, 1965, cited in *Summary of World Broadcasts*, ME/1965/A/2–3, September 19, 1965.

178. Cairo Home Service, "Cairo *Al-Akhbar* Comment on the Casablanca Conference," September 15, 1965, cited in *Summary of World Broadcasts*, ME/1961/A/2, September 16, 1965.

179. See, for instance, the comments by Lebanese President Charles Hilu. Beirut Home Service, September 18, 1965, cited in *Summary of World Broadcasts*, ME/1965/A/5, September 19, 1965.

180. The other factor was the split between Egypt and Saudi Arabia over the ongoing revolt in Yemen and King Faysal's proposed Islamic Pact, which Nasser interpreted as a direct challenge to his Arab nationalism. See Mutawi, *Jordan in the 1967 War*, p. 67; Kerr, *Arab Cold War*, pp. 109–110; Dann, *King Hussein*, pp. 149–50; Gerges, *Superpowers and the Middle East*, p. 186.

181. Damascus Domestic Service, "Nasir Reveals Weak Attitude Toward Syria," June 1, 1965, cited in *FBIS*, June 2, 1965, G3; Rabinovich, *Syria Under the Ba'ath*, pp. 167–68.

182. Cairo Domestic Service, "Nasir Opens Palestine National Congress," May 31,

1965, cited in *FBIS*, June 3, 1965, B1–17. Also see MENA, "Abd An-Nasir Grants Interview to *Al-Hurriyah*," Cairo, June 7, 1965, cited in *FBIS*, June 8, 1965, B1–4.

183. Cairo Domestic Service, "Nasir Opens Palestine National Congress," May 31, 1965, cited in *FBIS*, June 3, 1965, B1–17.

184. Syria, of course, made much of Nasser's statement and acknowledgment that he would not come to Syria's defense on just any grounds. The result was a heated war of words. See MENA, "*Al-Ahram* Replies to Syrian Criticism of Nasir," Cairo, June 3, 1965, cited in *FBIS*, June 3, 1965, B25–27; Damascus Domestic Service, " 'Certain Arab States' Pursue 'Two-Faced' Policy," June 2, 1965, cited in *FBIS*, June 3, 1965, G1–3. See Rabinovich, *Syria Under the Ba'ath*, pp. 168–69, for Syria's response to Nasser's speech.

185. Seale, *Struggle for Syria*, p. 104. Also see Rabinovich, *Syria Under the Ba'ath*, pp. 204–206; Hopwood, *Syria*, p. 47; Mufti, *Sovereign Creations*, pp. 173–76.

186. Rabinovich, *Syria Under the Ba'ath*, p. 209.

187. Damascus Domestic Service, "Al-Bath: Arabs Denounced Summit Long Ago," August 2, 1966, cited in *FBIS*, August 2, 1966, G1. Also see Gerges, *Superpowers and the Middle East*, p. 196.

188. Gerges, *Superpowers and the Middle East*, p. 197.

189. Dann, *King Hussein*, p. 152.

190. Although Nasser's actions were largely driven by regional politics of the moment, it was easier for him to recognize this Ba'athist regime that was more "local" in focus. Rabinovich, *Syria Under the Ba'ath*, p. 210.

191. Gamasy, *October War*, p. 89.

192. Samir Mutawi, "The Jordanian Response," in R. Parker, ed., *The Six-Day War: A Retrospective* (Gainesville: University of Florida Press, 1996), p. 175.

193. According to Mutawi, the Jordanians feared that this alliance spelled the end of Nasser's conservativism and constituted a trap from which he would not be able to extricate himself. Syria, in the Jordanian view, believed that it would triumph over Nasser whether there was a war or not and whether the Arabs won or lost. "Jordanian Response," p. 175.

194. Syria not only intended to embarrass Nasser but also to further its domestic political objectives of popularity and help bring down an Israeli government that it believed was teetering on the brink. Moshe Maoz, *Syria and Israel: From War to Peacemaking* (Oxford, England: Clarendon, 1995), pp. 94–98. According to Fred Lawson, Syria's willingness to escalate the conflict with Israel was related to Syrian domestic struggles regarding the political economy and government-military relations. *Why Syria Goes to War: Thirty Years of Confrontation* (Ithaca, N.Y.: Cornell University Press, 1996), pp. 47–49.

195. Mutawi, *Jordan in the 1967 War*, p. 73.

196. Ibid., p. 79.

197. Salibi, *Modern History of Jordan*, p. 218; Mutawi, *Jordan in the 1967 War*, p. 81.

198. Mutawi, *Jordan in the 1967 War*, pp. 77–78.

199. C. Ernest Dawn, "The Other Arab Responses," in Parker, *Six-Day War*, p. 155.

200. Mutawi, *Jordan in the 1967 War*, pp. 28, 85; Dawn, "Other Arab Responses," p. 158–59.

201. Kerr, *Arab Cold War*, pp. 126–27.

202. Gamasy, *October War*, pp. 26–27; also see Mark Tessler, *A History of the Is-raeli-Palestinian Conflict* (Bloomington: Indiana University Press, 1995), pp. 389–90.

203. Mutawi, *Jordan in the 1967 War*, p. 87.

204. Ibid., p. 90; Dawn, "Other Arab Responses," p. 159. See Dann, *King Hussein*, chap. 12, for a discussion of the months preceding the June war.

205. Mutawi, *Jordan in the 1967 War*, pp. 100–103, 162, 183.

206. Ibid., pp. 108–109, for discussions of the treaty.

207. Quoted in Salibi, *Modern History of Jordan*, p. 220.

208. Mutawi, *Jordan in the 1967 War*, pp. 100–101; also see Salibi, *Modern History of Jordan*, pp. 219–20.

209. A sure sign of their disarray appeared at the last Arab League Council meeting before the 1967 war; while the Arab states were on the verge of war, the only action they could muster was a resolution denouncing racial discrimination in the United States. Kerr, *Arab Cold War*, p. 125.

6. Sovereignty and Statism, 1967–1990

1. Quoted in Abdel Magid Farid, *Nasser: The Final Years* (Reading, England: Ithaca, 1994), p. 127.

2. Albert Hourani, *A History of the Arab Peoples* (Cambridge, Mass.: Harvard University Press, 1991), p. 442.

3. Malcolm Kerr, *The Arab Cold War* (New York: Oxford University Press, 1970), p. 129.

4. Mohamed Heikal, *The Sphinx and the Commissar* (New York: Harper and Row, 1978), pp. 261–62.

5. Adeed Dawisha, "Jordan in the Middle East: The Art of Survival," in P. Seale, ed., *The Shaping of an Arab Statesman: Abd al-Hamid Sharaf and the Modern Arab World* (New York: Quartet, 1983), p. 69.

6. A. Hourani, *History of the Arab Peoples*, p. 451; see the collection of essays in Giacomo Luciani, ed., *The Arab State* (Berkeley: University of California Press, 1990).

7. TAP, "Bourghiba Calls for Arab Unity Based on Islam," June 20, 1967, cited in *Foreign Broadcast Information Service* (hereafter *FBIS*), June 20, 1967, I22. Also see Amman Domestic Service, "Paper Says Immediate Summit Meeting Essential," *Al-Dustur*, July 10, 1967, cited in *FBIS*, July 10, 1967, D4.

8. Middle East News Agency (hereafter MENA), "Haykal Article Discusses Proposed Arab Summit," Cairo, July 13, 1967, cited in *FBIS*, July 14, 1967, B6–10.

9. MENA, "Iraq, Syria Submit Plans at Summit," Baghdad, June 18, 1967, cited in

FBIS, June 19, 1967, C1. Also see Baghdad Domestic Service, "Minister Says Holy War Depends on Unity," reported by MENA, June 18, 1967, cited in *FBIS*, June 19, 1967, C2.

10. Derek Hopwood, *Syria: 1945–86* (Boston: Unwin Hyman, 1988).

11. MENA, "Haykal Article Supports Arab Summit," Cairo, July 20, 1967, cited in *FBIS*, July 21, 1967, B8–9. See also Amman Domestic Service, "Haykal Article Reflects Positive Change," July 17, 1967, cited in *FBIS*, July 18, 1967, D3.

12. Tahseen Bashir, interview by author, Washington, D.C., April 2, 1996.

13. Ibid.

14. Amman Domestic Service, "Newspaper [*Al-Dustur*] Views Call for Summit Conference," June 19, 1967, cited in *FBIS*, June 19, 1967, D1–2.

15. "Amman's *Al-Dustur* on Heikal's Change of Opinion," July 17, 1967, cited in *Summary of World Broadcasts*, ME/2519/A/8, July 18, 1967.

16. Amman Domestic Service, "*Al-Dustur* Praises Nasir Call for Summit Talks," July 25, 1967, cited in *FBIS*, July 25, 1967, D1.

17. MENA, "Obstacles to Arab Summit Discussed," Damascus, June 29, 1967, cited in *FBIS*, June 30, 1967, F1.

18. Cairo Domestic Service, "Mahjub Opens First Meeting," August 1, 1967, cited in *FBIS*, August 2, 1967, I11–12.

19. Beirut RNS, "Tunisian-PLO Differences," August 3, 1967, cited in *FBIS*, August 4, 1967, I13.

20. MENA, "*Al-Ahram* Notes Achievements of Khartoum Talks," Cairo, August 8, 1967, cited in *FBIS*, August 9, 1967, B6.

21. MENA, "Arab Ministers to Seek Settlements," Cairo, August 4, 1967, cited in *FBIS*, August 7, I11.

22. George Corm, *Fragmentation of the Middle East: The Last Thirty Years* (London: Hutchinson, 1983), p. 53.

23. Beirut RNS, "Differences Remain After Baghdad Conference," August 22, 1967, *FBIS*, August 23, 1967, C2.

24. "Military Unity Cannot Be Delayed," *Al-Arab*, August 28, 1967; cited in *FBIS*, August 28, 1967, C1; Iraqi News Agency, "Economic Unity Should Precede Political Unity," *FBIS*, August 24, 1967, C3.

25. Anonymous source, interview by author, Amman, Jordan, September 3, 1995.

26. Cairo Domestic Service, "Proceedings of Final Session of Arab Summit," September 1, 1967, cited in *FBIS*, September 5, 1967, I12–15.

27. Anonymous source, interview by author, Amman, Jordan, September 3, 1995.

28. Amman Domestic Service, "King Husayn Interviewed on Arab Summit," September 4, 1967, *FBIS*, September 5, 1967, D1.

29. *Al-Dustur*, cited in *Summary of World Broadcasts*, ME/2561/A/6, September 6, 1967. Also see the editorials in the Baghdadi *Al-Fajr al-Jadid* and the Egyptian *Al-Akhbar al-Yawm*, reprinted in *Summary of World Broadcasts*, ME/2558/A/3, September 2, 1967, and ME/2559/A/4, September 4, 1967, respectively. See Fouad Ajami, *The Arab Predicament: Arab Political Thought and Practice Since 1967* (New York: Cam-

bridge University Press, 1981), for a more complete treatment of the symbolic significance of Khartoum.

30. MENA, *"Ath-Thawrah* Scores Arab Summit Resolutions," Damascus, September 2, 1967, cited in *FBIS*, September 5, 1967, G1.

31. Baghdad Domestic Service, "Arif Holds Press Conference on Arab Summit," September 3, 1967, cited in *FBIS*, September 5, 1967, C1.

32. A countermovement of radicalism was growing. See Ahmed Abdalla, *The Student Movement and National Politics in Egypt* (London: Al-Saqi Books, 1985).

33. Ajami, *Arab Predicament*, p. 71.

34. Mohamed Heikal, *Secret Channels* (London: HarperCollins, 1996), p. 133.

35. Nadav Safran, *Saudi Arabia: The Ceaseless Quest for Security* (Ithaca, N.Y.: Cornell University Press, 1988), pp. 141–42.

36. Farid, *Nasser*, p. 200; Heikal, *Secret Channels*, pp. 155–58.

37. Heikal, *Secret Channels*, p. 304.

38. Mark Tessler, *A History of the Israeli-Palestinian Conflict* (Bloomington: Indiana University Press, 1995), pp. 410–11.

39. Heikal, *Secret Channels*, p. 155.

40. Ajami, *Arab Predicament*, pp. 74–75.

41. Tunis Home Service, "Rabat Summit Proceedings of December 22," December 22, 1969, quoted in *Summary of World Broadcasts*, ME/3263/A/1, December 23, 1969.

42. Rabat Home Service, "King Hassan's Press Conference Following the Rabat Summit," December 24, 1969, cited in *Summary of World Broadcasts*, ME/3264/A/8, December 26, 1969.

43. Kamal Salibi, *The Modern History of Jordan* (London: I. B. Taurus. 1993), p. 236.

44. Amman Home Service,"Husayn's Reply to Nasir's Message of 19th September," September 20, 1970, quoted in *Summary of World Broadcasts*, ME/3488/A/11–15, September 21, 1970.

45. Amman Home Service, "King Husayn's Telegrams to Arab Kings and Presidents," September 20, 1970, quoted in *Summary of World Broadcasts*, ME/3488/A/13–14, September 21, 1970.

46. Cairo Radio, text of "Commentary by Salah as-Suwayfi," Voice of the Arabs, September 24, 1970, cited in *Summary of World Broadcasts*, ME/3492/A/4, September 25, 1970. Also see Hilmi al-Buluk, "Comment on the Jordan Situation," Voice of the Arabs, September 17, 1970, quoted in *Summary of World Broadcasts*, ME/3486/A/3, September 18, 1970.

47. Kerr, *Arab Cold War*, p. 151.

48. Libya's Muammar al-Qaddafi declared that he would cut off financial aid to Jordan, funnel weapons to the fedayeen, and was prepared to act unilaterally and militarily if the fighting against the Palestinians did not cease immediately. Then for good measure he accused Iraq of betraying the cause because it failed to intervene

militarily. Libyan Radio, "Lybian Statements and Comment on Jordan," September 20, 1970, cited in *Summary of World Broadcasts*, ME/3489/A/3–4, September 21, 1970.

49. Quoted in Amatzia Baram, "No New Fertile Crescent: Iraqi-Jordanian Relations, 1968–92," in J. Nevo and I. Pappe, eds., *Jordan in the Middle East, 1948–88: The Making of a Pivotal State* (London: Frank Cass, 1994), p. 120.

50. Damascus Home Service, "Statement by Syrian Information Minister, Hammud al-Qabbani," September 21, 1970, cited in *Summary of World Broadcasts*, ME/3489/A/7–8, September 22, 1970.

51. *Why Syria Goes to War: Thirty Years of Confrontation* (Ithaca, N.Y.: Cornell University Press, 1996), chap. 3. Fred Lawson links Syria's limited intervention to domestic political and economic struggles.

52. Algiers Home Service, "Algerian Message to Yasir Arafat and King Husayn," September 17, 1970, cited in *Summary of World Broadcasts*, ME/3486/A/8, September 18, 1970.

53. Farid, *Nasser*, p. 51; Dawisha, "Jordan in the Middle East," p. 65.

54. Kerr, *Arab Cold War*, p. 137.

55. Heikal, *Secret Channels*, p. 299.

56. Statement by Tahseen Bashir at press conference, reported by Cairo Home Service, September 22, 1970, cited in *Summary of World Broadcasts*, ME/3490/A/2, September 23, 1970.

57. Cairo Home Service, "Numayri's Cairo Press Conference on the 26th September," September 26, 1970, cited in *Summary of World Broadcasts*, ME/3494/A/1, September 27, 1970. Also see Cairo Home Service, "Exchange of Telegrams Between Nasir and Husayn," September 26, 1970, cited in *Summary of World Broadcasts*, ME/3493/A/7, September 27, 1970.

58. Amman Home Service, "Husayn's Broadcast to Armed Forces and Fedayeen," September 23, 1970, cited in *Summary of World Broadcasts*, ME/3490/A/7–8, September 24, 1970.

59. Salibi, *Modern History of Jordan*, p. 238.

60. Cairo Home Service, "Cairo Agreement on Jordan," September 27, 1970, cited in *Summary of World Broadcasts*, ME/3494/A/15–16, September 28, 1970.

61. Dawisha, "Jordan in the Middle East," p. 68.

62. Amman Home Service, "Cease-Fire Agreements in Jordan," October 10, 1970, cited in *Summary of World Broadcasts*, ME/3498/A/8–10, October 11, 1970.

63. An ongoing issue in Jordan's national identity was the place of Palestine in the national identity. Shirin Fathi, *Jordan: An Invented Nation?* (Hamburg: Deutsches Orient-Institut, 1994), pp. 210–11; Laurie Brand, "Palestinians and Jordanians: A Crisis of Identity," *Journal of Palestine Studies* 24, no. 4 (1995): 46–61. From 1950 through 1967 the Jordanian government attempted to "Jordanize" the Palestinians. But the loss of the West Bank and the growing number and radicalization of the Palestinians launched another consideration of Jordan's national identity. The events of 1970 further traumatized and stimulated that debate about the Jordanian national identity

and the authority of the Jordanian state, as did the ongoing question of whether the PLO or King Hussein represented the Palestinians.

64. Corm, *Fragmentation of the Middle East*, p. 32.

65. Safran, *Saudi Arabia*, pp. 156–60.

66. Alisdair Drysdale and Raymond Hinnebusch, *Syria and the Middle East Peace Process* (New York: Council on Foreign Relations Press, 1991), p. 108.

67. Corm, *Fragmentation of the Middle East*, p. 100. Egypt and Syria also undertook comparatively little coordination before the surprise attack, and such planning was thick with suspicion and mistrust. See Mohamed Abdel Ghani el-Gamasy, *The October War: Memoirs of Field Marshal el-Gamasy of Egypt* (Cairo: American University in Cairo Press, 1993), chap. 13; Saad el-Shazli, *The Crossing of the Suez* (San Francisco: American Middle East Research, 1980). Such suspicion led Egypt and Syria to not coordinate or fully disclose their military strategies and objectives. And their lack of coordination undermined the overall military campaign, most famous in the "pause" on the third day of the war after their initially impressive military advance. Gamasy, *October War*, chap. 24.

68. Abdel-Aziz Higazi, interview by author, June 10, 1987, Cairo, Egypt.

69. Saad Eddin Ibrahim, "Domestic Developments in Egypt," in W. Quandt, ed., *The Middle East: Ten Years After Camp David* (Washington, D.C.: Brookings Institution, 1988), pp. 19–62.

70. Ibid., p. 27.

71. Mohamed Heikal, *Autumn of Fury: The Assassination of Sadat* (New York: St. Martin's, 1983), p. 111; Ibrahim, "Domestic Developments in Egypt," p. 27.

72. Ghada Hashem Talhami, *Palestine and Egyptian National Identity* (New York: Praeger, 1992), chap. 6; Baghat Korany, "Egypt," in R. Brynen, ed., *Echoes of the Intifada* (Boulder, Colo.: Westview, 1991), p. 200; Ibrahim, "Domestic Developments in Egypt"; Abdel Monem Said Aly, "Egypt: A Decade After Camp David," in Quandt, *Middle East*, pp. 70–72; P. J. Vatikiotis, *Arab and Regional Politics in the Middle East* (New York: St. Martin's, 1984), p. 163.

73. Boutros Boutros-Ghali, *Egypt's Road to Jerusalem: A Diplomat's Story of the Struggle for Peace in the Middle East* (New York: Random House, 1997).

74. Vatikiotis, *Arab and Regional Politics*, p. 128.

75. Safran, *Saudi Arabia*, pp. 175–76.

76. Baghat Korany, "Political Petrolism and Contemporary Arab Politics, 1967–83," *Journal of Asian and African Studies* 21, no. 1/2 (1986): 68–80.

77. William Quandt, *Saudi Arabia in the 1980s* (Washington, D.C.: Brookings Institution, 1984), p. 34; Bassam Tibi, *Conflict and War in the Middle East, 1967–91* (New York: St. Martin's, 1993), p. 89.

78. Drysdale and Hinnebusch, *Syria and the Middle East Peace Process*, chap. 3; Moshe Maoz, *Syria and Israel: From War to Peacemaking* (Oxford, England: Clarendon, 1995), chaps. 7 and 9.

79. For discussions of the PLO during this period see Helena Cobban, *The Pales-*

tinian Liberation Organization: People, Power, and Politics (New York: Cambridge University Press, 1984); Moshe Shemesh, *The Palestinian Entity, 1959–74: Arab Politics and the PLO* (London: Frank Cass, 1988); Yezid Sayigh, *Armed Struggle and the Search for State: The Palestinian National Movement, 1949–93* (New York: Oxford University Press, 1997).

80. Gabriel Ben-Dor, "Nationalism Without Sovereignty and Nationalism with Multiple Sovereignties: The Palestinians and Inter-Arab Relations," in G. Ben-Dor, ed., *Palestinians and the Middle East Conflict* (Forest Grove, Ore.: Turtle Dove, 1979), pp. 148–49, 160.

81. Boutros-Ghali, *Egypt's Road to Jerusalem.*

82. Ismael Fahmy, *The Struggle for Peace in the Middle East* (Baltimore, Md.: Johns Hopkins University Press, 1983), pp. 108–109.

83. When the long-awaited Geneva peace conference opened on December 21, the only parties to the conflict that sent representatives were Israel, Egypt, and Jordan—the Syrian chair was empty. An international conference would not be held for another two decades.

84. Fahmy, *Struggle for Peace*, p. 83.

85. Safran, *Saudi Arabia*, p. 241.

86. Drysdale and Hinnebusch, *Syria and the Middle East Peace Process*, p. 110.

87. Fahmy, *Struggle for Peace*, pp. 96–97.

88. Safran, *Saudi Arabia*, p. 242.

89. Fahmy, *Struggle for Peace*, pp. 159–69.

90. Safran, *Saudi Arabia*, p. 244; Riyadh Home Service, "Saudi Reaction," September 2, 1975, cited in *Summary of World Broadcasts*, ME/4998/A/5, September 4, 1975.

91. Riyadh Home Service, "Saudi Comment on Arab Communists and the Sinai Agreement," September 22, 1975, cited in *Summary of World Broadcasts*, ME/5015/A/1, September 24, 1975.

92. Kuwait Home Service, "Kuwait Government Meeting—Sinai Disengagement," September 7, 1975, cited in *Summary of World Broadcasts*, ME/5002/A/10, September 9, 1975.

93. Amman Home Service, "King Husayn on Middle East Peace Prospects," November 24, 1975, cited in *Summary of World Broadcasts*, ME/5069/A/1–2, November 26, 1975.

94. Damascus Home Service, "Speech by Asad at October War Anniversary Celebration," October 6, 1975, cited in *Summary of World Broadcasts*, ME/5027/A/3–8, October 8, 1975. Also see Cairo Home Service, "Egyptian Comment on Speech by Asad," October 8, 1975, cited in *Summary of World Broadcasts*, ME/5027/A/3, October 10, 1975; Damascus Home Service, "Syrian Ba'ath Party Statement," September 3, 1975, cited in *Summary of World Broadcasts*, ME/4999/A/7, September 5, 1975; Damascus Home Service, "Syrian People's Assembly Statement on Sinai Agreement," September 23, 1975, cited in *Summary of World Broadcasts*, ME/5016/A/1–3, September 25, 1975;

Damascus Domestic Service, "Damascus Radio Assails As-Sadat Speech," March 15, 1976, cited in *FBIS*, March 16, 1976, H5.

95. Damascus Home Service, "Syrian Condemnation of Sadat's Statements on Sinai," February 21, 1976, cited in *Summary of World Broadcasts*, ME/5141/A/2–3, February 23, 1976.

96. Drysdale and Hinnebusch, *Syria and the Middle East Peace Process*, p. 117. The war of words between Egypt and Syria included a debate about their respective activities during the October War, particularly which was responsible for the "premature" halting of the advance after the third day of the war, which was the first to seek a cease-fire and for what purposes, and which sacrificed more during the war for the Arab cause. "Sadat's 15th September Speech at Meeting with ASU and TU Leaders," September 15, 1975, cited in *Summary of World Broadcasts*, ME/5009/A/1, September 17, 1975; "Syrian Reports of Criticisms of Sadat's 15th September Speech," *Ar-Ra'y al'Amm*, Kuwait, September 17, 1975, cited in *Summary of World Broadcasts*, ME/5011/A/2, September 19, 1975; Damascus Home Service, "Speech by Asad at October War Anniversary Celebration," October 6, 1975, cited in *Summary of World Broadcasts*, ME/5027/A/3–8, October 8, 1975.

97. "Iraqi Ba'ath Condemnation of Sinai Agreement," Baghdad Voice of the Masses, September 4, 1975, cited in *Summary of World Broadcasts*, ME/5000/A/1, September 6, 1975; "Iraqi Paper on Egyptian-Israeli Interim Agreement," *Ath-thawrah*, August 28, 1975, cited in *Summary of World Broadcasts*, ME/4994/A/2, August 30, 1975; "Iraqi Ba'ath Party Condemnation of Sinai Agreement," September 8, 1975, cited in *Summary of World Broadcasts*, ME/5000/A/1–8, September 9, 1975; "Iraq Criticism of Syria over Sinai Agreement," *Al-Jumhuriyah*, October 2, 1975, cited in *Summary of World Broadcasts*, ME/5023/A/5, October 3, 1975.

98. "Egyptian Comment," *Voice of the Arabs,* Cairo, September 2, 1975, cited in *Summary of World Broadcasts*, ME/4998/A/2, September 4, 1975.

99. Cairo Home Service, "Sadat's 4th September Speech at the Joint People's Assembly—ASU Meeting," September 4, 1975, cited in *Summary of World Broadcasts*, ME/5000/A/6–14, September 6, 1975.

100. "Sadat's 15th September Speech at Meeting with ASU and TU Leaders," September 15, 1975, cited in *Summary of World Broadcasts*, ME/5009/A/1, September 17, 1975.

101. Also see Cairo Home Service, "Ismail Fahmi's Statement to People's Assembly Committees," January 5, 1975, cited in *Summary of World Broadcasts*, ME/5101/A/8–10, January 7, 1975.

102. "Interview with President Sadat," *Al-Ahram*, February 3, 1976, cited in *FBIS*, February 3, 1976, D1–15.

103. In the war of words between Syria and Egypt, Egypt refused to be outdone. Cairo Radio broadcast that it was "difficult to believe that anyone would oppose" the agreement, "except, of course, a fool, an ignoramus, a cheap jacket, or an outbidder." Although the Ba'athists are also working toward the same goals, the broadcast con-

tinued, they will act irresponsibly in order to attract attention and engage in one-upmanship. Cairo Home Service, "Egyptian Denunciation of Syrian Ba'athists' 'One-Upmanship,'" November 24, 1975, cited in *Summary of World Broadcasts*, ME/5069/A/3–4, November 26, 1975. Other Egyptian commentaries accused Syria of voicing its objections as a method of extorting financial resources from other Arab states and accused Syria and Iraq of engaging in empty acts of "one-upmanships" that were designed to mask their empty gestures of Arabism. See "Egyptian Response to Criticism of the Sinai Agreement," cited in *Summary of World Broadcasts*, ME/5005/A/1–4, September 12, 1975.

104. See, respectively, Michael Barnett, *Confronting the Costs of War: Military Power, State, and Society in Egypt and Israel* (Princeton, N.J.: Princeton University Press, 1992); Anwar Sadat, *In Search of Identity* (New York: HarperBooks, 1978); Heikal, *Secret Channels*; Fahmy, *Struggle for Peace*, chap. 14.

105. Cairo Domestic Service, "President As-Sadat Addresses People's Assembly 26 November," November 26, 1977, cited in *FBIS*, November 28, 1977, D1–15; Cairo Domestic Service, "*Al-Ahram* Comments on Outcome of As-Sadat's Visit," November 22, 1977, cited in *FBIS*, November 22, 1977, D8.

106. Cairo Domestic Service, "As-Sadat Addresses Egyptian, Arab Peoples," September 18, 1978, cited in *FBIS*, September 19, 1978, D1. Also see MENA, "Ghali, Assembly Members Discuss Camp David Agreements," Cairo, October 3, 1978, cited in *FBIS*, October 4, 1978, D1–2. Also see "Media Reports People's Assembly Activities on Camp David," *FBIS*, October 16, 1978, D1–5; MENA, "Egyptian Cabinet Statement on Camp David Results," Egypt, September 19, 1978, cited in *Summary of World Broadcasts*, ME/5922/A/3–6, September 21, 1978; "Sadat's 2nd October Speech in the People's Assembly," Cairo, October 2, 1978, cited in *Summary of World Broadcasts*, ME/5933/A/1–15, October 3, 1978.

107. Cairo Domestic Service, "*Al-Ahram* Comments on Rejectionist Forces," September 22, 1978, cited in *FBIS*, September 22, 1978, D8; "*Al-Ahram* Editor Criticizes Opponents of Camp David Accords," *Al-Ahram*, Cairo, September 29, 1978, pp. 1, 3, cited in *FBIS*, October 4, 1978, D3–5; "*Al-Akhbar al-Yawm* Rejects Attempts to Expel Egypt from Arab League," *Al-Akhbar al-Yawm*, September 20, 1978, cited in *FBIS*, October 6, 1978, D7–8.

108. Cairo Domestic Home Service, "Sadat's 2nd October Speech in the People's Assembly," October 2, 1978, cited in *Summary of World Broadcasts*, ME/5933/A/1–15, October 3, 1978. For a detailed discussion of Camp David see Cairo Domestic Service, "Al-Sadat Grants Interview to Cairo Television," December 25, 1978, cited in *FBIS*, December 27, 1978, D1–24. In this interview he also linked Camp David to democracy in Egypt. Also see MENA, "Text of As-Sadat Interview with Kuwaiti Newspaper (*As-Siyasah*)," Cairo, November 9, 1978, cited in *FBIS*, November 13, 1978, D10–27.

109. MENA, "Paper Supports As-Sadat's Jerusalem Visit," November 19, 1977, cited in *FBIS*, November 21, 1977, C1; Cairo Domestic Service, "Sultan [of Oman] Supports As-Sadat's Visit to Israel," November 19, 1977, cited in *FBIS*, November 21, 1977, C1.

110. SNA, "Cabinet: Camp David not 'Final, Acceptable Formula for Peace,'" Riyadh, September 19, 1978, cited in *FBIS*, September 20. 1978, C3. Also see Iraq News Agency (hereafter INA), "Arab Foreign Minister Deliver Speeches at Conference," Baghdad, October 31, 1978, cited in *FBIS*, October 31, 1978, A3.

111. Safran, *Saudi Arabia*, p. 259.

112. Qatar News Agency (hereafter QNA), "Qatar Cabinet Statement on Camp David," and Gulf News Agency, "Bahrain Cabinet Statement on Camp David," September 20, 1978, cited in *Summary of World Broadcasts*, ME/5923/A/1–2, September 22, 1978.

113. Amman Domestic Service, "Amman Radio Comments on As-Sadat's Visit to Israel," November 25, 1977, cited in *FBIS*, November 28, 1977, F1–3. Also see Amman Domestic Service, "King Husayn Addresses Nation On As-Sadat Initiative," November 28, 1977, cited in *FBIS*, November 29, 1977, F1–3; Amman Television Service, "Jordan Reaction to Camp David Agreements," September 19, 1978, cited in *Summary of World Broadcasts*, ME/5922/A/6–8, September 21, 1978; Amman Television Service, "King Husayn's 10th October Speech," October 10, 1978, cited in *Summary of World Broadcasts*, ME/5940/A/6–10, October 12, 1978.

114. Heikal, *Secret Channels*, p. 259.

115. Baghdad Domestic Service, "Baghdad Commentary Assails As-Sadat's Speech," November 26, 1977, cited in *FBIS*, November 28, 1977, E23.

116. For the text of the Tripoli Declaration, see *Arab Report and Record* (December 1977): 1011.

117. Amman Domestic Service, "*Al-Dustur* Comments on As-Sadat's Visit to Israel," November 18, 1977, cited in *FBIS*, November 18, 1977, F2; Damascus Domestic Service, "As-Sadat's Trip to Israel Strongly Denounced," November 17, 1977, cited in *FBIS*, November 18, 1977, H1; SNA, "Royal Court Surprised by As-Sadat Initiative," Riyadh, November 18, 1977, cited in *FBIS*, November 21, 1977, C1–2; INA, "*Al-Jumhuriyah* Urges Overthrow," Baghdad, November 21, 1977, cited in *FBIS*, November 21, 1977, E6; Algiers Domestic Service, "Council of Ministers Condemns As-Sadat Trip," November 20, 1977, cited in *FBIS*, November 21, 1977, I1–2.

118. Damascus Domestic Service, "*Ath-thawrah* Outlines Secret Aims of Camp David Meeting," September 8, 1978, cited in *FBIS*, September 8, 1978, H1; "Reaction to Outcome of Camp David Conference," various news agencies, September 18, 1978, cited in *FBIS*, September 19, 1978, H1–2; Damascus Home Service, "Syrian Comment on Camp David Agreements," September 18, 197, cited in *Summary of World Broadcasts*, ME/5921/A/15, September 20, 1978; INA, "PLO Statement on Camp David Accords," and "Iraqi Statement on Camp David Accords," September 19, 1978, cited in *Summary of World Broadcasts*, ME/5922/A/1–3, September 21, 1978.

119. INA, "*Ath-Thawrah* Questions Syrian Stand Toward As-Sadat," Baghdad, November 23, 1977, cited in *FBIS*, November 23, 1977, E1. Also see "Iraqi Decisions in Response to Camp David," Baghdad Voice of the Masses, October 1, 1978, cited in *Summary of World Broadcasts*, ME/5932/A/5–7, October 3, 1978.

120. "Steadfastness Front Conference Opens in Damascus," *FBIS*, September 21, 1978, A1–3; SANA, "Final Statement, Proclamation," Damascus, September 25, 1978, A4–12. At the Baghdad summit Jordan circulated a working paper that called for a unified military command and more resources to the frontline states. Amman Home Service, "The Jordanian Working Paper," October 31, 1978, cited in *Summary of World Broadcasts*, ME/5958/A/9–10, November 2, 1978. See Joseph Meyer, "Introduction: The Steadfastness Group," *Middle East Review* 27, no. 1 (Fall 1984): 3–4, for a brief review of the group.

121. INA, "Text of Speech by President Ahmad Hasan al-Bakr of Iraq," Baghdad, November 2, 1978, cited in *Summary of World Broadcasts*, ME/5960/A/5–7, November 4, 1978.

122. Damascus Domestic Service, "Syrian Foreign Minister's Speech," October 30, 1978, cited in *FBIS*, October 31, 1978, A5; Damascus Domestic Service, "Syrian Draft Resolution," " October 31, 1978, cited in *FBIS*, November 1, 1978, A7–8. The "Arab People's Court" in Tripoli found Sadat a traitor against the Arab people for signing the "Stable David" accords. (JANA, "Arab People's Court Hears Case Against Sadat," Tripoli, October 29, 1978, cited in *FBIS*, October 31, 1978, I1. Also see Damascus Home Service, "Statement at End of Arab People's Conference," November 27, 1978, cited in *Summary of World Broadcasts*, ME/5982/A/2, November 30, 1978. Those who advocated punishing Egypt, however, also stated that they did not want to punish the Egyptian people who remained part of the Arab nation and who were led by a government that did not reflect its preferences. See Damascus Domestic Service, "Damascus Radio Demands Expelling Egypt from Arab League," October 14, 1978, cited in *FBIS*, October 17, 1978, H2–3; INA, "Saddam Husayn Press Conference on International Affairs," Baghdad, October 19, 1978, cited in *FBIS*, October 20, 1978, E1.

123. Safran, *Saudi Arabia*, p. 261.

124. Riyadh Domestic Service, "Saudi Minister's Speech," October 31, 1978, cited in *FBIS*, November 1, 1978, A1–3. Also see Cairo Domestic Service, "*Al-Akhbar* Comments on Baghdad Summit," October 30, 1978, cited in *FBIS*, October 20, 1978, D12; Riyadh Domestic Service, "Foreign Minister Comments on Baghdad Conference," October 28, 1978, cited in *FBIS*, October 30, 1978, C1.

125. Kuwait Domestic Service, "Foreign Minister on Egypt's Position, Baghdad Conference," October 30, 1978, cited in *FBIS*, October 31, 1978, C1; Gulf News Agency, "The Kuwait Working Paper," October 31, 1978, cited in *Summary of World Broadcasts*, ME/5958/A/10–11, November 2, 1978; Rabat Domestic Service, "Gulf States Oppose Action," November 4, 1978, cited in *FBIS*, November 6, 1978, A5; "Anti-Egyptian Measures Disclosed," *Ar'Ra'y*, Amman, November 6, 1978, p. 12, cited in *FBIS*, November 6, 1978, A19–20.

126. INA, "Arab Foreign Ministers Deliver Speeches at Conference," Baghdad, October 31, 1978, cited in *FBIS*, October 31, 1978, A4; QNA, "Foreign Ministry Spokesman on Egyptian-Israeli Treaty," Doha, March 27, 1979, cited in *FBIS*, March 28, 1979, C2.

127. Safran, *Saudi Arabia*, p. 262. On p. 309, Safran concludes that severing the connection with Egypt was palatable because its interests were already satisfied.

128. Anonymous source, interview by author, Amman, Jordan, September 5, 1996.

129. In the midst of this unrestrained acrimony was an unexpected stab at unification. Immediately before the Baghdad summit on October 26, 1978, Iraq and Syria announced that they had concluded a unity agreement. Declaring their intent to affirm a "qualitative change in their relations," they portrayed this agreement as a reaction to Camp David and a long overdue fulfillment of the desire for unity between the two Ba'athist regimes. INA, "The Iraqi-Syrian Charter Signed on 26th October," October 26, 1978, cited in *Summary of World Broadcasts*, ME/5954/A/1–3, October 28, 1978. A unity agreement, particularly one that had little prospect of success, was probably not the best antidote to Sadat's actions, but Iraq and Syria reached back into the past and Ba'athist ideology and pulled out a unification agreement. Although Iraq and Syria claimed that Camp David drove them to it, more likely causes were domestic forces and the imperative of regime survival. Malik Mufti, *Sovereign Creations: Pan-Arabism and Political Order in Syria and Iraq* (Ithaca, N.Y.: Cornell University Press, 1996), pp. 209–20; Eberhard Kienle, *Ba'ath Versus Ba'ath: The Conflict Between Syria and Iraq, 1968–89* (London: I. B. Taurus, 1990), chap. 4. The unity agreement disappeared with the night, replaced by the tried-and-true hostility and rivalry. Few cheered its birth and even fewer lamented or noticed its predictable demise.

130. INA, "Communique on Arab Summit Conference in Baghdad," Baghdad, November 5, 1978, cited in *Summary of World Broadcasts*, ME/5962/A/4–6, November 7, 1978. For Cairo's response see Cairo Home Service, "10 November Cairo Press on Baghdad Summit Conference," cited in *Summary of World Broadcasts*, ME/5966/A/3–5, November 12, 1978; "Cairo Press Critical of Baghdad Summit," *FBIS*, November 2, 1978, D1–5; Cairo Domestic Service, "Cairo Comments on Baghdad Summit Conference," November 6, 1978, cited in *FBIS*, November 7, 1978, D1–3.

131. The Kuwaiti paper *Ar-Ra'y al-'Amm* struck a puzzled face when it wrote that Sadat's flight to Jerusalem "is an odd situation. What is even more odd is that we are no longer afraid of causing an affront to the nation, violating its dignity and stabbing it in the heart with words and deeds and punishment for which until recently was execution and stoning." "Paper Criticizes As-Sadat Peace Initiative," *Ar-Ra'y al-'Amm* (Kuwait), November 12, 1977, p. 1, cited in *FBIS*, November 17, 1977, C1.

132. Also see Safran, *Saudi Arabia*, p. 311.

133. "Egyptian Anti-Arab Campaign: Pretext to Justify Separate Accords," *Ar-Ra'y al-'Amm* November 16, 1978, pp. 1, 19, cited in *FBIS*, November 21, 1978, C1.

134. Kuwait Domestic Service, "Cabinet Issues Statement on Camp David Results," September 20, 1978, cited from *FBIS*, September 20, 1978, C1; QNA, "*Al-Arab* Calls for Rejecting Camp David Results," Doha, September 19, 1978, cited in *FBIS*, September 20, 1978, C2–3; Emirates News Agency, "UAE: Statement Issued Rejecting Camp David Agreements," Abu Dhabi, September 21, 1978, cited in *FBIS*, September 22, 1978, C4.

135. Damascus Domestic Service, "Syrian Withdrawal," March 28, 1979, cited in *FBIS*, March 29, 1979, A6; "Khaddam Calls for Overthrow of Sadat," *Ash-Sharq al-Awsat*, London, March 24, 1979, cited in *FBIS*, March 27, 1979, H1–3; SANA, "Syrian Papers Call for Overthrow of Sadat," Damascus, May 31, 1978, cited in *Summary of World Broadcasts*, ME/6131/A/1, June 2, 1979.

136. Safran, *Saudi Arabia*, p. 230.

137. INA, "Arab Ministers Baghdad Meeting Resolution," Baghdad, March 31, 1979, cited in *Summary of World Broadcasts*, April 2, 1979, ME/6802/A/6–12.

138. Ali Hillal Dessouki, "Egyptian Foreign Policy Since Camp David," in Quandt, *Middle East*, p. 103; "Egyptian Reaction to Baghdad Meeting Resolutions," *Summary of World Broadcasts*, ME/6083/A/1–3, April 3, 1979; MENA, "2nd April Egyptian Statement on Baghdad Resolutions," Cairo, April 2, 1979, cited in *Summary of World Broadcasts*, ME/6084/A/4, April 4, 1979.

139. Cairo Radio, "Sadat's 5th April Address to Egyptian People's Assembly," April 5, 1979, cited in *Summary of World Broadcasts*, ME/6087/A/1–22, April 7, 1979; Cairo Radio, "Sadat's 11th April Address to the Nation," April 11, 1979, cited in *Summary of World Broadcasts*, ME/6092/A/3–10, April 13, 1979. Sadat also looked to the ulemas (religious authorities) to approve this peace treaty between a Muslim and non-Muslim nation (MENA, "Egypt: Al-Azhar Islamic Authorities on the Peace Treaty," May 9, 1979, cited in *Summary of World Broadcasts*, ME/6114/A/1–2, May 12, 1979).

140. Fahmy, *Negotiating for Peace*; Boutros-Ghali, *Egypt's Road to Jerusalem*.

141. Heikal, *Secret Channels*, p. 349.

142. Anonymous source, interview by author in Amman, September 5, 1996. Also see Muhammad Salih Ata Zahra, "National Security and Joint Arab Activity," *Al-Mustqbal al-Arabi*, no. 94 (December 1986): 16–35.

143. Heikal, *Autumn of Fury*, p. 72.

144. Isam Ni'man, "Peace Between the Arabs," *Al-Watan al-Arabi* 7, no. 333 (July 1, 1983): 36–37 (in Arabic); Mohammed Anis Salim, "Arab Schisms in the 1980s: Old Story or New Order?" *World Today* 38, no. 5 (May 1982): 175–84, and "The Future of Inter-Arab Relations," *Al-Mustqbal al-Arabi* 11, no. 115 (September 1988): pp. 126–54 (in Arabic); Muhammad Fadil al-Jamali, "Frank Words on the Crisis of Arab Unity Today," *Al-Mustqbal al-Arabi* 10, no. 109 (1988): 114–17 (in Arabic).

145. Ghassan Salame, "Inter-Arab Politics: The Return to Geography," in Quandt, *Middle East*, pp. 319–56; Ghassan Salame, "Integration in the Arab World: The Institutional Framework," in G. Luciani and G. Salame, eds., *The Politics of Arab Integration*, pp. 256–79 (New York: Croom Helm, 1988); George Joffe, "Middle Eastern Views of the Gulf Conflict and Its Aftermath," *Review of International Studies* 19 (April 1993): 177–99; Bassam Tibi, "The Simultaneity of the Unsimultaneous: Old Tribes and Imposed Nation-States in the Modern Middle East," in P. Khoury and J. Kostiner, eds., *Tribes and State Formation in the Middle East*, pp. 127–52 (London: I. B. Taurus, 1991).

146. Indeed, Saddam Hussein, who became president of Iraq in July 1979, tried to capitalize on Iraq's new leadership position by issuing in February 1980 an "Arab Na-

tional Charter," calling on other Arab states to join Iraq in a framework of security and economic cooperation. Although Hussein received a hearing from the other Arab states, they showed little interest in another pan-Arab security and economic institution.

147. Michael Barnett, "Identity and Alliances in the Middle East," in P. Katzenstein, ed., *The Culture of National Security: Norms and Identity in World Politics*, pp. 400–47 (New York: Columbia University Press, 1996).

148. "King Fahd on the GCC," *Ar-Ra'y al-'Amm*, November 19, 1984, cited in *FBIS*, 234, December 4, 1984, C3.

149. Tawfiq Abu Bakr, "The Flourishing of Arab Regionalism: Between Truth and Exaggeration," *Al-Arabi*, September 1984, pp. 61–63 (in Arabic).

150. Rabat Domestic Service, "King Hassan Announces Arab Summit for 7 August," July 27, 1985, cited in *FBIS*, July 29, 1985, A6–7.

151. Cairo Domestic Service, "Abd al-Majid on Coordination," May 22, 1989, cited in *FBIS*, May 23, 1989, p. 6. Also see Amman Domestic Service, " 'Text' of King Husayn's 24 May Summit Speech," May 25, 1989, cited in *FBIS*, May 26, 1989, pp. 7–8.

152. Rabat Television Service, "King Hassan Speaks," May 23, 1989, cited in *FBIS*, May 24, 1989, p. 10–11.

153. Amman Domestic Service, "Foreign Ministers Conference," November 20, 1980, cited in *FBIS*, November 21, 1980, A3–4.

154. Amman Domestic Service, "Text of King Husayn's Opening Address to Arab Summit," November 25, 1980, cited in *FBIS*, November 26, 1980, A1–8. The Egyptian newspaper *Al-Ahram* added that "King Husayn's portrayal of Arab disintegration inside the summit conference of Arab unity was clearer than any evidence." Cairo Domestic Service, "*Al-Ahram* Says Arab Summit Ended in Failure," November 28, 1980, cited in *FBIS*, December 4, 1980, D17.

155. Damascus Domestic Service, "Khaddam Address," November 21, 1980, cited in *FBIS*, November 24, 1980, A2. Also see Nihad al-Mashnuq, "Arab Wars Against Arabs," *Al-Nahar al-Arabi wal-Duwali*, March 15, 1982, pp. 6–7 (in Arabic).

156. Damascus Domestic Service, "King Husayn Speech, Summit Results Attacked," November 27, 1980, cited in *FBIS*, November 28, 1980, H1; Jerusalem Radio, "Syrian-Jordanian Relations," December 2, 1980, cited in *FBIS*, December 3, 1980, I1; Damascus Domestic Service, "Press Expresses Hope Jordan Has Learned 'Lesson,'" December 5, 1980, cited in *FBIS*, December 5, 1980, H1; Damascus Domestic Service, "Al-Asad Interviewed by Kuwaiti Newspaper," December 6, 1980, cited in *FBIS*, December 8, 1980, H1–4.

157. "Ghali Calls Amman Summit 'Camouflage' for Disarray," *Le Figaro*, Paris, November 26, 1980, p. 3, cited in *FBIS*, December 1, 1980, D1.

158. SPA, "Saudi Source on Postponement," Riyadh, November 26, 1981, cited in *FBIS*, November 27, 1981, A7; Amman Domestic Service, "Papers Regret Postponement of Arab Summit," November 26, 1981, cited in *FBIS*, November 27, 1981, F1–3; Damascus Domestic Service, "Radio Comments on Summit's Polarizing Impact,"

November 25, 1981, cited in *FBIS*, November 27, 1981, H1–2; MENA, "Mubarak October Interview on Fes, Arab Unity," Cairo, December 5, 1981, cited in *FBIS*, December 7, 1981, D1–2; Agence France-Presse, "Ghali: Summit Collapse Shows Arab Policy Fails," Paris, November 26, 1981, cited in *FBIS*, November 27, 1981, D1. Also see "Summit Failure Due to Conflicting Fronts," *Al-Ahram,* November 30, 1981, cited in *FBIS*, December 3, 1981, D1–2.

159. On the influence of Lebanon see Nadir Farjani, "On the Threshold of a New Era for Arab Ideological Activity," *Al-Mustqbal al-Arabi* 5, no. 48 (February 1983): 120–24 (in Arabic); Corm, *Fragmentation of the Middle East*, p. 204; Dessouki, "Egyptian Foreign Policy Since Camp David," p. 9.

160. Rabat Domestic Service, "King Hassan Announces Arab Summit for 7 August," July 27, 1985, cited in *FBIS*, July 29, 1985, A1.

161. Rabat Domestic Service, "King Hassan's Opening Address," August 7, 1985, *FBIS*, August 8, 1985, A1–2.

162. Amman Domestic Service, "Jordan King Husayn's Speech," August 7, 1985, cited in *FBIS*, August 8, 1985, A5. Also see Atif al-Ghamri, "The Extraordinary Summit Preferred Not to Confront Provocative Problems," Cairo Domestic Service, August 10, 1985, cited in *FBIS*, August 13, 1985, D2.

163. Malik Mufti, "A Brave New Subsystem: Inter-Arab Conflict and the End of the Cold War," unpublished 1997 manuscript, Tufts University, Boston.

164. Ibid., p. 28.

165. See, for instance, INA, "Iraq's Ramadan Addresses Summit," Baghdad, August 9, 1985, cited in *FBIS*, August 12, 1985, A3.

166. Taher al-Masri, interview by author, Amman, September 2, 1995.

167. Also see Gabriel Ben-Dor, "Jordan and Inter-Arab Relations," in Nevo and Pappe, *Jordan in the Middle East* p. 200.

168. Masri interview.

169. Amman Domestic Service, "Text of King Husayn's 24 May Summit Speech," May 25, 1989, cited in *FBIS*, May 26, 1989, pp. 7–10.

170. Ibid.

171. Rabat Television Network, "Mubarak Addresses Meeting," May 23, 1989, cited in *FBIS*, May 24, 1989, p. 11.

172. Makrom Muhammad Ahmad, "Chief Editor Views Egypt's Arab Role," *Al-Musawwar*, Cairo, May 19, 1989, pp. 4–6, cited in *FBIS*, May 24, 1989, pp. 20–23.

7. The End of the Arab States System? Arab Politics Since the Gulf War

1. Cairo Domestic Service, "Mubarak Gives News Conference 8 August," August 8, 1990, cited in *Foreign Broadcast Information Service—Near East and South Asia* (hereafter *FBIS-NES*)-90–153, August 10, 1990, p. 8.

2. Anonymous source, interview by author, Amman, Jordan, September 5, 1996.

3. For reviews of the Gulf War see Lawrence Freedman and Ephraim Karsh, *The Gulf War, 1990–91* (Princeton, N.J.: Princeton University Press, 1993); Dilip Hiro, *From Desert Shield to Desert Storm: The Second Gulf War* (New York: Routledge, 1992).

4. Iraq News Agency (hereafter INA), "Arab Power for Regional Peace," Baghdad, June 3, 1990, cited in *FBIS*, June 5, 1990, p. 16.

5. See Mohamed Heikal, *Illusions of Triumph: An Arab View of the Gulf War* (London: Fontana, 1993), for a detailed account of this period and the emerging crisis in Iraqi-Kuwaiti relations.

6. See Freedman and Karsh, *Gulf War*, for an excellent overview of the war. See Stanley Reshnon, ed., *The Political Psychology of the Gulf War: Leaders, Publics, and the Process of Conflict* (Pittsburgh, Pa.: University of Pittsburgh Press, 1993), for various statements on features of the crisis.

7. "The Arabs' Blackest Day," *Al-Ahram*, August 3, 1990, p. 1, cited in "Papers Regret Iraqi Invasion, Urge Swift Action," *FBIS-NES-90–150*, August 3, 1990, p. 10.

8. On August 3 the Arab League Ministerial Council condemned the invasion, demanded Iraq's unconditional withdrawal, and reminded all its members that the Arab League Charter is premised on sovereignty. Fourteen countries endorsed the resolution, whereas Yemen, Jordan, the PLO, Iraq, Sudan, and Mauritania abstained or voted against it. Middle East News Agency [hereafter MENA], August 3, 1990, cited in "MENA Carries Text," *FBIS-NES-90–151*, August 10, 1990, p. 1.

9. See Heikal, *Illusions of Triumph*, for a detailed account of the confusion and tensions behind the summit meeting.

10. Cairo Domestic Service, "Mubarak Gives News Conference August 8," August 8, 1990, cited in *FBIS-NES-90–153*, August 10, 1990, p. 8, 9.

11. Also see Heikal, *Illusions of Triumph*, p. 281.

12. Ibrahim Nafi, "It Is Not with Soldiers' Boots That We Determine the Future of Nations," *Al-Ahram*, August 4, 1990, pp. 1, 5, cited in *FBIS-NES-90–155*, August 10, 1990, pp. 10–12. Also see MENA, "Statement by Qatari Cabinet," August 8, 1990, cited in *FBIS-NES-90–154*, August 9, 1990, p. 20; Cairo Domestic Service, "A Positive Arab Move Is Imperative," August 4, 1990, cited in *FBIS-NES-90–151*, August 6, 1990, p. 19.

13. MENA, "Closed Summit Discussions Held 11 August," August 11, 1990, cited in *FBIS-NES-90–156*, August 13, 1990, p. 8.

14. MENA, "MENA Reports Arab Summit Resolutions 10 August," August 10, 1990, cited in *FBIS-NES-90–156*, August 13, 1990, pp. 1–2.

15. Cairo Domestic Service, "Mubarak Opens Arab Summit, Gives Speech," August 10, 1990, cited in *FBIS-NES-90–156*, August 13, 1990, pp. 2–4.

16. Sanaa Voice of Palestine, "PLO Leadership Issues Statement on Gulf," August 20, 1990, cited in *FBIS-NES-90–162*, August 21, 1990, pp. 2–3. The majority of the conference participants agreed that Arab countries should not give a "blanket approval or act as an umbrella for foreign intervention in the region." Ibrahim Nafi, "The Fruits of the Arab Summit," *Al-Ahram*, August 12, 1990, cited in *FBIS-NES-90–156*, August 13, 1990, p. 10.

17. Marc Lynch, *Contested Identity and Security: The International Politics of Jordanian Identity* (New York: Columbia University Press, forthcoming); Adam Garfinkle, "The Nine Lives of Hashemite Jordan," in R. Satloff, ed., *The Politics of Change in the Middle East* (Boulder, Colo.: Westview, 1993), pp. 99–100.

18. In *Illusion of Triumph* Heikal paints a Saudi Arabia that was quite fearful of allowing Western troops on its soil for fear of being stained by imperialism but equally hesitant to permit Arab troops on its soil for fear that the costs would prove tremendous.

19. Khaled Bin Sultan, *Desert Warrior: A Personal View of the Gulf War by the Joint Forces Commander* (New York: HarperCollins, 1995), p. 172; Shibley Telhami, "Arab Public Opinion and the Gulf War," in Reshnon, *Political Psychology of the Gulf War*, pp. 183–97.

20. Freedman and Karsh, *Gulf War*, p. 69; Heikal, *Illusions of Triumph*, p. 8. See, for instance, Bahgdad Domestic Service, "Saddam Calls Arabs, Muslims to Save Mecca," August 10, 1990, cited in *FBIS-NES-90–156*, August 13, 1990, pp. 45–46. One of the more stinging criticisms leveled at Saddam Hussein by other Arab leaders was that his invasion of Kuwait had set back the cause of Palestine—that it represented an unexpected gift to Israel and had divided and weakened the Arab world. Saddam Hussein responded to these charges with his notion of linkage, that is, exchanging his withdrawal for an Israeli withdrawal. Freedman and Karsh, *Gulf War*, p. 100.

21. Telhami, "Arab Public Opinion"; Dale Eickelman and James Piscatori, *Muslim Politics* (Princeton, N.J.: Princeton University Press, 1996), pp. 13–15; Emile Nakleh, "Regime Stability and Change in the Gulf: The Case of Saudi Arabia," in Satloff, *Politics of Change in the Middle East*, p. 119; James Piscatori, "Religion and Realpolitik: Islamic Responses to the Gulf War," in J. Piscatori, ed., *Islamic Fundamentalisms and the Gulf Crisis* (Chicago: American Academy of Arts and Sciences, 1991), pp. 3–18. Controversy has been considerable over how to interpret the so-called Arab street and whether the reaction was in support of Saddam Hussein or whether he became a vehicle for expressing long-standing grievances against the oil-wealthy Kuwaitis, the Arab states, and the West. In the *Illusions of Triumph*, pp. 286–87, 304, Heikal convincingly argues how the invasion of Kuwait and the subsequent Western intervention were opposed by those "in the street," but the latter raised greater anxieties and fears.

22. Cairo Domestic Service, August 11, 1990, cited in "Commentary Views Saddam Husayn Call for Jihad," *FBIS-NES-90–158*, August 15, 1990, p. 10; Damascus Domestic Service, August 15, 1990, cited in "Commentary Compares Iraqi, Israeli Withdrawals," *FBIS-NES-90–158*, August 15, 1990, p. 44. For a survey of the ideological contestation over the Gulf War see Eli Podeh, "In the Service of Power: The Ideological Struggle in the Arab world During the Gulf Crisis," *Conflict Quarterly* (Fall 1994): 7–25.

23. Telhami, "Arab Public Opinion."

24. King Fahd, interview by MBC Television, London, November 14, 1991, cited in *FBIS-NES-91–223*, November 19, 1991, p. 15.

25. Fahd al-Fanek, interview by author, Amman, September 1, 1995.

26. "President on Prospects for Arab Unity," *Al-Hayat*, cited in *FBIS-NES-84–054*, March 21, 1994, p. 25.

27. "League Chief Expects Arab Summit 'Next February,'" *Al-Sharq al-Awsat*, January 1, 1995, cited in *FBIS-NES-95–002*, January 4, 1995, pp. 7–8.

28. Also see Ibrahim Karawan, "Arab Dilemmas in the 1990s: Breaking Taboos and Searching for Signposts," *Middle East Journal* 48, no. 3 (Summer 1994): 433–54; Muhammad Faour, *The Arab World After Desert Storm* (Washington, D.C.: United States Institute of Peace Press, 1993), chaps. 4 and 5; Bernard Lewis, "Rethinking the Middle East," *Foreign Affairs* 71, no. 4 (Fall 1992): 99–119.

29. William Quandt, *Peace Process: American Diplomacy and the Arab-Israeli Conflict Since 1967* (Berkeley: University of California Press, 1993), p. 396.

30. Adnan Abu Odeh, interview by author, Washington, D.C., April 2, 1996.

31. "Faysal al-Husaini on Significance of Madrid," *La Republica*, Rome, p. 16, November 7, 1991, cited in *FBIS-NES-91–219*, November 13, 1991, p. 1. Many in the Arab world who opposed the Madrid talks largely viewed them as selling out the Palestinians. See, for instance, "Muslim Brotherhood Rejects 'Sell-Out' Talks," *Al-Shab*, October 22, 1991, p. 9–10, cited in *FBIS-NES-91–209*, October 29, 1991, p. 23.

32. For various statements on the multilateral talks see Steven Spiegel and David Pervin, *Arms Control and Regional Security*, vol. 1, and *The Environment, Water, Refugees, and Economic Cooperation and Development*, vol. 2, of *Practical Peacemaking in the Middle East* (New York: Garland, 1995); Bruce Jentleson, "The Middle East Arms Control and Regional Security (ARCS) Talks: Progress, Problems, and Prospects," Institute on Global Conflict and Cooperation Policy Paper, no. 26, September 1996, University of California at San Diego.

33. Algiers Voice of Palestine, "Qaddumi on Arab Coordination for Madrid Talks," October 31, 1991, cited in *FBIS-NES-91–212*, November 1, 1991, p. 37.

34. Oded Granot, "The Glue Is Beginning to Come Unstuck," *Ma'ariv*, 28 (March 1994): 2; cited in *FBIS-NES-94–062-A*, 31 March 1994, p. 3.

35. Interview with author, Cairo, March 16, 1996. Also see Yahya Sadowski, *Scuds or Butter?* (Washington, D.C.: Brookings Institution, 1992).

36. Jeffrey Alexander, "Citizen and Enemy as Symbolic Classification: On the Polarizing Discourse of Civil Society" in Michele Lamont and Marcel Fourier, eds., *Cultivating Boundaries* (Chicago: University of Chicago Press, 1992), p. 289; William Connolly, *Identity/Difference* (Ithaca, N.Y.: Cornell University Press, 1991), chap. 7.

37. Arab states also were beginning to contemplate the inclusion of Israel within a Middle East common market. See Agence France-Presse, "Impact of Israel on Middle East Common Market," *FBIS-NES-94–085*, May 3, 1994, p. 37; "Monetary Fund Official on Cooperation With Israel," *FBIS-NES-94–031*, February 12, 1994, p. 2; Sanaa Voice of Palestine, "Arab League Studies Middle East Market," *FBIS-NES-94–055*, March 22, 1994, p. 3.

38. Syrian vice president Abd al-Halim Khaddam, interview by Syrian Radio, No-

vember 14, 1995, cited in "Khaddam on al-Asad, Peace Process, Amman Summit," *FBIS-NES-95–220*, November 15, 1995, p. 61. For an expanded discussion of the change in Syria's Israel policy see Moshe Maoz, *Syria and Israel: From War to Peacemaking* (Oxford, England: Clarendon, 1995), chaps. 10 and 11.

39. "Text of King Husayn *Al-Ahram* Interview," *Al-Dustur*, Amman, February 19, 1995, p. 28, cited in *FBIS-NES-95–034*, February 21, 1995, p. 62.

40. Various interviews by author in Amman, August 30–September 10, 1995; "Opposition Figures, Parties Cited on Treaty," *Shihan*, October 22–28, 1994, cited in *FBIS-NES-94–206*, October 27, 1994, p. 30; "Opponents of Peace Accord Escalate Verbal Attacks," *Jordan Times*, October 26, 1994, cited in *FBIS-NES-94–208*, October 27, 1994, p. 32. Also see Lynch, *Contested Identity and Security*.

41. Interview of Crown Prince Hassan by Oded Granot, *Maariv*, October 27, 1995, p. 2, cited in *FBIS-NES-95–211*, November 1, 1995, pp. 70–71.

42. Fahmy interview.

43. See, for instance, Amos Elon, "The Thinking Men's War," *New York Times Magazine*, May 11, 1997, pp. 40–43.

44. Syrian Radio, "Calls for New Middle East, Normalization Criticized," February 23, 1995, cited in *FBIS-NES-95–036*, February 23, 1995, pp. 61–62. According to the secretary-general of the Arab League, a Middle Eastern market is possible only after "a comprehensive and just peace." MENA, "Arab League Chief on Regional Issues," April 14, 1995, cited in *FBIS-NES-95–073*, April 17, 1995, p. 1.

45. Prime Minister Rafia al-Hariri, "Al-Hariri on 'Race' for Normalization with Israel," Radio Free Lebanon, November 15, 1994, cited in Radio Free Lebanon, "Al-Hariri on 'Race' for Normalization with Israel," *FBIS-NES-94–220*, November 15, 1994, p. 43. Also see "Arabs Cautioned Against Rush to Normalize," *Al-Quds al-Arabi*, Jerusalem, December 29, 1994, p. 13, cited in *FBIS-NES-95–002*, January 4, 1995, p. 19.

46. *Rose al-Yusuf*, October 23, 1995, p. 10, cited in "Minister: No Regional Cooperation with Israel Before Peace," *FBIS-NES-95–207*, October 26, 1995, p. 63.

47. Damascus Syrian Arab Republic Radio, "Interview with *Tishrin*," November 14, 1995, cited in "Khaddam on al-Asad, Peace Process, Amman Summit," *FBIS-NES-95–220*, November 15, 1995, p. 61.

48. Abd-al-Bari Atwan, "Israel and Joining the League," *Al-Quds al-Arabi*, December 23, 1994, cited in *FBIS-NES*, December 30, 1994, p. 3.

49. Dooa el-Bey, "Mapping the Future," *Al-Ahram Weekly*, November 10–16, 1994, p. 1. Also see Saad Eddin Ibrahim, "Future Visions of the Arab Middle East," *Security Dialogue* 27, no. 4 (1996): 425–36, and the discussions that occurred at the conference sponsored by the Arab Thought Forum in Doha, Qatar, April 19–20, 1995, as described by Ali Oumlil, "Four Questions," *Arab Thought Forum* 2, no. 2 (1995): 1–5.

50. For the text of the Damascus Declaration see MENA, "Final Version of Damascus Declaration," *FBIS-NES-91–152*, August 7, 1991, pp. 1–2.

51. MENA, "Idea of Arab Force Deployed in Gulf Abandoned," November 13, 1991, cited in *FBIS-NES-91–220*, November 14, 1991, p. 1. As noted in Egypt's *Al-Ahram*, "We

have to acknowledge the apprehensions of the people in the Gulf, or at least some of them, who fear an *Arab* presence in the Gulf, because the past is not very encouraging." Ihsan Bakr, " 'Sensitivity' with Damascus Declaration Viewed," *Al-Ahram*, June 7, 1992, p. 9, cited in *FBIS-NES-92–114*, June 12, 1992, pp. 9–10. The secretary-general of the Arab League nearly pronounced the last rites for the Arab Collective Security Pact: "At the same time it must be clear that the concept of security is the biggest responsibility of each individual state. Each state determines the needs and boundaries of its security on its own, because this concerns its people and its future. We should basically assume that there should be no interference in any country's security. We must acknowledge and proceed from this basic principle," *FBIS-NES-92–232*, December 2, 1992, pp. 1–2. See also the Memorandum of Understanding signed between the Arab League and the GCC, cited in *FBIS-NES-92–034*, February 20, 1992, p. 3.

52. Zakariya Nil, "The Abu Dhabi Gulf Summit Face to Face with Most Important Topics of the House," *Al-Ahram*, December 12, 1992, cited in *FBIS-NES-92–241*, December 15, 1992, p. 10–11.

53. Abu Odeh interview.

54. Anwar-Ul-Haq Ahady, "Security in the Persian Gulf After Desert Storm," *International Journal* 49 (Spring 1994): 219–40.

55. The dynamics also led to a wide-ranging debate about the boundaries of the region. See, for instance, "Arafat Suggests Formation of Mideast 'Regional Order,' " *Al-Nahar*, February 14, 1994, cited in *FBIS-NES-94-030*, February 14, 1994.

56. Baghat Korany, "National Security in the Arab World: The Persistence of Dualism," in D. Tschirgi, ed., *The Arab World Today* (Boulder, Colo.: Westview, 1994), p. 166.

57. The preference for external security guarantees from pan-Arab states rather than the members of the Damascus Declaration became particularly visible in October 1994 when Iraqi troops amassed on the Kuwaiti border. Essentially, the GCC states could not be bothered by either Egypt or Syria and coordinated their military responses with the United States.

58. For a lengthier discussion of these developments in regional security, see Michael Barnett, "Regional Security After the Gulf War," *Political Science Quarterly* 111, no. 4 (Winter 1996–97): 597–618.

59. Correspondingly, whereas most regional symposiums before the Gulf War stressed the importance of sovereignty and political unity over democracy, since then the priority has been reversed. Nakleh, "Regime Stability and Change," pp. 133–34.

60. Fahmy interview.

61. Lotfi el-Khuli, interview by author, Cairo, March 18, 1996.

62. Nassaf Hitti, interview by author, Cairo, March 19, 1996.

63. Ibrahim Nafi, "Article Examines Future of Arab League," *Al-Ahram al-Duwali*, January 27, 1995, p. 5, cited in *FBIS-NES-95–052*, March 17, 1995, p. 5.

64. "Minister Expects Disturbances in the Region," *Al-Muharrir*, November 6, 1995, p. 6, cited in *FBIS-NES-95–215*, November 7, 1995, p. 50.

65. Shimon Peres, *The New Middle East* (New York: Holt, 1993).

66. Amos Elon, "Crumbling Cairo," *New York Review of Books*, April 6, 1996, pp. 32–36; Mohammed Sid-Ahmed, "The Arab League and the Arab State," *Al-Ahram Weekly*, April 6–12, 1995, p. 8.

67. See the comments by Ghayth Aramanzi, head of the Arab League's London office, at the conference on the New Middle East at London University's School of Oriental and African Studies on December 19–20, 1994. Reported in *FBIS-NES-95–022*, February 7, 1995, p. 7. Other league officials discounted such fears, saying that such talk revealed not an actual threat posed by Israel but rather a lack of confidence in the abilities of the Arab states. "League Plays Down Fears of Israeli Economic Domination," Dubai, January 9, 1995, cited in *FBIS-NES-95–005*, January 9, 1995, p. 4.

68. Anonymous source, interview by author, Amman, September 5, 1996.

69. Sid-Ahmed, "Arab League and the Arab State."

70. Mohammed Sid-Ahmed, "When Israelis Speak Arabic," *Al-Ahram Weekly*, March 30–April 5, 1995, p. 8.

71. "Peres Sees Membership in Arab League as Next Goal," *Ha'aratz*, December 21, 1994, pp. A1, 10, cited in *FBIS-NES-94–246*, December 22, 1994, p. 18; "Israel and Joining the Arab League," *Al-Quds al-Arabi,* December 23, 1994, p. 1, cited in "Israeli Request to Join League Shows Arab 'Humiliation,'" *FBIS-NES-94–251*, December 30, 1994, p. 2–3. Abdel al-Majid also was reported to have said that "Israel's joining the Arab League is not serious and belongs in the wastebasket." MENA, "Abdel al-Majid: No Place for Israel in Arab League," January 25, 1995, cited in *FBIS-NES-95–017*, January 26, 1995, p. 2.

72. Muhammed Bassouni, interview by author, Tel Aviv, August 24, 1995.

73. Hitti interview. Also see Egyptian Radio, "League Chief Speaks on the 50th Anniversary of the Arab League," March 22, 1995, cited in *FBIS-NES-95–056*, March 23, 1995, p. 1; "Article Examines Future of Arab League," *Al-Ahram al-Duwali*, January 27, 1995, p. 5, cited in *FBIS-NES-95–052*, March 17, 1995, p. 5.

74. Egyptian Radio, "Egyptian President Mubarak Gives Speech," March 22, 1995, cited in *FBIS-NES-95–056*, March 23, 1995, pp. 2–6.

75. Percy Cohen, *Modern Social Theory* (New York: Basic Books, 1968), p. 131.

76. Paul Noble, Rex Brynen, and Baghat Korany, "Conclusion: The Changing Regional Security Environment," in B. Korany, P. Noble, and R. Brynen, eds., *The Many Faces of National Security in the Arab World* (New York: St. Martin's, 1993), p. 281.

77. Egyptian Radio, "Egyptian President Mubarak Gives Speech," March 22, 1995, cited in *FBIS-NES-95–056*, March 23, 1995, pp. 2–6.

78. MENA, "Arab League Chief Addresses Meeting," September 20, 1995, cited in *FBIS-NES-95–183*, September 21, 1995, p. 3.

79. As a former minister of Jordan put it, "While Arab unity has died, reasons for it still make sense. If not for emotional concepts, then out of necessity. In this regard the idea of Arab unity is similar to Europe. Small states cannot survive unless they are part of a collection of states." Interview by author, Amman, Jordan, September 5, 1996.

8. The Making and Unmaking of Arab Politics

1. On the relevant distinction between historical and analytical particularism as it pertains to the study of the Middle East, see Fred Halliday, "The Middle East in International Perspective: Problem of Analysis," in R. Bush et al., eds., *The World Order: Socialist Perspectives*, pp. 201–20 (London: Polity Press, 1987).

2. See Robert Powell, "Anarchy in International Relations Theory: The Neorealist-Neoliberal Debate," *International Organization* 48, no. 2 (Spring 1994): 337–38; Ron Jepperson, Alexander Wendt, and Peter Katzenstein, "Norms, Identity, and Culture in National Security," in P. Katzenstein, ed., *Culture of National Security: Norms and Identity in World Politics*, pp. 33–75 (New York: Columbia University Press, 1996); Emanuel Adler and Michael Barnett, "Security Communities in Theoretical Perspective," in E. Adler and M. Barnett, eds., *Security Communities* (New York: Cambridge University Press, 1998); Alexander Wendt, *Social Theory of International Politics* (New York: Cambridge University Press, forthcoming); Emanuel Adler, "Seizing the Middle Ground: Constructivism in World Politics," *European Journal of International Relations* 3, no. 3 (September 1997): 319–63; Christian Reus-Smit, "The Constitutional Structure of International Society and the Nature of Fundamental Institutions," *International Organization* 51, no. 4 (Autumn 1997): 555–90.

3. Jepperson, Wendt, and Katzenstein, "Norms, Identity, and Culture"; Martha Finnemore, *National Interests in International Society* (Ithaca, N.Y.: Cornell University Press, 1996). For general statements on the social construction of interests, see Jutta Weldes, "Constructing National Interests," *European Journal of International Relations* 2, no. 3 (1996): 275–318; William Connolly, *The Terms of Political Discourse* (Princeton, N.J.: Princeton University Press, 1983), chap. 2; Jeffrey Isaac, *Power and Marxist Theory* (Ithaca, N.Y.: Cornell University Press, 1987).

4. The expectation that the Arab governments would further the goals of the wider community, moreover, can be linked to a related function of the Arab state's foreign policy: it was designed to give its citizens the sense that they were part of, and included in, a wider community. This is consistent with Clifford Geertz's understanding that one function of the foreign policy of the postcolonial state is to connect marginalized individuals to a community. "The Integrative Revolution," in C. Geertz, *The Interpretation of Cultures* (New York: Basic Books, 1973), p. 258. For the general point about the expressive features of group participation see Randall Collins, "On the Microfoundations of Macrosociology," *American Journal of Sociology* 86, no. 5 (March 1981): 984–1014; Jonathan Turner, *A Theory of Social Interaction* (Palo Alto, Calif.: Stanford University Press, 1988), pp. 49, 52–53, 59.

5. For statements on the potentially complementary character of sociological and economic models, see Peter Blau, *Exchange and Power in Social Life* (New Brunswick, N.J.: Transaction, 1992), p. xiv; Erving Goffman, *Strategic Interaction* (Philadelphia: University of Pennsylvania Press, 1969), pp. 85–145; Randall Collins, "Conflict Theory and the Advance of Macrohistorical Sociology," in G. Ritzer, ed., *Frontiers of Social*

Theory, pp. 69–87 (New York: Columbia University Press, 1990); Michael Hechter, *Principles of Group Solidarity* (Berkeley: University of California Press, 1987), p. 185; Barry Weingast, "A Rational Choice Perspective on the Role of Ideas and Shared Beliefs: State Sovereignty and International Cooperation," *Politics and Society* 23, no. 4 (1995): 449–64; Robert Bates and Barry Weingast, "Rationality and Interpretation: The Politics of Transition," paper presented at the Midwest Political Science Association Meetings, Chicago, March 1997; James Johnson, "Symbol and Strategy in Comparative Political Analysis," *American Political Science Association–Comparative Politics Newsletter* (Summer 1997): 6–9; Donald Searing, "Roles, Rules, and Rationality in the New Institutionalism," *American Political Science Review* 85, no. 4 (December 1991): 1239–60; Martin Hollis and Steve Smith, *Explaining and Understanding International Relations* (New York: Oxford University Press, 1991), p. 167.

6. David Carr, *Time, Narrative, History* (Bloomington: Indiana University Press, 1986), p. 166; also see A. P. Cohen, T*he Symbolic Construction of Community* (New York: Tavistock, 1985).

7. Carr, *Time, Narrative, History*, p. 163.

8. Ibid., p. 167.

9. For a survey of militarized disputes see Malik Mufti, "A Brave New Subsystem: Inter-Arab Conflict and the End of the Cold War," unpublished 1997 manuscript, Tufts University, Boston.

10. Paul Noble, "The Inter-Arab System," in B. Korany and A. Dessouki, eds., *The Foreign Policies of the Arab States* (Boulder, Colo.: Westview, 1984), p. 61.

11. Also see Stephen Walt, *The Origins of Alliances* (Ithaca, N.Y.: Cornell University Press, 1987), p. 149.

12. George Simmel, *Conflict and the Web of Group Affiliations* (New York: Free Press, 1955), chap. 2; Marc Howard Ross, *Culture of Conflict* (New Haven, Conn.: Yale University Press, 1993); Ann Swidler, "Culture in Action: Symbols in Strategies," *American Sociological Review* 51, no. 2 (April 1986): 273–86.

13. For a similar claim regarding the relationship between normative structure and the means of influence, see Rodney Hall, "Moral Authority as a Power Resource," *International Organization* 51, no. 4 (Autumn 1997): 591–622.

14. For a general argument on access to the media as applied to the Middle East, see Gadi Wolsfeld, *The Media and Political Conflict: News from the Middle East* (New York: Cambridge University Press, 1997), chap. 2.

15. Samir Mutawi, "The Jordanian Response," in R. Parker, ed., *The Six-Day War: A Retrospective* (Gainesville: University Press of Florida, 1996), p. 179.

16. Michael Williams, "Hobbes and International Relations: A Reconsideration," *International Organization* 50, no. 2 (Spring 1996): 213–37.

17. E. H. Carr, *The Twenty Years' Crisis* (New York: Harper Torchbooks, 1964), pp. 132–45.

18. Blau, *Exchange and Power in Social Life*, pp. 43–50. For general statements on power and symbols see Marshall Sahlins, *Culture and Practical Reason* (Chicago: Uni-

versity of Chicago Press, 1976), chap 5; Pierre Bourdieu and Loic Wacquant, *An Invitation to Reflexive Sociology* (Chicago: University of Chicago Press, 1992), pp. 12–15.

19. Pierre Bourdieu, "On Symbolic Power," in P. Bourdieu, *Language and Symbolic Power* (Chicago: University of Chicago Press, 1994), pp. 167–68.

20. See Robert Keohane, *After Hegemony* (Princeton, N.J.: Princeton University Press, 1984); Stephen Krasner, ed., *International Regimes* (Ithaca, N.Y.: Cornell University Press, 1982).

21. For various realist and neorealist statements see Walt, *Origins of Alliances*; Glenn Snyder, "Alliance Theory: A Neorealist First Cut," in R. Rothstein, ed., *The Evolution of Theory in International Relations*, pp. 83–104 (Columbia: University of South Carolina Press, 1992); Kenneth Waltz, *Theory of International Politics* (Reading, Mass.: Addison-Wesley, 1979), chaps. 6, 8.

22. On the symbolic function of organizations see Paul Dimaggio and Walter Powell, "Introduction," in P. Dimaggio and W. Powell, eds., *The New Institutionalism in Organizational Analysis*, pp. 1–40 (Chicago: University of Chicago Press, 1991); W. Richard Scott, *Institutions and Organizations* (Beverly Hills, Calif.: Sage, 1995).

23. The imperatives of political survival and "budget security" are also sources of many Arab alliances. See, respectively, Michael Barnett and Jack Levy, "The Domestic Sources of Alignments and Alliances," *International Organization* 45, no. 3 (Summer 1991): 369–96; Laurie Brand, *Jordan's Inter-Arab Relations* (New York: Columbia University Press, 1995).

24. Walt, *Origins of Alliances*, p. 149.

25. Both rationalist and sociological approaches recognize that norms are accompanied by sanctions. For rationalist approaches see Jack Knight, *Institutions and Social Conflict* (New York: Cambridge University Press, 1992); for sociological approaches see Talcott Parsons, *The Structure of Social Action* (New York: Free Press, 1968); Erving Goffman, *Relations in Public* (New York: HarperBooks, 1971).

26. Robert Axelrod, "An Evolutionary Approach to Norms," *American Political Science Review* 80, no. 4 (December 1986): 1095–1112.

27. Erving Goffman, *The Presentation of Self in Everyday Life* (New York: Anchor, 1959), and *Strategic Interaction*.

28. Dennis Wrong, *Power* (New Brunswick, N.J.: Transaction, 1988), chap. 9; Goffman, "The Interaction Order," *American Sociological Review* 48, no. 1 (February 1983): 5–7; Barry Barnes, *The Elements of Social Theory* (Princeton, N.J.: Princeton University Press, 1996), pp. 13–14; Hechter, *Principles of Group Solidarity*, p. 157.

29. Barry Buzan's concept of "concentric circles of commitment" builds on the recognition that some states are better able and more willing to adhere to the norms of the community than are others because of their "proximity" to certain core identities. "From International System to International Society: Structural Realism and Regime Theory Meet the English School," *International Organization* 47, no. 3 (Summer 1993): 349. But the case of Arab politics suggests that compliance is accomplished not simply by state identity, which presents an oversocialized view of state actors, but

also because governments want the social approval that comes from being viewed as part of the group.

30. Herbert Blumer, *Symbolic Interactionism: Perspective and Method* (Englewood Cliffs, N.J.: Prentice-Hall, 1969), p. 19; Harold Garfinkel, *Studies in Ethnomethodology* (Englewood Cliffs, N.J.: Prentice-Hall, 1967).

31. David Dessler, "What's at Stake in the Agent-Structure Debate?" *International Organization* 43, no. 3 (Summer 1989): 467. Also see Wendt, *Social Theory of International Politics*, chap. 4.

32. See Charles Tilly, "States and Nationalism in Europe, 1492–1992," *Theory and Society* 23 (1994): 131–46, for a discussion linking the demise of empires and the rise of nationalism.

33. See Richard Ned Lebow, "The Long Peace, the End of the Cold War, and the Failures of Realism," *International Organization* 48, no. 2 (Spring 1994): 252–59, for a good overview and criticism of the neorealist focus on the role of force for understanding international stability and change. On the polarity debate see Kenneth Waltz, "The Stability of the Bipolar World," *Daedalus* 93, no. 3 (Summer 1964): 881–909. On hegemonies see Robert Gilpin, *War and Change in World Politics* (New York: Cambridge University Press, 1981). On balances of power see Waltz, *Theory of International Politics*, chap. 6.

34. Dessler, "What's at Stake?" p. 455; William Sewall, "Three Temporalities: Toward an Eventful Sociology," in T. McDonald, ed., *The Historic Turn in the Human Sciences* (Ann Arbor: University of Michigan Press, 1996), p. 263; Rey Koslowski and Friedrich Kratochwil, "Understanding Change in International Politics: The Soviet Union's Demise and the International System," *International Organization* 48, no. 2 (Spring 1994): 216; George Herbert Mead, *Mind, Self, and Society* (Chicago: University of Chicago Press, 1934), p. 309.

35. Martin Kramer, "Middle East: Old and New," *Daedalus* 126, no. 2 (Spring 1997): 89–112; Saad Eddin Ibrahim, "Future Visions of the Arab Middle East," *Security Dialogue* 27, no. 4 (1996): 425–36.

36. For general statements on identity and threat see William Connolly, *Identity/Difference* (Ithaca, N.Y.: Cornell University Press, 1991); David Campbell, *Writing Security* (Minneapolis: University of Minnesota Press, 1992); Iver Neumann and Jennifer Welsh, "The Other in European Self-Definition: An Addendum to the Literature on International Society," *Review of International Studies* 17 (1991): 327–48.

37. Paul Noble, Rex Brynen, and Baghat Korany, "Conclusion: The Changing Regional Security Environment," in B. Korany, P. Noble, and R. Brynen, eds., *The Many Faces of National Security in the Arab World* (New York: St. Martin's, 1993), p. 281.

38. See Michael Barnett, "Nationalism, Sovereignty, and Regional Order in the Arab States System," *International Organization* 49, no. 3 (Summer 1995): 479–510; F. Gregory Gause III, "Sovereignty, Statecraft, and Stability in the Middle East," *Journal of International Affairs* 45, no. 2 (Winter 1992): 441–67.

39. On sovereignty as a focal point see Weingast, "A Rational Choice Perspective

on the Role of Ideas and Shared Beliefs."

40. Hedley Bull, *The Anarchical Society* (New York: Macmillan, 1977).

41. Emile Durkheim, *The Division of Labor in Society* (New York: Free Press, 1984), p. 173.

42. For the general claim see Koslowski and Kratochwil, "Understanding Change in International Politics"; Dessler, "What's at Stake?"; Wendt, *Social Theory of International Politics.*

43. See Richard Ned Lebow and Thomas Risse-Kappen, eds., *The End of the Cold War and International Relations Theory* (New York: Columbia University Press, 1994), for this broad point as it pertains to international relations theory.

44. Philip Abrams, *Historical Sociology* (Ithaca, N.Y.: Cornell University Press, 1982), p. 192.

45. Roger Owen, *State, Power, and the Making of the Modern Middle East* (New York: Routledge, 1992), p. 21.

46. Cairo Domestic Service, August 8, 1990, cited in "Mubarak Gives News Conference 8 August," *FBIS-NES*-90–153, August 10, 1990, p. 8.

47. Ghassan Salame, "Inter-Arab Politics: The Return to Geography," in W. Quandt, ed., *The Middle East: Ten Years After Camp David*, pp. 319–56 (Washington, D.C.: Brookings Institution, 1988).

48. Rex Brynen, "Palestine and the Arab State System: Permeability, State Consolidation, and the Intifada," *Canadian Journal of Political Science* 24, no. 3 (September 1991): 613.

49. As Charles Tilly aptly notes, "When things happen within a sequence affects how they happen." *Big Structures, Large Processes, and Huge Comparisons* (New York: Russell Sage, 1984).

Bibliography

Abbott, Andrew. 1983. "Sequences of Social Events: Concepts and Methods for the Analysis of Order in Social Processes," *Historical Methods* 16, no. 4 (Fall): 129–46.

———. 1992. "From Causes to Events: Notes on Narrative Positivism," *Sociological Methods and Research* 20, no. 4 (May): 428–55.

Abdalla, Ahmed. 1985. *The Student Movement and National Politics in Egypt*. London: Al-Saqi Books.

Abdel-Malek, Anouar. 1968. *Egypt: Military Society*. New York: Random House.

Abdel-Salam, Mohamed. 1994. "Intra-Arab State Conflicts." *Kurasat Istratijiya* [Strategic Papers], no. 23. Al-Ahram Center for Political and Strategic Studies, Cairo.

Abell, Peter. 1996. "Sociological Theory and Rational Choice Theory." In B. Turner, ed., *Blackwell Companion to Social Theory*, pp. 252–73. New York: Basil Blackwell.

Abercrombie, Nicholas. 1986. "Knowledge, Order, and Human Autonomy." In J. Hunter and S. Ainlay, eds., *Making Sense of Modern Times: Peter Berger and the Vision of Interpretive Sociology*, pp. 11–30. New York: RKP.

Abidi, Aqil Hyder Hasan. 1965. *Jordan: A Political Study, 1948–57*. New York: Asia Publishing.

Abrams, Philip. 1982. *Historical Sociology*. Ithaca, N.Y.: Cornell University Press.

Abu-Jaber, Faiz. 1969. "The Egyptian Revolution and Middle East Defense: 1952–55," *Middle East Forum* 45, no. 4 (December): 25–56.

Adler, Emanuel. 1997. "Seizing the Middle Ground: Constructivism in World Politics," *European Journal of International Relations* 3, no. 3 (September): 319–63.

Adler, Emanuel and Michael Barnett. 1998. "Security Communities in Theoretical Perspective." In E. Adler and M. Barnett, eds., *Security Communities*. New York: Cambridge University Press.

Adler, Emanuel and Peter Haas. 1992. "Conclusion: Epistemic Communities, World Order, and the Creation of a Reflective Research Program," *International Organization* 46, no. 1 (Winter): 367–90.

Ahady, Anwar-Ul-Haq. 1994. "Security in the Persian Gulf After Desert Storm," *International Journal* 49 (Spring): 219–40.

Ajami, Fouad. 1978–79. "The End of Pan-Arabism," *Foreign Affairs* 57, no. 5 (Winter): 355–73.

———. 1981. *The Arab Predicament: Arab Political Thought and Practice Since 1967.* New York: Cambridge University Press.

Alexander, Jeffrey. 1987. *Twenty Lectures.* New York: Columbia University Press.

———. 1992. "Citizen and Enemy as Symbolic Classification: On the Polarizing Discourse of Civil Society." In M. Lamont and M. Fourier, eds., *Cultivating Boundaries*, pp. 289–308. Chicago: University of Chicago Press.

Alexander, Jeffrey and Paul Colony. 1985. " 'Institutionalization' and 'Collective Behavior': Points of Contact Between Eisenstadt's Functionalism and Symbolic Interactionism." In E. Cohen, M. Lissak, and U. Almagor, eds., *Comparative Social Dynamics*, pp. 337–45. Boulder, Colo.: Westview.

Aly, Abdel Monem Said. 1988. "Egypt: A Decade After Camp David." In W. Quandt, ed., *The Middle East: Ten Years After Camp David*, pp. 63–93. Washington, D.C.: Brookings Institution.

Aminzade, Ronald. 1992. "Historical Sociology and Time," *Sociological Methods and Research* 20, no. 4 (May): 456–80.

Anderson, Benedict. 1990. *Imagined Communities: Reflections on the Origin and Spread of Nationalism.* 2d ed. New York: New Left.

Anderson, Lisa. 1991. "Legitimacy, Identity, and the Writing of History in Libya." In E. Davis and N. Gavrielides, eds., *Statecraft in the Middle East: Oil, Historical Memory, and Popular Culture*, pp. 71–91. Miami: Florida International University Press.

Ansari, Hameid. 1986. *Egypt: The Stalled Society.* Albany: State University of New York Press.

Ansari, Mohammad Iqbal. 1968. *The Arab League, 1945–55.* Aligarh, Pakistan: Aligarh Muslim University.

Antonius, George. 1965. *The Arab Awakening.* New York: Capricorn.

Arab Report and Record. Various years.

Aruri, Nasser. 1972. *Jordan: A Study in Political Development, 1962–65.* The Hague: Martinus Nijhoff.

Associated Press. 1997. "Jordan's King, in Frank Speech, Calls '67 War a Major Blunder," *New York Times*, June 6, p. A6.

Awad, Ibrahim. 1994. "The Future of Regional and Subregional Organization in the Arab World." In D. Tschirgi, ed., *The Arab World Today*, pp. 147–160. Boulder, Colo.: Westview.

Axelrod, Robert. 1986. "An Evolutionary Approach to Norms," *American Political Science Review* 80, no. 4 (December): 1095–1112.

Ayoob, Mohammad. 1993. "Unraveling the Concept: 'National Security' in the Third World," In B. Korany, P. Noble, and R. Brynen, eds., *The Many Faces of National Security in the Arab World*, pp. 31–55. New York: St. Martin's.

——. 1994. *Third World Security Predicament*. Boulder, Colo.: Lynne Reinner.

Ayubi, Nazih. 1995. *Overstating the Arab State*. London: I. B. Taurus.

al-Azm, Aziz. 1995. "Nationalism and the Arabs," *Arab Studies Quarterly* 17, no. 1/2 (Winter–Spring): 1–17.

Bach, Kent. 1975. "Analytic Social Philosophy: Basic Concepts," *Journal of the Theory of Social Behavior* 5, no. 2 (October): 189–214.

Badeeb, Saeed. 1986. *The Saudi-Egyptian Conflict over North Yemen, 1962–70*. Boulder, Colo.: Westview.

Bakr, Tawfiq Abu. 1984. "The Flourishing of Arab Regionalism: Between Truth and Exaggeration," *al-Arabi*, September, pp. 61–63 (in Arabic).

Baldwin, David, ed. 1993. *Neorealism and Neoliberalism*. New York: Columbia University Press.

Barakat, Halim. 1990. "Beyond the Always and the Never: A Critique of Social Psychological Interpretations of Arab Society." In H. Shirabi, ed., *Theory, Politics, and the Arab World*, pp. 132–59. New York: Routledge.

——. 1993. *The Arab World*. Berkeley: University of California Press.

Baram, Amatzia. 1990. "Territorial Nationalism in the Middle East," *Middle Eastern Studies* 26, no. 4 (October): 425–48.

——. 1994. "No New Fertile Crescent: Iraqi-Jordanian Relations, 1968–92." In J. Nevo and I. Pappe, eds., *Jordan in the Middle East, 1948–88: The Making of a Pivotal State*, pp. 119–60. London: Frank Cass

Barnes, Barry. 1988. *The Nature of Power*. Cambridge, Mass.: Polity.

——. 1996. *The Elements of Social Theory*. Princeton, N.J.: Princeton University Press.

Barnett, Michael. 1992. *Confronting the Costs of War: Military Power, State, and Society in Egypt and Israel*. Princeton, N.J.: Princeton University Press.

——. 1993. "Institutions, Roles, and Disorder: The Case of the Arab States System," *International Studies Quarterly* 37 (September): 271–96.

——. 1995. "Nationalism, Sovereignty, and Regional Order in the Arab States System," *International Organization* 49, no. 3 (Summer): 479–510.

——. 1996. "Identity and Alliances in the Middle East." In P. Katzenstein, ed., *The Culture of National Security: Norms and Identity in World Politics*, pp. 400–47. New York: Columbia University Press.

——. 1996–97. "Regional Security After the Gulf War," *Political Science Quarterly* 111, no 4 (Winter): 597–618.

Barnett, Michael and Jack Levy. 1991. "The Domestic Sources of Alignments and Alliances," *International Organization* 45, no. 3 (Summer): 369–96.

Batatu, Hanna. 1978. *The Old Social Classes and the Revolutionary Movements of Iraq*. Princeton, N.J.: Princeton University Press.

Bates, Robert and Barry Weingast. 1997. "Rationality and Interpretation: The Politics of Transition." Paper presented at the Midwest Political Science Association Meetings, Chicago, March.

Bechtold, Peter. 1973. "New Attempts at Arab Cooperation: The Federation of Arab Republics, 1971–?" *Middle East Journal* 27, no 2 (Spring): 152–72.

Be'eri, Eliezer. 1982. "The Waning of the Military Coup in Arab Politics," *Middle Eastern Studies* 18, no. 1 (January): 69–81.

Ben-Dor, Gabriel. 1979. "Nationalism Without Sovereignty and Nationalism with Multiple Sovereignties: The Palestinians and Inter-Arab Relations." In G. Ben-Dor, ed., *Palestinians and the Middle East Conflict*, pp. 143–71. Forest Grove, Ore.: Turtle Dove.

———. 1983. *State and Conflict in the Middle East*. New York: Praeger.

———. 1994. "Jordan and Inter-Arab Relations." In J. Nevo and I. Pappe, eds., *Jordan in the Middle East, 1948–88: The Making of a Pivotal State*, pp. 189–207. New York: Frank Cass.

Benford, Robert and Scott Hunt. 1992. "Dramaturgy and Social Movements: The Social Construction and Communication of Power," *Sociological Inquiry* 62, no. 1 (February): 36–55.

Berger, Peter. 1963. *Invitation to Sociology*. New York: Anchor.

———. 1966. "Identity as a Problem in the Sociology of Knowledge," *European Journal of Sociology* 7: 105–15.

Berger, Peter and Thomas Luckmann. 1967. *The Social Construction of Reality*. New York: Anchor.

Bermeo, Nancy, ed. 1997. "Notes from Annual Meetings: Culture and Rational Choice," *American Political Science Association–Comparative Politics Newsletter* (Summer): 5–21.

el-Bey, Dooa. 1994. "Mapping the Future," *al-Ahram Weekly*, November 10–16, p. 1.

Biersteker, Thomas and Cindy Weber. 1996. "The Social Construction of State Sovereignty." In T. Biersteker and C. Weber, eds., *State Sovereignty as Social Construct*, pp. 1–21. New York: Cambridge University Press.

Binder, Leonard. 1958. "The Middle East as a Subordinate International System," *World Politics* 10, no. 3 (April): 408–29.

———. 1962. "Nasserism: The Protest Movement in the Middle East." In M. Kaplan, ed., *The Revolution in World Politics*, pp. 152–74. New York: Wiley.

Blau, Peter. 1992. *Exchange and Power in Social Life*. New Brunswick, N.J.: Transaction.

Bloom, William. 1989. *Personal Identity, National Identity, and International Relations*. New York: Cambridge University Press.

Blumer, Herbert. 1939. "Collective Behavior." In R. Park, ed., *An Outline of the Principles of Sociology*, pp. 221–80. New York: Barnes and Noble.

———. 1969. *Symbolic Interactionism: Perspective and Method*. Englewood Cliffs, N.J.: Prentice-Hall.

Boden, Deirdre. 1990. "The World as It Happens: Ethnomethodology and Conversational Analysis." In G. Ritzer, ed., *Frontiers of Social Theory*, pp. 185–213. New York: Columbia University Press.

Bourdieu, Pierre. 1994. *Language and Symbolic Power*. Chicago: University of Chicago Press.

———. 1994. "On Symbolic Power." In P. Bourdieu, *Language and Symbolic Power*, pp. 163–70. Chicago: University of Chicago Press.

Bourdieu, Pierre and Loic Wacquant. 1992. *An Invitation to Reflexive Sociology*. Chicago: University of Chicago Press.

Boutros-Ghali, Boutros. 1997. *Egypt's Road to Jerusalem: A Diplomat's Story of the Struggle for Peace in the Middle East*. New York: Random House.

Brand, Laurie. 1994. "Economics and Shifting Alliances: Jordan's Relations with Syria and Iraq, 1975–81," *International Journal of Middle Eastern Studies* 26: 393–413.

———. 1995. *Jordan's Inter-Arab Relations*. New York: Columbia University Press.

———. 1995. "Palestinians and Jordanians: A Crisis of Identity," *Journal of Palestine Studies* 24, no. 4: 46–61.

Brockner, Joel and Jeffrey Rubin. 1985. *Entrapment in Escalating Conflicts: A Social Psychological Analysis*. New York: Springer-Verlag.

Brown, L. Carl. 1984. *International Politics of the Middle East*. Princeton, N.J.: Princeton University Press.

———. 1987. "The Middle East: Patterns of Change, 1947–87," *Middle East Journal* 41, no. 1 (Winter): 26–39.

———. 1988. "The June 1967 War: A Turning Point?" In Y. Lukacs and A. Battah, eds., *The Arab-Israeli Conflict: Two Decades of Change*, pp. 133–46. Boulder, Colo.: Westview.

———. 1994. "The Middle East After the Cold War and the Gulf War: Change or More of the Same?" In G. Downs, ed., *Collective Security After the Cold War*, pp. 197–216. Ann Arbor: University of Michigan Press.

Bruner, Jerome. 1986. *Actual Minds, Possible Worlds*. Cambridge, Mass.: Harvard University Press.

———. 1991. "The Narrative Construction of Reality," *Critical Inquiry* 18, no. 1: 1–21.

Brynen, Rex. 1991. "Palestine and the Arab State System: Permeability, State Consolidation, and the Intifada," *Canadian Journal of Political Science* 24, no. 3 (September): 594–621.

Brzoska, Michael and Thomas Ohlson. 1987. *Arms Transfers to the Third World, 1971–85*. Oxford, England: Oxford University Press for the Stockholm International Peace Research Institute.

Bull, Hedley. 1977. *The Anarchical Society*. New York: Macmillan.

Burke, Peter. 1991. "Identity Processes and Social Stress," *American Sociological Review* 56, no. 4 (December): 836–49.

Burns, Tom. 1992. *Erving Goffman*. New York: Routledge.

Buzan, Barry. 1993. "From International System to International Society: Structural Realism and Regime Theory Meet the English School," *International Organization* 47, no. 3 (Summer): 327–52.

———. 1995. "The Levels of Analysis Problem Reconsidered." In K. Booth and S. Smith, eds., *International Relations Theory Today*, pp. 198–216. College Station: Pennsylvania State University Press.

Buzan, Barry, Charles Jones, and Richard Little. 1993. *The Logic of Anarchy*. New York: Columbia University Press.

Calhoun, Craig. 1991. "Problem of Identity in Collective Action." In J. Huber, ed., *Micro-Macro Linkages in Collective Action*, pp. 51–75. Beverly Hills, Calif.: Sage.

Callinicos, Alex. 1995. *Theories and Narratives*. Durham, N.C.: Duke University Press.

Campbell, David. 1992. *Writing Security*. Minneapolis: University of Minnesota Press.

Carr, David. 1986. *Time, Narrative, History*. Bloomington: Indiana University Press.

Carr, E. H. 1964. *The Twenty Years' Crisis*. New York: Harper Torchbooks.

Chejne, Anwar. 1957. "Egyptian Attitudes Toward Pan-Arabism," *Middle East Journal* 11, no. 3 (Summer): 253–68.

Clapham, Christopher. 1985. *Third-World Politics*. Madison: University of Wisconsin.

——. 1996. *Africa and the International System: The Politics of State Survival*. New York: Cambridge University Press.

Claude, Inis. 1966. "Collective Legitimization as a Political Function of the United Nations," *International Organization* 20, no. 3 (Summer): pp. 337–67.

Clegg, Stewart. 1994. "Power and Institutions in Organization Theory." In J. Hassard and M. Parker, eds., *Toward a New Theory of Organizations*. New York: Routledge.

Cobban, Helena. 1984. *The Palestinian Liberation Organization: People, Power, and Politics*. New York: Cambridge University Press.

Cohen, A. P. 1985. *The Symbolic Construction of Community*. New York: Tavistock.

Cohen, Jean. 1985. "Strategy or Identity: New Theoretical Paradigms and Contemporary Social Movements," *Social Research* 52, no. 4 (Winter): 663–716.

Cohen, Percy. 1968. *Modern Social Theory*. New York: Basic Books.

Coleman, James. 1990. *The Foundations of Social Theory*. Cambridge, Mass.: Harvard University Press.

Collins, Randall. 1980. "Early Goffman and the Analysis of Face-to-Face Interaction." In J. Ditton, ed., *The View from Goffman*, pp. 52–79. New York: St. Martin's.

——. 1981. "On the Microfoundations of Macrosociology," *American Journal of Sociology* 86, no. 5 (March): 984–1014.

——. 1986. "Interaction Ritual Chains, Power, and Property." In J. Alexander, R. Munch, N. Smelser, and B. Gissen, eds., *The Micro-Macro Link*, pp. 193–206. Berkeley: University of California Press.

——. 1988. "The Durkheimian Tradition in Conflict Sociology." In J. Alexander, ed., *Durkheimian Sociology and Cultural Studies*, pp. 107–28. New York: Cambridge University Press.

——. 1990. "Conflict Theory and the Advance of Macrohistorical Sociology." In G. Ritzer, ed., *Frontiers of Social Theory*, pp. 69–87. New York: Columbia University Press.

Connolly, William. 1983. *The Terms of Political Discourse*. Princeton, N.J.: Princeton University Press.

———. 1991. *Identity/Difference*. Ithaca, N.Y.: Cornell University Press.

Cook, Karen, ed. 1986. *Social Exchange Theory*. Beverly Hills, Calif.: Sage.

Cook, Karen, Jodi O'Brien, and Peter Kollock. 1990. "Exchange Theory: A Blueprint for Structure and Process." In G. Ritzer, ed., *Frontiers of Social Theory*, pp. 158–81. New York: Columbia University Press.

Corm, George. 1983. *Fragmentation of the Middle East: The Last Thirty Years*. London: Hutchinson.

Dahrendorf, Ralf. 1968. "Homo Sociologicus." In R. Dahrendorf, *Essays in the Theory of Society*, pp. 15–25. Palo Alto, Calif.: Stanford University Press.

Dann, Uriel. 1989. *King Hussein and the Challenge of Arab Radicalism: Jordan, 1955–67*. New York: Oxford University Press.

———. 1994. "The Hashemite Monarchy, 1948–88: The Constant and the Changing— An Integration." In J. Nevo and I. Pappe, eds., *Jordan in the Middle East, 1948–88: The Making of a Pivotal State*, pp. 189–207. London: Frank Cass.

Davis, Eric. 1992. "State Building in Iraq in the Iran-Iraq War and the Gulf Crisis." In M. Mildarsky, ed., *The Internationalization of Communal Strife*, pp. 69–92. London: Routledge and Kegan Paul.

Davis, Eric and Nicolas Gavrielides, eds. 1991. *Statecraft in the Middle East: Oil, Historical Memory, and Popular Culture*. Miami: Florida International University Press.

Dawisha, Adeed. 1976. *Egypt in the Arab World: Elements of a Foreign Policy*. New York: Wiley.

———. 1983. "Jordan in the Middle East: The Art of Survival." In P. Seale, ed., *The Shaping of an Arab Statesman: Abd al-Hamid Sharaf and the Modern Arab World*, pp. 61–74. New York: Quartet.

Dawn, C. Ernest. 1991. "The Origins of Arab Nationalism." In R. Khalidi, L. Anderson, M. Muslih, and R. Simon, eds., *The Origins of Arab Nationalism*, pp. viii–xix. New York: Columbia University Press.

———. 1996. "The Other Arab Responses." In R. Parker, ed., *The Six-Day War: A Retrospective*, pp. 153–88. Gainesville: University Press of Florida.

Dessler, David. 1989. "What's at Stake in the Agent-Structure Debate?" *International Organization* 43, no. 3 (Summer): 441–74.

Dessouki, Ali Hillal. 1982. "The New Arab Political Order: Implications for the 1980s." In M. Kerr and E. Yassin, eds., *Rich and Poor States in the Middle East: Egypt and the New Arab Order*, pp. 319–47. Boulder, Colo.: Westview.

———. 1988. "Egyptian Foreign Policy Since Camp David." In W. Quandt, ed., *The Middle East: Ten Years After Camp David*, pp. 94–110. Washington, D.C.: Brookings Institution.

———. 1989. "Nasser and the Struggle for Independence." In W. R. Louis and R. Owen, eds., *Suez 1956: The Crisis and Its Consequences*, pp. 31–41. New York: Oxford University Press.

Dessouki, Ali Hillal and Baghat Korany. 1984. "A Literature Survey and Framework for Analysis." In B. Korany and A. Dessouki, eds., *The Foreign Policies of Arab States*, pp. 5–18. Boulder, Colo.: Westview.

Dimaggio, Paul and Walter Powell. 1991. "Introduction." In P. Dimaggio and W. Powell, eds., *The New Institutionalism in Organizational Analysis*, pp. 1–40. Chicago: University of Chicago Press.

Dittmer, Lloyd and Samuel Kim. 1993. "In Search of a Theory of National Identity." In S. Kim and L. Dittmer, eds., *China's Quest for National Identity*, pp. 1–31. Ithaca. N.Y.: Cornell University Press.

Douglas, Mary. 1986. *How Institutions Think*. Syracuse, N.Y.: Syracuse University Press.

Drysdale, Alisdair and Raymond Hinnebusch. 1991. *Syria and the Middle East Peace Process*. New York: Council on Foreign Relations Press.

Duri, A. A. 1987. *The Historical Formation of the Arab Nation*. New York: Croom Helm.

Durkheim, Emile. 1984. *The Division of Labor in Society*. New York: Free Press.

Edelman, Murray. 1988. *Constructing the Political Spectacle*. Chicago: University of Chicago Press.

Eickelman, Dale and James Piscatori. 1996. *Muslim Politics*. Princeton, N.J.: Princeton University Press.

Ekeh, Peter. 1974. *Social Exchange Theory: Two Traditions*. New York: Cambridge University Press.

Elon, Amos. 1996. "Crumbling Cairo," *New York Review of Books*, April 6, pp. 32–36.

———. 1997. "The Thinking Men's War," *New York Times Magazine*, May 11, pp. 40–43.

Emirbayer, Mustafa. 1997. "Manifesto for a Relational Sociology," *American Journal of Sociology* 103, no. 2 (September): 281–317.

Eppel, Michael. 1994. *The Palestine Conflict and the History of Modern Iraq*. London: Frank Cass.

Esposito, John. 1986. *Islam and Politics*. 3d ed. Syracuse, N.Y.: Syracuse University Press.

Evron, Yair. and Yaacov Bar-Siman-Tov. 1975. "Coalitions in the Arab World," *Jerusalem Journal of International Relations* 1 (Winter): 71–108.

Fahmy, Ismael. 1983. *The Struggle for Peace in the Middle East*. Baltimore, Md.: Johns Hopkins University Press.

Faksh, Mahmud A. 1993. "Withered Arab Nationalism," *Orbis* 37, no. 3 (Summer): 427–38.

Faour, Muhammad. 1993. *The Arab World After Desert Storm*. Washington, D.C.: United States Institute of Peace Press.

Farah, Tawfic, ed. 1987. *Pan-Arabism and Arab Nationalism: The Continuing Debate*. Boulder, Colo.: Westview.

Farid, Abdel Magid. 1994. *Nasser: The Final Years*. Reading, England: Ithaca.

Farjani, Nadir. 1983. "On the Threshold of a New Era for Ideological Activity," *al-Mustqbal al-Arabi* 5, no. 48 (February): 120–24 (in Arabic).

Fathi, Shirin. 1994. *Jordan: An Invented Nation: Tribe, State Dynamics and the Formation of National Identity*. Hamburg: Deutsches Orient Institut.

Fay, Brian. 1996. *Contemporary Philosophy of Social Sciences*. New York: Basil Blackwell.

Fierke, K. M. 1996. "Multiple Identities, Interfacing Games: The Social Construction of Western Action in Bosnia," *European Journal of International Relations* 2, no. 4: 470–71.

Fine, Gary. 1990. "Symbolic Interactionism in the Post-Blumerian Age." In G. Ritzer, ed., *Frontiers of Social Theory*, pp. 117–57. New York: Columbia University Press.

Finnemore, Martha. 1996. *National Interests in International Society*. Ithaca, N.Y.: Cornell University Press.

Foreign Broadcast Information Service. See United States Information Agency.

Frankel, Benjamin. 1997. "Restating the Realist Case: An Introduction." In B. Frankel, ed., *Realism: Restatements and Renewal*, pp. 3–14. New York: Frank Cass.

Freedman, Lawrence and Ephraim Karsh. 1993. *The Gulf War, 1990–91*. Princeton, N.J.: Princeton University Press.

Frey, Frederick. 1985. "The Problem of Actor Designation in Political Analysis," *Comparative Political Studies* 17, no. 2 (January): 127–52.

Fromkin, David. 1989. *A Peace to End All Peace: The Fall of the Ottoman Empire and the Rise of the Modern Middle East*. New York: Holt.

Gallman, Waldemar. 1964. *Iraq Under General Nuri: My Recollections of Nuri al-Said*. Baltimore, Md.: Johns Hopkins University Press.

el-Gamasy, Mohamed Abdel Ghani. 1993. *The October War: Memoirs of Field Marshal el-Gamasy of Egypt*. Cairo: American University of Cairo Press.

Gamson, William. 1985. "Goffman's Legacy to Political Sociology," *Theory and Society* 14: 605–22.

———. 1992. "The Social Psychology of Collective Action." In A. Morris and C. M. Mueller, eds., *Frontiers in Social Movement Theory*, pp. 53–76. New Haven, Conn.: Yale University Press.

———. 1992. *Talking Politics*. New York: Cambridge University Press.

Garfinkel, Harold. 1967. *Studies in Ethnomethodology*. Englewood Cliffs, N.J.: Prentice-Hall.

Garfinkle, Adam. 1992. *Israel and Jordan in Shadow of War: Functional Ties and Futile Diplomacy*. New York: St. Martin's.

———. 1993. "The Nine Lives of Hashemite Jordan." In R. Satloff, ed., *The Politics of Change in the Middle East*, pp. 85–118. Boulder, Colo.: Westview.

Gause, F. Gregory III. 1990. *Saudi-Yemeni Relations: Domestic Structures and Foreign Influence*. New York: Columbia University Press.

———. 1992. "Sovereignty, Statecraft, and Stability in the Middle East," *Journal of International Affairs* 45, no. 2 (Winter): 441–67.

Geertz, Clifford. 1973. "After the Revolution: The Fate of Nationalism in the New States." In C. Geertz, *The Interpretation of Cultures*, pp. 193–234. New York: Basic Books.

——. 1973. "The Integrative Revolution." In C. Geertz, *The Interpretation of Cultures*, pp. 255–310. New York: Basic Books.

——. 1973. "Politics of Meaning." In C. Geertz, *The Interpretation of Cultures*, pp. 311–26. New York: Basic Books.

Gellner, Ernest. 1983. *Nations and Nationalism*. Ithaca, N.Y.: Cornell University Press.

Gerges, Fawaz. 1994. *The Superpowers and the Middle East: Regional and International Politics, 1955–67*. Boulder, Colo.: Westview.

——. 1995. "The 1967 Arab-Israeli War: U.S. Actions and Arab Perceptions." In D. Lesch, ed., *The Middle East and the United States: A Historical and Political Reassessment*, pp. 189–208. Boulder, Colo.: Westview.

Gershoni, Israel. 1997. "Rethinking the Formation of Arab Nationalism in the Middle East, 1920–45: Old and New Narratives." In J. Jankowski and J. Gershoni, eds. *Rethinking Nationalism in the Arab Middle East*, pp. 3–25. New York: Columbia University Press.

Gershoni, Israel and James Jankowski. 1987. *The Search for Egyptian Nationhood*. New York: Oxford University Press.

——. 1995. *Redefining the Egyptian Nation, 1930–45*. New York: Cambridge University Press.

Giddens, Anthony. 1983. *Central Problems in Social Theory*. Berkeley: University of California Press.

——. 1984. *The Constitution of Society*. Berkeley: University of California Press.

——. 1987. "Erving Goffman as a Systematic Social Theorist." In A. Giddens, *Social Theory and Modern Sociology*, pp. 109–39. Palo Alto, Calif.: Stanford University Press.

Gilpin, Robert. 1981. *War and Change in World Politics*. New York: Cambridge University Press.

Glubb, John. 1957. *A Soldier with the Arabs*. London: Hodder and Stoughton.

Goffman, Erving. 1959. *The Presentation of Self in Everyday Life*. New York: Anchor.

——. 1963. *Behavior in Public Places*. New York: Free Press.

——. 1969. *Strategic Interaction*. Philadelphia: University of Pennsylvania Press.

——. 1971. *Relations in Public*. New York: HarperBooks.

——. 1974. *Frame Analysis*. Cambridge, Mass.: Harvard University Press.

——. 1983. "The Interaction Order," *American Sociological Review* 48, no. 1 (February): 1–17.

Goldberg, Jacob. 1993. *The Foreign Policy of Saudi Arabia: The Formative Years, 1902–18*. Cambridge, Mass.: Harvard University Press.

Gomaa, Ahmed M. 1977. *The Foundation of the League of Arab States*. London: Longman.

Gould, Stephen Jay. 1988. *Wonderful Life: The Burgess Shale and the Nature of History*. New York: Norton.

Granovetter, Mark. 1995. "Problems of Explanation in Economic Sociology." In N. Nohria and R. Eccles, eds., *Networks and Organizations: Structure, Form, and Action*, pp. 25–56. Cambridge, Mass.: Harvard Business School Press.

Green, Jerrold. 1986. "Are Arab Politics Still Arab?" *World Politics* 38, no. 4 (July): 611–25.

Griffin, Larry. 1992. "Temporality, Events, and Explanation in Historical Sociology," *Sociological Methods and Research* 20, no. 4 (May): 403–27.

Haas, Ernest. 1993. "Nationalism: An Instrumental Social Construct," *Millennium* 22, no. 3: 505–45.

Haim, Sylvia. 1976. *Arab Nationalism: An Anthology*. Berkeley: University of California Press.

Hall, Rodney. 1997. "Moral Authority as a Power Resource," *International Organization* 51, no. 4 (Autumn): 591–622.

Halliday, Fred. 1987. "The Middle East in International Perspective: Problem of Analysis." In R. Bush, G. Johnston, and D. Coates, eds., *The World Order: Socialist Perspectives*, pp. 201–20. London: Polity Press.

——. 1987. "State and Society in International Relations: A Second Agenda," *Millennium* 16, no. 2: 215–29.

——. 1990. "The Crisis of the Arab World: The False Answers of Saddam Hussein," *New Left Review* 184 (November–December): 69–74.

Halperin, Manfred. 1963. *The Politics of Social Change in the Middle East and North Africa*. Princeton, N.J.: Princeton University Press.

Hare, Paul and Herbert Blumberg, eds. 1988. *Dramaturgical Analysis of Social Interaction*. New York: Praeger.

Harik, Ilya. 1990. "Origins of the Arab States System." In G. Luciani, ed., *The Arab State*, pp. 1–29. Berkeley: University of California Press.

Hasou, Tawfig. 1985. *The Struggle for the Arab World: Egypt's Nasser and the Arab League*. Boston: Routledge and Kegan Paul.

Hassouna, Hussein. 1975. *The League of Arab States and Regional Disputes: A Study of Middle East Conflicts*. Dobbs Ferry, N.Y.: Oceana Publications.

Hechter, Michael. 1987. *Principles of Group Solidarity*. Berkeley: University of California Press.

Heikal, Mohamed. 1973. *The Cairo Documents*. New York: Doubleday.

——. 1978. "Egyptian Foreign Policy," *Foreign Affairs* 56, no. 4 (July): 714–27.

——. 1978. *The Sphinx and the Commissar*. New York: Harper and Row.

——. 1983. *Autumn of Fury: The Assassination of Sadat*. New York: St. Martin's.

——. 1987. *Cutting the Lion's Tail: Suez Through Egyptian Eyes*. New York: Arbor House.

——. 1993. *Illusions of Triumph: An Arab View of the Gulf War*. London: Fontana.

——. 1996. *Secret Channels*. London: HarperCollins.

Heritage, John. 1987. "Ethnomethodology." In A. Giddens and J. Turner, eds., *Social Theory Today*, pp. 224–71. Palo Alto, Calif.: Stanford University Press.

Hewedy, Amin. 1989. "Nasser and the Crisis of 1956." In W. R. Louis and R. Owen, eds., *Suez 1956: The Crisis and Its Consequences*, pp. 161–72. New York: Oxford University Press.

Hinnebusch, Raymond. 1988. "Egypt, Syria, and the Arab States System." In Y. Lukacs and A. Battah, eds., *The Arab-Israeli Conflict: Two Decades of Change*, pp. 179–97. Boulder, Colo.: Westview.

Hiro, Dilip. 1992. *From Desert Shield to Desert Storm: The Second Gulf War*. New York: Routledge.

Hollis, Martin. 1972. "The Man and the Mask: A Discussion of Role Theory." In J. A. Jackson, ed., *Role*, pp. 41–74. London: Cambridge University Press.

———. 1988. *The Cunning of Reason*. New York: Cambridge University Press.

———. 1994. *The Philosophy of Social Science: An Introduction*. New York: Cambridge University Press.

Hollis, Martin and Steve Smith. 1991. *Explaining and Understanding International Relations*. New York: Oxford University Press.

Holsti, K. J. 1970. "National Role Conceptions in the Study of Foreign Policy," *International Studies Quarterly* 14 (September): 233–309.

Hopwood, Derek. 1988. *Syria: 1945–86*. Boston: Unwin Hyman.

Hourani, Albert. 1946. *Syria and Lebanon: A Political Essay*. New York: Oxford University Press.

———. 1981. "Middle Eastern Nationalism Yesterday and Today." In A. Hourani, *The Emergence of the Modern Middle East*, pp. 179–92. New York: Macmillan.

———. 1983. *Arabic Thought in the Liberal Age, 1798–1939*. New York: Cambridge University Press.

———. 1991. *A History of the Arab Peoples*. Cambridge, Mass.: Harvard University Press.

———. 1991. "How Should We Write the History of the Middle East?" *International Journal of Middle Eastern Studies* 23 (February): 125–36.

Hourani, Cecil. 1947. "The Arab League in Perspective," *Middle East Journal* 1, no. 2 (April): 125–36.

Hovsepian, Nubar. 1995. "Competing Identities in the Arab World," *Journal of International Affairs* 49, no. 1 (Summer): 1–24.

Hudson, Michael. 1977. *Arab Politics: The Search for Legitimacy*. New Haven, Conn.: Yale University Press.

Hunt, Scott, Robert Benford, and David Snow. 1995. "Identity Fields: Framing Processes and the Social Construction of Movement Identities." In E. Larana, H. Johnston, and J. Gusfield, eds., *New Social Movements: From Ideology to Identity*, pp. 185–208. Philadelphia: Temple University Press.

Hurewitz, J. C. 1982. *Middle East Politics: The Military Dimension*. Boulder, Colo.: Westview.

———. 1989. "The Historical Context." In W. R. Louis and R. Owen, eds., *Suez 1956: The Crisis and Its Consequences*, pp. 19–29. New York: Oxford University Press.

Hurwitz, Roger. 1989. "Strategic and Social Fictions in the Prisoner's Dilemma." In J. Der Derian and M. Shapiro, eds., *International/Intertextual Relations: Postmodern Readings of World Politics*, pp. 113–34. New York: Lexington.

Hussein, King. 1962. *Uneasy Lies the Head*. London: Heineman.

Ibrahim, Saad Eddin. 1988. "Domestic Developments in Egypt." In W. Quandt, ed., *The Middle East: Ten Years After Camp David*, pp. 19–62. Washington, D.C.: Brookings Institution.

———. 1994. "Arab Elites and Societies After the Gulf Crisis." In D. Tschirgi, ed., *The Arab World Today*, pp. 77–88. Boulder, Colo.: Westview.

———. 1995. "Management of Ethnic Issues in the Arab World," *Kurasat Istratijiya* [Strategic Papers], no. 26. Al-Ahram Center for Political and Strategic Studies, Cairo.

———. 1996. "Future Visions of the Arab Middle East," *Security Dialogue* 27, no. 4: 425–36.

Isaac, Jeffrey. 1987. *Power and Marxist Theory*. Ithaca, N.Y.: Cornell University Press.

Ismael, Tariq. 1986. *International Relations of the Contemporary Middle East*. Syracuse, N.Y.: Syracuse University Press.

Jackson, R. and C. Rosberg. 1982. "Why Africa's Weak States Persist: The Empirical and Juridical in Statehood," *World Politics* 35, no. 1 (October): 1–24.

al-Jamali, Muhammad Fadil. 1988. "Frank Words on the Crisis of Arab Unity Today," *al-Mustqbal al-Arabi* 10, no. 109: 114–17 (in Arabic).

Jankowski, James. 1984. "Zionism and the Jews in Egyptian Nationalist Opinion, 1920–39." In A. Cohen and G. Baer, eds., *Egypt and Palestine*, pp. 315–31. New York: St. Martins.

———. 1997. "Arab Nationalism in 'Nasserism' and Egyptian State Policy, 1952–58." In J. Jankowski and J. Gershoni, eds., *Rethinking Nationalism in the Arab Middle East*, pp. 150–68. New York: Columbia University Press.

Jankowski, James and James Gershoni, eds. 1997. *Rethinking Nationalism in the Arab Middle East*. New York: Columbia University Press.

Jentleson, Bruce. 1996. "The Middle East Arms Control and Regional Security (ARCS) Talks: Progress, Problems, and Prospects." Institute on Global Conflict and Cooperation Policy Paper, no. 26, September, University of California at San Diego.

Jepperson, Ron, Alexander Wendt, and Peter Katzenstein. 1987. "Norms, Identity, and Culture in National Security." In P. Katzenstein, ed., *The Culture of National Security: Norms and Identity in World Politics*, pp. 33–75. New York: Columbia University Press.

Jervis, Robert. 1970. *The Logic of Images in International Relations*. New York: Columbia University Press.

———. 1988. "Realism, Game Theory, and Cooperation," *World Politics* 40, no. 3 (April): 317–49.

Joffe, George. 1993. "Middle Eastern Views of the Gulf Conflict and Its Aftermath," *Review of International Studies* 19 (April): 177–99.

Johnson, James. 1997. "Symbol and Strategy in Comparative Political Analysis," *American Political Science Association–Comparative Politics Newsletter* (Summer): 6–9.

Kadi, Leila. 1966. *Arab Summit Conferences and the Palestine Problem, 1936-50, 1964-66*. Beirut: PLO Research Center.

Karawan, Ibrahim. 1994. "Arab Dilemmas in the 1990s: Breaking Taboos and Searching for Signposts," *Middle East Journal* 48, no. 3 (Summer): 433–54.

Karpat, Kemal. 1988. "The Ottoman Ethnic and Confessional Legacy in the Middle
East." In M. Esman and I. Rabinovich, eds., *Ethnicity, Pluralism, and the State in
the Middle East*, pp. 35–53. Ithaca, N.Y.: Cornell University Press.

Katzenstein, Peter, ed. 1996. *The Culture of National Security: Norms and Identity in
World Politics*. New York: Columbia University Press.

Kedourie, Ellie. 1970. "The Chatham House Version." In E. Kedourie, *The Chatham
House Version and Other Middle Eastern Studies*, pp. 351–94. London: Weidenfeld
and Nicolson.

Keohane, Robert. 1984. *After Hegemony*. Princeton, N.J.: Princeton University Press.

Kerr, Malcolm. 1968. "Egyptian Foreign Policy and Revolution." In P. J. Vatikiotis, ed.,
Egypt Since the Revolution, pp. 114–39. New York: Praeger.

——. 1970. *The Arab Cold War*. New York: Oxford University Press.

——. 1972. "Regional Arab Politics and the Conflict with Israel." In P. Hammond and
S. Alexander, eds., *Political Dynamics in the Middle East*, pp. 31–68. New York:
American Elsevier.

——. 1983. "Arab Society and the West." In P. Seale, ed., *The Shaping of an Arab Statesman: Abd al-Hamid Sharaf and the Modern Arab World*, pp. 209–24. New York:
Quartet.

Kertzer, David. 1988. *Ritual, Politics, and Power*. New Haven, Conn.: Yale University
Press.

——. 1996. *Politics and Symbols*. New Haven, Conn.: Yale University Press.

Khadduri, Majjid. 1946. "Toward an Arab Union: The League of Arab States," *American Political Science Review* 40, no. 1 (February): 90–100.

——. 1960. *Independent Iraq: A Study in Iraqi Politics Since 1932*. New York: Oxford
University Press.

Khalaf, Issa. 1993. *Politics in Palestine: Arab Factionalism and Social Disintegration,
1939–48*. Albany: State University of New York Press.

Khalidi, Rashid. 1989. "Consequences of the Suez Crisis in the Arab World." In W. R.
Louis and R. Owen, eds., *Suez 1956: The Crisis and Its Consequences*, pp. 377–92.
New York: Oxford University Press.

——. 1991. "Arab Nationalism: Historical Problems in the Literature," *American Historical Review* 96, no. 5 (December): 1363–73.

——. 1991. "The Impact of the Iraqi Revolution on the Arab World." In R. Fernea and
W. Louis, eds., *The Iraqi Revolution of 1958: The Old Social Classes Revisited*, pp.
106–17. New York: I. B. Tauris.

——. 1997. *Palestinian Identity: The Construction of Modern National Consciousness*.
New York: Columbia University Press.

Khalidi, Rashid, Lisa Anderson, Muhammad Muslih, and Reeva Simon, eds. 1991. *The
Origins of Arab Nationalism*. New York: Columbia University Press.

Khalidi, Walid. 1978. "Thinking the Unthinkable: A Sovereign Palestinian State," *Foreign Affairs* 56, no. 4 (July): 695–713.

Khalil, Muhammad. 1962. *The Arab States and the Arab League: A Documentary Record*, vols. 1 and 2. Beirut: Khayat's.

al-Khalil, Samir. 1991. *The Monument: Art, Vulgarity, and Responsibility in Iraq*. Berkeley: University of California Press.

Khoury, Philip. 1982. "The Pragmatic Trend in Inter-Arab Politics," *Middle East Journal* 36, no. 3 (Summer): 374–87.

———. 1983. *Urban Notables and Arab Nationalism: The Politics of Damascus, 1860–1920*. New York: Cambridge University Press.

———. 1987. *Syria and the French Mandate*. Princeton, N.J.: Princeton University Press.

Khoury, Philip and Joseph Kostiner, eds. 1991. *Tribes and State Formation in the Middle East*. London: I. B. Taurus.

Kienle, Eberhard. 1990. *Ba'ath Versus Ba'ath: The Conflict Between Syria and Iraq, 1968–89*. London: I. B. Taurus.

———. 1993. "The Limits of Fertile Crescent Unity: Iraqi Policies Toward Syria Since 1945." In D. Hopwood, H. Ishaw, and T. Koszinowski, eds., *Iraq: Power and Society*, pp. 356–79. New York: Oxford University Press.

———. 1995. "Arab Unity Schemes Revisited: Interest, Identity, and Policy in Syria and Egypt," *International Journal of Middle Eastern Studies* 27: 53–71.

Kimmerling, Baruch and Joel Migdal. 1993. *The Palestinians*. New York: Free Press.

Kiser, Edgar. 1996. "The Revival of Narrative in Historical Sociology: What Rational Choice Theory Can Contribute," *Politics and Society* 24, no. 3: 249–71.

Klieman, Aaron. 1982. "The Arab States and Palestine." In E. Kedourie and Sylvia Haim, eds., *Zionism and Arabism in Palestine and Israel*, pp. 118–37. London: Frank Cass.

Knight, Jack. 1992. *Institutions and Social Conflict*. New York: Cambridge University Press.

Korany, Baghat. 1986. "Political Petrolism and Contemporary Arab Politics, 1967–83," *Journal of Asian and African Studies* 21, no. 1/2: 66–80.

———. 1988. "The Dialectics of Inter-Arab Relations, 1967–87," In Y. Lukacs and A. Battah, eds., *The Arab-Israeli Conflict: Two Decades of Change*, pp. 164–78. Boulder, Colo.: Westview.

———. 1991. "Egypt." In R. Brynen, ed., *Echoes of the Intifada*, pp. 195–214. Boulder, Colo.: Westview.

———. 1994. "National Security in the Arab World: The Persistence of Dualism," In D. Tschirgi, ed., *The Arab World Today*, pp. 161–78. Boulder, Colo.: Westview.

Korany, Baghat and Ali Hillal Dessouki. 1984. "The Global System and Arab Foreign Policies." In B. Korany and A. Dessouki, eds., *The Foreign Policies of Arab States*, pp. 19–40. Boulder, Colo.: Westview.

Koslowski, Rey and Friedrich Kratochwil. 1994. "Understanding Change in International Politics: The Soviet Union's Demise and the International System," *International Organization* 48, no. 2 (Spring): 215–48.

Kostiner, Joseph. 1993. *The Making of Saudi Arabia, 1916–38: From Chieftaincy to Monarchical State*. New York: Oxford University Press.

Kramer, Martin. 1993. "Arab Nationalism: Mistaken Identity," *Daedalus* 122, no. 3 (Summer): 171–206.

———. 1997. "Middle East: Old and New," *Daedalus* 126, no. 2 (Spring): 89–112.

Krasner, Stephen. 1988. "Sovereignty: An Institutional Perspective," *Comparative Political Studies* 21, no. 1 (April): 66–94.

Krasner, Stephen, ed. 1982. *International Regimes*. Ithaca, N.Y.: Cornell University Press.

Kratochwil, Friedrich. 1989. *Norms, Rules, and Decisions*. New York: Cambridge University Press.

Kreps, David. 1990. "Corporate Culture and Economic Theory." In J. Alt and K. Shepsle, eds., *Perspectives on Political Economy*, pp. 90–143. New York: Cambridge University Press.

Kuran, Timur. 1990. "Private and Public Preferences," *Economics and Philosophy* 6: 1–26.

Kyle, Keith. 1989. "Britain and the Suez Crisis, 1955–56." In W. R. Louis and R. Owen, eds., *Suez 1956: The Crisis and Its Consequences*, pp. 103–31. New York: Oxford University Press.

Lake, David and Robert Powell. Forthcoming. "Strategic Choice and International Relations." In D. Lake and R. Powell, *Strategic Choice and International Relations*. Princeton, N.J.: Princeton University Press.

Landis, J. R. 1971. *Sociology: Concepts and Characteristics*. Belmont, Calif.: Wadsworth.

Laroui, Abdallah. 1969. "Sands and Dreams." In G. Atyeh, ed., *Arab and American Cultures*, pp. 3–13. Washington, D.C.: AEI Press.

Lawson, Fred. 1991. "Syria." In R. Brynen, ed., *Echoes of the Intifada*, pp. 215–33. Boulder, Colo.: Westview.

———. 1996. *Why Syria Goes to War: Thirty Years of Confrontation*. Ithaca, N.Y.: Cornell University Press.

Layne, Linda. 1994. *Home and Homeland: The Dialogics of Tribal and National Identities in Jordan*. Princeton, N.J.: Princeton University Press.

Lebow, Richard Ned. 1994. "The Long Peace, the End of the Cold War, and the Failures of Realism," *International Organization* 48, no. 2 (Spring): 249–77.

Lebow, Richard Ned and Thomas Risse-Kappen, eds. 1994. *The End of the Cold War and International Relations Theory*. New York: Columbia University Press.

Lerman, Eran. 1995. "A Revolution Prefigured: Foreign Policy Orientation in the Postwar Years." In S. Shamir, ed., *Egypt: From Monarchy to Republic*, pp. 283–308. Boulder, Colo.: Westview.

Lesch, Anne Mosley. 1973. "The Palestine Arab Nationalist Movement Under the Mandate." In W. Quandt, F. Jabber, and A. Mosley Lesch, *The Politics of Palestinian Nationalism*, pp. 5–42. Berkeley: University of California.

Lesch, David, ed. 1995. *The Middle East and the United States: A Historical and Political Reassessment*. Boulder, Colo.: Westview.

Le Vine, Victor. 1984. "The Arab World in the 1980s: Have the Predicates of Politics Changed?" *Middle East Review* 26, no. 3 (Spring): 3–16.

Lewis, Bernard. 1992. "Rethinking the Middle East," *Foreign Affairs* 71, no. 4 (Fall): 99–119.

Little, T. R. 1956. "The Arab League: A Reassessment," *Middle East Journal* 10, no. 2 (Spring): 138–50.

Longrigg, Stanley. 1953. *Iraq, 1900 to 1950*. New York: Oxford University Press.

Louis, Wm. Roger. 1984. *British Empire in the Middle East, 1945–51: Arab Nationalism, the United States, and Postwar Imperialism*. New York: Oxford University Press.

———. 1984. "The Era of the Mandates System and the Non-European World." In H. Bull and A. Watson, eds., *The Expansion of International Society*, pp. 201–13. New York: Oxford University Press.

Louis, Wm. Roger and Roger Owen, eds. 1989. *Suez 1956: The Crisis and Its Consequences*. New York: Oxford University Press.

Luciani, Giacomo. 1990. "Introduction." In G. Luciani, ed., *The Arab State*, pp. xvii–xxxii. Berkeley: University of California Press.

Luciani, Giacomo, ed. 1990. *The Arab State*. Berkeley: University of California Press.

Luciani, Giacomo and Ghassan Salame. 1990. "The Politics of Arab Integration." In G. Luciani, ed., *The Arab State*, pp. 394–419. Berkeley: University of California Press.

Lukitz, Liora. 1995. *Iraq: The Search for National Identity*. London: Frank Cass.

Lunt, James. 1989. *Hussein of Jordan*. London: Macmillan.

Lynch, Marc. Forthcoming. *Contested Identity and Security: The International Politics of Jordanian Identity*." New York: Columbia University Press.

MacDonald, R. 1965. *The League of Arab States: A Study in the Dynamics of Regional Organization*. Princeton, N.J.: Princeton University Press.

Mach, Zdzislaw. 1994. *Symbols, Conflict, and Identity*. New York: State University of New York Press.

MacIntyre, Alisdair. 1981. *After Virtue*. South Bend, Ind.: University of Notre Dame Press.

Maddy-Weitzman, Bruce. 1993. *The Crystallization of the Arab State System*. Syracuse, N.Y.: Syracuse University Press.

Manning, Phillip. 1992. *Erving Goffman and Modern Sociology*. Palo Alto, Calif.: Stanford University Press.

Mansfield, Peter. 1973. *The Ottoman Empire and Its Successors*. New York: St. Martin's.

Maoz, Moshe. 1995. *Syria and Israel: From War to Peacemaking*. Oxford, England: Clarendon.

al-Mashnuq, Nihad. 1982. "Arab Wars Against Arabs." *al-Nahar al-Arabi wal-Duwali*, March 15, pp. 6–7 (in Arabic).

Mattar, Philip. 1988. *The Mufti of Jerusalem*. New York: Columbia University Press.

Mauss, Marcel. 1967. *The Gift: Forms and Functions of Exchange in Archaic Societies*. New York: Norton.

Mayer, Thomas. 1984. "Egypt and the 1936 Arab Revolt in Palestine," *Journal of Contemporary History* 19, no. 2 (April): 275–87.

——. 1984. "End of Pan-Arabism?" *Middle East Review* 26, no. 4 (Summer): 31–36.

McAdam, Doug, John McCarthy, and Mayer Zald. 1996. "Introduction." In D. McAdam, J. McCarthy, and M. Zald, eds., *Comparative Perspective on Social Movements: Political Opportunities, Mobilizing Structures, and Cultural Framing*, pp. 1–20. New York: Cambridge University Press.

McCall, George and J. L. Simmons. 1978. *Identities and Interactions*. New York: Free Press.

McCarthy, John and Mayer Zald. 1977. "Resource Mobilization and Social Movements: A Partial Theory," *American Journal of Sociology* 82, no. 6 (May): 1212–41.

McDonald, Robert. 1965. *The League of Arab States: A Study in the Dynamics of Regional Organization*. Princeton, N.J.: Princeton University Press.

Mead, George Herbert. 1934. *Mind, Self, and Society*. Chicago: University of Chicago Press.

Mearsheimer, John. 1995. "The False Promise of Institutions," *International Security* 19, no. 3: 5–49.

Mehdi, Mohammad. 1963. "The Cairo Declaration," *Middle East Forum* 49, no. 8 (Summer): 31–40.

Meyer, Joseph. 1984. "Introduction: The Steadfastness Group," *Middle East Review* 27, no. 1 (Fall): 3–4.

Mitchell, W. J. T., ed. 1980. *On Narrative*. Chicago: University of Chicago Press.

Molm, Linda. 1997. *Coercive Power in Social Exchange*. New York: Cambridge University Press.

Moore, Clement Henry. 1971. "On Theory and Practice Among the Arabs," *World Politics* 24, no. 1 (October): 106–26.

Morris, Aldon and Carol Mueller, eds. 1992. *Frontiers in Social Movement Theory*. New Haven, Conn.: Yale University Press.

Morris, Benny. 1993. *Israel's Border Wars*. New York: Oxford University Press.

Morrow, James. 1994. *Game Theory for Political Scientists*. Princeton, N.J.: Princeton University Press.

Most, Benjamin and Harvey Starr. 1984. "International Relations Theory, Foreign Policy Substitutability, and 'Nice' Laws," *World Politics* 36, no. 3 (April): 383–406.

Mouzelis, Nicos. 1991. "The Interaction Order and the Micro-Macro Distinction," *Sociological Theory* 10, no. 1 (Spring): 123–32.

——. 1995. *Sociological Theory: What Went Wrong?* New York: Routledge.

Mufti, Malik. 1996. *Sovereign Creations: Pan-Arabism and Political Order in Syria and Iraq*. Ithaca, N.Y.: Cornell University Press.

——. 1997. "A Brave New Sub-System: Inter-Arab Conflict and the End of the Cold War," unpublished manuscript, Tufts University, Boston.

Muller, Harald. 1993. "The Internalization of Principles, Norms, and Rules by Governments." In V. Rittberger, ed., *Regime Theory and International Relations*, pp. 361–88. New York: Clarendon.

Muslih, Muhammad. 1988. *The Origins of Palestinian Nationalism*. New York: Columbia University Press.

Mutawi, Samir. 1987. *Jordan in the 1967 War*. New York: Cambridge University Press.

———. 1996. "The Jordanian Response." In R. Parker, ed., *The Six-Day War: A Retrospective*, pp. 168–83. Gainesville: University Press of Florida.

Nafaa, Hassan. 1987. "Arab Nationalism: A Response to Ajami's Thesis on the 'End of Pan-Arabism.'" In T. E. Farah, ed., *Pan-Arabism and Arab Nationalism: The Continuing Debate*, pp. 133–51. Boulder, Colo.: Westview.

Nakleh, Emile. 1993. "Regime Stability and Change in the Gulf: The Case of Saudi Arabia." In R. Satloff, ed., *The Politics of Change in the Middle East*, pp. 119–44. Boulder, Colo.: Westview.

———. 1994. "The Arab World After the Gulf War: Challenges and Prospects." In E. Boulding, ed., *Building Peace in the Middle East: Challenges for States and Civil Society*, pp. 111–20. Boulder, Colo.: Lynne Reinner.

Nasser, Gamal Abdel. 1959. *Philosophy of the Revolution*. Buffalo, N.Y.: Smith, Keynes, and Marshall.

Neumann, Iver and Jennifer Welsh. 1991. "The Other in European Self-Definition: An Addendum to the Literature on International Society," *Review of International Studies* 17: 327–48.

Nevo, Joseph. 1994. "Introduction." In J. Nevo and I. Pappe, eds., *Jordan in the Middle East, 1948–88: The Making of a Pivotal State*, pp. 1–12. London: Frank Cass.

Ni'man, Isam. 1983. "Peace Between the Arabs," *al-Watan al-Arabi* 7, no. 333 (July 1): 36–37 (in Arabic).

Noble, Paul. 1984. "The Arab System: Opportunities, Constraints, and Pressures." In B. Korany and A. Dessouki, eds., *The Foreign Policies of Arab States*, pp. 41–78. Boulder, Colo.: Westview.

———. 1984. "The Inter-Arab System." In B. Korany and A. Dessouki, eds., *The Foreign Policies of the Arab States*, pp. 60–70. Boulder, Colo.: Westview.

Noble, Paul, Rex Brynen, and Baghat Korany. 1993. "Conclusion: The Changing Regional Security Environment." In B. Korany, P. Noble, and R. Brynen, eds., *The Many Faces of National Security in the Arab World*, pp. 275–302. New York: St. Martin's.

Nuseibeh, Hazem. 1983. "Arab Nationalism: Decades of Innocence and Challenge." In P. Seale, ed., *The Shaping of an Arab Statesman: Abd al-Hamid Sharaf and the Modern Arab World*, pp. 197–208. New York: Quartet.

Nutting, Anthony. 1958. *I Saw for Myself*. London: Hollis and Carter.

———. 1972. *Nasser*. London: Constable.

Nye, Joseph. 1993. *Understanding International Conflicts: An Introduction to Theory and History*. New York: HarperCollins.

Onuf, Nicholas. 1989. *World of Our Own Making.* Columbia: University of South Carolina Press.

Ortner, Sherry. 1984. "Theory in Anthropology Since the 1960s," *Comparative Study of Society and History* 26, no. 1 (January): 126–66.

Oumlil, Ali. 1995. "Four Questions," *Arab Thought Forum* 2, no. 2: 1–5.

Owen, Roger. 1983. "Arab Nationalism, Arab Unity, and Arab Solidarity." In T. Asad and R. Owen, eds., *Sociology of the "Developing Societies": The Middle East*, pp. 16–22. New York: Monthly Review Press.

———. 1992. *State, Power, and Politics in the Making of the Modern Middle East.* New York: Routledge.

Parker, Richard, ed. 1996. *The Six-Day War: A Retrospective.* Gainesville: University of Florida.

Parsons, Talcott. 1968. *The Structure of Social Action.* New York: Free Press.

Peres, Shimon. 1993. *The New Middle East.* New York: Holt.

Pfaff, Richard. 1970. "The Functions of Arab Nationalism," *Comparative Politics* 2, no. 2 (Spring): 147–68.

Pipes, Daniel. 1990. *Greater Syria: History of an Ambition.* New York: Oxford University Press.

Piscatori, James. 1986. *Islam in a World of Nation-States.* New York: Cambridge University Press.

———. 1991. "Religion and Realpolitik: Islamic Responses to the Gulf War." In J. Piscatori, ed., *Islamic Fundamentalisms and the Gulf Crisis*, pp. 1–28. Chicago: American Academy of Arts and Sciences.

Piscatori, James, ed. 1991. *Islamic Fundamentalisms and the Gulf Crisis.* Chicago: American Academy of Arts and Sciences.

Podeh, Eli. 1994. "In the Service of Power: The Ideological Struggle in the Arab World During the Gulf Crisis," *Conflict Quarterly* (Fall): 7–25.

———. 1995. *The Quest for Hegemony in the Arab World: The Struggle over the Baghdad Pact.* New York: E. J. Brill.

Pogany, Istvan. 1987. *The Arab League and Peacekeeping in Lebanon.* New York: St. Martin's.

Polkinghorne, Donald. 1986. *Narrative Knowing and the Human Sciences.* Albany: State University of New York Press.

Popitz, Heinrich. 1972. "The Concept of Social Role as an Element of Sociological Theory." In J. Jackson, ed., *Roles*, pp. 11–33. New York: Cambridge University Press.

Porath, Yehoshua. 1986. *In Search of Arab Unity.* London: Frank Cass.

Powell, Robert. 1994. "Anarchy in International Relations Theory: The Neorealist-Neoliberal Debate," *International Organization* 48, no. 2 (Spring): 337–38.

Psathas, George. 1980. "Early Goffman and the Analysis of Face-to-Face Interaction in *Strategic Interaction*." In J. Ditton, ed., *The View from Goffman*, pp. 52–79. New York: St. Martin's.

Pundik, Ron. 1994. *The Struggle for Sovereignty: Relations Between Great Britain and Jordan, 1946–51.* Cambridge, Mass.: Basil Blackwell.

Quandt, William. 1984. *Saudi Arabia in the 1980s.* Washington, D.C.: Brookings Institution.

———. 1993. *Peace Process: American Diplomacy and the Arab-Israeli Conflict Since 1967.* Berkeley: University of California Press.

Rabinovich, Itamar. 1972. *Syria Under the Ba'ath, 1963–66.* New York: Halstead.

———. 1991. *The Road Not Taken.* New York: Oxford University Press.

———. 1995. "Egypt and the Palestine Question Before and After the Revolution." In S. Shamir, ed., *Egypt: From Monarchy to Republic,* pp. 325–39. Boulder, Colo.: Westview.

Rahmy, Ali Abdel Rahman. 1983. *The Egyptian Policy in the Arab World.* Washington, D.C.: University Press of America.

Rawls, A. W. 1987. "The Interaction Order Sui Generis: Goffman's Contribution to Social Theory," *Sociological Theory* 5, no. 2 (Fall): 136–49.

Rejwan, Nissim. 1974. *Nasserite Ideology: Its Exponents and Critics.* New York: Wiley.

Reshnon, Stanley, ed. 1993. *The Political Psychology of the Gulf War: Leaders, Publics, and the Process of Conflict.* Pittsburgh, Pa.: University of Pittsburgh Press.

Reus-Smit, Christian. 1997. "The Constitutional Structure of International Society and the Nature of Fundamental Institutions," *International Organization* 51, no. 4 (Autumn): 555–90.

Rhoads, John. 1991. *Critical Issues in Social Theory.* College Station: Pennsylvania State University Press.

Ross, Marc Howard. 1993. *Culture of Conflict.* New Haven, Conn.: Yale University Press.

Rubin, Barry. 1981. *The Arab States and the Palestine Conflict.* Syracuse, N.Y.: Syracuse University Press.

Ruggie John. 1986. "Continuity and Transformation in the World Polity." In R. Keohane, ed., *Neorealism and Its Critics,* pp. 131–57. New York: Columbia University Press.

Sabit, Adel M. 1989. *A King Betrayed: The Ill-Fated Reign of Farouk of Egypt.* New York: Quartet.

Sadat, Anwar. 1978. *In Search of Identity.* New York: HarperBooks.

Sadowski, Yahya. 1992. *Scuds or Butter?* Washington, D.C.: Brookings Institution.

Safran, Nadav. 1988. *Saudi Arabia: The Ceaseless Quest for Security.* Ithaca, N.Y.: Cornell University Press.

Sahlins, Marshall. 1976. *Culture and Practical Reason.* Chicago: University of Chicago Press.

Salame, Ghassan. 1988. "Integration in the Arab World: The Institutional Framework." In G. Luciani and G. Salame, eds., *The Politics of Arab Integration,* pp. 256–79. New York: Croom Helm.

———. 1988. "Inter-Arab Politics: The Return to Geography." In W. Quandt, ed., *The*

Middle East: Ten Years After Camp David, pp. 319–56. Washington, D.C.: Brookings Institution.

——. 1990. " 'Strong' and 'Weak' States: A Qualified Return to the *Muqaddimah.*" In G. Luciani, ed., *The Arab State*, pp. 29–64. Berkeley: University of California Press.

Salame, Ghassan, ed. 1987. *The Foundations of the Arab State*. New York: Croom Helm.

Salem, Paul. 1994. *Bitter Legacy: Ideology and Politics in the Arab World*. Syracuse, N.Y.: Syracuse University Press.

Salibi, Kamal. 1988. *A House of Many Mansions: The History of Modern Lebanon Reconsidered*. Berkeley: University of California Press.

——. 1993. *The Modern History of Jordan*. London: I. B. Taurus.

Salim, Mohammed Anis. 1982. "Arab Schisms in the 1980s: Old Story or New Order?" *World Today* 38, no. 5 (May): 175–84.

——. 1988. "The Future of Inter-Arab Relations," *al-Mustqbal al-Arabi* 11, no. 115 (September): 126–54 (in Arabic).

Satloff, Robert. 1994. *From Abdullah to Hussein: Jordan in Transition*. New York: Oxford University Press.

Sayigh, Fayez. 1958. *Arab Unity: Hope and Fulfillment*. New York: Devin-Adair.

Sayigh, Yezid. 1997. *Armed Struggle and the Search for State: The Palestinian National Movement, 1949–93*. New York: Oxford University Press.

Sayigh, Yezid and Avi Shlaim, eds. 1997. *The Cold War and the Middle East*. New York: Oxford University Press.

Schelling, Thomas. 1980. *The Strategy of Conflict*. Cambridge, Mass.: Harvard University Press.

Schenkein, Jim, ed. 1978. *Studies in the Organization of Conversational Interaction*. New York: Academic.

Schiebe, Karl. 1986. "Self-Narratives and Adventure." In T. Sabine, ed., *Narrative Psychology: The Storied Nature of Human Conduct*, pp. 129–51. New York: Praeger.

Schlenker, Barry. 1996. *Impression Management: The Self-Concept, Social Identity, and Interpersonal Relations*. Monterey, Calif.: Brooks/Cole.

Schön, Donald and Martin Rein. 1994. *Frame Reflection: Toward the Resolution of Intractable Policy Controversies*. New York: Basic Books.

Scott, W. Richard. 1995. *Institutions and Organizations*. Beverly Hills, Calif.: Sage.

Seale, Patrick. 1986. *The Struggle for Syria*. New Haven, Conn.: Yale University Press.

Searing, Donald. 1991. "Roles, Rules, and Rationality in the New Institutionalism," *American Political Science Review* 85, no. 4 (December): 1239–60.

Sela, Avraham. 1988. "The Changing Focus of the Arab States' System," *Middle East Review* 20, no. 3 (Spring): 41–54.

——. 1997. *The Decline of the Arab-Israeli Conflict: Middle East Politics and the Quest for Regional Order*. Albany: State University of New York Press.

Sen, Amartya. 1977. "Rational Fools: A Critique of the Behavioral Foundations of Economic Theory," *Philosophy and Public Affairs* 6 (Summer): 317–44.

Sewall, William. 1992. "Introduction: Narratives and Social Identities," *Social Science History* 16, no. 4 (Winter): 479–88.

———. 1992. "A Theory of Structure: Duality, Agency, and Transformation," *American Journal of Sociology* 98, no. 1 (July): 1–29.

———. 1996. "Three Temporalities: Toward an Eventful Sociology." In T. McDonald, ed., *The Historic Turn in the Human Sciences*, pp. 245–80. Ann Arbor: University of Michigan Press.

Sharabi, Hisham. 1965. "The Transformation of Ideology in the Arab World," *Middle East Journal* 19, no. 4 (Autumn): 471–86.

Sharma, J. P. 1990. *The Arab Mind: A Study of Egypt, Arab Unity, and the World*. Delhi: H. K. Publishers.

el-Shazli, Saad. 1980. *The Crossing of the Suez*. San Francisco: American Middle East Research.

Shemesh, Moshe. 1988. *The Palestinian Entity, 1959–74: Arab Politics and the PLO*. London: Frank Cass.

Shimshoni, Johnathan. 1993. *Israel and Conventional Deterrence: Border Wars from 1953 to 1970*. Ithaca, N.Y.: Cornell University Press.

Shlaim, Avi. 1988. *Collusion Across the Jordan: King Abdullah, the Zionist Movement, and the Partition of Palestine*. New York: Columbia University Press.

Sicker, Martin. 1989. *Between Hashemites and Zionists: The Struggle for Palestine, 1908–88*. New York: Holmes and Meier.

Sid-Ahmed, Mohammed. 1995. "The Arab League and the Arab State," *al-Ahram Weekly*, April 6–12, p. 8.

———. 1995. "When Israelis Speak Arabic," *al-Ahram Weekly*, March 30–April 5, p. 8.

Silberman, Neil Asher. 1989. *Between Past and Present: Archeology, Ideology, and Nationalism in the Modern Middle East*. New York: Holt.

Simmel, George. 1955. *Conflict and the Web of Group Affiliations*. New York: Free Press.

———. 1971. "Group Expansion and the Development of Individuality." In D. Levine, ed., *George Simmel: On Individuality and Social Forms*, pp. 251–93. Chicago: University of Chicago Press.

Simon, Reeva. 1997. "The Imposition of Nationalism on a Non-Nation State: The Case of Iraq During the Interwar Period, 1921–41." In J. Jankowski and J. Gershoni, eds. *Rethinking Nationalism in the Arab Middle East*, pp. 87–105. New York: Columbia University Press.

Sivan, Emmanuel. 1987. "The Arab Nation-State: In Search of a Usable Past," *Middle East Review* 19, no. 3 (Spring): 21–30.

Smith, Anthony. 1991. *National Identity*. Reno: University of Nevada Press.

Smith, Charles. 1992. *Palestine and the Arab-Israeli Conflict*. 2d ed. New York: St. Martin's.

Snow, David and Robert Benford. 1988. "Ideology, Frame Resonance, and Participant Mobilization." In B. Klandermans, H. Kriesi, and S. Tarrow, eds., *From Structure to Action*, pp. 197–217. Greenwich, Conn.: JAI Press.

———. 1992. "Master Frames and Cycles of Protest." In A. Morris and C. Mueller, eds., *Frontiers in Social Movement Theory*, pp. 133–55. New Haven, Conn.: Yale University Press.

Snow, David, E. Rochford, S. Worden, and R. Benford. 1986. "Frame Alignment Processes, Micromobilization, and Movement Participation," *American Sociological Review* 51, no. 3 (August): 464–81.

Snow, David, L. Zurcher, and S. Ekland-Olson. 1980. "Social Networks and Social Movements: A Microstructural Approach to Differential Recruitment," *American Sociological Review* 45, no. 5 (October): 787–801.

Snow, Peter. 1972. *Hussein: A Biography*. London: Barrie and Jenkins.

Snyder, Glenn. 1992. "Alliance Theory: A Neorealist First Cut." In R. Rothstein, ed., *The Evolution of Theory in International Relations*, pp. 83–104. Columbia: University of South Carolina Press.

Spiegel, Steven and David Pervin. 1995. *Arms Control and Regional Security*, vol. 1 of *Practical Peacemaking in the Middle East*. New York: Garland.

———. 1995. *The Environment, Water, Refugees, and Economic Cooperation and Development*, vol. 2 of *Practical Peacemaking in the Middle East*. New York: Garland.

Spruyt, Hendrik. 1994. *The Sovereign State and Its Competitors: An Analysis of Systems Change*. Princeton, N.J.: Princeton University Press.

Stevens, Georgiana. 1957. "Arab Neutralism and Bandung," *Middle East Journal* 11, no. 2 (Spring): 139–52.

Stinchcombe, Arthur. 1968. *Constructing Social Theories*. Chicago: University of Chicago Press.

Stone, Lawrence. 1981. "The Revival of the Narrative: Reflections on a New Old History." In L. Stone, *The Past and the Present Revisited*, pp. 74–93. London: Routledge and Kegan Paul.

Strauss, Anselm. 1978. *Negotiations*. San Francisco: Jossey-Bass.

Stryker, S. 1980. *Symbolic Interactionism: A Social Structural Perspective*. Reading, Mass.: Benjamin/Cummings.

Sultan, Khaled Bin. 1995. *Desert Warrior: A Personal View of the Gulf War by the Joint Forces Commander*. New York: HarperCollins.

Susser, Asher. 1994. "Jordan, the PLO, and the Palestine Question." In J. Nevo and I. Pappe, eds., *Jordan in the Middle East, 1948–88: The Making of a Pivotal State*, pp. 211–28. London: Frank Cass.

Swidler, Ann. 1986. "Culture in Action: Symbols in Strategies," *American Sociological Review* 51, no. 2 (April): 273–86.

Talhami, Ghada Hashem. 1992. *Palestine and Egyptian National Identity*. New York: Praeger.

Tarbush, Mohammad. 1982. *The Role of the Military in Politics: A Case Study of Iraq to 1941*. Boston: Kegan Paul.

Tarrow, Sidney. 1994. *Power in Movement*. New York: Cambridge University Press.

Taylor, Alan. 1982. *The Arab Balance of Power System*. Syracuse, N.Y.: Syracuse University Press.

Telhami, Shibley. 1990. *Power and Leadership in International Bargaining: The Path to the Camp David Accords*. New York: Columbia University Press.

——. 1993. "Arab Public Opinion and the Gulf War." In S. Reshnon, ed. *The Political Psychology of the Gulf War: Leaders, Publics, and the Process of Conflict*, pp. 183–97. Pittsburgh, Pa.: University of Pittsburgh Press.

Tessler, Mark. 1995. *A History of the Israeli-Palestinian Conflict*. Bloomington: Indiana University Press.

Thelen, Kathleen and Sven Steinmo. 1992. "Historical Institutionalism in Comparative Politics." In S. Steinmo, K. Thelen, and F. Longstreth, eds., *Structuring Politics: Historical Institutionalism in Comparative Analysis*, pp. 1–32. New York: Cambridge University Press.

Tibi, Bassam. 1981. *Arab Nationalism*. New York: St. Martin's.

——. 1988. "Structural and Ideological Change in the Arab Subsystem." In Y. Lukacs and A. Battah, eds., *The Arab-Israeli Conflict: Two Decades of Change*, pp. 147–63. Boulder, Colo.: Westview.

——. 1991. "The Simultaneity of the Unsimultaneous: Old Tribes and Imposed Nation-States in the Modern Middle East." In P. Khoury and J. Kostiner, eds., *Tribes and State Formation in the Middle East*, pp. 127–52. London: I. B. Taurus.

——. 1992. "Religious Fundamentalism and Ethnicity in the Crisis of the Nation-State in the Middle East." Working Paper 5.4, Center for German and European Studies, University of California, Berkeley.

——. 1993. *Conflict and War in the Middle East, 1967–91*. New York: St. Martin's.

Tilly, Charles. 1984. *Big Structures, Large Processes, and Huge Comparisons*. New York: Russell Sage.

——. 1994. "States and Nationalism in Europe, 1492–1992," *Theory and Society* 23: 131–46.

Torrey, Gordon. 1964. *Syrian Politics and the Military, 1945–58*. Columbus: Ohio State University Press.

Tripp, Charles. 1993. "The Iran-Iraq War and the Iraqi State." In D. Hopwood, H. Ishaw, and T. Koszinowski, eds., *Iraq: Power and Society*, pp. 90–115. New York: Oxford University Press.

Turner, Jonathan. 1988. *A Theory of Social Interaction*. Palo Alto, Calif.: Stanford University Press.

Turner, Ralph. 1978. "The Role and the Person," *American Journal of Sociology* 84, no. 1 (July): 1–23.

United States Information Agency. *Foreign Broadcast Information Service*. Various Years. Middle and Near East.

Vaisse, Maurice. 1989. "France and the Suez Crisis, 1955–56." In W. R. Louis and R. Owen, eds., *Suez 1956: The Crisis and Its Consequences*, pp. 131–44. New York: Oxford University Press.

Vatikiotis, P. J. 1967. *Politics and the Military in Jordan: 1921–57*. London: Frank Cass.

———. 1971. *Conflict in the Middle East*. London: Allen and Unwin.

———. 1978. *Nasser and His Generation*. New York: St. Martin's.

———. 1984. *Arab and Regional Politics in the Middle East*. New York: St. Martin's.

Vincent, R. J. 1991. "Order in International Politics." In J. B. D. Miller and R. J. Vincent, eds., *Order and Violence*, pp. 38–64. New York: Oxford University Press.

al-Wafi, Mahmud Abu al-Jamid. 1981. "The Arab Summit Conferences as Method for Mutual Accommodation," *al-Mustqbal-al-Arabi* 31 (September): 67–81 (in Arabic).

Walt, Stephen. 1987. *The Origins of Alliances*. Ithaca, N.Y.: Cornell University Press.

Waltz, Kenneth. 1964. "The Stability of the Bipolar World," *Daedalus* 93, no. 3 (Summer): 881–909.

———. 1979. *Theory of International Politics*. Reading, Mass.: Addison-Wesley.

Weber, Max. 1978. *Economy and Society*. Berkeley: University of California Press.

Weingast, Barry. 1995. "A Rational Choice Perspective on the Role of Ideas and Shared Beliefs: State Sovereignty and International Cooperation," *Politics and Society* 23, no. 4: 449–64.

Weldes, Jutta. 1996. "Constructing National Interests," *European Journal of International Relations* 2, no. 3: 275–318.

Wendt, Alexander. 1992. "Anarchy Is What States Make of It: Anarchy and the Social Construction of Power Politics," *International Organization* 46, no. 2 (Spring): 391–426.

———. 1994. "Collective Identity Formation and the International State," *American Political Science Review* 88, no. 2 (June): 384–96.

———. Forthcoming. *Social Theory of International Politics*. New York: Cambridge University Press.

White, Hayden. 1973. *Metahistory*. Baltimore, Md.: Johns Hopkins University Press.

Wildavsky, Aaron. 1992. "Indispensable Framework or Just Another Ideology? Prisoner's Dilemma as an Antihierarchical Game," *Rationality and Society* 4, no. 1: 8–23.

Williams, Michael. 1996. "Hobbes and International Relations: A Reconsideration," *International Organization* 50, no. 2 (Spring): 213–37.

Wilson, Mary. 1988. *King Abdullah, Britain, and the Making of Jordan*. New York: Cambridge University Press.

Wolsfeld, Gadi. 1997. *The Media and Political Conflict: News from the Middle East*. New York: Cambridge University Press.

Wrong, Dennis. 1988. *Power*. New Brunswick, N.J.: Transaction.

———. 1994. *The Problem of Order*. New York: Free Press.

Yousif, Abdul-Salaam. 1991. "The Struggle for Cultural Hegemony During the Iraqi Revolution." In R. Fernea and W. Louis, eds., *The Iraqi Revolution of 1958: The Old Social Classes Revisited*, pp. 172–96. New York: I. B. Tauris.

Zahra, Muhammad Salih Ata. 1986. "National Security and Joint Arab Activity," *al-Mustqbal al-Arabi*, no. 94 (December): 16–35 (in Arabic).

Zald, Mayer N. 1996. "Culture, Ideology, and Strategic Framing." In D. McAdam, J. McCarthy, and M. Zald, eds., *Comparative Perspective on Social Movements: Political Opportunities, Mobilizing Structures, and Cultural Framing*, pp. 261–74. New York: Cambridge University Press.

Zartman, I. W. and A. G. Kluge. 1984. "Heroic Politics: The Foreign Policy of Libya." In B. Korany and A. Dessouki, eds., *The Foreign Policies of the Arab States*, pp. 175–96. Boulder, Colo.: Westview.

Zeine, Zeine. 1960. *The Struggle for Arab Independence: Western Diplomacy and the Rise and Fall of Faisal's Kingdom in Syria*. Beirut: Khayat's.

Zubaida, Sami. 1993. "The Nation State in the Middle East." In S. Zubaida, *Islam, the People, and the State: Political Ideas and Movements in the Middle East*, pp. 121–82. London: I. B. Taurus.

Index

129–33, 137, 138–39; Yemen War, 139,
167, 168; *see also* Arab states and
Israel; Arab states and unification;
Arab states and sovereignty; Arab
states and West; Egypt
Netanyahu, Binyamin, 225, 226, 235
New Middle East, 231
1967 war, 156–59; and Arab League,
313*n*209; effects of, 161–64; explanations of, 3; and fragmentation, 2, 3,
267, 268; symbolic entrapment and,
47, 156–59, 248, 258; *see also* Arab
states and Israel; Arab states and
sovereignty
normative fragmentation. *See*
fragmentation
normative integration. *See* integration
normative structure: defined, 2, 29,
277*n*8; and susceptibility to symbols,
39–40, 44–46, 244–49; and power, 7,
10–11, 40; changes in, x, xi, 7, 8–11,
12–13, 17–18, 23–24, 37–39, 40, 49,
241–42, 244–46, 255–56, 261–62; *see
also* Arabism; norms
Norms: and Arab relations with Israel,
18, 20, 21–22, 23, 38, 71–72, 85–86,
91–98, 148–52, 153–55, 164–65, 165–66,
167–71, 173–74, 174–76, 182, 186–87,
187–90, 192–96, 198–200, 229–33, 235,
249, 258, 261, 268–69; and Arab
relations with the West, 17, 21, 38,
66–68, 86–87, 103–19, 128, 227–29,
234–35, 257, 261; of Arabism, ix,
viii–ix, 17–18, 49; constitutive, 18, 30;
defined, 30; and identity, 18, 27, 29,
30–31, 48, 49–50; regulative, 30;
contestation, ix, 7, 8–11, 37–39, 40,
219–20, 241–42, 244–46, 255–56;
compliance with, 11, 34–36, 37,
48–49, 253–55; and interactions, 7; of
international society, 207–8; and
order, 6, 262–63; and social control,

7–8, 28; of sovereignty, 13, 17, 18, 20,
21, 23, 29, 30–32, 77–82, 86, 98–103,
121–22, 129–39, 144–46, 147–48,
151–53, 165–67, 171–74, 176–80, 200–1,
204–9, 221–26, 227–29, 235, 257–58,
258, 262–64, 269–70; *see also* Arab
states and Israel; Arab states and
Palestine; Arab states and sovereignty; Arab states and unification;
fragmentation; integration; symbolic exchanges
Numairi, Gaafar Mohamd, 179
Nutting, Anthony, 110

Oman, 193, 195
Ottoman Empire, 57, 58, 60

Palestine, 87–98, 235; and Arab League,
88; and Arab public opinion, 72;
Arab states' intervention in, 85–86,
91; King Abdullah and, 93–96; and
rise of Arab nationalism, 68–72; 1936
strike, 69; symbolic competition
and, 71, 88–90; and UN, 89; and
unification, 288*n*69; *see also* Arab
states and Israel; Arafat, Yasir;
Palestine Liberation Organization
Palestine Liberation Organization
(PLO), 16; on Bourguiba, 151; on
Camp David, 193; creation of,
149–50; and Declaration of Principles, 222; on disengagement agreements, 189; and Gulf War, 218, 222;
and Jordanian civil war, 176–80; and
Madrid talks, 221; and peace process,
185–86; on Rogers initiative, 175;
symbolic power of, 249; *see also*
Palestine, Arab states and Israel
Palestine National Congress, 154
path dependence, 19
Peel Commission, 71
Peres, Shimon, 222, 231, 251